ALL HONOURABLE MEN

All Honourable Men:
The Social Origins of War in Lebanon

Michael Johnson

Centre for Lebanese Studies
in association with
I.B.Tauris Publishers
LONDON • NEW YORK

Published in 2001 by The Centre for Lebanese Studies, Oxford
in association with I.B.Tauris & Co Ltd
Victoria House, Bloomsbury Square, London WC1B 4DZ
175 Fifth Avenue, New York NY10010
Website: http://www.ibtauris.com

In the United States and Canada distributed by St Martin's Press
175 Fifth Avenue, New York NY 10010

ISBN 1 86064 715 4

A full CIP record for this book is available from the British Library
A full CIP record for this book is available from the Library of Congress

Library of Congress Catalog card: available

Typeset in BerkeleyOldstyle by Oxford Publishing Services
Printed and bound in Great Britain by Biddles Ltd, Guildford and King's
Lynn

For Catherine

Contents

Lebanese Confessional Communities

Sunni Muslims
Orthodox Muslims. Sunnis were the coreligionists of the Ottomans. According to the 1932 French Mandate census, they were the second largest community in Lebanon (after the Maronites). As a result, the premiership of Lebanon is reserved for a Sunni. Now probably the third largest community.

Shi'a Muslims
Heterodox Muslims. The Shi'a split from the Sunnis in the seventh century. In 1932 they were the third largest community. The speakership or chair of the Lebanese parliament is reserved for a Shi'a. Now they are the largest community in Lebanon.

Druze
Heterodox Muslims. The Druze split from the Shi'a in the eleventh century.

Maronites
Lebanese Catholics whose church entered into union with Rome in the twelfth century. In 1932 they were the largest Lebanese community. The presidency of Lebanon is reserved for a Maronite. Now they are probably the second largest community.

Greek Orthodox
Members of the eastern Orthodox church, which finally broke with the western Catholic church in the eleventh century.

Greek Catholics
Their church split from the Greek Orthodox in the seventeenth century and formed a uniate church with Rome in the eighteenth.

Armenian Orthodox and Armenian Catholics
Armenian immigrants to Lebanon.

Other Christians
Syrian Orthodox, Syrian Catholics, and Protestants. The latter are mainly the descendants of those converted by American missionaries. Also small groups of Assyrians or Nestorians, and Chaldaean Catholics.

For sizes of communities, see table on page 3.

Chronologies of Lebanese History

Regimes

BC to 395	Roman empire.
395–636	Byzantine empire.
636–61	Arab Muslim caliphate (second to fourth caliphs).
661–750	Umayyad caliphate (Damascus).
750–1258	Abbasid caliphate (Baghdad).
909–1171	Fatimid caliphate (Cairo).
1058–1157	Seljuk sultanate (Isfahan, Persia).
1097–1291	Crusader kingdoms.
1171–1250	Ayyubi sultanate (Cairo): Saladin (Salah ad-Din ibn Ayyub) and his family.
1250–59	Ayyubi rule continues in Syria.
1250–1517	Mamluk sultanate (Cairo).
1453–1922	Ottoman sultanate (Istanbul).
1516–1831	Ottoman rule in Lebanon.
1831–40	Egyptian rule, under Ibrahim Pasha, in Lebanon.
1840–1918	Ottoman rule in Lebanon.
1518–1697	Ma'ni emirate in Lebanon.
1697–1842	Shihabi emirate in Lebanon.
1842–60	Two governorates of Lebanon.
1861–1915	Autonomous governorate (*mutasarrifiyya*).
1915–18	Ottoman military rule during first world war.
1918–20	French occupation after the war.
1920–43	French Mandate: French rule under mandate from the League of Nations. Lebanon enlarged (*Grand Liban*) to include: the coastal region and the cities of Tripoli, Beirut, Sidon and Tyre; the northern region of Akkar; southern region of Jabal (Mount) Amil; and the eastern region of the Bekaa valley.
1943	Lebanese independence.
1958	Civil war.
1975–90	Civil wars.
1990	'Second republic' established.

Post-independence presidencies

1943–52	President Bishara al-Khouri.
1952–58	President Camille Chamoun.
1958–64	President Fu'ad Shihab.
1964–70	President Charles Helou.
1970–76	President Suleiman Frangieh.
1976–82	President Elias Sarkis.
1982	President-elect Bashir Gemayel (assassinated).
1982–88	President Amin Gemayel.
1988	Rival executives: General Michel Aoun (Maronite) and Salim al-Huss (Sunni).
1989	President René Moawad (assassinated).
1989–98	President Elias Hrawi.
1992	Rafiq al-Hariri (Sunni Muslim) becomes prime minister. Nabih Berri (Shi'a Muslim) elected speaker (chairman) of parliament.
1998	General Emile Lahoud (former army commander) elected president. Like all Lebanese presidents, he is a Maronite Christian. Salim al-Huss replaces Hariri as prime minister.
2000	Rafiq al-Hariri replaces Huss as prime minister.

Confessional harmony and conflict

19th century	Increased acreages on Mount Lebanon given over to silkworm production, and an expansion of the grain trade, contribute to a growth of new market towns and new classes of merchants, petty commodity producers and rich peasants.
	After the French revolution of 1789, ideas of liberal nationalism spread throughout Europe and eventually influence the growth of Arab and Lebanese nationalisms.
1821–30	Greek revolution against Ottoman rule. Greece becomes independent. This gives some inspiration to Lebanese nationalists.
1831–40	Egyptian rule. Encouraged by Ibrahim Pasha (Egyptian governor of Syria and Lebanon), American Presbyterian missionaries move their printing press from Malta to Beirut and begin to establish new schools. Catholic missions respond. Lazarists reopen men's college at Ayn Tura on Mount Lebanon. They and the Jesuits establish many schools in Lebanon.
1840	Overthrow of Egyptian rule and the re-establishment of Ottoman authority. Druze lords return from exile to reclaim

	estates confiscated by the Lebanese emir (a client of Egypt) and distributed to a predominantly Christian bourgeoisie.
1841	Disputes over land lead to Druze–Christian fighting.
1842	Abolition of the emirate. Lebanon divided into two governorates.
1845	More Druze–Christian fighting.
1847	Jesuits establish a printing press.
1858–59	Maronite Catholic peasants, encouraged by their clergy, rebel against their Maronite landlords in the Kisrawan district of Mount Lebanon.
1860	Druze lords in the Shouf region retain the loyalty of their Druze peasantry and the peasant revolt degenerates into a confessional war. In less than four weeks, 11,000 Maronites and other Christians are massacred by Druze (and some other Muslim) fighters and 4000 die from starvation and disease. In Damascus a further 5000 Christians are slaughtered by Sunni Muslims. The Arab nationalist Butrus al-Bustani (a Maronite who had converted to Protestantism) appeals to his fellow Christians in his weekly journal *Nafir Suriyya* (Clarion of Syria) to love their enemies and work to create a national community based on a common language and culture.
1861	Lebanon becomes an autonomous Ottoman province or 'Mutasarrifate' (*mutasarrifiyya*) under European protection, and feudal dues and obligations are abolished.
1880	A clandestine nationalist group of Christians and Muslims calls for the independence of Syria in union with Lebanon.
1913	A high point of Muslim–Christian unity in Beirut: the Committee of Reforms leads a multi-confessional movement of merchants for local Arab autonomy within the Ottoman empire.
1918–20	Arab and British armies take Damascus from the Ottomans. Emir Faisal is crowned king of Syria, but he is deposed by the French. France and Britain divide Ottoman Syria. Widespread opposition from Muslims and Orthodox Christians to a Maronite-dominated Greater Lebanon separated from Syria.
1936	Franco–Lebanese treaty; Muslim–Christian fighting in Beirut; notables from both confessions mediate. After his visit to the Berlin Olympics, Pierre Gemayel founds the predominantly Maronite, Lebanese nationalist, Phalanges party (*al-kata'ib*). Some Sunni Muslim leaders begin to revalue their interests in relation to Greater Lebanon and Syria.

1943	After Muslim merchants have come to see the advantages of a Lebanese separation from Syria, Maronite Catholic and Sunni Muslim leaders agree to an unwritten National Pact as the basis for a multi-confessional nation state. Lebanon becomes independent.
1948	Creation of the state of Israel in part of the formerly British Mandate territory of Palestine. In the warfare that follows, some 700,000 Palestinians flee or are expelled. Around 110,000 settle in refugee camps in Lebanon. By the early 1970s, the Palestinian population in Lebanon would number approximately 400,000.
1956	The Suez war: Israel, Britain and France invade Egypt after the nationalization of the (British and French owned) Suez canal. As a result of US pressure, however, their armies withdraw. The Egyptian president, Jamal Abdul Nasser, becomes the hero of Arab nationalism and inspires Lebanese Sunni Muslims with ideas of pan-Arab unity.
1958	The pro-western, and anti-Nasserist, President Camille Chamoun plans to amend the Lebanese constitution so that he can extend his term of office. Muslim grievances, Maronite fears and factional disputes between Lebanese leaders lead to a short civil war: 2500 people are killed and there is confessional fighting in Beirut. The war ends after the leaders agree to a compromise.
1958–70	The Shihabist regimes (of President Fu'ad Shihab and his successor Charles Helou) divert resources to Lebanon's underdeveloped Muslim periphery, but this encourages capitalist farming on landed estates. Predominantly Shi'a sharecroppers are forced off the land and into the slums and shanty towns of Beirut.
1964	Formation of the Palestine Liberation Organization (PLO).
1967	The Arab–Israeli 'six day' war is followed by increased commando activity by the PLO against Israel from bases in Lebanon.
1969	Yasser Arafat becomes leader of the PLO. Serious and prolonged fighting occurs between the PLO and the Lebanese army.
1970	Suleiman Frangieh is elected president and forms an anti-Shihabist government. The *Deuxième Bureau* (security apparatus) is purged, weakening the state's ability to control the PLO and Lebanese militias.
1970–75	Inflation, unemployment, strikes and demonstrations are rife. Lebanese 'leftists' (predominantly Muslim) are armed and trained by the PLO; periodic fighting breaks out between the

Lebanese army and PLO; there are clashes between the PLO and predominantly Maronite militias (particularly the Phalangists).

1975–76   Civil war with 25,000–40,000 killed; 'ethnic cleansing' and massacres.

1976   Syria invades to prevent a defeat of the Maronite militias, leading to the military defeat of the PLO and Lebanese National Movement (LNM).

1977   Kamal Jumblat, Druze leader of the LNM, assassinated by agents of Syria.

1978   Israel invades southern Lebanon to attack PLO forces and establishes a 'buffer zone' under the control of a Maronite-led militia.

Tony Frangieh (Suleiman's son), his wife, baby daughter and members of his household and militia are killed by a Phalangist squad (under the command of Samir Geagea) in an intra-Maronite war for control of Christian Lebanon. Syrians bombard Christian quarters of East Beirut.

Imam Musa as-Sadr, the Shi'a spiritual leader and founder of the Shi'a militia, Amal, disappears without trace while on a visit to Libya. The Shi'a begin to turn against Arab nationalist parties in the LNM.

1979   The Iranian revolution is an inspiration to Lebanese Shi'a, many of whom now see Amal as more representative of their interests than the secular leftist parties of the LNM.

1980   The Iran–Iraq war is fought by proxy in the suburbs of Beirut, first between Amal and a Palestinian group backed by Iraq. Deteriorating relations with the PLO, which acts like an army of occupation in Shi'a southern Lebanon, lead to fighting spreading to the south. Periodic clashes between Amal and the PLO and its LNM allies continue until the Israeli invasion in 1982 creates a temporary alliance.

The Phalangists defeat their major Maronite rival, the Tigers militia led by Camille Chamoun's son Dany. As a result, Bashir Gemayel (the second son of Phalanges founder Pierre) becomes the master of most of Maronite Lebanon, commanding a unified militia called the Lebanese Forces.

1982   The Israelis invade Lebanon and besiege Beirut in order to neutralize the PLO; the Syrians retreat to northern Lebanon; PLO fighters are evacuated from Lebanon under the supervision of a US-led multinational force.

Bashir Gemayel is elected president of Lebanon (by a barely

quorate parliament), but he is assassinated by a pro-Syrian agent before he takes office. Maronite militias blame the Palestinians and massacre hundreds of civilians in the Beiruti quarters of Sabra and Shatila. As the PLO fighters had been expelled, the quarters were defenceless. Amin Gemayel (Bashir's elder brother) is elected president.

1983   Fighting between Palestinian factions in northern Lebanon leads to a Syrian intervention against Yasser Arafat who is forced to leave Lebanon (eventually establishing the PLO's headquarters in Tunisia).

The Shouf war: as the Israelis withdraw from Lebanon, Druze and Maronite militias fight for control of the Druze region of Mount Lebanon. Walid Jumblat (Kamal's son and Druze leader) announces an alliance between the Shi'a and Druze forces, backed by Syria. The Druze expel the Lebanese Forces (commanded by Samir Geagea) from the Shouf; many civilians are killed; thousands of Maronites and other Christians flee from the fighting. The US navy shells Druze positions from the sea. Shi'a suicide bombers kill 241 US marines and 58 French soldiers in Beirut, demoralizing the multinational forces.

1984   The Shi'a Amal militia takes the Sunni quarters of West Beirut from government control; the multinational forces withdraw from Lebanon.

1985   Opposing 'concessions' to Syria, Samir Geagea mounts a rebellion within the Lebanese Forces against leaders sympathetic to President Amin Gemayel. Fighting between rebel Lebanese Forces and Sunni and Druze militias around Sidon leads to the flight of thousands of Christian civilians. A movement called 'Women Against War' marches to the parliament building.

Start of the 'war of the camps': the Shi'a Amal militia besieges Palestinian quarters in southern Beirut in an attempt to remove Palestinian fighters who had infiltrated back into Lebanon (some via Druze territory). Druze and Amal forces unite to defeat the Sunni Murabitun militia in West Beirut, but later fight each other.

1986   Amal continues its war of the camps with a renewed siege in southern Beirut. The secular and multi-confessional trade union confederation organizes a demonstration against the war.

1987   More Shi'a–Druze fighting in Beirut; the Syrian army enters the western quarters of the city to restore order. More protests against the war are organized by the trade unions. After the start of the Palestinian uprising (*intifada*) in December against the Israeli occupation of the Gaza and West Bank, Nabih Berri, the leader of Amal, announces an end to the war of the camps.

1988   War between Amal and a rival Shi'a militia, the Iranian-backed Hizballah, in Beirut. Syria enters the Shi'a suburbs of Beirut to restore order. More protests against the war are organized by the trade unions.

President Amin Gemayel resigns at the end of his term of office, and parliament is unable to elect a successor. Two rival executives: General Michel Aoun (Maronite commander of the Lebanese army) in Christian territory, and Salim al-Huss (Sunni prime minister) in Syrian-controlled (predominantly Muslim) Lebanon.

1989   Heavy fighting between General Aoun's forces (backed by Iraq) and the Syrian army and its Lebanese allies in and around Beirut. Hundreds killed, many of them civilians. The rump of the Lebanese parliament elected in 1972 meets in Ta'if, Saudi Arabia, and negotiates the 'Ta'if agreement' as the basis for peace: more powers for the Sunni prime minister and Shi'a speaker of the parliament; the ratio of Christian and Muslim deputies in parliament changed from 6:5 to 1:1. Soon after his election by the parliament, President René Moawad is assassinated. Elias Hrawi replaces him.

1990   Months of fighting (this time within the Christian enclave) take place between General Michel Aoun's forces and a rival Maronite faction (Samir Geagea's Lebanese Forces) that wants to negotiate with the Syrians and their Lebanese allies. Iraq invades Kuwait. Syria's support for the US-led coalition in the Gulf war leads, it seems, to the USA (and indirectly Israel) giving Syria *carte blanche* to pacify Lebanon. Michel Aoun's forces routed and he successfully seeks sanctuary in the French embassy; he is later exiled to France.

The civil or uncivil wars that had started in April 1975, and had killed more than 100,000 people, come to an official end. Dany Chamoun, his wife and two small sons are murdered. An opponent of Syrian intervention, Chamoun is presumed to have been killed by pro-Syrian agents, but Samir Geagea is eventually held responsible.

1991   All Lebanese and Palestinian militias are disarmed with the exception of Hizballah, which is allowed to continue fighting the Israelis and their Lebanese allies (the 'South Lebanon Army') in the Israeli 'security zone' in southern Lebanon.

1992   Secular strikes and demonstrations stimulated by a currency crisis and inflation take on the character of a popular uprising with, in many places, anti-Syrian slogans. The prime minister resigns and a new government is formed to supervise parliamentary elections (the first since 1972). Major Christian parties boycott the elections in protest against continuing Syrian occupation and the gerrymandering of constituencies to favour pro-Syrian warlords. Thus pro-Syrian Christian deputies are elected. Amal and Hizballah candidates defeat traditional leaders in Shi'a constituencies. Rafiq al-Hariri, a billionaire contractor with joint Saudi–Lebanese citizenship, is appointed extra-parliamentary prime minister. He encourages foreign investment in postwar reconstruction, and commits his personal fortune to the cause. Nabih Berri, the leader of Amal, becomes speaker of the parliament.

1994   Despite helping the Syrians to depose General Michel Aoun, Samir Geagea and the Lebanese Forces do not co-operate with the new regime in Lebanon. After a bomb attack on a Maronite church, the government accuses Geagea of being responsible and dissolves the Lebanese Forces, preventing it from becoming a political party.

1995   Although found innocent on the bombing charge, Samir Geagea is sentenced to life imprisonment for the murder of Dany Chamoun and his family in 1990.

Parliament amends the constitution to extend President Elias Hrawi's term of office until 1998.

1996   Israeli attacks against Hizballah and civilian targets in southern Lebanon lead to an upsurge of national feeling: there are demonstrations of solidarity and a national day of mourning for the dead.

Second general election after the end of the civil wars. Christians generally ignore calls for a boycott from exiled Maronite leaders (Michel Aoun, Amin Gemayel and Dany Chamoun's brother Dory). Prime Minister Rafiq al-Hariri and his electoral allies do well in Beirut. Hizballah loses some seats. Parliament is dominated by two blocs: Rafiq al-Hariri's and Nabih Berri's.

Demonstrations and protests are organized by the Lebanese trade union confederation and other groups against bans on public demonstrations and the closing down of a number of opposition radio and TV stations. Troops are deployed on the streets of Beirut at the end of November to prevent a general strike and demonstrations. Michel Aoun, Amin Gemayel and Dory Chamoun form an exile grouping to press for Syrian withdrawal and the re-establishment of Lebanese sovereignty.

1998   President Hrawi fails in his attempts to introduce civil marriage in Lebanon. Local elections are held throughout Lebanon: opposition Christians, including Dory Chamoun, are elected; there are Hizballah successes at the expense of Amal.

Emile Lahoud is elected president after Elias Hrawi's extended term of office comes to an end. Salim al-Huss becomes prime minister and forms a government of technocrats committed to economic reforms and the eradication of corruption.

2000   Israel withdraws from south Lebanon, the South Lebanon Army militia collapses, and Lebanese authority is restored. President Hafiz al-Asad dies. His son, Bashar, takes over as president of Syria.

Third general election after the end of the civil wars. Constituencies are gerrymandered to ensure election of pro-Syrian candidates. Rafiq al-Hariri becomes prime minister after he and his allies win all the seats in Beirut.

1

An Auto-Critique

1. Lebanon and confessionalism

First, a Lebanese joke told to me in 1972. Marilyn Monroe dies and goes to heaven. At the pearly gates, Saint Peter tells her that unfortunately there is no bed available at such short notice. Perhaps she would like to share? He takes her into his office where the three great patriarchs, the prophets Moses, Muhammad and Jesus, are playing with two dice. They agree to play for a night with her. The Prophet Moses throws two fives and feels very excited. Then the Prophet Muhammad throws two sixes and looks smug. No one can beat him. Jesus reminds them the contest is not yet over and picks up the dice. He throws two sevens!

'Oh please, Jesus,' protests the Prophet Muhammad, 'this is no time for one of your miracles!'

We are not informed whether Ms Monroe agreed to sleep with the winner. In a male-dominated society, the assumption is she was not offered a choice. What the story demonstrates is that Jesus was either a dishonourable cheat (if the teller were a Muslim) or he had superior powers and therefore commanded respect (if the teller were a Christian). In either event, the joke illustrates the tensions of a 'patriarchal society' divided along the lines of confession or religion, and it confronts some of the issues addressed in this book, including the cultural values of 'respect' and 'honour'.

When I heard the joke, all those years ago and before the start of the civil wars, Lebanon was often referred to as the 'Switzerland of the Middle East'.

1

Despite large income differentials between rich and poor, the banking and trading economy of Beirut ensured that Lebanon was a relatively prosperous nation state. With magnificent mountain scenery, fertile soil and a warm Mediterranean climate, Lebanon seemed peculiarly blessed. Tourists from the Arab Gulf and Europe came to enjoy these natural advantages, eat the fine food of Lebanese and French cuisines, and indulge other senses in the nightclubs and casinos of Beirut. As the publicity brochures claimed, it was even possible to ski on the mountains in the morning and on the sea in the afternoon. It was a beautiful country, and it was said that when God created Lebanon, the other countries were jealous. Why should this tiny land on the eastern shores of the Mediterranean be so favoured with mountains, streams and rivers, with forested slopes and the fertile plain of the Bekaa? God, so the story goes, saw that the complaints were just, and to correct the imbalance he created the Lebanese.

By the middle of the twentieth century, if not earlier, Lebanon had a highly competitive and acquisitive population. In Beirut, the banking and financial centre of the Arab Middle East, most people were employed in the service sector, competing with each other for jobs and markets. In the countryside, peasant individualism and the increasing commercialization of agriculture contributed to a competitive society that was in many ways similar to that of the city. There was apparently little 'civic' consciousness or sense of community, and where there were communitarian attachments they often contributed to further division.

Roughly half the population of Lebanon confessed to Christianity and half to Islam, and these two communities were in turn fragmented into a number of sects, thus potentially setting Christian against Christian and Muslim against Muslim. The major Christian division was between Catholics (Maronite, Greek, Armenian and Syrian) and eastern Orthodox (Greek, Armenian and Syrian), and there was also a number of Protestants. Muslims were divided into the orthodox Sunnis and heterodox Shi'a, and there was a relatively large minority of Druze, a confession that because of the belief in the transmigration or reincarnation of souls could hardly be said to be Muslim at all. (As can be seen from the table below, there used to be a small Jewish community during the period of the French Mandate; but since the creation of Israel in 1948, and the succession of Arab–Israeli wars, most Jews have left the country).

Of these sects, the Maronite Catholic and Greek Orthodox Christians, and the Sunni, Shi'a and Druze Muslims, are the most important. Traditionally, the Maronites lived on Mount Lebanon (*Mont Liban*), although since the latter half of the nineteenth century many have migrated to Beirut where they live alongside other Christians in the eastern half of the city. The Druze are concentrated in the Shouf region of the mountains (*jabal ash-shuf*) to the south of Beirut, and the Shi'a in the Mount Amil (*jabal 'amil*) region in southern Lebanon and in the Bekaa valley to the east of the Mount Lebanon range. In the 1960s large

Confessional composition of the Lebanese population:
1932 census figures and 1984 estimates

Confession	1932 Population	1932 %	1984 Population	1984 %
Shi'a	154,208	19.6	1,100,000	30.8
Sunnis	175,925	22.4	750,000	21.0
Druze	53,047	6.8	200,000	5.6
Muslims	383,180	48.8	2,050,000	57.3
Maronites	226,378	28.8	900,000	25.2
Greek Orthodox	76,522	9.7	250,000	7.0
Greek Catholics	45,999	5.9	150,000	4.2
Armenian Orthodox	25,462	3.2		
Armenian Catholics	5,694	0.7		
Armenians			175,000	4.9
Syrian Orthodox	2,574	0.3		
Syrian Catholics	2,675	0.3		
Other local churches	528	0.1		
Protestants	6,712	0.9		
Other Christians			50,000	1.4
Christians	392,544	50.0	1,525,000	42.7
Jews	3,518	0.4	no figures available	
Others	6,301	0.8	no figures available	
Total Population	785,543	100.0	3,575,000	100.0

Sources: 1932 census figures from Hourani 1946: 121.
1984 estimates from Johnson 1986: 226.
Note: There has been no census of confessions since the French Mandate.

numbers of Shi'a migrated to Beirut where they tended to live in the southern suburbs, often as neighbours to the Palestinian refugees (mostly Sunni, but a number of Christians too) whose camps had been established there in 1948–49 after they had fled from the new state of Israel. As coreligionists of the ruling Ottomans, the Sunnis usually lived in the coastal cities of Tripoli, Beirut and Sidon where imperial protection was greatest, although there is a substantial rural community in the northern Akkar region of the mountains. Because the Greek Orthodox tended to have good relations with the Sunni authorities, many of them settled in Beirut, and in the nineteenth century a number of rich merchant families built their mansions outside the old city walls to establish the Christian quarter of al-Ashrafiyya in the heart of what is now East Beirut.

Confessional identity had long been built into the judicial and administrative structures of the state. Under the rule of the Sunni Muslim Ottomans, the *millet* system had allowed each Christian and Jewish community to manage its communal affairs under its own leadership, particularly with regard to personal law and the provision of educational and welfare services. The freedom allowed to the different sects varied. Such heterodox Muslims as the Shi'a did not have their own millet and usually had Sunni law imposed upon them. But in the Lebanese mountains, the political and judicial systems were virtually autonomous from imperial authority, and the heterodox Druze and Shi'a were often governed by their own principles as much as their Christian neighbours.

After the defeat of the Ottoman empire in the first world war, the Arab provinces of the Levant were divided between Britain and France under the 'mandate' of the League of Nations. In Lebanon the French Mandate (1920–43) maintained a system of confessional law in matters to do with marriage, divorce and inheritance, and also confirmed confessional representation in the liberal-democratic polity. In 1943 independent Lebanon inherited a system in which the presidency of the republic was by convention reserved for a Maronite Catholic (who belonged to the supposedly largest sect according to the 1932 census). The premiership was similarly reserved for a Sunni, and the office of speaker or chair of the parliamentary assembly for a Shi'a. Seats in the elected assembly were distributed in a ratio of six Christian to five Muslim deputies, in rough proportion to the supposed size of the various sects in the population.

This political and judicial system was the one in place at the start of the Lebanese civil war in 1975 and, with relatively minor amendments, was the one re-established after the official end of the wars in 1990. Seats in the parliament are now distributed in an equal ratio of Christians and Muslims. But even though it is generally accepted that the Shi'a have become the largest sect (because as a poor and rural community, they had a higher birth rate), the presidency is still reserved for a Maronite, and the premiership for a Sunni. Under the new arrangements, the Shi'a speaker has considerably more power than before and forms part of a triumvirate. But the Maronite president and Sunni prime minister remain symbolically, and in some respects actually, more influential.

The extent to which this system contributed to the outbreak of civil hostilities, by encouraging confessional identification and tension, is not the major concern of this book, although some familiarity with the way the system worked (and works) is essential for following an argument about the causes and content of confessional conflict. It is especially important for making an assessment (in the final chapter) of the prospects for reconstruction and reform in what has been called Lebanon's 'Second Republic'.

Of greater importance, however, are the values of patriarchy, honour and respect that are partly exemplified in the story of Marilyn Monroe's first night in heaven. By acting in a way some might consider dishonourable, Jesus commands respect. This is a reflection or intimation of a wider set of cultural values which include the normative requirements that 'honourable men', or men who seek the respect of others, should defend and fight for their status, family and community, should control the behaviour of 'their' women and adolescent sons, and should be prepared to demonstrate their honour by imposing shame on others.

2. Class and client

It seems to me that an understanding of Lebanese patriarchy, and a culture of honour and shame, is crucial if we are to make sense of the emotional aspects of confessional conflict — matters I now realize I neglected in my earlier work, *Class and Client in Beirut* (Johnson 1986). Looking back at that book, I feel there are at least two things wrong with it. First, it is perhaps too materialist or neo-Marxist in its approach, and certainly it fails to deal adequately with the emotional affectivity of confessional allegiance in Lebanese society. Secondly, it ends on too gloomy a note, arguing that even if a Syrian or some other external intervention were to end the years of warfare, there was no social class which could perform the unifying role played by the 'commercial-financial bourgeoisie' that had created independent Lebanon in the 1940s.

In relation to the latter point, I argued that Lebanese independence in 1943 came about largely as a result of an informal compact between leading merchants and financiers who belonged to the Christian and Sunni Muslim communities or confessions. They agreed they should co-operate in building a liberal political system that would encourage a free economy based on Beirut and its hinterland lying within the borders of 'Greater Lebanon' (*Grand Liban*), the territory defined by the French mandatory authorities after the first world war (Johnson 1986: 25–6). In alliance with rural landlords, political representatives of the commercial and financial bourgeoisie took control of the state and implemented policies to promote the trading, banking and insurance sectors of the economy (Johnson 1986: 119 ff).

As confessional conflict was quite simply 'bad for business', political leaders usually sought to moderate the prejudices of their followers and, in the cities, they developed sophisticated political machines to distribute patronage and control their clients (Johnson 1986: chapters 3 and 4). Even when a complex combination of internal and external factors gave rise to a short civil war in 1958, the leaders of most factions generally tried to prevent the conflict degenerating into confessional fighting and eventually effected a compromise that contributed to a decade of peaceful economic and social development (Johnson 1986: chapters 5 and 6).

The Lebanese civil war that began in 1975 was thus caused mainly by developments external to what I called the 'clientelist system' of political control (Johnson 1986: chapter 4) which had so effectively sustained a relative order since independence. Two communities were excluded from the clientelist system: the Palestinian refugees who were not citizens of Lebanon and were therefore unable to trade votes for services; and the recent Shi'a migrants to Beirut who were registered to vote in their villages and were thus excluded from the patronage structures of the city. Both groups were susceptible to radical politics and came to be seen as a threat to the Lebanese political system, Palestinians swelling the ranks of one or other faction within the Palestine Liberation Organization, and many Shi'a joining Lebanese leftist parties.

In addition, the governments and intelligence agencies of various Arab states and Israel interfered in Lebanese politics, and their intervention was largely centred on the growth of the Palestinian 'armed presence' that provided perhaps the single most important *casus belli* (Johnson 1986: 174–8), promoting Maronite fears and radicalizing popular Muslim feeling. Many Christians, particularly Maronite Catholics, saw Lebanon as their refuge, a place where they liked to say they were able to ring their church bells on Sundays, where they were not submerged in a sea of Islam. The growing alliance between some Arab governments, Palestinian commandos and popular Muslim movements in Lebanon was thus seen as a threat to the Maronite 'nation' and its prerogatives. In particular, the guerrilla activities of the Palestine Liberation Organization against Israel from its Lebanese bases made it appear that the PLO was a 'state within a state' that invited Israeli reprisals against the Maronite 'homeland'.

As the warfare progressed, the larger banks, insurance companies and trading houses moved out of Beirut to such places as Cyprus, Jordan and the Gulf, and Paris, London and New York. It became clear that the commercial-financial bourgeoisie and its international partners no longer needed Lebanon as a territorial base (Johnson 1986: 225). Indeed, the breakdown of the old elite consensus and the collapse of state authority led to a war economy (Johnson 1986: 200–3) that the major players had every interest in maintaining. Against this background I ended my book by arguing 'there appeared to be no national class — neither bourgeoisie nor any other — which was conscious of its common interests and able to constitute a point of unity in the midst of communal diversity' (Johnson 1986: 226).

This interpretation assumed that political control must necessarily be imposed from above by a ruling class with a direct economic interest in confessional harmony, and that militant confessionalism was a characteristic of most or many members of the 'lower classes'. Both assumptions are oversimplified or wrong.

While I would still want to argue that the clientelist structures of the prewar Lebanese state were remarkably effective in providing the framework for an overall order, I now realize that I underestimated the extent to which diffuse systems of power existed in civil society that also contributed to social stability. Towards the end of this book, I make use of Michel Foucault's work on 'surveillance' (1975; 1976) to elaborate this theme. But as an indicator to the direction of my current thinking about Lebanon, it is worth mentioning here some points made in Theodor Hanf's excellent study of the civil wars (1993), published soon after they had ended.

First, it is clear that although most Lebanese identified themselves in one way or another with their confessional community, this did not necessarily mean they were prepared to fight and die for it, nor did they usually approve of the atrocities committed against the 'Other'. Only a minority was involved in the fighting, and a large majority favoured a democratic solution to the various conflicts. The opinion survey of economically active Lebanese conducted by Hanf and his associates in 1987 indicates that 80 per cent of respondents favoured a form of 'consociational' democracy in which power would be shared by the leaders of the various confessions (Hanf 1993: 519–34).

Secondly, organized opposition to the war did develop in the latter half of the 1980s. In 1985 a movement called 'Women Against War' marched on parliament. The secular and multiconfessional confederation of trade unions, the *Confédération Générale des Travailleurs Libanais* (CGTL), led mass protests against the war, involving tens of thousands of participants, in 1986, 1987, 1988 and 1990. And such professional groups as the Association of Lawyers, the Medical Association, and Association of Engineers excluded representatives of the militias from their governing bodies (Hanf 1993: 639–40). All these events demonstrated the strength and vitality of the organizations of civil society, auguring well for any postwar settlement and demonstrating that significant sections of that society could live together in confessional harmony without the imposed order of a ruling class.

8

All Honourable Men

3. Honour and vengeance

Nevertheless, it has to be said that such antiwar movements developed relatively late, after the fighting and massacres of 1975–76, the Syrian intervention in 1976, the bombardment of Christian East Beirut by Syrian artillery in 1978, and the siege and bombing of Muslim West Beirut by Israel, and the massacres of Sabra and Shatila, in 1982. By the mid-1980s most Lebanese were thoroughly tired of war, and yet a significant minority — 10 per cent of Hanf's sample — still favoured a total victory for their faction. 'This economically frustrated, highly militant group has no difficulties in imagining the expulsion of all opponents,' wrote Hanf (1993: 533), and 'the presence of one or several groups with profiles of this nature are a godsend to any political force in or out of the country that has an interest in perpetuating tension.'

It is this 10 per cent — probably more at different stages of the civil war (or wars) — that needs explaining. It represents those who subscribed to the uncompromising values of kinship and confession, of communal defence and aggression, of massacre and 'ethnic cleansing'. *Ad-dam ma bisir may*, 'blood never becomes water,' is a Lebanese proverb much more redolent with symbolic meaning than the equivalent saying in English, and it serves as a text for subsequent chapters of this book.

Intimately connected with the notion of 'blood' are the values of honour and shame, and a culture of violence and heroism. Although a majority of people in prewar Lebanon did not necessarily subscribe to such values, there were sufficient numbers who admired the violent hero to give rise to a politics structured around male honour, feuding and vengeance. As warfare became the norm in the 1970s, more and more people were sucked into a vortex of blood and revenge. An upper-class Sunni woman, for example, wrote in her diary of her hatred for the Christian (overwhelmingly Maronite) Phalangist militia after the massacre of Muslim civilians on 'Black Saturday' in December 1975:

Pierre Gemayel, the Phalangist leader, ... is issuing appeals for a return to sanity and calm. Sanity! ... You do not listen to someone ... who has shed the blood of three hundred and sixty-five people to *cleanse his honour.* ... At this moment I want the Mourabitouns [*murabitun*, a Sunni Muslim militia] or anybody else to give the Phalangists back twice as good as we got. I would like them to go into offices and kill the first seven hundred and thirty defenceless Christians they can lay their hands on.

(Tabbara 1979: 54; my emphasis)

Prior to the war, Lina Mikdadi Tabbara had no real sense of her Muslim identity. As a civil servant married to an architect and living in an apartment in one of Beirut's most fashionable quarters, she lived a life of ease, she tells us, in her 'well-feathered Lebanese nest' (Tabbara 1979: 1). In common with other members of the elite she had close friends in most of the confessions. She was, however, part of a social and political system in which the values of kinship, honour and revenge seemed to be prominent aspects of the culture. As we shall see, these values helped to create a political order in Lebanon after independence in 1943. Unfortunately, they later became transformed in such a way as to promote the most appalling atrocities in the civil wars of the 1970s and 1980s.

Tabbara's honest account of her emotions at a particular stage of the civil war demonstrates that even members of the liberal secular elite could be motivated by feelings of communal hurt, pride and vengeance. Although, like Tabbara, most of them later modified their views of self and Other, many Lebanese experienced similarly powerful emotions at one time or another during the years of warfare.

4. Ethnicity and massacres

In the Lebanese capital of Beirut is a Palestinian district or quarter named Shatila. There, one evening in September 1982, a group of Christian militiamen came to the door of Leila's house. They were mostly in their teens or early twenties. Perhaps there were older men amongst them, but they were all *shabab*, a term the Lebanese use to describe young males — and armed men who have not grown up. This gang of thugs had already murdered a family of eight children and their parents. Leila and her father went out to meet them.

'This is my father,' she said. 'He is 60 years old. Don't kill him. What has he done to you?'

'Shut up, you bitch,' said a militiaman carrying an axe. 'Don't say a word or we'll rape and kill you.'

The father was axed to death.

Leila's 17-year-old sister came running out screaming, 'Father, father! Why did you kill him?'

They shot her dead.

One of them asked, 'Is this a girl or a boy? We thought she was a boy.'

Another used the axe to cut the sister's arm and hand into pieces. They grabbed her gold bangles and rings. They tore away her earrings and pulled off her necklace. Leila turned from the men and knelt down to put back the top of her father's skull on his head. They pushed her away and took the money from his pocket and a ring from his finger.

'Don't move, you bitch,' said one, and they stole jewellery from her body and money from her bag.

Then they went next door to the house of Leila's aunt and uncle. The women were forced out and the militiamen entered and slaughtered the men and boys. A 13-year-old was burnt alive with a flame-thrower (Leila's testimony in Lamb 1984: 550–1).

Apart from her sister, Leila and her female relatives were fortunate: they were not killed. Also, none of them was raped. Other women and girls in Shatila and the neighbouring quarter of Sabra were. A Lebanese journalist describes the aftermath of the massacre in which over a thousand Palestinian and Lebanese civilians were killed by Phalangists and other Christian militiamen:

> At the southern entrance to Shatila, a row of shanty dwellings has been levelled by the shelling, burying the occupants alive. Fifty yards beyond lies a heap of bodies. ... One has been castrated, others maimed with knives. A group of five women are sprawled across a sandheap. One lies spread-eagled on her back, her torn blouse exposing mutilated breasts; beside her the severed head of a child. ... A woman moans endlessly over a corpse, waving a blood-soaked identity card. 'My brother, this is my brother ... he is Lebanese, not Palestinian.' ... Down an alleyway the bodies of two young girls of 11 or 12 years of age lie side by side, their legs splayed in a posture of rape. ... In a darkened backroom, a group of bodies huddles in the corner, father and mother clutching their two small sons and new-born baby. Another new-born baby is found alive, playing in the arms of his dead mother. His father's body dangles from a window frame. A pregnant woman has been disembowelled and the foetus flung across the room.
>
> (Safa Zaitoun's testimony in Lamb 1984: 562–4)

A survivor (in an anonymous testimony in Lamb 1984: 567–8) recalls: 'They separated the men and the boys from the rest and ordered them to lie on the ground. Then they shot them all. We screamed and ran to the men. ... They shot two women dead and wounded three others. Then they picked out three young girls, tied them up and raped them right in front of us.' And another (Om Kayed in Lamb 1984: 565) tells us: 'I nearly went off my head over Om Mubarak. She was nine months pregnant. They ripped her open with a long knife, tore out the child and scattered her insides. Then they finished her off with bullets.' Virtually all the dead in Sabra and Shatila were unarmed civilians. Most victims were robbed. Some were raped, some mutilated: breasts, penises and testicles were cut away, Christian crosses carved into the flesh and, in one case, 'the members of a baby cut off and disposed on an ironing board in a circle around his head' (Randal 1990: 15).

This was not the first ethnic massacre in Lebanon or the last. One of the earliest atrocities occurred at the end of May 1975 when a Shi'a Muslim gang called the Knights of Ali (*fityan 'ali*) set up a roadblock outside the Bashoura cemetery in Beirut and abducted and killed around fifty Christians. The bodies were left among the graves, 'their penises neatly severed and stuffed in their mouths' (Randal 1990: 78). Then came the massacres of Black Saturday in December 1975 and the Karantina in January 1976. After the Maronite Phalangist militia and their allies had slaughtered or driven out the Palestinian and Lebanese population of the old quarantine area of Beirut's port, the slums and shacks of the shanty town were bulldozed to create a level empty space that later became the site of the Christians' military headquarters. The list of massacres goes on and on: Bashoura, Beirut's Black Saturday, Dubayya, the Karantina, Damour, Jisr al-Basha, Tal az-Zaatar, Khiam, Ehden, Safra-Marine, Zahle, Sabra and Shatila, the Shouf, the Shi'a–Palestinian 'war of the camps'.

The Palestinian and Lebanese Muslim revenge for the Karantina was 'merciless' (Fisk 1990: 99). Perhaps as many as 350 Christians were killed in the seaside village of Damour. Young women were raped; babies were shot in the head; houses were looted and dynamited.

> But the plunder did not end there. The cruel young men who follow every civil war army made their way to Damour, some of them as high on hashish as the Phalangists had been at Karantina. Many of them were Lebanese Muslims, part of [the] 'Leftist Alliance'. Some were Palestinians. And at some point — no one knows exactly which day — they vented their wrath on the old Christian cemetery, digging up the coffins and tearing open the gates of vaults, hurling Damour's past generations across the graveyard.
>
> (Fisk 1990: 99–100)

After Damour the Christians avenged themselves on Tal az-Zaatar, the 'hill of thyme' where thousands of Palestinians had made their homes. When the quarter or 'camp' finally surrendered to the besieging Christian forces in August 1976, hundreds had died from wounds, gangrene and starvation. The victorious militias then proceeded to slaughter hundreds more. Bodies — alive as well as dead — were dragged through the streets behind jeeps and cars, and according to one report some Palestinians were burnt at the stake (*Economist*, 4 December 1976). As with the Karantina, Tal az-Zaatar was then obliterated with bulldozers and explosives.

A mother and her six children, fleeing from Tal az-Zaatar, were stopped by militiamen belonging to the Guardians of the Cedars (*hurras al-arz*). This party was one of the most extreme Maronite groups and had chosen its name to demonstrate a loyalty to Lebanon — which has a cedar tree as the motif on its national flag — and to indicate a defence of Lebanese Christians for whom the cedar was a cherished symbol of their homeland. The gunmen informed the mother that they would shoot all her children save one. She should choose the child to be spared.

Apparently she eventually made a choice. The men shot that one first and then killed all the others. As what seemed like a final act of cruelty they left the mother alive (Tabbara 1979: 162–3).

Lina Tabbara asks her friend, a sympathetic Maronite priest, why children are killed. The despairing cleric replies, 'Because they grow up' (Tabbara 1979: 163). And a former officer of the Lebanese police, a Maronite known as Abu Arz (Father of the Cedars) and leader of the Guardians, explains to the press, 'If you feel compassion for the Palestinian women and children, remember they are Communists and will bear more Communists' (Randal 1990: 91).

5. Modernization and confessionalism

Analyses of confessional, communal or ethnic identification and conflict can be broadly divided into three types, depending on the emphases of their authors: 'situational', 'primordial', and 'syncretic'. Some would argue that only the primordial approach really gets to grips with the strength of feeling exhibited by those responsible for massacres in the Lebanese civil wars, and it now seems to me to be unsatisfactory to reduce such emotion, as the 'structuralists' or 'situationalists' — including myself — have tended to do, to material self-interest and differential access to economic and political resources (Hechter 1975; 1986; Johnson 1986). Doing so obscures the emotional affectivity that undoubtedly exists within the rival factions in confessional and ethnic conflict. It is equally inadequate, however, to adopt a dogmatically primordial stance and see ethnic or communal ties as existing from the beginning of social history and thus as fundamental and determining characteristics of society and politics. An article written by Clifford Geertz (1963) is often given as an example of this approach, although he is very careful to qualify his position (Gurr 1993: 367 n4). Talking of the *'assumed "givens"* of social existence', he argues that 'congruities of blood, speech, custom, and so on, *are seen to have* an ineffable, and at times overpowering, coerciveness in and of themselves ... *at least in great part* by virtue of some unaccountable absolute import attributed to the very tie itself' (Geertz 1963: 109, my emphases). Geertz attaches considerable analytic significance to primordialism, but his is a description of the way ethnic nationalists themselves see the ties of blood and birth. It is their analysis, not Geertz's, that argues primordial or ethnic ties are 'natural' to the human condition.

Some, such as James McKay (1982), George Scott (1990) and Ted Gurr

(1993), have offered a third, syncretic approach. However, in their attempt to give weight to both emotional and structural factors, these authors seem to skirt around what lies at the heart of the problem. When one hears or reads accounts of confessional and ethnic conflict, of the rape of girls, the cutting open of the wombs of pregnant women, and the castration of men, one seeks a 'rational' explanation of such 'irrational' behaviour. But materialist accounts of the origins of ethnic identity need to be supplemented by a full analysis of the emotional aspects of ethnic conflict. It is relatively easy to give a structural or situational explanation of confessional identity in terms, for example, of class structure and an uneven development of the economy, but to understand the affectivity of confessional violence we need to probe deeper into the values of civil society.

As a starting point, it is useful to situate Lebanon in its Mediterranean rather than Arab or Middle Eastern context. What is striking about the civil wars in Lebanon is that the style of violence was so gruesome and nasty, as it was in Bosnia and other provinces of the former Yugoslavia. The aim, it seems, was not just to kill the 'Other' but to kill in particularly brutal ways, involving the violation and mutilation of the bodies of men and women, and thus the utter degradation and humiliation of the enemy community. Here ideas of the nature of self and person are crucially important, ideas closely related to the notions of individual honour and shame. There is a vast literature on honour in the Mediterranean region, and I draw upon some of this in the second chapter of this book. My intention is to demonstrate that such values maintained a degree of social and political stability in independent Lebanon from 1943 until the outbreak of civil war in 1975, but that subsequently the imposition of shame on communal enemies contributed to an almost complete breakdown of order and a virtual 'demonization' of the Other.

Leadership in independent Lebanon was associated with an aggressive assertion of honour. Political bosses recruited a clientele of supporters who pledged their votes in elections in return for jobs, welfare and other patronage services. But supporters also admired a leader who was prepared to use force to promote his and his clients' interests. Many also admired the middle-level leaders of the 'street' or village who had often established themselves as 'men of honour' by killing a rival. As these strong-arm men were usually petty criminals, political bosses would offer them protection from the law enforcement agencies in return for their organizing abilities as popular leaders. In some respects the political system — particularly in the cities — worked as a kind of 'mafia' with the bosses acting as 'godfathers' to their clients, offering personal services in return for support, and providing protection to strong-arm racketeers in return for their organizing the clientele. This point is made in passing in sections 1 and 4 of the second chapter, but is more fully developed in section 6 where a comparison is made between the Lebanese political system and the Calabrian mafia or *'ndrangheta*.

Conflict between political leaders often took the form of feuding, a limited form of violence between men of honour that was governed by rules about the proportionality of injury and vengeance. In the civil wars, however, some political bosses and their militias imposed a vengeance or punishment on their opponents that was out of all proportion. Clearly a sense of communal honour involving wholesale massacres and 'ethnic cleansing' is not the same as the personal sense of honour held by those who use a limited degree of violence to advance their claims to leadership.

Honour, then, is a changing cultural attribute, and in order to understand how it is socially reproduced in different socioeconomic and political conjunctures, I turn in the third chapter to a discussion of Lebanese history. Because many social anthropologists consider a heightened sense of male personal honour to be a particular characteristic of Mediterranean societies, I think it worth spending a short time (in chapter 3, section 2) on an account of the way the concept was used or manipulated in southern Europe prior to the modern period. This might be something of a diversion, but I want to show how notions of honour and heroism are pre-Christian values that seem to have been reproduced in Europe as the ideology of a warrior nobility in opposition to the power of the church. Whether, as at least one author has suggested (Dromgoole 1997), this moral code was derived from classical Greek myths is ultimately beside the point (although it is an idea with interesting possibilities). What is important is that, prior to the modern period, honour in Europe was largely an expression of the aristocracy's right to rule. It was concerned with what Michel Foucault (1976: 197) called the 'symbolics of blood', and with the exercise of arbitrary power and domination over peasants and other 'commoners'.

This was the form it took in 'feudal' Mount Lebanon, and the main concern of chapter 3 is to show, first, how the lords of the Mountain imposed their domination on the peasantry within a hierarchy of honour; second, how 'feudalism' was challenged by capitalism and associated liberal values; and third, how a different form of honour became more widespread as the old agrarian order broke down. Section 3 of the chapter discusses the main social and economic changes that occurred in the nineteenth century: an expansion of mission schools and the dissemination of ideas derived partially from the French revolution of 1789, the extension of the market and new forms of agricultural production; the challenge of the Maronite church to the landlord system; increasing competition for land that now had a commercial value; and peasant revolts and confessional conflict. Then section 4 shows how commoners claimed a right to exercise honour that previously had been largely monopolized by the landlords. Maronite peasant revolutionaries emerged who had a strong-arm style of leadership and they entered into a violent competition for land that led in 1859 to the expulsion of Maronite landlords from the Kisrawan district of the Mountain, and in 1860 to a war between Maronites and Druze that involved the massacres of thousands of Christians. We shall see how the partial collapse of the agrarian order led to a situation in which confessional identity provided a sense of community in an increasingly individualistic and competitive society. After the Christian peasants had expelled their Maronite landlords, Druze lords made appeals to their coreligionist peasants by claiming the Maronites were coming to steal their land. The massacres were a result of the warfare that followed.

Thus the development of capitalism undermined an order based on the inherited honour of warrior lords; and with the development of peasant-proprietorship, it became a quality to which all men could aspire in a society influenced by the idea of what I call an 'egalitarian ethic'. To approach this subject, section 5 of chapter 3 starts with a more detailed consideration of the Calabrian mafia to show the way honour and feuding could provide a sense of order in a highly competitive and 'disordered' rural environment. It is also argued that in an ecology where land and water are limited an ethic or 'myth' of egalitarianism develops, perhaps to control what would otherwise be an unbridled competition for scarce resources. Within this ethic, competition for honour is sanctioned but is controlled by social rules about the proper conduct of feuding. In turn, an assertion of honour allows some to become leaders of village society and to acquire a greater proportion of land and other resources to which, under the terms of the egalitarian ethic, they are not morally entitled.

After the rural upheavals of 1859–60, the Ottomans abolished feudal rights and exactions in the mountains and new leaders began to establish themselves. However, they were not usually created by an assertion of honour through feuding or mafia activity, and so we cannot conclude that rural leaders emerged in Lebanon in the way they seemed to have done in the Calabrian region of southern Italy. Apart from those leaders who might have emerged from the feuds between leading families or clans in the northern district of Zgharta, most parliamentarians in Christian Mount Lebanon came from the professions or established commercial backgrounds (see chapter 3, section 5).

In contrast to the oppressive domination of the landlords, however, the new leaders of the twentieth century subscribed to an egalitarian ethic (or myth) and a form of 'populism' that reflected the necessity to win votes in an increasingly democratic political system. As in the city, leadership on the Mountain was still hierarchical and very much associated with the values of aggressive honour. But it was exercised within a context of liberal democracy and was in marked contrast to the landlord domination that persisted in the Sunni Muslim Akkar region in the far north of the country, and in the predominantly Shi'a regions of the Bekaa valley and southern Lebanon.

Chapter 3 ends (in section 6) with a speculation about whether the values of feuding and honour on the Mountain were then imported into the city. Some Lebanese believe this to have happened, and they even see the mountain feud to be, in some sense, a determinant of confessional conflict. The historian Kamal Salibi (1988: 163–5), for example, argues that a 'heritage of bitter mountain feuds' was absorbed into the modern political system, and that these feuds were an aspect of 'mountain tribalism', which in the nineteenth century had been 'perpetuated by religious and sectarian differences' providing the tribes with 'confessional labels and fighting banners'.

I disagree with some of the implications of this approach and argue that although feuding and confessional conflict share some similar notions of honour, they are in fact different phenomena. As I point out in chapter 2 (section 7), the feud was a 'damage-limitation exercise', whereas confessional conflict was unconstrained and whole communities were destroyed in massacres. In addition, although confessional massacres first occurred in a rural context, the civil wars a century later were determined much more by urban factors than any rural tradition. So there are two crucial distinctions that inform my argument: first, the difference between feuding and confessional war; and second, the difference between the confessional war in 1860 and the wars in the 1970s and 1980s.

The massacres of 1860 were the result of disputes about the ownership of land. The wars of the latter half of the twentieth century, by contrast, were largely conditioned by a reproduction of confessional consciousness as a response to the pressures of urban life. Maronite fighters in 1975 might have thought they 'remembered' the appalling events of 1860 when undefended Christian communities had been exterminated — and the notion of 'collective memory' is something to which I refer at a number of points in my argument. But this 'memory' does not indicate that there was an unbroken line of communal fear and hatred from 1860 to 1975. There were certainly confessional tensions and conflicts, the most serious being the short civil war of 1958, but as we shall see (in chapter 2, section 3) that was more a secular factional conflict between political bosses than a war between Christians and Muslims. The war that started in 1975 was the result of special conditions largely related to the role of the Palestinians in Lebanon, not an enduring hatred between Maronites and Muslims. And, as I explain below, the hatred that was unleashed had more to do with the nature of patriarchy and the 'sexually repressive family' in the city than any memory of past rural conflict.

Feuding between confessional groups did occur with some regularity in modern Lebanon, but it was much like feuding *within* confessions — limited and often settled by mediation (see chapter 3, section 6). Confessional war was quite different. It involved a far higher degree of ethnic identification and a 'demonization' of the Other that made it largely immune to mediation. Specifically, it involved a sense of ethnic or 'romantic' nationalism which was a response to the emotional traumas of a competitive urban existence. To explain these traumatic emotions, it is perhaps helpful to look at psychoanalytic accounts of ethnic identity and conflict. These — along with some comparative material drawn mainly from the Indian subcontinent — are considered in the fourth chapter (section 3).

The use of such psychoanalytic concepts as 'splitting' and 'narcissistic hurt and rage', however, leads us into uncharted territory where many hazards await us. It is therefore argued, in section 4 of chapter 4, that we need to develop a sociology of ethnicity or confessionalism that, informed by the insights and 'metaphors' of psychoanalysis, takes account of the emotional aspects while still holding on to the structural or situational determinants of conflict. Incorporated in this sociology are the cultural notions of blood, kinship and — above all — patriarchy, and in section 5 I consider Hisham Sharabi's account of 'neo-patriarchy' in the Arab world (1988).

Hopefully, the discussions of honour and shame, of psychoanalytic theory, and of patriarchy and the pressures generated within the urban family will help to rectify the lack of a full analysis of confessionalism in *Class and Client*. But before turning to a brief introduction to the argument about patriarchy, it is worth mentioning another aim of this study — that is to situate confessional conflict and such associated values of honour and shame in what might be termed a process of 'modernization'. I hesitate to use this term so many years after so many sociologists and others subjected 'modernization theory' to often devastating critiques, André Gunder Frank (1969) being one of the first, and Samih Farsoun and Lisa Hajjar (1990) being more recent critics and concerned to demonstrate the theory's inadequacy in the context of the Middle East. These days, I suppose, a social scientist anxious to receive the accolade of his peers would be better advised to work with a theory of 'postmodernism' or that other fashionable concept of 'globalization' (and I will not provide the references as there are so many, one hardly knows where to start). But 'modernization' is still a useful word to describe a process that first developed in Europe in the eighteenth century, and in the Middle East in the nineteenth. As a process it includes, among other things, the development of capitalism, industrialization, nationalism, urbanization, and the earlier stages of globalization, as well as rather more specific developments such as structures of 'surveillance' replacing arbitrary repression, and the nuclear family superseding different forms of the extended family.

This will all become clearer as the argument develops in subsequent chapters, but as a starting point it is perhaps necessary to differentiate my use of the concept 'modernization' from the theory that is often associated with it. To oversimplify somewhat, the theory assumed that 'modern' values of rationality, achievement, universalism and the like would gradually diffuse into 'traditional' societies and replace the values of irrationality, ascription, and particularism. The 'pattern-variables' of Talcott Parsons (1952; Parsons and Shils 1951) were manipulated by sociologists of development to explain the 'modernization' process, and there was an assumption that such values as honour and shame, patriarchy and ethnicity, were the residues of an earlier traditional society that would one day be eliminated by the inexorable advance of rationality and science.

My point is that these values, far from being the cultural remainders of tradition, are in many respects the creations of modernity (and I now dispense with the quotation marks around this awkward word and its derivatives). As we shall see in chapter 4 (section 2) tribalism in southern Africa, for example, was not a problem brought to the city from a traditional rural society but, on the contrary, migrant workers from a countryside where social relations had little or nothing to do with ethnicity actually created a tribal identity as a support network in the new mining towns. A similar point will be made about Lebanon where, for example, Shi'a migrants to Beirut in the 1960s became far more conscious of their confessional identity in response to the social and psychological pressures of urban life.

Indeed the evidence from Africa, India and the Middle East suggests that urbanization is the single most important stimulator of tribal, communal, confessional or, to use the generic term, 'ethnic' identity. Other factors are obviously important, however, and we have seen how confessional conflict first erupted, in the mid-nineteenth century, in rural Lebanon. The spread (or 'globalization') of the ideas of nationalism in the nineteenth century might also have had a marginal influence on the Maronites, so one could argue that capitalism, urbanization and nationalism were all possible determinants of ethnic identity. And, in turn, all three phenomena can be conveniently labelled as part of a modernization process. Some might say that ultimately capitalism determined everything else, which I suppose I came close to doing in *Class and Client*. But that seems too reductionist and loses sight of some of the crosscutting influences of the different aspects of modernity.

Having briefly discussed ethnicity, what of such other modern values as honour and patriarchy? Clearly, similar values existed in pre-modern rural society (see, for example, chapter 3, section 2), but the crucial point is that they were reproduced in an urban (or urbanized) context in new and different forms (which is why, incidentally, Hisham Sharabi talks of *neo*-patriarchy). Honour in 'feudal' or agrarian society was a determinant of leadership and domination, most obviously by lords over peasants, and was largely concerned with notions of 'blood', the historical depth of genealogies, and the marriage alliances that cemented dynastic power. With the development of urbanization, a process started that Michel Foucault (1976: 197) encapsulated in his point about the 'symbolics of blood' being replaced with the 'analytics of sexuality'.

Foucault argues that, in Europe during the early years of the nineteenth century, the male members of the sexually repressed bourgeoisie became concerned with a patriarchal project to control women and children. Very significantly, they imposed controls on the sexuality of their families that reflected their concern for clean and healthy descent (Foucault 1976: 159–60). They seem to have been motivated more by a desire to create a new class-based genealogy than by tracing the historical lineages of particular families; and the 'honour' of these 'neopatriarchs' came to reside in the control of their women's 'shame' (see chapter 4, section 5).

Although there are differences between the neopatriarchy of nineteenth-century Europe and that of the modern Middle East, the similarities are far more significant. In Europe women were controlled by theories and practices relating to their 'nervousness', their 'unreliability' and their 'hysteria'. In the Middle East and some other Mediterranean countries, women are seen as sexually threatening to the order of society and are to varying degrees secluded from the males they might seduce. Thus it seems that compared with pre-modern agrarian society, honour in an urbanized Lebanon is perhaps more concerned with the control of women than with the imposition of domination on lesser men.

The honour of men in modern Lebanese society was increasingly determined by the proper behaviour of their women, and by their ability to protect their wives, daughters and sisters from becoming shamed. This was an onerous burden, and the need to control women (and young men) could create a rebellious reaction that required more controls in a depressing cycle of greater repression. As we shall see in chapter 4, 'romantic' or ethnic nationalism, articulated in Lebanon by such confessional organizations as the predominantly Maronite Phalanges party, laid great stress on family values, on women as mothers of the nation, and men as the defenders of their family and community. The romantic nationalism of Maronite and Muslim particularists provided myths of origin for their respective communities and a sense of security and status for patriarchs, their women and their adolescent sons. Discipline, authoritarianism and strong leadership were highly valued and reflected, buttressed and justified the patriarch's role in the sexually repressive family. Women were valued as mothers and the providers of hearth and home. And the party and militia structures of ethnic nationalism provided opportunities for young men to behave in an obstreperous or even violent fashion not sanctioned by the repressive family — but they did so in an organizational context that required submission to a cause and its patriarchal leader.

This sense of belonging and security was particularly comforting in the often frightening world of the city where men were forced to compete with each other for jobs, markets or other ways of making a living and providing for their family. This is not to deny the competitive individualism of the countryside, particularly in those areas of Mount Lebanon where smallholding agriculture predominated (chapter 3, sections 4 and 5). That individualism was also a result of modernity, specifically of capitalism and the commercialization of agriculture. For many of the Shi'a migrants to Beirut, however, the city was much more competitive than the landed estates from which they had been expelled by their lords in the 1960s. Life as a sharecropper had been hard and poor, but the often harsh domination of the landlords had been tempered by the occasional act of kindness, perhaps the granting of a loan, help with medical treatment, or simply the landlord's presence at a family wedding or funeral. As we shall see in chapter 2, the status hierarchy in agrarian society was in many respects a willing or consensual dependence of those without honour on their honourable lords. Sharecropping peasants knew their place and, although they might have resented the arbitrary cruelty of their landlord, they had little choice in the matter and therefore little opportunity to imagine a different social order. Ultimately the lord provided land and the means to scratch a living. He also provided a secure order. When the Shi'a landlords of southern Lebanon turned to mechanized farming in the 1960s and expelled their peasants, thousands of migrants made their way to the slums and shanty towns of Beirut. Betrayed by their lords, divorced from the land that had fed them, their sense of order was shattered, and in the city they had to compete with other members of a growing sub-proletariat or 'under-class' for scarce jobs and housing. No wonder so many of them eventually turned, in the 1980s, to their Shi'a confessional organizations in a search for a moral and social security (see chapter 4, section 2).

Confessionalism, then, created order in a disordered economy and society, and we shall see that this was important for the urban 'salariat' and small-property owners as well as the sub-proletariat. Confessionalism created community out of chaos, and provided a discourse that explained a confusing and unjust world. Not only did it provide a sense of belonging but also, by defining a hated Other, it gave people someone to blame for the misery of urban life.

There were, however, other forces at work in the modernization process, and it is here that Michel Foucault's analysis of surveillance (1975) is important. During the nineteenth century, he argues, European society created 'carceral' or cellular structures such as workhouses, factories, barracks, asylums, hospitals and schools that resembled the cell-structure of the prison. These divided people into production lines, platoons, wards and classrooms where workers, soldiers, patients and pupils were held under the eye or 'gaze' of social authority. Such carceral structures were not necessarily imposed by a bourgeois state in the interests of capitalism, but were often generated by civil society itself. Doctors and nurses created the ward, teachers the classroom, and thus there developed a network of 'micro-powers' in which people policed themselves and developed self-discipline in place of an order structured by domination.

In chapter 4 (section 5) I argue that carceral structures and self-surveillance also developed in urban Lebanon in the nineteenth and twentieth centuries. Schools, hospitals, commercial networks, and the like created sophisticated structures in civil society that made a significant contribution to social order. Ultimately, even trade unions came into their own as civic organizations. Prior to the civil wars they had been weak and largely under the domination of powerful politicians and other representatives of the commercial-financial elite (Johnson 1986: 41). By the late 1980s, however, they were in the forefront of the multiconfessional opposition to the warlords.

My use of the concept of surveillance suggests a more optimistic future for postwar Lebanon than my despairing conclusion to *Class and Client*. I was wrong to assume that order could only be imposed from above and that 'ordinary' Lebanese were incapable of taking control of their own destiny. Nevertheless, a recognition of the significant role played by the institutions of civil society should not obscure the fact that the latter continue to compete with neopatriarchal structures of domination. The final chapter of this book points to some serious problems in the Second Republic, not least of which are the close controls imposed on trade union activity by the state, and the continuation of a confessional system of representation in a polity still controlled by a repressive regime.

6. Ethnicity and history

Although I want to understand the emotions of confessional and ethnic conflict, it should be clear by now that I am not adopting a 'primordial' approach to the subject. Unfortunately such an analysis is often implicit in other accounts of Lebanese politics and society, and all too often explicit. During the civil wars of the 1970s and 1980s many journalistic accounts in newspapers and other media saw confessional conflict as a 'fact' of Lebanese history. It was almost as if there had been an unbroken line of confessional antagonism ever since the Muslim Arab conquest of the eastern provinces of the Christian Byzantine empire in the seventh century. The line had continued through the Crusades by European Christians to take possession of the holy places of Syria and Palestine in the eleventh, twelfth and thirteenth centuries, and on through the subordination of Christians under a succession of Muslim rulers, the last being the Ottomans who controlled Lebanon from the early sixteenth century until 1918 (apart from a brief Egyptian interregnum in the 1830s).

There is no doubt that in terms of the 'collective memories' of the various protagonists in Lebanon's civil wars, a period like the Crusades provided a rich source of myths. The PLO's Palestinian Liberation Army in Syria was known as the 'Hittin brigade' after the victory of Salah ad-Din al-Ayyubi (Saladin) and his troops over the Frankish forces at Hittin in Palestine in 1187 (Cooley 1973: 23). Palestinians and Lebanese Muslims drew a parallel between the Zionist 'occupation' of Israel and the Crusades, taking comfort from the fact that after two centuries or so the European knights had been expelled. Maronites 'remembered' that they had fought alongside the Franks, and the Phalangist militia came to see itself as the modern equivalent of a knightly order like the Templar warrior monks (see chapter 2, section 7). But it is mistaken to assume from this that Muslims and Christians have always 'remembered' the Crusades with equal intensity down through the generations to the modern period.

Even in more academic writing there is an assumption that confessional identification is deeply embedded in Lebanese history. Helena Cobban (1985), for example, sees the politics of Lebanon in terms of an 'inter-sect system' that dates back to the fourteenth century when she incorrectly assumes that the original Shi'a inhabitants of the Kisrawan district of Mount Lebanon had been expelled by Maronite settlers from the north (Cobban 1985: 36). In fact the major migrations of Maronites started in the sixteenth century, and the Shi'a were finally persuaded or forced to leave in large numbers during the eighteenth century (Salibi 1988: 103–6). Apart from this historical inaccuracy, there is some superficial logic to Cobban's argument. The inter-sect system involved the different communities of Lebanon accepting the dominance of one sect over the others, with another sect or confession in a supportive second place. Under the 'emirate' or princedom of Mount Lebanon, which had been established by the Ottomans in the early sixteenth century and lasted until 1842, the Druze were the dominant community. In the last years of the emirate the Maronites challenged the Druze, eventually reducing them to second place, despite an initial Christian defeat in 1860.

With the creation of Greater Lebanon in 1920, the Sunnis of the coastal cities, and the Shi'a of the Bekaa valley and the southern mountains, were incorporated into the system. The Maronites maintained their 'prime' position in the new arrangement, with the Sunnis in second place. Eventually the Shi'a challenged the Maronites for 'primacy within the system' and the years of warfare after 1975 represent, for Cobban (1985: 211–12), not 'a period of decay' but one of 'transition' comparable to that which had occurred in the nineteenth century.

The problem with this sort of approach is its underlying primordialism. Cobban (1985: 218) talks of 'the rushing resurgence of the atavisms of a long-gone age'. The civil wars of the twentieth century are seen as virtually the same as the wars of the nineteenth — just another round of conflict in a sectarian system. After the bloodshed, Cobban believes, everything could return to normal with a Shi'a dominance that, we might add, would presumably persist for another hundred years when some other sect would challenge for primacy. It seems that Lebanon is doomed to a cycle of conflict between confessions — communities that, in Clifford Geertz's words (1963: 109), are the 'givens' of Lebanese 'social existence' and are 'unaccountable' except in terms of the 'coerciveness' of the ties of 'blood'.

Another reading of Lebanese history might emphasize the long periods of communal harmony. We could point to the fact there were hundreds of years of relative harmony from the time of the Crusades until the gradual expulsion of the Shi'a from the Kisrawan in the seventeenth and eighteenth centuries (and even then many Shi'a left with money paid as compensation for their land). Then there was communal peace from the time of the Maronite migrations until the Druze–Maronite wars of the mid-nineteenth century, and again from 1860 until 1975. However, this too would be something of an oversimplification, and we shall see that there were periodic outbreaks of confessional tension and fighting throughout the nineteenth and twentieth centuries.

The important point is that the different confessional conflicts in Lebanese history were not the result of an unchanging, always-existing, primordial consciousness. The Crusades were the result of a European invasion inspired by Pope Urban's religious appeal to the nobility in 1095, by a certain sense of piety on the part of some of the knights who responded, and by the prospect of booty and plunder for most others. The tensions between Maronite settlers and Shi'a peasants did not involve large-scale massacres comparable to those that had occurred during the Crusades or would occur again in 1860 and 1975–90, and so they could hardly be described as confessional warfare. The conflict was more like that which we find throughout pre-modern history when one tribe migrated into the area of another. The massacres of 1860, by contrast, were the result of the differential mobilization of Maronite and Druze peasants in terms of their incorporation into a new market economy, and of their differential access to western educational and trading influences. As we shall see (in chapter 3, section 3), Maronite Christians benefited more than the Druze from Catholic mission schools and contact with western merchants, and they acquired an acquisitive ethic earlier than the Muslims. Then, after the peasant revolts in 1858–59, the Druze came to fear that the Maronites would take their land, and so they fought a war in which thousands of Christians were slaughtered.

Finally, the wars of the 1970s and 1980s started because the commandos of the Palestine Liberation Organization were using Lebanon as a base to attack Israel and were arming and training a number of predominantly Muslim parties and militias. The PLO believed they needed the support of these militias to prevent the Maronite (and Sunni) political establishment from expelling them from a country that was increasingly subjected to Israeli reprisal raids. Not surprisingly, the protagonists defined themselves along confessional lines, the Muslims with a sense of a wider Arab nationalism and the Maronites holding to a specifically Lebanese identity. But had it not been for the PLO's militarization of Lebanese politics (and the responsive militarization of the Maronites), all the socioeconomic and confessional tensions in Lebanon could have been contained by the Lebanese state (see chapter 2, section 6, and chapter 4, sections 4 and 6).

Central to my argument is the crucial fact that the twentieth-century conflict was in large part one between competing nationalisms, and this indicates a significant difference compared with the events of 1860. We shall see (in chapter 3, section 3) that apart from some minor influences, nationalism was not a major issue in 1860. Competing ideas of nationality developed in the late nineteenth and early twentieth centuries and were an urban not a rural phenomenon. In addition, the ethnic or romantic nationalisms that emerged in the twentieth century were far more the result of rural–urban migration and social change in the city than any rural conflict over land (chapter 4).

In other words, serious confessional conflict first emerged as an early modern phenomenon in a rural social formation and it was later reproduced in another form at a later stage of the modernization process as a result of urbanization. Confessionalism is not a residue from antiquity or 'traditional' society. It is something that is re-created, like honour and shame, as part of a process of social reproduction in the nineteenth and then again in the twentieth centuries.

2

Honour and Confession

At least three different types of honour existed in Lebanon prior to the civil wars of the 1970s and 1980s. First there was honour in the sense of nobility, the prestige that attached to a man of high birth. In those areas of the countryside where landlordism persisted, this form of honour was largely defined in terms of family genealogies that could be traced back over many generations — sometimes to the seventeenth century or even earlier — and it was associated with an arbitrary and oppressive power exercised by the lords over their peasants. In the city, by contrast, the most influential political leaders or 'za'ims' (*zu'ama*) often belonged to notable merchant families that had established themselves relatively recently in the nineteenth or early twentieth centuries. Their high birth and prestige buttressed a leadership that, in the context of a liberal democracy, was more responsive to the needs of their followers or 'clients' who were given patronage such as jobs and welfare in return for their political support.

A second form of honour was the respect claimed by a man who was willing to use violence to establish and maintain his leadership. This was more associated with the za'ims' lieutenants or 'qabadays' (*qabadayat*), most of whom had claimed honour by killing or otherwise defeating a rival. Many of these leaders of the street or urban quarter were criminals and racketeers, but particularly amongst the poor they were admired popular leaders and were protected by their high-status patrons in return for their organizing and policing the za'ims' clienteles. In parliamentary elections, for example, qabadays provided security for the 'political machine' and ensured that their political bosses' clients voted as they were directed (Johnson 1997).

Finally, a third type of honour related to men's control of 'their' women. For many Lebanese, the honour of their family was enshrined in the proper behaviour of wives and daughters, and honourable men were required to ensure that the women in their family did not become shamed or act in a shameless way. This notion of conjugal or sexual honour was of immense concern to patriarchal heads of families in all social classes, and we shall see how the rape of enemy women in the civil wars could be interpreted as a calculated insult to the men who should have protected them.

The complexities of these different forms of honour are discussed in the first five sections of this chapter. Then in section 6, I show how an heroic culture of honour contributed to the maintenance of an effective and relatively efficient sociopolitical order in Lebanon during the 1950s, 1960s and early 1970s.

Personal honour in prewar Lebanon was associated with feuding, a limited form of violence in which some men would kill to assert and defend their honour and leadership but where there were socially defined rules that emphasized proportional acts of vengeance rather than widespread slaughter and massacre. Soon after the fighting started in 1975, however, a new form of honour was 'reproduced' in confessional and ethnic conflicts in which the protagonists seemed to be motivated by a desire to impose a complete shame on their communal enemies by employing rape, pillage and 'ethnic cleansing' as strategies of war. The differences between personal and communal honour, and between limited feuding and confessional war, are discussed in section 7, prior to a concluding section that introduces the notion of the 'social reproduction' of honour which forms a large part of the next chapter's subject matter.

1. Nobility and respect

Despite disagreements and differences in approach, many anthropologists in the 1960s and 1970s tended to see the Mediterranean region as a distinct cultural entity with the 'honour and shame' dichotomy as a central if not defining characteristic (Peristiany 1965; Pitt-Rivers 1965; Schneider 1971; Black-Michaud 1975; Davis 1977). In the 1980s the ubiquity and homogeneity of honour began to be questioned (Herzfeld 1980; 1984; 1985; Wikan 1984; Brandes 1987) and it was argued that other 'moral principles' were more prominent, perhaps as a result of social change or what David Gilmore called 'rapid modernization'. Nevertheless, in editing a collection of papers on the subject in 1987, Gilmore could still argue that the critics of the orthodox approach 'would probably all agree that these "other" moral principles ... hospitality, respect, and honesty, are also specifically Mediterranean values which can and do complement the classic honor/shame system' (Gilmore 1987: 3).

Having said that, all would probably also agree with Carol Delaney (1987:

35) that the concepts of honour and shame were 'not uniform and constant throughout the Mediterranean area'. Even a cursory reading of the literature reveals that the notion of honour was used in a variety of ways in different societies, and this perhaps explains why so many different analyses were offered by social anthropologists.

The problem about honour is its inherent ambiguity and the ambivalent attitudes people have to those who are said to possess it. What might be seen as honourable behaviour by some people in society can be considered dishonourable by others, and while people might recognize someone as honourable there could be a degree of resentment involved in doing so. We can illustrate this, and give an indication of one difference of opinion in the literature, by referring to John Davis's review of the subject in 1977.

Davis took issue with J. K. Campbell (1964) and C. Lison-Tolosana (1966) who appeared to deny a connection between honour and economic and political power. It was a careful argument in which Davis (1977: 100) stated quite clearly that the stratification of honour could not be 'assimilated to class or organizational rank' in an exact or simple way. However, honour could be seen as 'a system of stratification' that 'describes the distribution of wealth in a social idiom, and prescribes appropriate behaviour for people at the various points in the hierarchy' (Davis 1977: 98). The rich have more honour than the poor, and thus they can insult inferior men and seduce or violate their women (Davis 1977: 91), demand and obtain respect, and at the same time — for honour binds leaders and led together — they and the poor see their relationship as a '*co-operative* dependence of those who have less honour on those who have more' (Davis 1977: 98, my emphasis).

This is a crucial point, and we shall see how honour in modern Lebanon was closely connected with other forms of stratification such as class and power. Campbell (1964: 306) was surely correct, however, when he suggested that a rich man could be without honour; and, as we shall see, it is important to differentiate honour from other forms of status, such as nobility for example, just as it is essential to follow the well-known prescriptions of Max Weber (1948) and distinguish between the stratifications of class, status and power (discussed below). They may overlap in important ways, but in order to prepare the ground for demonstrating the extent and nature of the overlap, it is as well to make clear distinctions at the outset.

In relation to the distinction between honour and nobility, Davis pressed his critique of Campbell by pointing out that 'families with very high prestige can do things which, if they had less, would be dishonourable' (Davis 1977: 95), and he used Campbell's reference to an 'incestuous' marriage between cousins (Campbell 1964: 267) to illustrate his point. Davis argued that Campbell's

account of Sarakatsan shepherds in the mountains of northern Greece showed
how a high-status couple from a leading lineage had honour despite their incest.
In fact, Campbell's account does not necessarily demonstrate this was the case;
but if the shepherds did continue to recognize the family's honour, presumably
they were using the concept to describe other attributes of behaviour or birth
and were overlooking what must otherwise have been seen by them as a dishonourable union.

What is honourable or acceptable in one social class or status might not be so
in another. Often it seems that, even within a single class or stratum, there is
considerable disagreement over what is honourable. Ultimately, it is Julian Pitt-
Rivers who was right when he wrote that 'respect and precedence are paid to
those who claim it and are sufficiently powerful to enforce their claim. ... *On the
field of honour might is right*' (Pitt-Rivers 1965: 24–5, my emphasis).

Further consideration of the literature on honour is probably counter-
productive. The exchanges in academic journals between social anthropologists
reveal that there is much confusion in the academy about what is being
discussed. More importantly, confusion also reigns in the societies that the
anthropologists study. The overarching sociological concept of honour includes
a variety of different indigenous meanings, and the latter are usually less precise
than those wielded by the academics. Let us start with the proposition that
when it comes to defining what is honourable, all that can be said with any
degree of certainty is that 'might is right'.

Thus the honour we are initially concerned with is the *respect* accruing to a
man (and only rarely to a woman) as a result of his use of implicit or explicit
force. It is similar to the respect paid to Jesus by those who admired his cunning
use of miraculous powers to win a night with Marilyn Monroe (see chapter 1,
section 1), but who might at the same time have felt that the use of those
powers made him a dishonourable cheat or even a bully. In the end, Jesus
imposed his will by the use of a superior power.

Honour as 'respect' should be distinguished from the essentially urban
concept of nobility or notability. Notables, who usually inherit their status, may
sometimes have respect as well, but their role in Lebanon before the civil wars
— or at least in Beirut and other cities — often depended more on their families'
wealth, political involvement, and reputation for philanthropy, going back over
at least one or two generations. Roles more directly associated with respect were
those of *za'im* and *qabaday* (Johnson 1997). Za'ims were powerful parliamentarians who operated as patriarchal political bosses at the head of a clientele that
included armed retainers or qabadays. The latter were strong-arm leaders of the
'street', urban quarter or village, who had emerged from the 'common people'
after using force to establish their claims to leadership.

Many Lebanese despised these leaders, but it is remarkable how many others admired them. One way of claiming the status of qabaday was to kill an enemy, a rival, or anyone who showed insufficient respect, and such 'honourable' behaviour was at least grudgingly admired by part of the local population and adulated by a significant minority. Because 'honour crimes' were treated leniently by the courts, and za'ims were prepared to influence the judges, qabadays did not usually serve long sentences for murder. Also, much of their activity as pimps, protection racketeers and smugglers was ignored by the police who, so long as they were paid off in one way or another, were prepared to tolerate a controlled level of criminality.

In effect, some sectors of the Lebanese political system operated like a patriarchal 'mafia' with the za'ims acting as godfathers to their clientele. They would offer protection from the law to the popular leaders of the street and village in return for the qabadays' organizing and controlling the clients and occasionally mobilizing armed men to fight for their patrons' interests (Johnson 1986: 82–95).

As a result of this violent style of leadership, political conflict between za'ims sometimes — and between qabadays relatively often — took the form of vendetta or feuding. Some social anthropologists make refined distinctions between the concepts of 'feud', 'blood feud' and 'vendetta'. In his famous study of the Nilotic Nuer people in Sudan, for example, E. E. Evans-Pritchard (1940: 150) distinguished the general concept of feud from the 'specific institution' of 'blood feud', while others have emphasized the difference between a limited feud (or blood feud) and vendetta. Thus, for some, blood feud properly refers to a system of violence in which the culturally accepted *lex talionis* or law of retaliation insists on a directly proportional vengeance of a life for a life, while vendetta involves 'unrestricted killing between two groups in a society' (Beattie 1966: 150). Vendetta is not the same as war, however, and a 'degree of social control is always implicit' (Beattie 1966: 150). I would normally be prepared to use these terms interchangeably. However, in the interests of clarity, for the most part I will dispense with the concept of vendetta and use 'feud' or 'blood feud' to refer to a limited form of conflict between self-defined groups in society where the parties to the dispute accept that vengeance should be broadly proportional, though not necessarily exactly so. Limited homicide, and the emphasis on seeking mediation to end the feud, distinguish this form of conflict from war where killing is more or less unrestricted and not easily subject to a mediated resolution.

Feuding between qabadays in Lebanon was similar to that identified by Jacob Black-Michaud who argued that honour in a society with a weak central authority or state is a prize won in 'the successful prosecution of feud' (Black-

Michaud 1975: 184) and serves to create and legitimize leadership. 'In feuding societies,' he wrote, 'honour and power are synonymous' (Black-Michaud 1975: 178). In Lebanon, however, people could have power without honour or, like most of the 'street-level' qabadays, they could have great honour but only limited power. Once more it is clear that a careful distinction must be made between honour and other forms of stratification.

Max Weber's distinctions are a useful starting point. In his well-known essay on the subject (1948, first published as part of a larger work in German in 1921) he defined three types of stratification. His definition of economic 'class' was similar to Karl Marx's 'relations of production', although Weber emphasized relations determined by people's opportunities in the economic market. 'Status' referred more to patterns of consumption than production, and was defined in terms of a person's 'style of life' and social prestige. In Lebanon such statuses as honour and notable family are marks of prestige — as are confessional categories insofar as Muslims, and particularly Shi'a, are (or certainly were) generally considered to be of a lower social status than Christians. Finally, Weber's concept of 'party' referred to the stratification of political power, about which more later (in section 6 of this chapter).

In discussing the status of honour, a consideration of a number of social classes might be significant. Generally speaking, we might assume that in the city the commercial-financial bourgeoisie would have more honour or prestige than the petty bourgeoisie (or lower middle class) and considerably more than the sub-proletariat (the unemployed, semi-employed, or 'under-class'). But by becoming a qabaday, a member of the sub-proletariat could lay claim to respect and would be recognized as honourable. In the countryside, landlords were invariably seen as having more honour than the peasants, but even here a peasant could become a qabaday. Similarly, in relation to political power, a strong and brave man could command considerable respect or honour, but he might have only limited opportunities in the political system.

2. Honour and shame

There are a number of words in Arabic that can be translated as 'honour' (Kressel 1988; 1992) but they all have shades of meaning that demonstrate the complexity of the concept I am trying to define. In discussing the system of honour in the northern Lebanese region of Akkar, Michael Gilsenan (1989; 1996) distinguishes between two local concepts used when he conducted his fieldwork in 1971–72. The word *karama* was used to describe 'personal honour and integrity', while *sharaf* referred to honour in the sense of 'controlling the sexual purity of group and individual' (Gilsenan 1989: 214). It seemed to me that in Beirut, however, *sharaf* was often used to imply high rank or nobility, with some suggestion that this was an inherited quality. Someone who was *sharif* was honourable, respectable and distinguished, with a connotation of being high-born. The word *sharif* is also commonly used for a descendant of the Prophet Muhammad, which again indicates the 'ascriptive' content of this form of honour.

Another word with a similar meaning is *wajh* which literally means face or countenance. In English the idea of losing face is associated with a loss of *respect*, but in Lebanon — at least in the Sunni Muslim quarters of Beirut where I conducted my fieldwork in 1972–73 — the derived word *wajih* was used for a local notable who was usually of high *birth*. A more 'achieved' (as opposed to 'ascribed') quality was contained in the word *muhtaram*, meaning honoured, revered and, very significantly, respected. From the same root is derived *ihtiram*, meaning respect or deference.

These are perhaps subtle nuances, but the distinction is clear enough. Honour in my sense of *sharaf* can be used to define a notable's status that is buttressed by — although not necessarily synonymous with — high birth and inheritance. *Ihtiram*, on the other hand, is a much more active concept and implies a degree of moral or physical force. It is the Arabic word probably closest to the Italian mafia's concept of 'respect'.

In fact the differences between Gilsenan's and my interpretations of *sharaf* are not as great as they might first appear. Although, in the rural society of north Lebanon, the word was 'particularly identified with the control of women's sexuality', the suggestion that the low-born peasants could possess such honour was regarded by the high-born landlords and their armed retainers as 'a source of mockery or a social solecism' (Gilsenan 1996: 189). As we shall see (in section 4 of this chapter) only those possessed of a genealogy could exercise *sharaf* in Akkar and protect the honour of their women. The peasants had no real knowledge of their descent, certainly no written genealogy, and were seen as lacking both history and honour. One might even say that in the local discourse of honour this lack of a socially recognized descent contributed to, or even caused, the peasants' inability to prevent the violation of their women by their high-born lords.

Although Beirutis also used *sharaf* to describe sexual honour, a perhaps more precise concept was *'ird*. Whatever their inherited status, many men would claim and then seek to protect *'ird* by imposing sometimes draconian controls on their wives, daughters and sisters. Clearly the same notion of conjugal and sexual honour existed in both places, but in Akkar it was restricted to those with a noble descent, while in the city it was an attribute that could be held by the humble as well as the strong. In fact, many Lebanese would argue that *'ird* is a quality that all possess. No longer something 'claimed', it is simply there within the family to be preserved and protected. This remains a powerful normative value in contemporary Lebanon, as indeed does the idea of respect and the associated honour codes of vengeance and feuding. While only a minority of Lebanese are prepared to carry the protection or promotion of honour as far as committing acts of violence, such behaviour is not unusual. As Massoud Younes (1999: 9–10) points out, Lebanese newspapers regularly carry reports of honour crimes and blood vengeance, and his account of a father shooting a pregnant but unmarried daughter in January 1999 is just one example of the continuing social significance of honour and shame.

In summary, although there are differences in the local usage of particular words, analytically we can differentiate at least three concepts of honour in modern Lebanon: being high-born or of high status; having (or 'imposing') respect; and preserving honour or 'ird in the sense of defending the 'shame' of women. Although it cannot be easily translated into Arabic, the notion of women having shame or 'sexual modesty' (Black-Michaud 1975: 218) rather than honour is a recurring theme in the literature on the Mediterranean and demonstrates the way honour is 'closely associated with sex' as Julian Pitt-Rivers (1961: 114) once put it with customary bluntness. Honour is a fundamental property of men whose task it is to defend their women's shame from assault and ensure they do not descend into a shameless state. The woman's hymen is the boundary of that shame. Once it is broken the husband 'can come and go as he pleases, as he, but no one else, may enter his fields with ease' (Delaney 1987: 40, paraphrasing sura 2 of the Koran). If another enters the 'field of shame' then the husband or other responsible males, such as brothers or father, are shamed themselves, thus making male honour in the sense of 'ird particularly vulnerable (as we shall see in section 7) in the violation of women in war.

As an aside, it is perhaps worth mentioning that some exceptional (or mythological) women may demand and obtain respect. A particularly colourful example drawn from another part of the Middle East is Aziza al-Fahla, who was one of the few women among the *futuwwat* of Cairo in the early part of the twentieth century. The *futuwwat* were the equivalent of the qabadays of Beirut, and it was written of Aziza that, 'One blow from her hand was enough to knock any man to the ground. A blow with her head would split a stone' (quoted in translation in El-Messiri 1977: 243).

Also, many militias in the Lebanese civil wars recruited some women as fighters. This seems to have been a response to feminist pressures, which were carried from Europe into the cosmopolitan society that existed in Beirut. Such women, however, were still stereotyped: they were token women, beautiful young fighters or the avenging mothers of male martyrs (Sharara 1978: 14–15). Or they were some other bizarre construct of a male imagination. In his history of the Maronites, Butrus Daw (1978: 17 and 39–50) traced the women of the Christian militias back to the Phoenician goddess Astarte. The 'daughters of Ashtarata', he tells us, became 'the Lebanese women who invaded the world and spread the elements of civilization', and this 'Amazonate' that was 'renowned for chivalry' became 'a symbol of the women fighters in the Lebanese war of 1975' (quoted in translation in Khuri 1990: 158).

There was not, however, much evidence of chivalric values. To be accepted by their male comrades the militia women had to be more courageous and more bloodthirsty. Two Israeli journalists, Ze'ev Schiff and Ehud Ya'ari (1986: 17), describe how in 1976 a military delegation from their country to the Maronite enclave in Lebanon met with two female fighters, one of whom carried a plastic bag of amputated fingers and the other a bag of earlobes. These were their trophies cut from the men they had killed. Similarly, American and European journalists in Beirut claimed to have met up with a group of 'uniformed young women' on the front-line 'who proudly showed them a sack of male genitalia' (Randal 1990: 78).

3. Nobility and honour

When I lived in Beirut in the early 1970s, status was socially defined in a number of different ways, but one important indicator was family background. Some families or clans were considered to be high-born or notable, while others were of middle or inferior status. The word family (*'a'ila*) is used here to refer to a patrilineal kinship group, bearing the same surname and having the same confession, that traced its descent from common ancestors. Such families in Beirut and its hinterland could be several thousand strong, but despite the fact that nearly all of them had members who were politically insignificant, economically poor, or of low social status, people perceived some families as being socially pre-eminent. This status, as it were, 'rubbed off' on to all members of the clan, so that my laundry man, for example, was held in some esteem by the predominantly poor inhabitants of our quarter in Beirut because he belonged to a middle to high-status Sunni Muslim family. Despite his low-status occupation and the fact that he did not usually have much to do with his rich and high-status kin, the local washerman was seen as well connected and possessed of a certain amount of prestige and influence.

My neighbours tended to identify a notable family (*bayt ma'ruf*: 'known house') in terms of the core lineages' history of wealth, philanthropy and political activity going back at least one or two generations. This status was usually inherited by the direct descendants of nineteenth and early twentieth-century merchants, while in the countryside nobility was more often associated with the families of landlords who could trace their ancestry through many generations of local power. Michael Gilsenan's study, for example, shows that while many landlord families in the Sunni region of Akkar had, by the early 1970s, sold their land, or had lost their political power, they were still known as 'beys' (originally an Ottoman rank), a status that was largely based on their possession of detailed genealogies back to a single Kurdish ancestor in the seventeenth century (Gilsenan 1996: 41–2). Similarly, the Jumblat family, Druze landlords or their descendants in the Shouf region of Mount Lebanon, claimed descent from a Kurdish warlord who in the early seventeenth century had rebelled against the Ottomans in northern Syria and briefly established an emirate. When the rebellion failed, the Jumblats were said to have found refuge in the Lebanese mountains, becoming a dominant landlord group in the 1690s (Joumblatt 1982: 26–7; Salibi 1965: 10).

We shall see that landlord power was often arbitrary and onerous, and the stories or 'narratives' (Gilsenan 1996) of peasants told of the harsh exaction of work and tribute imposed upon them. By contrast, the urban notables' status was more usually associated with a reputation for generosity and philanthropy extended to their poorer kin and neighbours. The way they were described to me in Beirut, the prestige of early twentieth century notables in effect required that they gave assistance to the poor, providing jobs, money and welfare, as well as mediating in disputes and performing other political services. With the growth of parliamentary democracy under the French Mandate (1920–43), however, active political leadership in Lebanon became a virtual monopoly of political bosses (za'ims) who had a more coercive and forceful style and who, in the cities, organized sophisticated political machines to recruit and control a clientele of supporters (Johnson 1986).

As a rank in the democratic political system, the term *za'im* was probably first applied to Lebanon's rural parliamentarians who were the descendants of such old landed families as the Druze Jumblats in the Shouf region of the Mountain (*Mont Liban*), and the Shi'a As'ads in southern Lebanon. A second type of rural za'im emerged in Christian Mount Lebanon from families that rose to political prominence during the late nineteenth and early twentieth centuries. Camille Chamoun, from the Shouf market town and administrative centre of Dayr al-Qamar, who was president of Lebanon from 1952 to 1958, was by profession a lawyer and his father had been a civil servant in the finance department of the Lebanese autonomous province or governorate (*mutasarrifiyya*) of the Ottoman empire. Another president, Suleiman Frangieh (1970–76), from the mountain district of Zgharta in north Lebanon, belonged to a family who, although they had some land, seem to have acquired most of their wealth through trade and other business activities. His paternal grandfather had served as a district administrator during the period of the *mutasarrifiyya*, and his father had been a member of parliament under the French Mandate (Goria 1985: 36 and 123; Harris 1997: 112).

The followings of these rural za'ims, particularly those from landlord families, tended to be more stable than the clienteles of urban bosses, and were in some areas buttressed by values of consensual fealty rooted in a 'feudal' past. Nevertheless, relations between rival landlords were often highly competitive and it seems that their forceful reputation for honour was even more important than in the city for maintaining the respect of their followings. Violence against one's rivals was certainly not a hindrance to political advancement in an 'heroic society' (Gilsenan 1996: 57).

During the 1960 elections, for example, Sabri Hamada, the Shi'a za'im and landlord of the northern Bekaa valley, got into a quarrel during the campaign and shot and wounded an army officer who was supervising the electoral process. Hamada was returned from his constituency with a substantial majority and, despite the fact that the security forces' investigation of the shooting incident was not yet completed, he was elected by the parliament to be its chairman or speaker (Kerr 1960: 270). More remarkably, Suleiman Frangieh, the Maronite za'im of Zgharta, was elected president of Lebanon by the parliament in 1970, even though he and his gunmen had in 1957 fought a battle with a rival clan that had resulted in a number of fatalities. Shooting his rivals was one thing, but where they were killed was quite another. The shoot-out had taken place in a church in the Zgharta district, during or (depending on the teller of the story) just prior to a requiem mass for a local parishioner (Gilmour 1983: 44; Glass 1990: 300–1; Gordon 1980: 56; Randal 1990: 125–6; and see chapter 3, section 5, below).

It should be clear that one of the characteristics distinguishing a za'im from other notables was the respect (*ihtiram*) attached to his role. Like other notables a za'im inherited nobility, but he had to assert himself in violent and heroic acts against his enemies and others who thwarted him. During the civil war, of course, opportunities for feuding and demonstrating honour increased. A well-known case is the intra-Maronite vendetta between the Frangiehs and Gemayels. Following the distinction made in the first section of this chapter, I use the word 'vendetta' here to emphasize the relatively unrestricted degree of violence involved in this particular 'feud'. But although this conflict between two Maronite political families was in some respects *sui generis*, it does illustrate several characteristics of what might be described as the Lebanese political culture of honour and heroism.

Up until the late 1970s, the various Maronite militias usually co-operated in the civil war against their common enemies (Palestinians and Lebanese Muslims and 'leftists'). However, after the Syrians had imposed a fragile truce in 1976, intra-confessional tensions came to the fore. Eventually Bashir Gemayel used his position as the commander of the Phalangist militia to impose his hegemony over other Maronite forces and bring most of them into a unified structure under his command. One of his first moves was to strike against the power of the former president of Lebanon, Suleiman Frangieh, in northern Lebanon. In particular, he wanted to weaken the family's militia under the command of Suleiman's son, Tony, and also he was apparently determined to take over some lucrative construction rackets that the Frangiehs were said to control (Hanf 1993: 235 ff; Randal 1990: 121 ff).

In June 1978 a force of Phalangists entered the Frangiehs' northern strong-hold in the district of Zgharta and attacked their summer residence in the mountain village of Ehden. During the assault Tony Frangieh, his wife and baby daughter were gunned down, along with some 25 other people. Bashir's father, Pierre Gemayel (who had founded the Phalanges party in 1936), was said to have been horrified by this brutal slaughter. Many Maronites and other Catholics, however, considered it to have been a regrettable necessity, and the Ehden incident helped to establish Bashir Gemayel as a respected leader of his community. His election as president of Lebanon in August 1982 was greeted with great jubilation, and his subsequent assassination a month later was mourned by a Maronite community shaken by tremendous grief.

The reaction of the Frangieh clan and their supporters was predictable. The story is told that Suleiman Frangieh said he could understand why members of his family had been slaughtered, but he was particularly concerned that a household pet had been shot as well. 'Why did they kill the dog?' he asked. His intention was obvious: he would have Bashir Gemayel and his family killed like animals in retaliation for the deaths of Tony Frangieh and the others.

At the funeral, the mourners wore light colours because black could only be worn after the Frangiehs' honour had been avenged; and the bodies were not buried but kept in a crypt to await the day when revenge was exacted (Randal 1990: 128 and 152). Many Phalangists were killed in the following years and attempts were made on the lives of Bashir and Pierre Gemayel, in one of which Bashir's baby daughter was blown to pieces along with a number of bodyguards. Although it was not always clear who was behind these killings, there were plenty of bloodcurdling threats coming from the Frangieh camp. On the first anniversary of Tony Frangieh's death, a mass was said in Zgharta and the priest, a man of God no less, allegedly declared: 'All those who profaned Ehdene will be killed, particularly those of the Gemayel clan, those and their descendants for generations until not a single man or woman remains' (Randal 1990: 131).

When Bashir was finally killed by a massive bomb in the Phalanges party headquarters, an agent of Syria, not the Frangiehs, was found to have been responsible. But there was widespread rejoicing in Zgharta. Suleiman Frangieh praised God for his mercy and expressed his deep regret that he had not been the instigator of his enemy's death (Randal 1990: 152). Later, in 1983 at a Lebanese peace conference in Geneva, Suleiman Frangieh and Amin Gemayel (Bashir's brother) entered into an emotional and public embrace which some considered marked the end of the vendetta (Johnson 1986: 207). Others, however, interpreted Frangieh's hugs and kisses as the actions of a wily old fox lulling an intended victim into a false sense of security.

Such violent feuding between political families was relatively rare in Lebanon before the civil wars of the 1970s and 1980s, and when it happened it tended to take place between the subalterns rather than the za'ims themselves. The most serious fighting between za'ims occurred in the brief civil war of 1958, and then it was noteworthy that the major leaders refrained from killing or ordering the killing of each other. This was also the case in the first rounds of the civil war in 1975–76. Indeed, even after the Druze za'im, Kamal Jumblat, was assassinated in 1977, the various warlords still seemed to operate according to an unwritten rule that leaders should usually be spared so that negotiations could eventually be conducted to bring about a cease-fire between their followers. It is almost certainly the case that with a few exceptions like Tony Frangieh, most of the prominent Lebanese leaders who were killed died at the hands of either Syrian or other external agencies.

The protection of za'ims and warlords was part of the honour code of feuding and helped to maintain a semblance of negotiation at various stages of the civil wars. It was also a survival of an elite solidarity that had been so central to what some political scientists called a 'consociational' system in Lebanon (Hudson 1976; Dekmejian 1978). This concept referred to an alliance of moderate communal leaders who, in the interests of stability, accepted within the association of the 'consocies' the relative dominance of one of the communities (in Lebanon, the Maronites). Prior to the wars most za'ims, in common with elites in other 'consociational democracies' (Lijphart 1977; Nordlinger 1972), co-operated with each other in maintaining political order, moderating their confessional appeals and seeking to contain the sectarian allegiances of their followers.

The za'ims were either members of or closely linked to the commercial and financial elite, and they recognized that the trading and banking sectors of the economy depended on political and social stability. By the end of the 1960s, even the landlord za'ims had become part of this elite by diversifying into mechanized capitalist farming or by investing in the service sector of the economy. And the control of the state by what I have called a 'commercial-financial bourgeoisie' was a linchpin of the prewar order and provides much of the explanation for Lebanon's relative stability from independence in 1943 until the early 1970s (Johnson 1986; and see section 6 below).

The requirement that za'ims should control their clienteles in the interest of order meant it was sometimes difficult for them to exhibit their honour. Their followers often perceived them as communal champions, or thought they ought to be, but as members of a consociational elite one of their functions was to promote confessional harmony. Nevertheless, an important attribute of an honourable man was his readiness to defend his community, and za'ims were occasionally forced to adopt a communal stance. The role of the Beiruti Sunni, Sa'ib Salam, in the civil war of 1958 is a case in point.

As with most other za'ims, Salam had inherited his role from his father. Salim Salam had been an import–export merchant and Sa'ib inherited much of his wealth. The father had also had a strong-arm style of leadership that kept him closely in touch with the Sunni Muslim 'street'. It was alleged that, in 1922, he had been involved in the plot to assassinate a francophile Sunni who had accepted a position as director of the interior in the French administration. As a family, the Salams were renowned for their bravery and aggressive heroism. Salim's grandfather, for example, was a petty merchant who had supposedly killed, with his bare hands, one of a band of Greek pirates who had raided Beirut in the 1820s (Johnson 1986: 67–70).

In the 1950s Sa'ib Salam was able to demonstrate similarly honourable characteristics. After a *coup d'état* in 1952, the new Egyptian regime led by President Jamal Abdul Nasser adopted such radical policies as land reform and the nationalization of the Suez canal. When Britain and France, the owners of the canal, were forced by the United States to abandon their retaliatory invasion of Egypt in 1956, Nasser became the hero of the Arab world. While not necessarily supporting Egyptian 'socialism', the Sunni street in Lebanon turned to Nasserist Arab nationalism as a framework for expressing grievances against 'imperialism' generally and, specifically, against a pro-western Lebanese state that seemed to favour the Maronites and other Christians. Sensitive to popular feeling, Sa'ib Salam resigned from the Lebanese cabinet in protest against President Camille Chamoun's refusal to break off diplomatic relations with Britain and France. He then joined Nasserist and anti-government demonstrations and, in one of these, received a wound to his head when security forces opened fire on the crowd and killed at least five people (Qubain 1961: 54–5).

During the civil war in 1958 Sa'ib Salam became the leader of a predominantly Sunni insurrection in Beirut, and the destruction of part of his house during a night of shelling demonstrated his and his family's valour in battle. For most of the city's Muslim population, Salam was their communal hero and champion. By contrast, the previously dominant Sunni za'im of Beirut, Sami as-

Sulh, who collaborated with President Chamoun as his prime minister, was virtually excommunicated by his community. However, although he could exhibit honour in 1958, Salam was still restricted by the necessity to contain communal violence. His quarrel with the Maronite president had far more to do with a factional dispute between Lebanese za'ims than any confessional antagonism. Despite confessional fighting during the war, the conflict began because President Chamoun had interfered in the elections of 1957 to ensure a majority in the parliament that would nominate him for a second period of office. The excluded za'ims who had lost their parliamentary seats went to war, supported by some elected allies; and the leaders on *both* sides of the conflict included Muslims and Christians, who usually worked hard to prevent communal fighting between their followers.

After some months of fighting in the summer of 1958, and after 2000 deaths (small beer compared with the slaughter of the wars in the 1970s and 1980s), the za'ims effected a compromise in the interests of political and economic order. President Chamoun was allowed to complete his term of office and General Fu'ad Shihab, the commander-in-chief of the army who had remained neutral during the war, was elected by parliament to take his place. Apart from the fact that it would have been difficult for one side to defeat the other decisively (particularly after the intervention of US marines as a peace-keeping force), many leaders of the various factions seemed to have been motivated by a recognition that civil war was bad for business. Thus the commercial-financial elite's tradition of confessional moderation was maintained, concessions were made on both sides and old enemies became reconciled, to the extent that Sa'ib Salam and Camille Chamoun were close political allies in the late 1960s (Johnson 1986: chapters 5 and 6).

The requirements of the consociational system and the necessity to form multiconfessional coalitions to compete for patronage in parliament and government meant that za'ims, particularly in the cities, ran the risk of alienating sections of their confessional clienteles. The electoral system, described by Albert Hourani (1966: 26) as possibly 'the most important contribution made by the French to the political life of Lebanon', provided for multimember constituencies with seats reserved for the numerically dominant confessions in the locality. To be elected, a candidate usually had to ally with candidates from other sects in an 'electoral list' so as to win the support of the allies' confessional followings. Thus candidates had to moderate their sectarian appeals to their own clientele to make the necessary alliances with za'ims from other confessions. Similarly, a Maronite who wanted to become president, or a Sunni who wanted to be prime minister, had to build a multiconfessional bloc in the parliament in order to be elected. While all this was functional for the consociational system, it could be dysfunctional for the solidarity of the confessional link between a za'im and his clientele. In addition, the wealth and power a za'im acquired through politics could become a source of resentment on the part of his clients, especially if plentiful supplies of patronage in the form of jobs, welfare, credit and other services were not always forthcoming.

It was here that inherited honour was so important in maintaining the consent of the dependent clientele and legitimizing what might otherwise have been seen as a more or less coercive form of leadership. The use of qabadays to police the urban political machine — principally by ensuring that clients voted as directed in elections or provided other services to their za'im — meant that the dependent clients sometimes became resentful or even rebellious. But by laying claim to the status of notable, the urban za'im was placed at the head of a social hierarchy that was generally accepted as a natural order extending back into the Ottoman period. And in so doing, he was able to paint a normative gloss over the more bullying aspects of his political organization.

In the cities, notable families could not trace their genealogies back as far as those in the countryside. Nevertheless, the wealth of merchants and financiers had been legitimately acquired by the hard work and thrift of their ancestors, and older people remembered their philanthropy, piety and public service. In the romantic myths of the city, the ancestors of modern za'ims, and notables generally, were invariably portrayed to me as morally upright men who genuinely cared for the less fortunate in their communities. This was often done to make a comparison with the selfishness and moral disorder that my informants saw around them in the early 1970s, but it was also, I think, a reflection of the more egalitarian world of the city compared with landed estates in the countryside.

4. Agrarian society and the city

The urban merchants and financiers might have been rich, but they did not hold a monopoly of economic resources in the way landlords did in relation to land. At least theoretically, city-dwellers could improve their socioeconomic status; and just as there was a free economic market, so there was a market in political leadership. If one's patron did not provide, one could usually find another. Thus leadership in the city, and in its mountain hinterland where there was a small-holding peasantry, was always less stable than in the regions of landed estates. It was also less oppressive and more responsive to the wishes and ideologies (Arab nationalism, for example) of the clienteles. The honour of the urban za'im had to be earned: it could not be imposed.

By contrast, landlord families had exercised their authority and will for many generations, some of them for centuries. The modern descendants of 'feudal' lords clearly had more honour than their dependants. There was never any question of it. And to paraphrase John Davis (1977: 98), the peasants generally accepted the 'co-operative dependence' of the less honourable on those who had more. Of course, there were myths about the way landlords cared for the peasantry, about their generosity in advancing credit or in providing welfare assistance; and just as the urban myths contained many elements of truth, so presumably did their rural counterparts. But it seems that the co-operation of the peasantry extended even to the endurance of what the Lebanese called *zulm* — injustice, oppression or tyranny — and the landlord's honour was often associated with an arbitrary and harshly imposed form of rule.

As already intimated, in some areas of rural Lebanon landlordism had long since been done away with. For example, the Maronite peasants of the Kisrawan district had expelled their lords in the revolt of 1858–59; and although some of those lords later regained possession of their land, the growth of capitalist relations of production in the nineteenth century had contributed to the growth of a class of peasant proprietors on the Mountain (see chapter 3, section 3, below). But certainly until the 1960s, the peripheral regions in the north, south and east of the country remained under the control of powerful and coercive lords. It was the reformist regime of President Fu'ad Shihab (1958–64) that created the conditions for the gradual breakdown of this rural order by improving communications, providing electricity and piped water, and encouraging investment. As we shall see, the expulsion of sharecroppers and other tenants under the impulse of commercial and mechanized farming was to have far-reaching consequences that would lead to the civil wars of the 1970s and 1980s. For the moment, however, we should note the way the landlord system operated before it was disabled.

Even after relations of wage labour and capitalist agriculture had become established in the remote — and overwhelmingly Sunni Muslim — Akkar district of northern Lebanon, Michael Gilsenan found, in 1971–72, a status system which, although different from its predecessor, was still structured around lords, qabadays and honour. He presented a sorry picture of the lords' retainers, their mythologizing of the 'sword and horse', their swaggering bravado, their 'profound contempt' for work and the peasantry, their reckless and 'spendthrift display'. The qabadays' economic position as bailiffs and estate managers had been almost completely undermined, but they and 'the less successful of the lords' remained 'imprisoned in an ideology of honour and the traditional "feudal" relations on which honour is based.' Honour had become 'more and more a ritualized model of expression that less and less reflected the emerging realities, even though men still [held] it up as a mirror of the truth' (Gilsenan 1977: 169–70).

In his extended and excellent treatment of the oral 'narratives' or storytelling of Akkaris, Gilsenan (1996) distinguishes three status groups which (rather like castes in India) were historically related to the stratifications of class and power. At the top of the hierarchy were the 'beys' (*bakawat*), traditionally landlords, who traced their genealogies (often *written* in an elaborate Arabic calligraphy) to a common Kurdish (and Sunni) ancestor in the seventeenth century. Below them were the 'aghas' (*aghawat*) who, like the beys, were the holders of an Ottoman rank. They had been, and some still were, the armed retainers of the landlords, acting as bodyguards, agents and enforcers. As with the beys, they too claimed a foreign, non-Arab origin. They were Circassian Sunnis and, although there was disagreement about when they arrived in Akkar (some said the late nineteenth century, some earlier) there was a belief that they were descended from common ancestors. At the bottom of the hierarchy were the *fellahin*, the peasants and labourers (also Sunnis) who effectively had no genealogy and therefore no history, or none worth mentioning (Gilsenan 1996: 47–51).

The *fellahin* were said to be indigenous inhabitants of the region who had lost their freedom and land to the beys, or had 'fled' from another region nearby. Bey (*bak*) and agha narratives spoke of their own 'noble flight' to Akkar after 'armed confrontation or personal combat', and stressed their assumption of power immediately upon arrival in their new home. By contrast, the myths of peasant origin emphasized 'displacement of the weak and dispossessed' (Gilsenan 1996: 51). While some lords had become *déclassés*, their sons working in lower status jobs as clerks in the city or as officers in the police or army, and while some members of peasant families had risen in status through emigration or education, becoming businessmen or members of the liberal professions, a status hierarchy of nobility still prevailed in Akkar. This was defined in terms of genealogy and the marriage and property alliances that had preserved the hegemony of at least some of the lords and their retainers.

The inherited honour of nobility was supported by imposing a sense of respect on others. Narratives about the beys and aghas illustrated the way they had exhibited their honour in the past, and their actions claimed respect in the present. Men would enter into 'verbal duelling', telling stories about past incidents or seizing the initiative in conversation, employing mockery and irony to score points off one another (Gilsenan 1996: 206 ff and passim). During the election campaign of 1972, in an act of 'calculated effrontery', a young bey sat ostentatiously playing through his fingers his expensive amber *misbaha* (rosary), with one leg crossed over his knee and the sole of his shoe turned 'in the face' of an elderly agha, a famed hunter who, in the 1950s, had been the companion and chief retainer of a great lord (Gilsenan 1996: 255). The same bey quarrelled over money with a young and impetuous agha who then went around threatening the lord. Outside a café in the coastal town of Tripoli the lord taunted the agha, who drew his pistol. The bey drew his own gun and shot the agha dead. Just like that, 'six bullets pumped into him as he lay on the ground' (Gilsenan 1996: 259).

During the famine in the first world war, an agha had in jest promised a lord his olive grove if the bey would give him the orange he was eating. The lord handed him the fruit. Later, in the lord's reception room, now in front of witnesses, the bey held his agha to his word and asked for the olive grove. The agha, who was an honourable man, immediately replied, 'Take it,' ending a narrative that illustrated the 'cunning' but devastating honour of the lords and the spendthrift bravado and 'manly display' (*murajul*) of the aghas (Gilsenan 1996: 115–19).

Many of the stories and actions of the beys and aghas demonstrated their absolute contempt for the peasantry, and their cruel and capricious domination of their subordinates. Some years before, a lord had killed a *fellah* working on the scaffolding around his mansion. He had shot him 'to test his new rifle' or simply 'because he felt like it' (Gilsenan 1996: 8 and 191). More recently, an agha and a *fellah*, friends or at least cronies, had quarrelled over a prostitute they had picked up in Tripoli. The *fellah*, Ali, had pulled a knife and stabbed his companion. The wound was not serious, but blood had been shed and the aghas organized their revenge against a man without status who had had the temerity to harm one of their own. Men grew their beards as a 'sign of intention', and eventually a young member of an agha family was chosen to inflict punishment. The youth, Abdallah, went to the village shop owned by Ali. 'Do you want it here in the shop or outside?' he asked. The *fellah* grabbed a gun, but the young agha was too quick for him and 'emptied his revolver into Ali's chest'. Abdallah, without any sign of fear, then turned his back on a crowd of *fellahin* who had seen the killing and calmly walked away, a hero to his peers. 'You have returned a man!' he was told by an agha elder (Gilsenan 1996: 159 ff).

Contempt for the *fellahin* was also shown in the attitude of beys and aghas to peasant women. The poorest were 'theirs for the taking' (Gilsenan 1996: 189–90). In October 1971, the newspapers reported the rape of a 13-year-old girl by a landlord's son in front of her parents, who were forced to watch by the violator's armed retainers (Gilsenan 1996: 39–40). This incident led to protests organized by a peasant union, demonstrating that changes were beginning to take place, that peasants were no longer prepared to be entirely subservient to their lords. Nevertheless, the narratives of the beys and aghas told of a regular violation of women, revealing a complete lack of honour (or what local people called *sharaf*) on the part of the *fellahin* men who were unable to protect their women from shame. The elite strata 'guarded and preserved the sanctity of their women, while showing deliberate disregard for that of the men beneath them'

(Gilsenan 1996: 189). In other words, it was men who were dishonoured by the rape of women, and it is significant that the men who protested about the peasant condition in 1971 did so in terms of their 'own violation' rather than that of their women (Gilsenan 1996: 191).

Clearly, the violence of domination in agrarian society was greater and more arbitrary than that in the city. The urban narratives told to me stressed the manipulation of followings rather than the coercion of dependants. As we shall see in the next section of this chapter, the urban za'ims did establish coercive structures of qabadays to control their political machines or clienteles. Many followers or clients also showed great respect when meeting their za'im, kissing his hand and using the most elaborate language to flatter and plead with him. They also used such honorific titles as bey (bak) or sheikh to address their urban boss. The Sunni za'im, Sa'ib Salam, was called 'Sa'ib Bey', and the leader of the Phalanges party, Pierre Gemayel, was 'Sheikh Pierre', titles their families had inherited from the Ottoman period. But it would be inconceivable for an urban za'im, 'because he felt like it', to shoot a man who might vote for him, and it would be a great scandal if a za'im or a member of his family were to rape a woman. Qabadays might sometimes behave like that, not the bosses.

The urban za'ims liked to portray themselves as liberal and humane men who sometimes, reluctantly, had to get their hands dirty in the rough and tumble of political faction-fighting. But they had to respond to their electorate, and that meant the Muslim za'ims sometimes even had to mouth slogans that smacked of socialism, or something very much like it, as when Sa'ib Salam, and other Sunni bosses in such cities as Tripoli and Sidon, adopted a populist Nasserist stance in the 1950s. To be successful, an urban za'im had to provide for his following, materially in terms of jobs, welfare services and other patronage, and morally in terms of being sensitive to the ideologies of the street.

The urban za'im's style of leadership might have been partly modelled on rural domination, and it was not mere sloganeering when the Lebanese left described the polity as 'political feudalism' (al-iqta' as-siyasi). Urban za'ims themselves could recognize this. Sa'ib Salam, for example, once told me that he thought the term za'im had been brought to Beirut by Shi'a migrants from a 'feudal' countryside during the period of the French Mandate. But it is significant that he then went on to say, with some embarrassment, that he did not like the associated connotations of zulm or tyranny. It is true that sometimes an urban za'im would behave with some of the arbitrariness of a landlord. Rashid Karami, the Sunni za'im of Tripoli, was a prime example. He slapped the faces of subordinates who offended him and, on one famous occasion when laying a wreath on his father's grave at an Independence Day celebration, he told three of his bodyguards to lie on the muddy ground so he could walk over their backs rather than get his shoes dirty (Goria 1985: 69; *An-Nahar*, 23 November 1970). But this was a za'im who had been born in a village, and who was the boss of a relatively small northern town with close connections to the neighbouring agrarian districts of Akkar and Zgharta. Za'ims in the sophisticated world of Beirut would simply not behave like that, or at least they were not supposed to behave like that.

Despite exceptions, the point still holds that urban za'ims generally manipulated rather than coerced their followings. They often felt awkward about the connotations of *zulm* or tyrannical oppression that attached to their role, embarrassed, I should add, not just in the company of a European researcher, but also with their peers and many of their subordinates. Their status, if not their power, owed far more to their membership of notable bourgeois families, as carriers of a tradition of probity and philanthropy, than to their use of force.

They were also, as members of a consociational business elite, mediators rather than aggressive fighters for political power. They were prepared to fight if their interests were severely threatened, as when a number of them were excluded from power by President Camille Chamoun in the 1950s (Qubain 1961). But as we have seen (in section 3) the war of 1958 was soon ended in a negotiated settlement, and former enemies even became allies within a few years. Similarly, Sa'ib Salam and rival za'ims were prepared to mobilize their armed followings in 1970 during a contest for the presidency of a Sunni Muslim charitable association (*al-maqasid*) that had within its gift large quantities of educational, medical and other welfare services that could be used as patronage. But the violence was largely confined to qabadays and other partisans firing their guns in the air, rather than at each other, and the dispute was ended quickly and peacefully after negotiation (Johnson 1978).

As far as I know, although there were shoot-outs in the city between qabadays that had been ordered by their leaders, no urban za'im ever killed or ordered the killing of another za'im prior to the civil wars of the 1970s and 1980s. Such a breach of the norm of mediation only occurred in a rural context, as when Suleiman Frangieh and his gunmen killed members of a rival clan in Zgharta in 1957 (see section 3), or when a za'im from Akkar was shot dead in the early 1950s, apparently at the instigation of a rival.

Before returning to our comparison of urban and agrarian leadership, the latter story is perhaps worth telling. Just before the parliamentary elections of 1953, a Sunni candidate in Akkar, Muhammad al-Abboud, was killed while leaving the presidential palace. His father, a bey with a fearsome reputation (it was he who had shot a *fellah* 'to test his new rifle'), decreed that the body should not be buried until the killing had been avenged. Later the father had another son on whose small shoulders, it was assumed, lay the requirement to avenge his brother. He, very sensibly, was sent to school in Switzerland for his safety. During the 1958 civil war the father too was shot, while being driven through Beirut. He died from his wounds. Meanwhile, Muhammad al-Abboud's body lay in a coffin, draped with a Lebanese flag, in his deserted palace on the edge of a village in the foothills of Akkar. It was still there when Michael Gilsenan arrived in 1971 (Gilsenan 1996: 29 ff).

The precise differences between rural domination and urban leadership are perhaps difficult to distinguish. There are so many caveats to be inserted into the argument that the crucial distinctions can become obscured. Despite the exceptions, however, the most important and significant point is that urban leadership in Lebanon, particularly in Beirut, was conditioned by the city, by its economy, family structure, and *new* sense of honour. In a service economy of trade and finance, the extended kinship structures of agrarian society were replaced by the nuclear family; a sense of community based on the hierarchy of lords, retainers and peasants was replaced by competitive individualism; and honour became more an issue of success in the economic market than something determined by inheritance. Inherited status was still very important for providing a sense of community and order, but it was not as pronounced as it was in agrarian society. In the peripheral regions of Lebanon where landlords completely dominated their peasants, genealogy and the 'symbolics of blood' (Foucault 1976: 197) were, along with a monopoly of land and force, the determinants of power. In the city, inherited status was largely a normative gloss on power.

In agrarian society, the symbolics of blood demanded respect, and the power and honour of landlords was exemplified in arbitrary violence and the shaming of subordinates. In the city, leaders exercised a certain amount of coercion in controlling their followers, but excessive force could lead to clients seeking another patron to protect them. In addition, the urban electorate was fickle in its allegiance, and there was a relatively high turnover of members of parliament in elections. Those za'ims who were linked to the governing faction and its patronage tended to get elected, while those in opposition often found it difficult if not impossible. By contrast, za'ims in agrarian society tended to win elections even when they belonged to an opposition faction.

Urban za'ims were respected not so much for an imposition of domination on their followers, but for their willingness to use a controlled degree of force against other za'ims or other communities. Even in these cases, za'ims were also required, by the norms of the consociational and economic systems, to limit their violence and seek a negotiated settlement to their disputes. As we have seen, warfare was usually considered bad for business.

In the city, most men could at least aspire to honour, and honour in the sense of *'ird* (sexual honour) became a value that all men could claim. No longer were men subordinate to a lord who could seduce or rape 'their' women with impunity. A discourse of neopatriarchy developed which told men that they could be the moral equals of their rulers and that they had the right to defend their women, and therefore themselves, from shame.

Most urban men simply got on with it, and worked hard to provide for their family, while keeping a watchful eye on their sisters, wives, daughters and adolescent sons. For them, as we shall see in chapter 4, life was a precarious balance between respectability and shame. Some, though, broke with the norms of respectable bourgeois life and claimed honour in the sense of respect. By becoming a qabaday and entering into a network of racketeering and crime, a young man could establish himself on the margins of the urban political economy, over time perhaps becoming a rich businessman. He could also become a minor player in the political system.

The urban sociopolitical system was to a considerable extent structured by a mafia of protection and racketeering situated in a highly competitive economy. But although this mafia involved violence and coercion, it was largely a case of qabadays attacking each other or preying upon outsiders, such as the owners of bars and nightclubs from whom money was extorted for their 'protection'. Za'ims, in turn, provided protection from the law to the qabadays, but they were not despots like the landlords. They covered their forceful style with a veneer of bourgeois respectability, and they restrained those qabadays who tried to exploit or dominate the members of a potential electorate. Qabadays and their urban bosses were not remnants of an old agrarian order but part of a relatively new one that had developed with urbanization and capitalism.

5. Respect and honour

Many Lebanese would derive the word *qabaday* from the Arabic verb 'to grasp or hold' (*qabada*), but the same word is found in Turkish (*kabadayi*) and is used to describe someone who has the characteristics of a 'swashbuckler' and maybe a bully, who is tough and has 'guts'. The Turkish form is in fact a combination of two words: *kaba*, meaning common or vulgar, and *dayi* or maternal uncle. The word was first used in Lebanon during Ottoman times and, despite the raised eyebrows of some of my anthropologist friends, the fact that *kabadayi* can be translated as something like 'wicked uncle' (and a maternal one at that) seems to me significant.

It can be argued that a mother's brother (a maternal uncle) occupied an ambiguous kinship role in Ottoman Muslim societies in which patrilateral parallel-cousin marriage was the normative ideal. Such a marriage would be considered incestuous by Catholic and Orthodox Christians, but in Lebanese

Muslim society there was a strong norm that it was preferable for a man to marry his father's brother's daughter (FBD). This meant that bachelors would see their paternal uncle as a potential father-in-law who should be treated with respect and courtesy. The mother's brother, on the other hand, was someone with whom young men could have a more relaxed, friendly and joking relationship. In a structural sense, the maternal uncle was morally linked to a young man's family through the mother but was nevertheless something of an outsider. This would have been the case even in a strict 'FBD-marriage' family in which the maternal uncle would be the grandson of the young man's great-grandfather and a patrilateral first cousin to the young man's father. Structurally, the mother's brother always belonged to a different kinship segment and was therefore a potential threat to paternal authority.

FBD marriages might be less common today, but they are by no means entirely out of fashion. In Beirut between 1940 and 1980 there was a relatively stable proportion of marriages contracted between patrilateral parallel cousins, amounting to approximately 5 per cent of all marriages or 8 per cent of Muslim marriages (Khlat 1989: 46–50; and see chapter 4, section 2 below). And as Carol Delaney argues (1987: 43), even though such marriages are less popular in Muslim societies than they were, there is still a sense in which they are 'an exemplar of the more pervasive symbolic logic of sexuality'. This logic defends patriarchy, the family, and an ideal of endogamy and the protection of patrimony, all of which are in turn closely tied up with the notions of honour and shame. According to the norms of this logic, the mother's kin are outside the moral community of the patrilineal family and its patrimony; and as her protector against any unreasonable behaviour on the part of her husband, the mother's brother is inevitably a threat to the patrilineal group. Clearly the Turkish origin of the word indicates the contradictory nature of the qabaday who could be brave and fearless in the defence of his community, and therefore a symbol of patriarchal order, but who at the same time was also unpredictably violent and capable of creating much disorder.

For many, the urban qabaday was a moral leader. He was a man of the people, a helper of the weak and poor, a protector of the quarter or neighbourhood, and a communal and confessional champion. For the patriarchal za'im and the political system as a whole, however, he was a potential threat as a popular leader of the street. Because, as one Beiruti expressed it to me, qabadays were leaders 'pushed forward by the masses', a za'im had to co-operate with them even though he might have resented having to deal with young (and not so young) thugs who were often involved in protection rackets, gun-running and smuggling.

Ordinary citizens also had ambivalent attitudes toward the qabaday.

Although he conformed to the code of honour and was heroic, physically strong, quick-witted and possessed of other 'masculine virtues', he also had the negative characteristics of bullying and sometimes very violent behaviour. Thus not only the elite resented the qabaday but even some of the poor called him *az'ar*, a thug or a scoundrel. However, despite his aggressive style of leadership many people saw the qabaday as more of a 'social bandit' (Hobsbawm 1959) than a robber of the poor, and one of the street leader's most important tasks was to defend and fight for his quarter and confessional community.

Many of the most prominent Muslim qabadays in Beirut in the 1960s and early 1970s had established themselves during the 1958 civil war when they had attacked the loyalist Christian quarters in the eastern part of the city and had defended the Sunni quarters against the Phalangists and other fighters supporting President Chamoun's regime. Similarly, in the post-1975 wars, Muslim qabadays fought in the ranks of Nasserist and other 'progressive' militias against the 'rightist' militias of the Maronites and their allies (Johnson 1986: 178 ff).

The character of the qabaday's honour is well illustrated by a shooting incident and its aftermath that occurred in Beirut in 1973 (Johnson 1986: 2–3). Asad Awad and Kamal al-Askari (an alias, 'Kamal the Soldier') were qabadays in their respective quarters of al-Ashrafiyya and al-Musaytiba. As the Ashrafiyya was a Christian quarter and the Musaytiba lay in the heart of the city's Muslim districts, it was almost inevitable that the two men should be rivals. In addition, there were rumours that the Muslim qabaday had started to muscle in on the Christian's protection racket. One night the Christian was dancing at a night-club with a young woman and he became angry when it appeared his rival was making eyes at her. Leaving his partner, he walked over to Askari's table and threatened him. A quarrel ensued and Awad drew his pistol, pointing it at the Muslim's chest.

Askari responded as the honour code demanded. In order not to lose face, he pulled out his own gun. Having drawn their weapons, honour now required that unless they were restrained by others, the two qabadays should use them. No one intervened quickly enough, so they shot each other dead.

There was some relief that both had died, because this meant there was not likely to be a feud of blood vengeance. Many people, however, expressed great sadness at the death of one or other of these brave young men in their twenties. In keeping with Muslim tradition, Kamal al-Askari's funeral was held the day after he died. Many friends and supporters crowded into the streets around the Musaytiba mosque, and young men fired their Kalashnikov machine rifles into the air to show their respect for a comrade who had faced up to his rival and had therefore died an honourable death. As the crowds grew, the funeral developed into a demonstration of the quarter's own honour and solidarity.

Armed youths moved from house to house, firing their cannonades as a tribute to the local inhabitants as well as their fallen leader, his honour rubbing off on all of them and reinforcing their identification with their locality and coreligionists.

Until this event I had assumed that only a small minority of my neighbours admired the qabadays. The youths who hung around on street corners or congregated in the coffee shops on the Basta road were attracted by the macho style of the street leaders and some aspired to be qabadays themselves, but I was surprised by the number of middle-aged and older people who attended the funeral. Some had been drawn there by curiosity, but others participated out of genuine respect and dutifully joined the cortège to the cemetery.

After the ceremony, I visited an elderly merchant in the quarter who used to delight in telling me about the old days when the qabadays had been 'real' men of honour, helping the poor and imposing authority by their physical presence rather than force of arms. He was not so much of a romantic that he denied their racketeering, and he often qualified his respect for them. Occasionally he treated them as something of a joke as, for example, when he laughed about the 'uniform' they had worn in the early twentieth century — a fez, moustache, cummerbund, dagger, pistol and short cane, and baggy trousers (*shirwal*) drawn in tight below the knee and weighted with pebbles ('to make them swing,' he said). But he always favourably compared this earlier generation with the thugs of his neighbourhood, whom he apparently held beneath contempt.

When I made some flippant remarks about what I had been told of Askari's involvement in prostitution, and began to joke about the manner of his death, the merchant stopped me before I had gone too far. He was evidently disappointed by my lack of respect. 'Kamal was my friend,' he said. 'He was a good man who helped the poor.'

I soon learnt that, in the 'popular' quarters of Sunni Beirut, even some members of the educated middle classes might admire at least one qabaday and would reserve the term *az'ar* for a street leader who belonged to an opposing political faction. In a competitive social environment, it seemed, the qabaday represented some semblance of local order and could even be seen as something of a philanthropist.

The vast majority of my neighbours had no aspiration to claim a qabaday status for themselves and would not have dreamt of behaving in an aggressively 'honourable' way. Young and alienated young men often talked the discourse of honour, but once they married they tended to provide for their families in a conventional manner and sought employment in the legal economy. Education was highly valued as a means for social advancement, as was hard work generally. Nevertheless, the local economy was very competitive: the poor competed with each other for jobs and services, petty traders for markets, and salaried employees for posts in the office hierarchy. Unemployment was an ever-present threat and some people opted for emigration (to the Arab Gulf and elsewhere) as a solution. In this individualistic and competitive world, people would seek out an intermediary (*wasta*) who could help them. This could be a relative or friend of the family; but for many their most influential patron was a za'im, and access to the za'im often depended on an introduction through a local qabaday who could vouch for the client's reliability in terms of voting and other forms of political support (Johnson 1986: 85–9 and 94–5).

High-status and influential people could obtain direct access to a za'im. Qabadays were particularly important as the recruiters and enforcers of that part of the za'im's organization composed of low-status, poor and politically weak clients. And the reason za'ims incorporated qabadays in this way was that they were usually admired by the clients they controlled. They were men of honour *par excellence*. They exacted swift and violent revenge for any attack on their person, their kin or community. They were heroes who would rather die in avenging an offence against their honour than face the ignominious shame of ignoring it. But becoming a qabaday did not set a person apart from his neighbours, for a major component of his honour was that he remained a popular man closely in touch with the street, providing services as a mediator between clients and za'im, a settler of disputes and a protector of people and property.

In many ways, this local order was extremely effective. Some of my Maronite and other Christian acquaintances were horrified when they learnt where I was living in West Beirut. 'Those Muslims!' one said. 'You will be robbed and your wife raped.' In fact, my wife was far safer walking alone at night in our poor and scruffy quarter than she would have been in London. We never worried about being mugged or burgled. Even though political tensions were mounting in the early 1970s, before the civil war there was little or no crime in our quarter apart from 'honour crimes' that were essentially an intra-qabaday affair. There was certainly a degree of domestic violence, and there was always the threat of coercion associated with protection, prostitution and other criminal and 'political' rackets. But criminal violence tended to happen 'downtown' in and around the bars and nightclubs rather than in our residential neighbourhood. We were very quickly welcomed into a local community in which everyone knew everyone else's business and where people looked out for each other. The social order that existed in the Basta and neighbouring Muslim quarters was more than something imposed by the qabadays, and I do not want to exaggerate their role. But there can be little doubt that there was a sense that members of the local community preferred to police themselves rather than rely on the conventional forces of law and order.

In terms of their political role, qabadays were especially important in parliamentary elections. Although the extent of direct vote-buying was probably exaggerated, tactics that were alleged to have been used included buying the identity cards of those poorer electors who could be induced by small sums of money. Those voters who were considered unreliable would not have their identity cards returned until after the polls had closed (thus denying them the ability to identify themselves to the staff at the polling station), while others were escorted to the polling booths by the qabadays, given their identity card and a ballot paper that had already been filled in, and supervised while they cast their vote.

Violence was sometimes used to threaten and undermine opposing za'ims' electoral machines, and to protect machines from attack. Those za'ims who were members of the opposition faction in parliament were particularly vulnerable to subversion by the police and security forces who would often arrest opposition qabadays, on real or trumped up charges, to prevent their organizing their patrons' machines. In retaliation, those qabadays who had escaped arrest would intimidate pro-regime za'ims and their clienteles. The amount of violence in elections varied according to the political situation, but most elections were remembered for minor incidents of beatings and shootings, and some for gun battles between rival groups of partisans or for the dynamiting of election workers' homes and za'ims' offices (Johnson 1986: 85–8).

The tactic of arresting opposition qabadays before elections demonstrates again their criminal reputation, but not all strong-arm leaders of the street were necessarily involved in protection, smuggling and prostitution rackets. Some were able to establish themselves in such legal occupations as security guards and taxi drivers to begin with, perhaps later becoming the bosses of stevedores and boatmen in Beirut's port, or the owners of haulage or trucking companies, or businessmen with interests in bars, nightclubs, restaurants or cinemas. The za'ims could help with this by providing loans, facilitating contracts or securing government concessions. In Beirut, for example, the port was run by a parastatal authority, and za'ims could influence the granting of concessions to unload ships, store goods and transport imports to their markets in Lebanon and Syria (Johnson 1986: 20–1 and 88–94).

When I lived on the edge of the popular Sunni quarter of the Basta (in 1972 and 1973), Faruq Shihab ad-Din (a Sunni) was a partner in a trucking company operating out of the port. Although he was known by the superior title of *rayyis* (from *ra'is* or 'chief'), he had a qabaday style of leadership, lived in the Basta and was closely associated with the port workers who were his neighbours. He was a man of the street, despite his wealth and influence. He was also a supporter and friend of Sa'ib Salam, and I was told that his za'im had assisted his rise to fortune. The local myth or 'narrative' was that he was involved in the 'port mafia' and had been protected by his za'im in return for political services. In 1970, for example, he had helped mobilize support for Salam when the latter faced a challenge to his presidency of the Sunni charitable association, the Islamic Maqasid Society of Beirut (*jam'iyyat al-maqasid al-khayriyya al-islamiyya fi bayrut*). At that time Shihab ad-Din had styled himself as the chief of an organization called *shabab ahya bayrut*, literally The Young Men of the Quarters of Beirut, although in this context *shabab* referred less to their youth than to the fact that they were men who might bear arms. As we have seen (in section 4) the Maqasid election in 1970 involved rival contenders deploying their armed supporters and I was told that, as the boss of a network of qabadays, Rayyis Faruq had played a key role in organizing the Salamist faction.

Sa'ib Salam's opponent in the 1970 election was Osman Dana ('Uthman ad-Dana), a rival Sunni za'im who unsuccessfully tried to register a large number of his supporters as members of the Maqasid assembly, the body charged with electing the board of directors and its president. Although Salam and Dana had previously made temporary and expedient alliances by standing on the same 'list' in the parliamentary elections of 1960, 1964 and 1968, they were nevertheless rivals for high office and in the long term were intent on excluding the other from parliament. Control of the Maqasid's charitable schools, colleges and hospital was an essential part of their respective strategies, and this explains why the presidential election in 1970 was fought against a background of threatened violence (Johnson 1978).

One of Dana's lieutenants in the Maqasid dispute was Ibrahim Qulaylat, whose men took their guns to the street in what turned out to be a failed attempt to force the Lebanese government into overturning the re-election of Sa'ib Salam as president of the charity. Qulaylat had established himself as a qabaday in the civil war of 1958, when at the age of 16 he had fought as a partisan of Salam and the other insurrectionists in Beirut. Although Salam eventually fell out with President Nasser of Egypt and became associated with Saudi Arabia, Qulaylat remained fiercely loyal to the Nasserist cause. In 1960 he was briefly held by the police while in the Saudi capital, Riyadh, and was questioned about a Nasserist plot to assassinate King Saud. Later, in 1966, he was arrested by the Lebanese authorities for the murder of a pro-Saudi newspaper editor in Beirut. Most people believed he had ordered the killing at the behest of his Egyptian paymasters, but after what seemed like high-level pressure on the court he was acquitted in 1968 and returned home from prison to a street party organized by his jubilant supporters in the popular Sunni quarter of Tariq al-Jadida (Johnson 1986: 83–4). Clearly the assassination of an anti-Nasserist editor was an honourable act for many Muslims in Beirut, and

Qulaylat was an immensely respected man in his neighbourhood. He was
known not just for his bravery and violent acts, but also for his influence with
the za'im Osman Dana, who for many years in the 1960s was a minister in the
government.

The urban qabaday provided some sense of order in a disordered world and
yet, at the same time, he embodied in his person many of the attributes of that
world. Quick-witted, cunning, socially mobile and, above all, aggressively competitive, unpredictable and violent, he represented an exaggerated microcosm of
the society he ordered. It is this contradiction, this paradox, that provides the
key to an understanding of the qabaday's success as a street leader. It was his
ability to combine naked self-interest with concern for the local community,
and to mediate within the context of honour between competition and co-
operation, instability and order, that legitimated his role as the za'im's
lieutenant.

6. Honour and the state

In *Class and Client in Beirut*, I think I exaggerated the all-encompassing
pervasiveness of what I called 'competitive service capitalism' (Johnson 1986:
103–10 and 220–3). I did recognize the development of oligopoly and discussed
the emergence of class-based politics in the early 1970s; but in attempting to
provide materialist explanations for the individualistic nature of Lebanese
society and for a clientelist structure of politics that responded to and promoted
individualism, I may have underestimated the extent of industrial development
and overestimated the social instability of the service sector. Nevertheless, I still
stand by what I wrote when I summarized clientelism:

> [E]xcept for a brief period in the 1970s, competitive [service] capitalism
> and an associated clientelist system continued to determine the character
> of Beirut's political economy. Even the developments of the first half of
> the 1970s did not pose an overwhelming threat to clientelism. Many of
> the so-called leftist groups were little more than clientelist structures
> whose leaders paid unemployed young people to fight in their militias.
> And had it not been for the intervention of external forces, such as the
> Palestinians, Israelis and certain Arab regimes, the clientelist system
> might well have contained the social pressures directed against it.
>
> (Johnson 1986: 105)

It was inevitable that having established an argument about the efficiency
and functionalism of clientelism, I would look outside the system for an explanation of its collapse (Johnson 1986: chapter 7). The Palestinians, who as non-

citizens (and therefore non-voters) were excluded from the system, armed the militias of the class-based 'counter-structure' (Johnson 1986: 105 and 168–9) led by Kamal Jumblat, a za'im from the Shouf region of the Mountain who was prepared to break the rules of the system by interfering in the politics of localities other than his own. Parochial leadership had been a crucial norm of clientelism, and za'ims did not usually encroach on another's patch. Jumblat wanted to be president of Lebanon, but as a Druze was excluded from an office reserved for a Maronite. He therefore tried to change the system by building a national coalition, based mainly in Beirut and the other coastal cities of Tripoli and Sidon. He was helped in this by a number of factions in the Palestine Liberation Organization (PLO) anxious to find Lebanese allies who would support them in their struggle for their homeland. In particular, they wanted to prevent their being forced out of Lebanon which, after King Hussein's army had expelled them from Jordan in 1970–71, was their one remaining front-line base on an Israeli border. But if the Palestinians felt insecure in Lebanon, many Lebanese were threatened by the armed units of the PLO. Indeed, since the 1969 'Cairo agreement' between the Lebanese government and the PLO, Palestinians had the right to police their own camps and districts and thus looked as though they were completely outside the controls of the state (see the end of the first section of chapter 4).

The 'leftist' and predominantly Muslim militias in Jumblat's National Movement (*al-haraka al-wataniyya*) were attractive to another group of people who, like the Palestinians, were excluded from the clientelist system. Working-class and sub-proletarian Shi'a immigrants in the suburbs of Beirut, many of them former sharecroppers forced off the land by the commercialization of agriculture, had become divorced from their lords in southern Lebanon (some of whom had actually expelled them from their land). Still registered to vote in their natal villages, they were not recruited into the clientele of a city boss and found it difficult to gain access to jobs, welfare and other urban patronage. Falling outside the controls of clientelism, they were thus more easily recruited into leftist and communal militias that were seeking to change the political system.

Encouraged by the latter and helped by Palestinian organizations and some Arab governments, the Sunni qabadays in Beirut and other cities also became more political and began to challenge their za'ims. After the death of President Nasser in 1970, Ibrahim Qulaylat (see above in section 5) had first become a client of the radical faction in Egypt and then, after its defeat by President Anwar Sadat, he turned to the Libyan regime of Colonel Mu'ammar Qadhafi (Goria 1985: 112 n30). Previously, in common with many of the more radical Sunni qabadays, he had been protected and controlled by the *Deuxième Bureau*, the internal security apparatus run by officers loyal to President Fu'ad Shihab

who after his term of office (1958–64) was still very influential behind the
scenes of Lebanese politics. The new regime established after the election of
Suleiman Frangieh as president in 1970, however, was largely composed of
people who had been excluded from power by President Shihab and his successor Charles Helou (1964–70). The members of the new government purged
the *Bureau* of their 'Shihabist' rivals and, as a result, there was no effective control of the qabaday and criminal networks that were now receiving arms,
training and finance from some groups within the PLO and from such radical
regimes as those of Iraq and Libya (Johnson 1986: 178–80).

Gradually, Maronite leaders came to fear Palestinian, Muslim and 'leftist'
militancy, and believed that the Sunni as well as Shi'a za'ims had lost control of
their clienteles. As a result, the Maronite za'ims began to break with the old elite
consensus that had contained confessional conflict reasonably effectively since
the latter part of the nineteenth century, and they built up their militias as the
'surrogates' and 'defenders' (Stoakes 1975) of the Lebanese state.

Parts of this explanation involve 'intra-systemic' factors. The social consequences of capitalist farming, the politicization of the qabadays, and a breaking
of the consociational consensus, had always been possibilities and were
developments that the system could not easily contain. But had it not been for
the external interventions of the Palestinians and foreign intelligence agencies
(such as the Libyans, Syrians, and Israelis) the various conflicts would not have
become as militarized as they did.

Although there are some problems with his more detailed interpretations
(see chapter 4, section 4, below), Theodor Hanf's analysis of the available data
shows how Shihabist reforms in the 1960s had served to reduce dramatically
Christian hegemony in the civil service and to increase educational opportunities for Muslims. Although Christians were still better represented in the
upper and middle classes, and Muslims — especially the Shi'a — formed a large
percentage of the urban sub-proletariat or 'under-class', the social stratification
of the two confessional groups remained broadly similar and confessional
inequality remained 'within bounds' (Hanf 1993: 105). Because Shi'a access to
mass education and their migration to the city were relatively recent events,
they were by far the poorest and most deprived of the various communities.
Many Shi'a, however, expressed their grievances more in class than confessional
terms; and despite the militant rhetoric of its leader (chapter 4, section 2), the
demands of their communal pressure group (the Imam Musa as-Sadr's Movement of the Deprived, *harakat al-mahrumin*) did not challenge the Lebanese
power structure in any fundamental way but merely amounted to a moderate
programme of social reform.

Overall, 'social and economic disparities' had 'narrowed enormously' since independence (Hanf 1993: 105); and although a series of strikes and demon-strations in the early 1970s caused some problems, the employers and security forces were able to contain them (chapter 4, section 4). The clientelist system of political control was socially threatened during this period, but on the eve of the war, although the external pressures were dangerous, it still seemed to be in place.

As a 'system' (Johnson 1986: 97–115) clientelism represented a complex articulation of the Lebanese class and status structures with what Max Weber (1948) described as the 'party' structure of political power. The relative stability of the system from 1943 to the early 1970s was in large part due to the unity of the multiconfessional commercial-financial bourgeoisie, a class with clear inter-ests in political stability, the promotion of a free economy, and a limited role for the state. It was not that the state was weak by default. Rather, the dominant class wanted to keep it weak in the sense of limiting its intervention in the economy.

Political order and control were not neglected, however, and were provided by the party or 'state' structure of patron–client relations descending from the patriarchal za'ims — many of whom were members of the dominant class — through the qabadays and other sub-patrons to the individualistic middle classes, sub-proletariat and peasantry. By exchanging patronage for personal support, the za'ims were usually able to contain the confessional and other divisions among their dependent clients; and by making judicious use of the state security forces, they could control their qabaday lieutenants who relied on them for protection from the law.

The clientelist structure of the Lebanese state was, for many years, remark-ably successful. In the cities and in areas of peasant proprietorship, where loyalties to the za'ims were more fickle and contingent than they were on the landed estates, disciplined political parties like the Phalanges (Entelis 1974; Khalaf 1976) or sophisticated political machines were established with quasi-bureaucratic forms of organization to distribute patronage and maintain sup-port. And in the pursuit of political order and stability, these organizations were often very adept at manipulating the clients' loyalties to such status groups as family, neighbourhood and confession (Johnson 1986: 52–79, 83–95, 110–14 and 127–35).

Urban za'ims would organize their clienteles into family or neighbourhood groups, working in 'popular' areas through clan or quarter qabadays, and else-where through 'respectable' notables or brokers. They would also associate themselves with religious charities and educational foundations, such as the Islamic Maqasid Society in Beirut which provided important sources of patron-age and also helped identify the za'im with the notable families' tradition of philanthropy and community leadership. Sa'ib Salam's success as a za'im in Beirut owed much to his presidency of the Maqasid in the 1960s and 1970s. Owning office blocks and other real estate in Beirut, this Sunni foundation was able to run a number of primary and secondary schools, a teacher training college, a nursing school, and a relatively large and modern hospital in Beirut, as well as giving land and financial assistance to such organizations as a Muslim old people's home, an orphanage, and the Muslim Boy Scouts. Managed by an assembly of members and a board of directors that were dominated by men who belonged to the notable Sunni families of Beirut, the Maqasid Society distributed free or subsidized education, health care and other welfare services in a communal context that continually reminded the recipients of patronage they were part of a status hierarchy that had provided for a number of generations. The hierarchy was led by a za'im who was closely associated with rich Sunni notables whose fathers or grandfathers had founded the charity in the latter part of the nineteenth century, and these families continued, in a modern context, a tradition of communal philanthropy and solidarity (Johnson 1986: 14–15, 46–7 and 51–3).

Manipulations of such loyalties helped legitimate the leadership roles in the clientelist structure, and this process was very much tied up with notions of honour: the honour or propriety of families whatever their status; the honour or high-born eminence of za'ims and other notables; the honour or respect claimed by patriarchal leaders. The relationship between the political honour of the za'ims and the familial honour found in the wider society was complex, but there can be little doubt, as Massoud Younes (1999: 173–81) argues, that the two reinforced each other in a variety of ways. In particular, it seems that the one was legitimated by the other in what we might describe as a perceived 'natural' order.

Only someone with contempt for the law and the status norms of authority could object to this order. And the honourable qabaday, so admired by some sections of the clientele, was just such a person. Za'ims could contain qabaday anarchy by helping some strong-arm leaders to establish themselves in legitimate business. But this created a further difficulty, as a rich businessman might become divorced from the street he was supposed to control. He might even be killed by an up and coming qabaday who wanted to take his place. In the end there had to be a superior force to control the political underworld, and this was provided by the police and security forces who could be ordered by the za'ims to imprison criminal qabadays who stepped out of line. Za'ims could also order the killing of a particularly recalcitrant qabaday, who could be shot while 'resisting arrest' or simply dispatched by a paid assassin. Although I cannot point to a documented case of a za'im ordering the execution of a qabaday in

Beirut, many people claimed that it had happened, and it certainly occurred elsewhere in Lebanon as is clear from references to the killings of 'outlaws' in Michael Gilsenan's account of Akkar (1996). The ultimate penalty for disloyalty was always implicit in the system, and urban qabadays had to accept their role as middle-level leaders. It was difficult for them to challenge the za'ims and their system, and it was only after the Lebanese state had collapsed in the first rounds of the civil war in 1975–76 that the strong-arm men were able to establish themselves as leaders independent of their former patrons and protectors.

This account of how honour and honourable leaders were incorporated into the Lebanese state contrasts with much anthropological writing that seems to see the continued existence of honour in the Mediterranean region as somehow being the result of a weak political authority. John Davis (1987: 24–5) makes the point well, citing Julian Pitt-Rivers (1961), Anton Blok (1974) and others. Blok, he argues, has something like 'a vacuum theory' of the political role of the mafia: if the state is too weak to impose order, another order based on family and honour takes its place.

Pino Arlacchi's accounts (1979; 1983) of the Italian Calabrian mafia (the *'ndrangheta*) make a similar point. His theory about the relationship between honour, leadership and 'permanent transition' (a concept he uses to describe a social formation not fully transformed by capitalism) is very suggestive and helped me develop an analysis of Lebanese clientelism (Johnson 1986: 103 ff). The *'ndrangheta* racketeers and their style of honour and leadership were, it seems, particularly well adjusted to operating within the Calabrian environment of a highly competitive market, small-scale units of production and distribution, unstable and rapid social mobility, a fragmented and individualistic society and, very significantly, a weak central authority or state (see chapter 3, section 5, below).

It is certainly the case that the particularism of honour is opposed to the universalism of a 'legal-rational' state, and my argument about the failure of 'technocratic' reformism in the 1960s can easily be used to support the point (Johnson 1986: 149–57). Despite their attempts to reform the Lebanese state and economy, Presidents Fu'ad Shihab and Charles Helou remained prisoners of the clientelist system and were not able to limit the power of the za'ims in the localities. The election of President Suleiman Frangieh in 1970 and subsequent acts like the purging and weakening of the *Deuxième Bureau* represented a reassertion of the values of honour and family against an attempt to extend the universalism of the state. In the 1960s, 'Shihabism' had been a reformist programme that used new state planning structures and government investment to provide services according to universal rather than particularist principles'. Piped water and electricity were extended to all the villages of Lebanon's underdeveloped periphery, not just those controlled by za'ims who belonged to a dominant faction; a social security programme was introduced for all Lebanese employees, not as patronage for favoured clients; and state schools were established to supplement the private schools run by za'ims and confessional foundations (Johnson 1986: 137–45, 153 and 218–19). Because this state provision threatened the patronage networks of the za'ims, and because the state's internal security apparatus was used to subvert qabadays who had previously been manipulated and protected by urban bosses, a reactive parliamentary coalition eventually emerged that was able to defeat (by one vote) the Shihabist presidential candidate (Elias Sarkis) in 1970. After the election of President Frangieh, the Shihabist experiment came to an end and the za'ims asserted their parochial and particularist power once more (Johnson 1986: 159–64).

However, what might be described as the Lebanese 'political mafia' did not merely fill a vacuum left by a weak central authority. This particular mafia was not usually in *opposition* to the state. Since the time of the French Mandate it had been an important apparatus *of* the state, distributing resources, socializing the citizenry, channelling demands and support, and providing for political control and order. It might have been a rough and ready order, and it could not prevent a short civil war and some confessional conflict in 1958. But it was nonetheless effective in holding together what one author called a 'precarious republic' (Hudson 1968) and another an 'improbable nation' (Meo 1965).

The Lebanese political system may not have measured up to the civility or civic culture enjoined on it by some of the contributors to an influential collection of essays edited by Leonard Binder (1966) and published during the Shihabist period. But it worked well enough and, under the circumstances, might have been the best that could reasonably have been hoped for. And the fact that it failed cannot be held against it too strongly. The external pressures in the 1970s were so great they would probably have destroyed a more 'developed' and civic-minded state as well.

7. Confessionalism and war

Once the civil war had started, the potential horror of a culture of honour and shame was quickly revealed. After some years of violent (but limited and eventually mediated) clashes between Palestinian commandos and Lebanese security forces, between Palestinians and predominantly Maronite militias, and between rival Muslim and Christian gangs in Beirut, uncontrollable war broke out on 13 April 1975. In the morning, armed men drove past a Maronite church where the Phalangist leader, Pierre Gemayel, was attending a service. They opened fire and killed four people, including Gemayel's bodyguard and two other members of the Phalanges. Later in the day, vengeful Phalangists attacked a bus carrying Palestinians and Lebanese Muslims to the Tal az-Zaatar refugee camp. 27 passengers and three bystanders were killed and 19 wounded. Fierce fighting then broke out in the suburbs of Beirut.

There is little point in my summarizing the background to the war and the complex and internecine conflicts of the 1970s and 1980s. Accounts elsewhere are legion (and for example, books in English include Ajami 1986; Barakat 1977; 1988; Cobban 1985; Fisk 1990; Gilmour 1983; Gordon 1980; Goria 1985; Haley and Snider 1979; Hanf 1993; Harris 1997; Johnson 1986; Khalaf 1987; Khalidi 1979; Khazen 2000; Norton 1987; Owen 1976; Rabinovich 1984; Randal 1990; Salibi 1976; Sayigh 1994; Schiff and Ya'ari 1986; Tabbara 1979).

What needs to be stressed here is that, freed from structural constraints, the honour of the various protagonists was expressed in a violent and anarchic fashion. Vengeance killings became indiscriminate and brutish. Hostages were taken at roadblocks on the basis of the confession entered on the victims' identity cards. Some were exchanged, but many others killed. And the killings were accompanied by rape, torture and mutilation. The values of feud and honour gave way to communal violence, 'ethnic cleansing' and what at other times would have been considered reprehensible and dishonourable behaviour.

The mutilations and other acts of war were heavy with symbolism. Male bodies were castrated to strike at their manhood and reproductive capacity. Women were raped not just to provide recreation for the fighters but also to dishonour the victims' men who should have protected them. The wombs of pregnant women were cut open to destroy the accursed progeny of the hated Other. Eyes, the windows to the soul, were gouged out perhaps to destroy the spiritual as well as physical enemy. Churches and mosques were destroyed or burnt down; graveyards were dug up with bulldozers; everything that represented the Other had to be destroyed, erased, obliterated.

The sexual imagery of some of this is obvious. For decades, Muslims and Christians had lived with myths about each other's women. Some Christian men saw Muslim women as docile, compliant, seductive and sensual, as 'odalisques', the harem women of the seraglio. It was an erotic perspective similar to that peddled by European Orientalists in their literature and art (Said 1978). And it was matched by the view which some Muslim men had of Christian women, that they were modern, progressive, advanced — little more than whores. In times of peace men might lust after the women of the Other but to interfere with them invited reprisals, and 'honour crimes' were usually treated leniently by the courts. For a time this 'entente' shielded women in the early days of the civil war (Sharara 1978: 12). Women were rarely taken hostage and those who were were quickly released. Often, militiamen on roadblocks did not ask to see women's identity cards. To harm a woman was *haram*, *'ayb*, shameful. Why, it was said, even during the terrible massacres of 1860 (see below, and chapter 3, section 3) some Christian women and girls of the Mountain did not flee from the Druze because it was known that honourable men would not touch women.

Gradually, however, the boundaries were crossed and men entered the Other's field of shame. After all, honour was in part an expression of communal pride and vengeance. It required that any attack against one's own people or their property should be repaid and, as the protagonists became inured to violence, large-scale massacres and associated rapes became more common.

Many of the massacres were perpetrated by Maronite militias against non-Lebanese communities: the Palestinians, Kurds and Syrians of the Karantina (January 1976), and the Palestinians of Tal az-Zaatar (August 1976) and Sabra and Shatila (September 1982). It would seem that a single community, convinced of its moral superiority and with a strong sense of solidarity, was more likely to impose communal punishment on a large scale than a coalition of nationalities and confessions such as the Palestinians and Lebanese National Movement.

Sometimes, however, units of the latter coalition did massacre their opponents. In the Christian village of Damour in January 1976, the Palestinians and their Lebanese allies raped and slaughtered the inhabitants and wrecked the cemetery, digging up the coffins and scattering bones and bodies (see chapter 1, section 4). But despite some exceptions, the point about 'single communities' still holds. It seems that Muslim massacres of Christians tended to occur when the Muslims concerned were of the same sect and bound together by a local sense of honour and solidarity — as, for example, in the massacres of Christians by the Druze after the assassination of Kamal Jumblat in March 1977 and during the bloody and unpleasant Shouf war of 1983.

What is important to recognize is that such slaughter not only served as a deterrent and therefore conformed to the cultural rule that honourable men should defend their community, but it was also retributive — a just and many would say divinely sanctioned punishment for the outsiders' affront to the community's honour. In addition, it provided an effective method of clearing the community's territory of 'foreigners'.

The Druze considered the Shouf mountain (to the south-east of Beirut) to be their 'homeland'; but since the massacres of 1860, they had lived peacefully alongside their Christian neighbours, many of them in confessionally mixed villages. It is generally accepted now that the Syrians were responsible for Kamal Jumblat's murder in 1977, the motive being to weaken the Lebanese National Movement that opposed the Syrian army's 'peace-keeping' intervention in 1976. Almost inevitably, though, Christians were blamed and many of them killed in revenge. It may be that those killings were an 'isolated incident' (Hanf 1993:

275), but in 1983 the presence of Christian militiamen, who had established bases in the Shouf during the Israeli invasion of 1982, was considered a defilement of the Druze homeland. In the warfare that followed the Israeli withdrawal, Christian civilians as well as militiamen were slaughtered as the Druze expelled their enemies. In August 1983, on the eve of some of the fiercest fighting of the Shouf war, Walid Jumblat (Kamal's son and leader of the Druze militia) was exultant. 'It will be a carnival,' he said, 'a bloody carnival' (Hanf 1993: 279). His men fought fiercely for the honour of their community, and over 160,000 Christian civilians fled from the Shouf and the southern slopes of Mount Lebanon, probably the largest population displacement in all the years of the Lebanese wars (Randal 1990: 360–1).

As we have seen (in chapter 1, section 4), among the earliest cases of ethnic cleansing were the massacres of the Karantina and Tal az-Zaatar in 1976. Other Muslim slum districts and Palestinian 'camps' overrun by Maronite forces in that year included the Maslakh, Dubayya and Jisr al-Basha. In all cases, the surviving civilians were driven out and most of their homes obliterated so they could never return. The Karantina and the Maslakh were neighbouring slum settlements, parts of them on Maronite church land, close to Beirut's port and the road from Christian East Beirut to the north. This road passed through Christian suburbs on the coast until it reached the Palestinian camp of Dubayya and then continued to the small Maronite port of Junieh. Similarly, Tal az-Zaatar and Jisr al-Basha were Palestinian quarters on the road from East Beirut to the Maronite stronghold on Mount Lebanon. Thus in addition to strategic considerations, these massacres and their aftermath served to restore territory to the Maronite homeland, in the same way as a 'cleansed' Shouf would create a Druze homeland in 1983.

Virtually any atrocity could be justified in the purification of the land. I remember a conversation in 1977 with a Maronite university student, who always struck me as an intelligent and considerate person. When she berated me over my sympathy for Lebanese Muslims and cited cases of militiamen raping, torturing and killing innocent Christians, I argued (perhaps naively) that whereas the leadership of the National Movement tried to prevent such horrific practices, the leaders of the Phalanges and other Maronite militias seemed to employ terror, rape and massacre as instruments of policy. I expected her to be angry and dispute my assertions, but her response was to shrug her shoulders and say quite calmly, 'But it's *our* country.'

The uncompromising pride involved in that statement provides a clue to the 'honour' with which I am trying to grapple. It is clearly different from honour in prewar Lebanon. The latter was associated with *limited* conflict, not all-out war. The honour code and the 'ritual of familial justice' (Younes 1999: 45–69 and

116–38) restricted the extent of feuding, and elaborate rules about hospitality and sanctuary helped to ensure that usually only an eye for an eye or a life for a life was taken in revenge. Because Asad Awad and Kamal al-Askari achieved the singular effect of killing each other when they fired their pistols in a Beirut nightclub (see section 5 above), no one countenanced further vengeance. There was certainly a norm that sometimes honour required repayment with interest, but unrestrained warfare between individuals or families could seriously undermine social order. Thus, as Jacob Black-Michaud (1975: 194) pointed out in his analysis of feuding in the Mediterranean region, the rules and structure of the feud generally served to contain the conflict.

Mediation is intrinsic to the feud (Middleton and Tait 1958: 20). The Druze businessman and former president of Middle East Airlines, Najib Alamuddin, tells us that, although 'blood feuds are a stern reality' on Mount Lebanon, men are 'required' to mediate if they are 'equally related' to the protagonists (Alamuddin 1993: 58 and 70). A man should be a partisan of his cousin if the latter is feuding with an outsider, but the same man is obliged to work for peace if two of his cousins are engaged in a feud with each other.

Mediation was sometimes achieved in remarkable ways. One story, told to me in 1973, about a feud in a Druze village illustrates the way religious belief could be mixed with the values of kinship and patrimony to bring about the resolution of conflict. In a sense what happened was stronger than mediation, for the solution depended on the arbitration of a soul that had transmigrated from a man who had been killed in an earlier round of the dispute. The Druze believe their souls pass into another body when they die, and it is not unusual for them to make highly informed claims that they are the reincarnations of others. Interestingly, these claims often relate to a violent death, and during and after the civil war many Druze children claimed to be incarnations of coreligionists who had died in the hostilities. This story, though, comes from before the war. Two families were arguing in a field about where the boundary between their lands lay. The dispute dated back a long time and blood had been shed a number of times. A boy, a child of some eight or nine years, picked up a stick and drew a line in the earth. When asked what he was doing, he said he was marking the boundary as it had been agreed at the last round of negotiation, long before he was born.

His father asked him how he knew this, and the boy replied that he was the reincarnation of a man the father had killed in the feud. When the child revealed details of the shooting that only the dead man and his killer could have known, his father embraced his former adversary who was now his son. The line scratched in the ground was accepted as the boundary and the feud ended, for how could the two families quarrel over land when the property was now,

through the boy, part of the patrimony of both? How could the father countenance killing his enemy again, now that he was his son, and how could the
rival family pursue a feud against a man who had fathered their own brother?

The possibility that the father had deliberately coached the boy was dis-
counted. It seemed that both families wanted the feud to end. It had been costly
in terms of lives, and all were seeking a way out of a resumption of hostilities.
Feuds are not usually pursued with great enthusiasm beyond the initial
exchanges of blood. The round of vengeance is an onerous duty from which
most men eventually want to escape, if only the code of honour would allow
them to do so. The evocative title of Massoud Younes's book (1999) on blood
vengeance in Lebanon, *Ces morts qui nous tuent*, 'the dead who kill us', is an
indication of the dreadful tragedy that the code imposes on its adherents.

The feud, then, is a damage-limitation exercise. Confessional conflict in
Lebanon was, by contrast, unlimited. Whole communities were destroyed in
massacres; urban quarters and refugee 'camps' were bulldozed and obliterated;
even the dead were destroyed by digging up graveyards. There were no rules to
restrain the bloodshed. At the level of the political elite there could still be
attempts at mediation and compromise; but such interventions were essentially
external to the exchange of death, not intrinsic to it like the rules of proper
behaviour in feuding. The fact that women and children could be killed in confessional fighting was just one demonstration that this form of conflict was quite
unlike feud. It was war.

Similarly, the myths of origin and collective memories were of a different
order. Tales of individual heroism, insults and quick-witted responses were the
prewar currency of the 'poetics of manhood' (Herzfeld 1985) or the 'word of
honour' of men (Gilsenan 1989). Michael Gilsenan shows how, in a village in
northern Lebanon, *murajul* or 'manly performance' in telling tales of honour was
closely associated with comedy and joking, whereby a man of honour could be
admired by one part of the audience but treated as a buffoon in another
(Gilsenan 1989; and see chapter 5, section 1, below). The collective memories
of confessionalism were a much more serious business. Stories of oppression
and resistance could go back to the Crusades if not earlier, and — to give one
dramatic example — the massacre of thousands of Maronites by Druze fighters
in 1860 was a relatively recent affront to communal honour that could not be
allowed to happen again. In less than four weeks, around 11,000 Maronites and
other Christians had been slaughtered and 4000 died from starvation and
disease. Most were killed by the Druze, but many died at the hands of Sunnis
and Shi'a, and a further 5000 Christians were massacred by Sunnis in Damascus
(Salibi 1965: 80–107; and see chapter 3, section 3, below).

These horrifying statistics help to explain the equally grisly massacres perpetrated by Maronite militias, a century later, in the 1970s. Undefended Christian communities had been extinguished in 1860. It was therefore essential to make the first strike against those Palestinians and Lebanese Muslims who appeared to be challenging Maronite hegemony in modern Lebanon.

The nature of heroism was different too. The heroes of the feud were usually common men who, like everyone else, had their weaknesses — who could be *az'ar*, a scoundrel, hooligan or thug, as well as *qabaday*. But some heroes of confessional conflict could take on a spiritual aura: if they died they were martyrs (*shuhada*) and, more than this, some were canonized. After the Lebanese Shi'a imam, Musa as-Sadr, disappeared in mysterious circumstances and was presumably assassinated while on a visit to Libya in 1978, many Shi'a hailed him as another 'Hidden Imam', like the one who had disappeared in the ninth century and who Shi'a believe will one day return to establish a reign of justice on earth (Ajami 1986; Norton 1987; Sayigh 1994: 173).

Bashir Gemayel was, in effect, not only canonized but also deified by some Maronites after his assassination in 1982. The faithful saw tears of oil running from some of his portraits that were hung on trees and balconies and pasted on walls all over the Maronite enclave on Mount Lebanon and in East Beirut. This was a miracle that was commonly associated with Catholic saints, and the Lebanese Forces (the unified Maronite militia created by Gemayel under Phalangist control) was transformed by the martyrdom of its leader to become what some described as a 'monastic order', comparable to the Knights Templar, the warrior monks of the Crusades. Great significance was attached to the fact that when the bomb exploded at the Phalanges party headquarters, Sheikh Bashir was in his early thirties, the age of the Lord Jesus at the time of his crucifixion. The day of the explosion was the feast-day for the Exaltation of the Holy Cross. Only an hour or so before he was killed, Gemayel had given a speech in the Convent of the Cross where his sister was a nun. He spoke standing under a large crucifix that had the inscription, 'By this sign you will vanquish.' He had come as a saviour in the image of Christ with a mission (*risala*) to save the Maronite homeland. He forgave those who hurt him, but he never forgave those who harmed Lebanon. He declared war on the enemies of Lebanon as Christ had declared war on the Anti-Christ. And just as Jesus had to be killed by the Jews, so Bashir had to die at the hands of Muslims. But as Jesus rose from the dead, so in a sense did Sheikh Bashir who was still a presence in his community and continued to influence events (Hage 1989: 381 ff).

At the beginning of the civil war the leaders of most militias, whether they were Arab or Lebanese nationalists, had been motivated by essentially secular ideologies of what can be loosely defined as the 'left' and 'right'. Leading units in the Lebanese National Movement included the Progressive Socialist Party (*al-*

hizb at-taqaddumi al-ishtiraki) led by Kamal Jumblat (which although a predominantly Druze party did have a social democratic programme), the Lebanese Communist Party (CPL), and the 'new-left' Communist Action Organization (*munazzamat al-'amal ash-shuyu'i*). By the mid-1980s, however, the communist parties had no influence at all, and such leaders as Walid Jumblat of the Progressive Socialist Party had been sucked into the sectarian discourse of their clienteles. Indeed some leaders of previously secular militias blatantly manipulated and encouraged sectarian practices. Ideological politics had gradually retreated before the powerful forces of clan and confessional allegiance. It had become impossible to talk of a political left and right in Lebanon when the most extreme forms of communalism motivated the vast majority of the fighters and many of their leaders.

An example of the degeneration of Lebanese politics was the way the former qabaday, Ibrahim Qulaylat (see section 5 above), the leader of the Sunni Murabitun militia in Beirut, issued statements in 1985 against his Shi'a enemies in the name of the Caliph Yazid. Yazid was the Sunni leader whom Shi'a abominate because he was responsible for the killing of Husayn ibn Ali in the seventh century; and Husayn, whose martyrdom is a foundational event in Shi'a mythology, is the most revered of all the imams (see chapter 4, section 2). The name of Qulaylat's militia came from the Arabic *murabit*, a word that conjures up images of a soldier who fights for Sunni Islam on a hostile frontier. And the use of Yazid's authority was a calculated sectarian insult, a reminder of Shi'a shame, from a Sunni leader who in the 1970s had been at least influenced by Nasserism and the other secular and progressive currents in the Lebanese National Movement (Johnson 1986: 213).

8. Honour and reproduction

The concept of honour and its associated values in Lebanon changed over time. In agrarian society, honour was essentially a system of domination. With the development of a free peasantry, however, it became associated with more egalitarian values (see chapter 3, sections 3 and 4, below), a trend that was strengthened by urbanization. Honour still provided legitimation for a patriarchal political order. Now, though, even men from humble social backgrounds could lay claim to it by asserting themselves against others in acts of violence that had previously been the prerogative of the lords and their retainers. In a normative sense, all men who were not subjected to the control of landlords had an 'equal opportunity' to be honourable in modern Lebanon. The use of the male noun is crucial here because, of course, women continued to be excluded. Women remained the 'property' of men, the difference being that they now 'belonged' to their husbands or fathers instead of their lords. Any man who aspired to honour would defend 'his' women from violation by others and would protect his family from impurity by imposing a sexual discipline on wives, daughters and sisters — even, occasionally, to the point of killing those who became shameless.

These 'egalitarian' values of honour were manipulated to considerable effect by the Lebanese political elite, particularly in the city and its urbanized mountain hinterland. Za'ims and qabadays were admired by sufficiently large sections of the population as men of honour and this legitimated a clientelist state structure that provided a social and political order in independent Lebanon. There were many who were critical of this system. For example there were those known as the *tiknuqratiyyin* — lawyers, doctors, and university lecturers, economists, engineers and other 'technocrats' who supported and worked for Shihabist reformism in the 1960s. Many educated people deplored the coercion and corruption in the system, and some — Christians as well as Muslims — joined secular communist and socialist parties. But in 1972, in the last general election held before the start of the civil war, liberal technocrats and radical leftists who stood for parliament were usually overwhelmingly defeated by the za'ims and their allies (Johnson 1986: 162–3, 167–8 and 180–1). Clearly, the clientelist system with its political culture of honour was still firmly in place not long before the outbreak of hostilities.

In warfare honour changed again. It became more a matter of domination than egalitarianism. People increasingly identified more closely with a social group larger than their nuclear or extended family, and as the confession was ideally endogamous (see chapter 4, section 2, below), it was still a kinship group and governed by the same patriarchal values as before. But whereas men had previously competed with each other largely to *protect* the honour of themselves and their families, they now fought to *dominate* and impose shame on a socially defined Other. Rather like the lords of Akkar had shamed those they considered to be lacking in noble descent, so the militiamen in the civil wars employed arbitrary violence against a despised, and in some respects subhuman, enemy.

Where do such values come from? It is unsatisfactory to suggest that honour and shame are unchanging phenomena deeply embedded in Lebanese culture that can be picked up now and again to be used as resources in political domination, economic competition or confessional conflict. But by considering a process of social reproduction, whereby the norms and values adopt different forms at different historical and socioeconomic conjunctures, we might arrive at a fuller understanding of the difficult and sometimes nebulous concepts of honour and shame.

This is the subject of the next chapter which starts by locating honour in its wider Mediterranean context prior to the modern period, and then proceeds to consider the growth of a personal sense of honour associated with an 'egalitarian ethic' in nineteenth-century Mount Lebanon. This development challenged the notion of honour as an ideology of social domination, and was associated with peasant revolts against landlords and the partial overthrow of 'feudalism' in the Kisrawan region of the Mountain. The collapse of a 'feudal order' also led to a new sense of community based on the confession, and I argue that personal and confessional honour grew in tandem during the early modern period. Confessionalism was contained during much of the twentieth century, but under the impulse of urbanization (and the external pressures on Lebanon) it eventually emerged as a dominant ideology in the 1970s and 1980s. Although the effects of rural–urban migration are touched on in the next chapter, a fuller treatment is given in chapter 4. Chapter 3 is largely concerned with providing an historical background, and with speculating on the repro-duction of honour in the early stages of modernization.

3

Honour and History

Economic and cultural contacts between Europe and Lebanon developed dramatically in the nineteenth century. But Mount Lebanon was in some senses part of the Mediterranean world considerably earlier, and in many respects it had little in common with the other Arab provinces of the Ottoman empire. Thus although 'Arab' notions of honour presumably had some influence on Lebanese culture, it is perhaps more useful to start a history of honour in Lebanon by focusing on Europe. This serves two purposes: first, it directs us away from a mistaken assumption that honour is a specifically Arab or Islamic concept (see section 1 below); and second, a consideration of the 'timocratic' culture of warrior nobles in Europe (in section 2) provides a background for an understanding of the way landlords in pre-modern Lebanon legitimated their domination of the peasantry.

It is not possible, however, to demonstrate that the Lebanese 'learnt' honour from Europe. Indeed, it would be wrong even to try to do so. Notions of honour and shame are more or less prominent in so many different geographic locations and historical periods that an explanation for their existence is better found in a consideration of the structure of particular societies and economies than in any dubious notion of cultural diffusion. In sections 3 to 5 of this chapter I offer a structural explanation for personal honour in nineteenth and twentieth-century Mount Lebanon, first considering the honour of domination exercised by 'feudal' lords and then a more 'populist' form that had existed to a degree before the nineteenth century (particularly in isolated parts of the Mountain where 'feudalism' had not been fully established) but which became far more prominent

70

as the lords gradually lost their power. I argue that the development of mercantile and agricultural capitalism, coupled with the propagation of liberal values through the educational system, undermined the old 'feudal order' in which honour seems to have been largely monopolized by the lords. With the development of a free peasantry, honour became a quality that all or most men could claim in a society influenced by the idea of an 'egalitarian ethic'. To introduce the latter concept I expand, in section 5, on my earlier mention of the Calabrian mafia (chapter 2, section 6) to show the way honour and feuding could provide a sense of order in a highly competitive economy and society. I then discuss the argument that in a rural ecology where land and water are limited, an ethic or 'myth' of egalitarianism develops which imposes social controls on the competition for scarce resources. Despite a hierarchy of wealth and power, social inequality is in effect denied by the egalitarian ethic and normative limits are imposed on accumulation. But although the ethic implies that *all* resources are limited, it does seem to sanction an assertion of honour and this allows some to become peasant leaders and to acquire a greater proportion of land or other assets to which, under the terms of the ethic, they are not properly entitled.

In this discussion, I consider the way the social anthropologist Jacob Black-Michaud (1975) modified an earlier account of the 'image of limited good' (Foster 1965) and argued that in Mediterranean 'feuding societies' the claiming of honour was the means by which leaders were created in a society where all other 'goods' were limited. In the Lebanese case, however, the most powerful rural leaders who emerged after the formal abolition of 'feudalism' in 1861 were not usually created by an assertion of honour through feuding, and most parliamentarians in Christian Mount Lebanon came from the professions or mercantile backgrounds. Nevertheless, these new leaders did subscribe to some sort of egalitarian ethic which in part reflected the necessity to win votes in a liberal democracy, and this was quite different from the landlord ethic of domination that persisted in the Akkar region in the north, the Bekaa valley, and southern Lebanon.

Another central theme of this chapter is the development in the nineteenth century of confessional identities. These represented another 'functional' set of normative values providing a sense of security and community in a new, competitive, capitalist environment. Alongside a populist sense of individual honour, communal honour also became more pronounced; and the assertion of Christian peasants' honour in their rebellion against the abuses of their Maronite landlords in 1858–59 led to a confessional conflict between Maronites and Druze in 1860 in which thousands of Christians were massacred. These events and the role of the Maronite church and Druze landlords in encouraging confessional identification are analysed in section 3.

After considering the 'reproduction' of personal and confessional honour in modern Lebanon (section 4) and the case of intra-Maronite feuding in the northern district of Zgharta (section 5), the chapter ends (in section 6) with a discussion of the proposition that the mountain feud was exported to the city where it contributed to confessional conflict in the twentieth century. Although this idea is suggestive, I argue that feuding and confessional conflict should be interpreted as quite different phenomena. As we have seen in chapter 2 (section 7), the feud was a damage-limitation exercise, whereas confessional conflict was without constraint and led to the ethnic cleansing of whole communities. And as we shall see in chapter 4, although confessional massacres occurred in a rural context in the nineteenth century, the civil wars of the 1970s and 1980s were determined much more by urbanization and competing ideas of nationalism than any agrarian tradition.

1. Lebanon and the Mediterranean

Although many social anthropologists have interpreted honour in a Mediter-ranean peasant or shepherd context and have seen the region as a 'distinct cultural entity' (see chapter 2, section 1), those who concentrate on the Arab world have tended to locate the subject within a theory about segmentary lineages or 'tribalism' in desert societies. Some ethnographies of segmentation do deal with communities like the predominantly sedentary Berbers of the Atlas mountains in Morocco (Gellner 1969), but the theory developed primarily out of the study of desert nomads which shifts the focus from a Mediterranean to an Arab context. Some beduin societies in north Africa might be described as geographically Mediterranean, but segmentary lineage theory has been applied to peoples in Arabia and Yemen who are in no sense related culturally to the peasants of southern Europe.

Put simply, studies of beduin and other segmentary societies have argued that the lineage or kinship structure provides a political and social order in the absence of a strong central authority or state. The theory can be summed up in the Arab proverb: 'I against my brother, my brother and I against our cousin, my cousin and I against the stranger.' Thus a man might quarrel with his brother over their inheritance, but would unite with him in a dispute with their cousin. Ultimately the larger lineage or descent group would unite in a feud with a kinship group more distantly related, so although there are many lines of fission in the society, the different segments do at times combine, or fuse, to fight a more distant enemy. This fusion — along with sometimes elaborate norms and structures of mediation — helps to resolve the conflicts between close relatives.

The theory of 'fission and fusion' was first developed by E. E. Evans-Pritchard in relation to the African Nilotic society of the Nuer (1940), but his later work

(1949) on the Sanusi of Cyrenaica (in eastern Libya) helped to place the theory more firmly in a beduin Arab context. Evans-Pritchard seemed to see segmentation as a description of the way tribal societies actually worked. But starting with Emrys Peters (1967) social anthropologists have tended to see it as an ideology, to which nomads might cling as a normative code about the way they ought to behave, but which had little social or political reality when it came to actual feuds over animals, women or honour. Clifford Geertz (1971: 22) was even moved to write that the Arab proverb should be recast as: 'The stranger and I against the whole lot of my horse-stealing relatives.'

The arguments about segmentary theory and the way lineage alliances did or did not structure feuding and honour need not detain us. A useful critical review of the subject can be found in Lila Abu-Lughod's discussion of anthropological approaches to the Arab world (1990). The important point for us is that the link made between beduin segmentation and feuding has helped to create the impression that notions of honour and shame are somehow peculiarly Arab. This is not just a European or western interpretation: the Iraqi sociologist Sana al-Khayyat, for example, also writes of 'the Arab concept of honour' (Khayyat 1990: 21) when discussing *'ird* and the repression of women in her country. Obviously *'ird* (sexual honour) is an Arabic word, but the concept is not specifically Arab. Nor, incidentally, is it Islamic as Jan Goodwin (1995) and many others would have us believe. Even such a serious approach to the subject as Mai Ghoussoub's (1987) sees the 'eternal masculine' in the Arab world as largely a result of Islam. If it serves no other purpose, my concentration on the Mediterranean region should dispel what sometimes amount to 'Islamophobic' assumptions.

Through migration, trade, and regional politics, Lebanon had many contacts with beduin societies, and some Lebanese have told me that the feud and values of honour came to them from a cultural exchange between the Mountain and the desert. As we shall see, some pre-Islamic poetry of a beduin origin was centrally concerned with honour and shame, and it is likely that this literature and the society it described were two influences among many on Lebanese culture. But Lebanon also traded in the Mediterranean; and amongst its Christian population, cultural ties with Europe were probably more influential. We should not exaggerate this. To a considerable extent, the Mountain remained culturally isolated from Europe for a long time after the end of Crusader influence in the thirteenth century. Nevertheless, Maronite priests continued to study in Rome, particularly after the establishment of the Maronite College at the Vatican in 1584. These clerics founded a few village schools whose graduates were often employed as secretaries by Druze as well as Maronite landlords. In the early seventeenth century Fakhr ad-Din II, the Druze emir or prince of the Lebanese Mountain, granted protection to Catholic missionaries, and in the eighteenth century such orders as the Franciscans and Jesuits were influential at the court of the emirs as well as in the villages.

Politically there were links with Europe too. Fakhr ad-Din II, for example, entered into an alliance with the Italian Medici dynasty and spent five years (1613–18) in exile in Tuscany where, according to a modern Druze historian, he was 'dazzled by Florentine architecture', exporting it to Lebanon on his return (Alamuddin 1993: 88). There is much myth-making about Fakhr ad-Din's progressive attitudes, but there is also evidence to demonstrate some truth in the stories told about the Druze emir, both in the account written by one of his secretaries and in the use he made of Italian advisers to help him reform his Lebanese administration (Salibi 1988: 158–60). The alliance with the Tuscans, however, did not last when it became clear that the emir could not co-operate with their territorial ambitions in Syria. After wars against neighbouring provinces had expanded his territory, the Ottomans counter-attacked and the Medicis failed to support him. Defeated in battle, Fakhr ad-Din was deposed in 1633 and executed by strangulation two years later in Istanbul.

Far more enduring was the link with France. In 1535 the Ottoman sultan, Suleiman the Magnificent, had entered into a 'capitulatory' treaty with Francis I in reward for the French king's assistance against the Habsburg empire. This granted various rights and immunities to French traders and paved the way for France becoming the protector of all Catholics in the Ottoman empire. Over subsequent centuries a close relationship developed between the Maronites and their European patrons; and partly as a result of tax concessions to French traders and local merchants protected by France, Maronite silk producers prospered and became more powerful on the Mountain. As an indication of growing Christian influence, at the end of the eighteenth century the Sunni Shihabi emirs converted to Maronite Christianity (Harik 1968; Hitti 1957; Salibi 1965).

This admittedly sketchy history provides a justification for seeing Lebanon as part of a Mediterranean world long before the modern period. Trade would increase considerably during the nineteenth century, and a revival of education led to what some have called a cultural 'awakening' as the Lebanese became exposed to modern European ideas. But although many of the best intellectuals among the graduates of the Maronite College — such as the Vatican librarian and orientalist scholar Joseph Simonius Assemanus (1687–1768) — tended to stay in Europe prior to the nineteenth century, and although education was limited to a privileged few, it would be wrong to assume that Lebanon was completely isolated from Latin Christendom during the 'dark ages' of Ottoman rule.

Kamal Salibi (1965: 120 ff) might have been right to see the cultural revival of the nineteenth century as something so dramatic that it really was as if the

Lebanese were waking from a long sleep. Certainly, in terms of historical explanation, that century is far more important for me than any speculation about the pre-modern period. Nevertheless, in a later work Salibi (1988: 158 ff) does recognize the 'subtle influences' that affected Lebanon, and particularly the Maronites, before the eighteenth and nineteenth centuries, and so some consideration of the Mediterranean culture of honour during the period of the European Renaissance might be useful in the sense of providing an historical context.

But although there is a degree of concern with cultural diffusion, what follows in section 2 is more a use of history as illustration or 'analogy' than a discussion of causal explanations. Any attempt to make a direct link between the aristocratic honour system in Renaissance Europe and similar systems of honour in Lebanon would be at best highly speculative, and at worst quite simply wrong. What can be said, however, is that the honour tragedies of seventeenth-century Spanish playwrights, for example, do provide a rich source for a consideration of the social content of honour as domination, as do the related discussions of classical Greek and medieval Arab notions of an heroic culture.

2. Honour and the European Renaissance

A driving cultural force of the 'rebirth' of European art was the revival of antiquity which during the fourteenth and fifteenth centuries stimulated a renewed interest in Greek and Roman art, philosophy and literature. A key aspect of classical culture involved the myths of ancient Greek heroes and the gods, and these formed the subject matter of many Renaissance paintings and sculptures. Similarly, the rediscovery of Aristotle's *Poetics* generated an interest in Greek drama and tragedy. Aristotle taught that the subject of tragedy was the hero who is morally elevated above ordinary men, but who is brought down by the tragic flaw of *hamartia* or error of judgement. As the tragedy unfolds, the actions of the hero provoke the cathartic emotions of pity and fear.

Classical tragic drama was first revived in Italy. In *Sofonisba*, for example, Giangiorgio Trissino (1478–1550) followed the technical prescriptions of Aristotle and told the story of Hannibal's sister (Sophonisba) who took poison rather than be taken alive by the Romans. But although the subject of heroism was given some treatment in Italian literature, it was usually associated with such other values as chivalry that tempered the uncompromising and cruel heroics of the Greek and Roman myths. Italian heroic poetry, for example, developed out of the *cantari* or sung poems that traditionally used themes drawn from the legends of Charlemagne and King Arthur. Perhaps the best known of the Italian romances is the sixteenth-century epic poem *Gerusalemme liberata* (Jerusalem Liberated) which took as its theme some mythological events of the first Crusade. Its author, Torquato Tasso (1544–95), paid careful attention to the rules of classical Greek and Latin poetry but his subject matter was clearly influenced by Christian and chivalric values.

In the sixteenth century, a number of Spanish playwrights also wrote classical tragedies but, as the theatre historian Melveena McKendrick (1992: 57) puts it, this genre was something of 'a dead end'. Far more significant were the honour tragedies of Lope de Vega (1562–1635) and Pedro Calderón de la Barca (1600–81). These dealt with contemporary Spanish — as opposed to classical — themes of honour, Lope concentrating on the absolutist domination of the feudal nobility and peasant resistance to it, Calderón on the code of conjugal honour that required a nobleman to kill his wife if she appeared to be adulterous.

Nevertheless, in discussing the work of Lope de Vega, Nicholas Dromgoole sets the Spanish honour plays in a classical Greek context. He points out that during the protracted reconquest of Spain from the Moors, Christian scholars became exposed to Greek texts that had been preserved in Arabic in the libraries of the Muslim civilization. This is uncontroversial. After the king of Castile and León had captured Toledo in 1085, for example, the mosque library of the city was found to contain Arabic translations of Aristotle (Mansfield 1985: 58). Rather more contentious is Dromgoole's emphasis on the heroic culture of Greek texts as a determinant of the Spanish nobility's honour. A central element of Greek culture, he says, was 'a highly developed sense of male personal honour' (Dromgoole 1997: 16), and this was in marked contrast to such Christian values as humility, penitence and forgiveness, mercy, charity and love. 'Greek ideas about honour,' he argues, 'arrived at a remarkably convenient time to underpin the struggle for supremacy between Church and State' (Dromgoole 1997: 19). In other words, the honour code of Greek heroes became the ideology of secular rulers who were intent on establishing their power and authority.

Dromgoole's discussion of Homer's *Iliad* reminds us how Achilles and his followers initially refused to fight at Troy because Agamemnon, the Greek commander-in-chief, had slighted the hero's honour. On reading Book I of Homer's epic poem, we might think that the quarrel over the slave-girl Briseis was a squalid affair, that Achilles was a spoiler, and an honourable man should have fought alongside his compatriots despite having lost his woman. But this was a matter of great importance to the respect that Achilles demanded as his due. Agamemnon had stolen Briseis, a woman who belonged to the hero, and a profound sense of personal honour would not let Achilles fight. It was a higher debt of honour that eventually resolved the dispute. After his squire and friend, Patroclus, was slain by Hector, Achilles rejoined the fray and killed the Trojan leader. Again Achilles demonstrated his uncompromising honour. When a wounded Hector invoked the names of the gods and pleaded — not for his life but for his body to be returned in honour to his parents — Achilles replied, 'Die! ... As for my own death, let it come when Zeus and the other deathless gods decide' (Homer 1950: 407). He then mutilated and insulted Hector's body by cutting its ankle tendons, tying the feet to a chariot and dragging it through the dust. Later of course, Achilles was killed by Hector's brother Paris, whose arrow was guided to the hero's vulnerable heel by the god Apollo, the son of Zeus.

Greek men of honour certainly defied the gods and, like Achilles, were prepared to take the consequences. Dromgoole, however, makes the further assertion that the Greek hero became the model for many aristocrats and noblemen throughout Catholic Europe. Turning their back on Christian values, he argues, they glorified satisfaction instead of penitence, vengeance instead of forgiveness, cruelty instead of mercy. An elaborate code of honour was established, and by meeting the obligations that this imposed the aristocrat was required to be publicly 'jealous of his honour' and ready to risk his life in its defence. In this he distinguished himself from those he dominated (Dromgoole 1997: 22).

In Lope de Vega's play, *Fuenteovejuna* (Well or Fountain of the Sheep), the *comendador* or lord of Fuenteovejuna is praised and honoured by the villagers for his brave deeds in battle, but he treats them with contempt, seducing the young women, married as well as single, eventually employing rape against those who refuse him. When a peasant is brave or foolish enough to support his cousin in her resistance, he is stripped naked, tied to a tree, and viciously flogged.

The personal honour of the nobility was a recurring theme in Spanish drama during the seventeenth century. In contrast to Lope, Pedro Calderón concentrated on conjugal honour. Three of his plays — *El médico de su honra* (The Physician or Surgeon of His Honour), *A secreto agravio, secreta venganza* (Secret Insult, Secret Vengeance), and *El pintor de su deshonra* (The Painter of his Dishonour) — deal with a nobleman who comes to believe that his wife is unfaithful. All three wives are in fact innocent, but they are killed by their husbands because they threaten to bring public shame to their men. In two of the plays, the putative lovers are killed too. In one, however, the lover is the king's brother, a prince 'and therefore immune' (McKendrick 1992: 147). This highly significant exception occurs in 'The Surgeon of His Honour'.

In the latter tragedy, Don Gutierre has his wife bled to death, but since he acted according to the code of honour the king condones what a modern audience would call murder. Noble women must be chaste and modest and accept, whatever the rights and wrongs of a particular case, that appearance is all and their life is not worth living if they have shamed their husband. As Doña

Leonor says, 'The end of honour is the end of life' (Calderón 1991: 34). At the close of the play she agrees to marry Don Gutierre, despite her knowing he has killed his first wife. When he reminds her he has 'already been the surgeon of [his] honour', she replies: 'If I am ever sick, Gutierre, do not hesitate to cure me' (Calderón 1991: 100).

Despite his uncompromising sense of honour in relation to his women, Gutierre nevertheless makes it clear that he will not seek vengeance against the man who has shamed him because the alleged adulterer is the king's brother, a royal prince with a higher status and power than a don. The king should punish the prince, not a mere nobleman who would not have the right. This is honour as a system of domination; there is nothing egalitarian about it. The code is adamant that those who socially have less honour should not harm those who have more. When they do, the consequences can be dreadful.

In Lope de Vega's *Fuenteovejuna* the abused peasants finally come to the end of their tether and kill the *comendador*, whereupon King Ferdinand sends a judge to identify and punish the offenders. The villagers — women and children as well as men — are put to the torture, and the audience hears their heart-rending screams of agony from off-stage. The peasants stand firm, however, refusing to name the actual killers, and after hearing their account of their lord's cruelty the king pardons them. While Lope challenges the notion that the poor and powerless do not possess honour (thus illustrating again the ambiguity of the code), his plays can only end in the peasants' favour by the intervention of the higher authority of the monarch. In another of Lope's plays, *Peribáñez*, the eponymous peasant, who protects his wife's virtue by killing his lascivious *comendador*, throws himself on the mercy of the king's justice. Melveena McKendrick's discussion of these tragedies makes the crucial point that when the king pardons the peasants in *Fuenteovejuna* and *Peribáñez*, he does not condone what they have done. 'Any justification of their action has to be implicit,' she argues, 'for the royal authority to which seigneurial authority yields depends no less than any other on the recognition and acceptance of hierarchical order' (McKendrick 1992: 90).

Although a somewhat revolutionary playwright could argue honour was classless (and as we shall see, that even women could be said to possess it), ultimately Lope de Vega had to accept that in practice the code buttressed an absolutist order in which only the military nobility, and ultimately only their monarch, could exercise honour with impunity. In Pedro Calderón's *El médico de su honra*, the king not only pardons but also condones Gutierre's bleeding his wife to death because the don's action conforms to the honour code of the nobility. In Lope's *Fuenteovejuna* the king only pardons the peasants who ultimately do not truly possess honour.

The idea that this notion of noble honour was originally derived from classical Greek culture is, at least, suggestive. In the poetry of Homer, 'hero' can be translated as something like 'gentleman' or 'noble', and the link between honour and nobility is amply demonstrated in the poet's account of the siege of Troy. We might, if we were so inclined, go further. In the fourth century BC the conquests of Alexander the Great carried the culture of Hellenism east as far as India; and stories of his deeds are still told in many languages. Iranians might remember him for his aggression against Persia, but such poets as Firdousi in the tenth century and Nizami in the twelfth kept the romance of Iskander alive. In terms of heroic action and arbitrary power, the myths of Alexander are similar to those of Homer's *Iliad*. And it is interesting to reflect for a moment on the fact that many societies in modern Greece, Turkey, the Arab Middle East, Iran, Afghanistan, and the Indian subcontinent, have highly developed concepts of honour and shame. The Urdu notion of *izzat*, for example, derived from the Arabic '*izza* (might, power, standing, glory), has connotations of a forceful sense of prestige and reputation, and is the word most commonly used in India for male honour in its various manifestations.

All this is intriguing but it is, of course, nothing more than speculation. We should return swiftly to the Mediterranean where enough confusion already awaits us. Here, all we can say with any degree of certainty is that the idea of honour during the Renaissance was influenced by a number of cultural strands. The plays of Lope de Vega, if not of Pedro Calderón, illustrate, for example, how other values of justice and some notion of 'rights' modified the Greek ideal. In contrast to Calderón's opinion of women, in Lope's *Fuenteovejuna* it is Laurencia, a woman who has been raped and therefore defiled and shamed, who urges the indecisive men to blood vengeance against the *comendador*. The honour code of the nobility would normally define a shamed woman as a social outcast, but Lope makes the peasant Laurencia a leader of men. Even more remarkable, she and other peasant women enthusiastically join their men in the slaughter. 'Cut him up for mincemeat!' cries one; 'let's drink his blood,' says another. As Laurencia goes in for the kill, she tells the others, 'My knife's so thirsty that it's shaking' (Lope 1997: 83–4). Some might seek classical precedents for this, but in Greek myths mortal women were more usually portrayed as demure wives and mothers, and significantly often as captives or the spoils of war.

Lope's portrayal of the women in the village of Fuenteovejuna is difficult to interpret. His audience is invited to sympathize with those who were raped by the *comendador*, but what about the horrific act of vengeance when they cut their tormentor apart? 'Torn to pieces by women!' exclaims the captain of the lord's guard when he looks in horror at his master's body (Lope 1997: 84).

Perhaps this is a dramatic device to stimulate the tragic catharsis of fear: fear of a violent, female, peasant passion stimulated by intolerable oppression; fear of sexual and social disorder. Perhaps the screams of the women, heard as they are tortured by the king's investigators, begin to restore the balance. They are brave and do not reveal the killers' identities. But surely they deserve some punishment? In the end it is the wise and just king who imposes order, not only by pardoning the killers, but also by putting the village under his personal rule. 'And we'll watch you carefully,' he warns (Lope 1997: 98).

Lope's ideas about a just monarch and fairness and decency in the treatment of the weak and poor perhaps owe more to another group of myths that influenced ideas about an heroic culture during the Renaissance. Legends about the Emperor Charlemagne (742–814) and his paladin or knight Roland had been told and sung for centuries, as had the Arthurian romances that influenced them. These laid great stress on the code of chivalry, where a knight was not only brave in battle but also pious and generous, a righter of wrongs, and a champion of the underdog. This was a courtly ideal — often honoured more in the breach than the observance — but there is no doubt that the values of chivalry influenced the treatment of honour in European tragic drama.

Arabic literature, too, dealt with the complexity of honour (Lichtenstadter 1974). Long before the European Renaissance, the writings of the sixth century warrior poet, Antara ibn Shaddad, and the oral myths that developed from them, created a beduin romance about his heroic deeds and love for the beautiful Abla, a story that is still told today in the Arab Middle East. Later, the Syrian poet Abu Tammam (807–46) collected together a large number of pre-Islamic poems handed down by the oral tradition of the beduin, and the first book of his anthology contained poems about manliness, heroism and solidarity, vengeance, feuding and bravery in battle. These values gave the collection its title, *Al-hamasa*, a word that reflected a zealous enthusiasm for the honour code. For centuries the desert nomads had structured and contained their kinship rivalries within a tribal organization and an associated ideology of blood vengeance and honour (Eickelman 1967), and it is difficult to see how they were influenced by the ancient Greeks.

Histories and romantic legends about the lives of the Prophet and his successors also dealt with heroes and heroism but, like Christianity, Islam enjoined on its adherents such values as charity for the poor, justice under the law, and equality before God. As law was divine — revealed by Allah to the Prophet Muhammad — the supremacy of codified rules over arbitrary power was possibly more pronounced than in Christian Europe where Roman and Germanic law was secular, creating a division between church and state that was quite unlike the unity of an 'Islamic theocracy'. The Tunisian historian Ibn

Khaldun (1333–1406) emphasized the central role played by 'asabiyya — clan or tribal solidarity based on blood relationships — in the creation of states. In its ideal or 'abstract' sense, kinship or lineage solidarity stands in opposition to revealed law and ideas about the 'common good', but Ibn Khaldun was clear that states would be stable (and truly Islamic) only if they combined 'asabiyya with the common good that came from obedience to divine law (Hourani 1967: 22).

Ideas of the common good were also expressed in the myths and legends of Arab or Muslim heroes. Although he was by origin a Kurd, Salah ad-Din or Saladin (1138–93) was the epitome of the Muslim Arab hero. As ruler of Egypt and Syria he recaptured Jerusalem from the Crusaders in 1187, sparing the lives of those who surrendered. This was in marked contrast to the appalling massacre of Muslims and Jews that had occurred when the Christian knights had overrun the city in 1099 — a savage atrocity demonstrating that chivalry was an ideology, not necessarily a guide to actual behaviour. The impression created of Salah ad-Din by such Arab historians as his secretary Imad ad-Din (an impression, incidentally, largely confirmed by Christian chroniclers of the time) was of a brave fighter, fiercely loyal to the Muslim cause but hospitable to his captives and generous to their leaders. He was said to be chivalrous in his treatment of women and the powerless, honest and direct, just and fair, pious and devout (Runciman 1978).

The tension between chivalry and domination in the literary treatment of honour reflected the political tension between notions of equality before Allah or God and the requirements of rule. More often than not, spiritual ideas about equality were subordinated to the claims of a temporal power; and without being drawn into the controversy of 'Orientalism' (see chapter 4, section 5, below), it cannot be denied that there was an authoritarian strand in Islam that legitimated absolutism. A saying attributed to the Prophet told the faithful: 'Do not abuse those who bear rule. ... If they do evil, they shall bear the burden, and your duty is to endure patiently' (quoted in Mansfield 1985: 72). And in the histories written by modern Orientalist academics we can find plenty of passages from Arab and Ottoman scholars expressing similar sentiments. Of course, there are modern historians who give a fuller interpretation of the complexities of Arab political thought. Albert Hourani, for example, points out that the Abbasid theologian al-Ghazali (1058–1111) qualified his insistence that people should obey an evil and unjust sultan by saying that Muslims should criticize such rulers if it were safe to do so. In the end, though, the criticism should be silent if speaking out would encourage civil strife (Hourani 1967: 6).

None of this should surprise us. Before, during and after the Renaissance much the same was said by the theologians and political philosophers of

Christian Europe. Although Christianity taught that the merciful were blessed and the meek would inherit the earth, the values of the sermon on the mount could always be conveniently ignored by the injunction to render Caesar his due. There was, however, a tension between the values of Christianity and state-craft, and the Italian political theorist, Niccolò Machiavelli (1469–1527), became associated with 'Old Nick' himself in the diatribes of Catholic clerics against his 'diabolical' text. There was also an informative and intellectual link between the contemporary exercise of secular power and the revival of antiquity. Machiavelli's *The Prince* contained numerous references to classical heroic leaders, including Achilles, Alexander the Great and various Roman emperors; and his conceptualization of *virtù* was largely derived from the Latin equivalent, *virtus*, of the Greek word *heros*. *Virtù* was the quality that a success-ful prince needed to influence fortune (*fortuna*) and impose good government. In his translation of *The Prince* (Machiavelli 1961), George Bull usually gives the word 'prowess' for *virtù*, but he and Machiavelli also demonstrate the other con-notations of bravery, pride and strength, willpower and glory (*gloria*), ruth-lessness and honour (*onore*).

We would expect the political manual of a Renaissance intellectual to be replete with classical references and concepts, but it is significant that Machiavelli's epitome of an efficient prince was not a Greek hero but the con-temporary duke of Romagna, Cesare Borgia (1476–1507). Borgia's ruthless, bloody and often cruel rise to power was observed by Machiavelli at first hand when he was sent by the government of Florence as an emissary to the duke's court in Rome. More than any other leader, Cesare Borgia was the model that *The Prince* urged the Florentine Medici dynasty to emulate. Like the Borgias, Machiavelli was concerned with practical politics, not mythology.

Ultimately, the European military nobles did not need a Greek code of ethics to justify their domination or to help them in the struggle between church and state. They were probably encouraged by heroic myths, but even before the Hellenization of European culture they had not usually countenanced any true submission to a religion of benevolence and humility. To do so would be pro-foundly offensive to their self-esteem. Max Weber explains this particularly well:

> The life pattern of a warrior has very little affinity with the notion of a beneficent providence, or with the systematic ethical demands of a trans-cendental god. Concepts like sin, salvation and religious humility have not only seemed remote from all elite political classes, particularly the warrior nobles, but have indeed appeared reprehensible to [their] sense of honor.
>
> (Weber 1966: 85, first published in German in 1920–21)

It seems that most if not all nobles who owned serfs or slaves — or who dominated their peasants to a degree that approached ownership — had what Plato (428/7–348/7 BC) called a 'timocratic' culture, similar to that which the Greek philosopher observed in classical Sparta where a military aristocracy exercised complete domination over their slaves and helots (serfs). In such a culture, personal ambition and the pursuit of honour (*timé*) were guiding principles in determining a capacity for ruling others, but similar timocracies have existed throughout history without any evidence of a direct link to the 'original' Greek model. It is interesting, for example, to consider Plato's account of the timocratic character alongside an account of honour in a much later slave society, that of the American 'old south'. Plato started his discussion by making a comparison with Glaucon, his competitive intellectual associate, and said of the Spartan timocrat:

> He must be rather more self-willed [than Glaucon], and rather less well-read, though not without intelligent interests; ready to listen, but quite incapable of expressing himself. He will be harsh to his slaves, because his imperfect education has left him uncertain of his superiority to them; he will be polite to his equals and obey his superior readily. He will be ambitious to hold office himself, regarding as qualifications for it not the ability to speak or anything like that, but military achievements and soldierly qualities, and he'll be fond of exercise and hunting.
>
> (Plato 1955: 319)

And here John Franklin writes about the slave owners' honour in the southern states of the USA during the nineteenth century:

> It was something inviolable and precious to the ego, to be protected at every cost. ... The honor of the Southerner caused him to defend with his life the slightest suggestion of irregularity in his honesty or integrity; and he was fiercely sensitive to any imputation that might cast a shadow on the character of the women in his family. To him nothing was more important than honor. Indeed, he placed it above wealth, art, learning, and the other 'delicacies' of an urban civilization and regarded its protection as a continuing preoccupation.
>
> (Franklin 1964: 34–5)

Of great importance for an understanding of honour as domination is the way Franklin goes on to argue that the slave master's sense of honour was a reflection of an absolute humiliation of slaves which the master had learnt to recognize and impose in childhood. As Orlando Patterson (1982) puts it, it is the 'degradation of the slave' that nurtures honour, first in the child's relationship with his slave nanny, and later with other slaves whom he is encouraged to discipline and hurt. This degradation is 'a ready object for the exercise of his sense of power' (Patterson 1982: 99), and it is the ability to humiliate others that generates a sense of honour in relation to free men and women too.

Patterson (1982: 79–80) and others (for example, Greenberg 1996: 7 and 148 n15) draw on recent anthropological accounts of Mediterranean honour to elaborate their theme in relation to slavery in the 'old south' and elsewhere. I think this is possibly inappropriate because of the differences between the honour of slave masters and other despots and that of free pastoralists and peasants in the modern Mediterranean region. Nevertheless, in most if not all timocratic cultures, honour is a 'zero-sum game'; and Patterson's accounts of slavery in classical Greece and Rome, European and African tribal societies, Arab and Indian civilizations, and the southern states of America, demonstrate that extreme forms of social domination seem always to promote some form of timocracy in which the honour of the dominant is the inverse of the degradation and humiliation of the dominated.

We shall return to the notion of a zero-sum (in section 5 of this chapter) when I consider honour in the context of an 'egalitarian ethic' in Lebanese peasant society. Here it is only necessary to conclude the discussion of warrior nobles by emphasizing the point about the neutrality of cultural diffusion. Like American slave owners, feudal lords in Europe might have had some knowledge of classical timocracies, but they did not necessarily learn honour from them. Although it might have stimulated the imagination of literate aristocrats, the revival of antiquity in the Renaissance probably had a broadly neutral effect on the honour of the aristocracy and lords. Rather, they developed their own languages, discourses and practices of honour within different and varied structures of domination that shared one characteristic: the degradation of those whose labour and bodies the lords and their ancestors had exploited over many generations.

It was not until the eighteenth century that the arbitrary and despotic rule of the European aristocracy began to be challenged systematically. On the eve of that 'enlightened' time, the English philosopher John Locke argued in his *Two Treatises of Government* (1690) that governance should be by popular consent, and revolution was a proper response to a regime that neglected the protection of 'life, liberty and property'. His ideas were to influence the first modern rebellion against absolutism when the American colonists started their war for freedom from the British crown in 1775. These were revolutionary ideas and it would take some time for them to become a conventional wisdom. Only a few years before Locke's treatises, his compatriot Thomas Hobbes had written *Leviathan* (1651), a spirited advocacy of absolutist monarchy and aristocratic honour that demonstrated the continuing vitality of timocratic notions of rule. Liberal ideas would, however, develop and spread during the period of the Enlightenment; and in the next section of this chapter, we shall see how such values were to contribute to a change in the relationship between ruler and ruled, not only in Europe but also in parts of Lebanon.

3. Lebanon and the nineteenth century

Until 1842, when the emirate (princedom) was abolished by the Ottomans and divided into two provinces or governorates, Mount Lebanon comprised a number of 'feudal cantons' — ultimately in the gift of the emir — covering the mountains of the Lubnan in the north, the Kisrawan in the centre, and the Shouf in the south, and extending west down to the coast, and east to the edge of the Bekaa. In 1861, the two governorates were combined into one, and Mount Lebanon remained an autonomous province of the Ottoman empire until the first world war. The Lebanese emirate and the later governorates of Mount Lebanon included a much smaller area than the *Grand Liban* (Greater Lebanon) created by the French in 1920. The Akkar mountains and plain to the north, the Bekaa valley to the east, and the Amil mountains and hills in the south were all outside its borders, as were the predominantly Sunni Muslim cities of Beirut and Tripoli on the coast. Dayr al-Qamar in the Shouf was the seat of the emir, although in the early nineteenth century Bashir II built his palace a few miles above the town at Beiteddine. For most of the time, the emir was subject to the Ottoman vali (*wali*) or governor of Sidon, whose capital was the coastal city of Acre (now Akko in Israel), and in the nineteenth century the governorates were supervised from Beirut or Damascus.

It might not be entirely correct to describe precapitalist agrarian society in Lebanon as 'feudal', but insofar as the lords of the mountains had effective ownership of their landed estates, the term has some comparative value. The lords were not merely 'tax farmers' or tribute collectors who could be moved around by the imperial authorities from one area to another, as they were in some other parts of the Ottoman empire under the *iltizam* system. The mountainous terrain and the distance from urban centres of authority contributed to the development of a relatively autonomous power structure. Over time the lords had established local dynasties, and the right to collect tribute was passed down from father to son in much the same way as it was in feudal Europe.

At the end of the sixteenth century the Druze emir of the Shouf, Fakhr ad-Din II, had been able to extend his domains so that by the early years of the seventeenth century he had brought the northern Maronite districts into a political unit which, apart from the payment of tribute and the occasional incursion of imperial armies, became virtually independent of Ottoman rule. As we have seen (in the first section of this chapter) Fakhr ad-Din was deposed by the Ottomans in 1633 and executed in 1635, but his dynasty survived until its male line ended in 1697. It was then replaced by the Shihabi emirate (Sunni at first, and later after the conversion of the Shihabs in the late eighteenth century, Maronite). These emirates set a pattern of two levels of relative autonomy: the emir's with respect to the Ottoman pasha or vali on the coast; and the feudal landlords' in relation to the emir. So long as tribute or taxes were paid, there was usually little interference by one level in the affairs of the others, although factional disputes at each level of the system did involve the intervention of higher and lower authorities (Chevallier 1971; Harik 1968; Hourani 1981; Khalaf 1977; Polk 1963; Salibi 1965; 1988).

The name used to describe the feudal system was *al-iqta'*, and the hereditary holder of a *muqata'a* or fief was known by the Turkified Arabic title of 'muqataaji' (*muqata'ji*). The muqataajis held the right to collect tribute in their domain and keep a relatively large proportion of it, and some of them also had legal ownership of land within and outside their fiefdom. Subordinate to them were, first, peasant proprietors who paid only taxes to their muqataaji, and second, tenants who usually farmed their terraced plots on a sharecropping basis, renting their land from muqataajis or other owners.

It is very difficult to determine the proportion of cultivators who owned their land rather than rented it. The French traveller, the Comte Constantin François de Volney, who visited Lebanon in the early 1780s, gave the impression that it was a very high percentage but, as Iliya Harik (1968: 27) points out, he did not make clear distinctions between tenants and proprietors. Writing at roughly the same time as Volney, the Maronite historian Shayban al-Khazin, who belonged to a muqataaji clan, claimed that in his family's fiefdom of the Kisrawan most land belonged to smallholding peasants (Harik 1968: 27). This, however, does not accord with recent research. Kamal Salibi, for example, tells us that by the nineteenth century the Khazins were the 'actual owners of all but the northernmost strip of Kisrawan' and their peasants were 'virtually their serfs' (Salibi 1988: 113; cf Fawaz 1994: 43).

Ilya Harik's history of Lebanon (1968) suggests that the patchy documentation available to us gives an impression of a relatively high percentage of peasant proprietors outside the Kisrawan, and this seems to be confirmed for the Druze region of the Shouf by William Polk's account (1963) which I discuss in more detail at the end of the fourth section of this chapter. Taking these two accounts together with Kamal Salibi's indicates that peasant ownership of small holdings was more likely to be found in the northern and southern districts of

Mount Lebanon where 'tribal' or clan forms of social organization were more pronounced than in the central Kisrawan district. As we shall see (in section 4), the peasants and sheikhs of the northern districts resisted an imposed subordination to muqataajis. In the southern districts of the Shouf, although there were Druze muqataajis who held extensive 'tax farms' and owned large estates, factional rivalry between them probably meant they were unable to force many of their 'tribal' or factional followers to accept a legal status of tenants-at-will because they needed their support as warriors. Nevertheless, landlordism was not confined to the Kisrawan, and the power of muqataajis was such that they could sometimes forcibly reduce peasant proprietors to sharecropping tenants.

Estimates that Harik (1968: 68 n73) derives from a probably reliable contemporary source suggest that in the early nineteenth century peasant proprietors owned a third of the land on Mount Lebanon and the nobles and church owned two thirds. Another estimate — 'a rather liberal one', says Harik — claims that Maronite monasteries owned almost a quarter of the Mountain by the middle of the nineteenth century (Churchill 1853, III: 88–9; Harik 1968: 112). These figures, therefore, suggest that in the early nineteenth century peasant smallholders owned something over 30 per cent of the land, the church (mainly monastic orders) owned less than 25 per cent, and muqataajis and other nobles owned over 40 per cent.

Under the impulse of capitalism, the feudal system was challenged and formally ended in the nineteenth century. In the late eighteenth century and early 1800s, in response to European demand, an increased acreage in Lebanon and Syria was given over to mulberry trees and silkworm production in the mountains and to the cultivation of grain in the Bekaa valley. This, in turn, transformed some villages into market towns and led to the growth of handicraft and machine production. As we shall see, the emergence of new social classes of merchants, craftsmen and 'yeomen farmers' promoted social upheavals that culminated in the Kisrawan peasant revolt of 1858–59 and the abolition of feudal dues and obligations in 1861 (Dubar and Nasr 1976: 51–9; Saba 1976; Chevallier 1971; Smilianskaya 1966).

In contrast to my speculative account of an earlier history, we can now begin to see a clearer link between European ideas and social changes in Lebanon. In 1831 Muhammad Ali — the pasha or governor of Egypt who had effectively broken away from the Ottoman empire — further challenged the sultan by ordering an invasion of Ottoman Syria. By 1832 the army led by his son Ibrahim had completed the conquest, and Ibrahim Pasha became governor of Syria (and Lebanon, although the emirate continued to exist). Like his father, Ibrahim could see the value of western education in the development of a modern army and economy, and he encouraged Christian missionaries to provide this. In

1834 a group of American Protestants moved their printing press from Malta to Beirut and began to establish schools in the city and on the Mountain. The printing of religious and secular material in Arabic revolutionized education, and Catholic missionaries were quick to respond to the Protestant challenge. The Lazarists reopened a Catholic higher-education college at Ayn Tura in the Kisrawan, while the Jesuits started new schools in Beirut, Sidon, Mount Lebanon, and the Bekaa valley. Then, in 1847, the Jesuits established their own printing press to rival the Protestants' (Antonius 1938: 35–51; Hitti 1957: 452–69; Salibi 1965: 132–8).

The Catholic mission schools expanded local knowledge of French language and culture, and this contributed to a radical influence in Lebanon. The French revolution of 1789 had had a profound effect in Europe. The idea of a transfer of power from the monarch to the people, and slogans about 'freedom, equality and brotherhood', were of immense consequence. The subjects of the monarch had become French *citizens* and there was now, in popular imagination if not in fact, a fusion of state and nation. Drawing inspiration from the American Declaration of Independence signed 13 years earlier, the French assembly had voted, in August 1789, for the Declaration of the Rights of Man (*et du citoyen*, to give its full title and significance). This document declared all were equal before the law, and it summed up the new sense of liberal nationalism with the bold statement: 'Sovereignty resides in the nation.' Such ideas were fundamentally subversive of autocratic monarchy and especially the multiethnic empires of the Ottomans, Habsburgs and Russian tsars. The Greeks, for example, started their revolt against the Turkish Ottomans in 1821 and, with the support of the European powers (Britain, France and Russia), won their independence in 1830.

The French revolution represented a not altogether distant threat to the Lebanese lords. The Maronite historian Haydar Ahmad Shihab (1761–1835), a cousin of Emir Bashir II, wrote that its effect was to destroy the social order which monarchy so effectively provided (Hourani 1967: 58). For others, though, the events in Europe inspired an optimistic vision of the future. When Ibrahim Pasha attempted to introduce a modern system of taxation, disarm the civilian population and introduce conscription, he was eventually faced with a mass rebellion on the Mountain. A proclamation issued by the leaders of the revolt in 1840 included a reference to the Greek nation's recent success against the Ottomans: 'Already the Greeks have given us an example, and secured their freedom with the help of God' (quoted in Hourani 1967: 62).

The insurgents knew their revolt against Egyptian rule would bring about the restoration of Ottoman authority, and they pledged their loyalty to the sultan. But as Albert Hourani points out, 'the idea of freedom' was in their proclamation 'by implication', and the rebels were aware of where such an idea had been manifested most fully. They appealed to the French, who at the time supported the Egyptians, to join the other European powers who favoured the return of the Ottomans:

> France, that great and magnanimous nation which has spread freedom in every place and has shed so much blood over the centuries to establish liberty in its government ... now refuses us her powerful support so that we may enjoy this same blessing.
>
> (Quoted in Hourani 1967: 62)

It was not until the turn of the century that the ideas of nationalism, Arab and Lebanese, began to be expressed more coherently in Beirut and Mount Lebanon. In 1840 it was the value of freedom that was uppermost, and it was a limited and indigenous form of liberty that the rebels espoused. They wanted the autonomy they had enjoyed before Ibrahim Pasha's reforms. They opposed the increased tax demands and, very significantly in a culture of heroism and honour, they resisted a forced conscription and demanded the right to go on bearing arms.

The history of nineteenth-century Lebanon is immensely complicated, involving dynastic disputes within the nobility, an increasing involvement of the European powers in local conflicts, and a number of changes of regime (Harik 1968; Khalaf 1987; Polk 1963; Salibi 1965; 1988). Two developments, however, are particularly important for our discussion of honour. These are, first, a growing peasant assertion against the abuses of the feudal system and, second, the emergence of confessional conflict. Although the two topics are intimately related and difficult to treat separately, it is useful to start with confessionalism in order to give a clearer sense of the political chronology of the century.

Confessional consciousness was no doubt influenced by nationalism in Europe, and perhaps the Maronites particularly were inspired by the success of the Greek war of independence in which Christians had thrown off the yoke of Muslim power. But disputes over land were far more significant. After centuries of communal harmony, serious confessional fighting first broke out in 1841. Druze and Maronite leaders had collaborated in 1840 to support the overthrow of Ibrahim Pasha and his Lebanese client, Emir Bashir II. They and their armed supporters had helped Turkish troops, assisted by the navies and armies of Britain and Austria, to re-establish Ottoman rule in Syria (with the deposed emir's cousin, Bashir III, appointed as the new prince of the Mountain). But during and after the hostilities, Druze feudal lords returned from exile to reclaim the estates that had been confiscated under Ibrahim Pasha's governorship and distributed to a predominantly Christian peasantry. The inevitable disputes over the ownership of land led to growing tensions between the Druze and Christian communities.

Prior to the Egyptian conquest, Emir Bashir II had consolidated his rule by turning against his former ally, Sheikh Bashir Jumblat, a Druze muqataaji who had become richer and more powerful than the emir. In 1824 Bashir's army had destroyed Jumblat's palace in the Shouf mountain village of Mukhtara, and the emir then confiscated the muqataaji's lands. After a failed counter-attack in 1825, Jumblat was taken prisoner and strangled to death in Acre on the orders of the Ottoman vali of the province of Sidon. Thus Druze opposition to Egyptian rule was largely a result of their hostility to Bashir II (who had switched his loyalty from the Ottomans with the success of the Egyptian invasion).

Land was confiscated from a number of Druze lords during the 1830s, and by the time they returned to Lebanon in 1840–41 some of their former Christian peasants had prospered from silk and other cash crops. Understandably, after Bashir Jumblat's sons came home, the rich peasantry and an emerging Christian bourgeoisie resisted their attempts to re-establish their rule; and when Sheikh Naman Jumblat sent rent-collectors to the village of Jezzine three of them were killed. Prior to this incident a quarrel between Maronites and Druze over an alleged case of poaching had led to an attack on a Druze village in which 18 people had died. Such events led, in 1841, to confessional war and a Druze revolt against the new emir, Bashir III, that spread throughout the Shouf region and claimed many lives. More fighting between Christians and Druze occurred in 1845, and thus by 1860 considerable resentment had built up on both sides which, as we shall see, contributed to the bloody massacres of that year (Harik 1968: 245–54; Polk 1963: 216–19; Salibi 1965: 40–52; Khalaf 1987: 45–61; Alamuddin 1993: 113–27).

The new emir, Bashir III, was under strong pressure from the restored Ottoman authorities to resist the demands of the landlords as these were contrary to the provisions of the *tanzimat-i khayriye* ('beneficent reforms') which sought to modernize the administration of the empire. One aspect of these reforms involved land tenure. Not only was it necessary to weaken the landed nobility throughout the empire so as to improve the effectiveness of central rule and increase revenues by taxing the peasantry directly, but also the reformers believed that, by granting secure tenure to the cultivators, agriculture would develop as it had in Europe. The first 'noble rescript' or decree relating to the *tanzimat* had been issued by the sultan in 1839, and seems to have been largely a result of British influence (Kedourie 1992: 36–7). It is therefore significant that Richard Wood, an emissary from the British embassy in Istanbul, should have approached Bashir III and 'desired' him not to allow the Lebanese lords to re-acquire a 'right over the peasants in order to despoil them of their produce' as this would go against the principles of the *tanzimat* (quoted in Choueiri 1988: 66).

Bashir's indecision and defeat by the Druze revolt led to his being deposed by the Ottomans in 1842. In keeping with the *tanzimat* aim of promoting local government, the emirate was ended in the same year and replaced by two governorates (the 'double *qa'immaqamiyya*'), the northern one administered by a Maronite *qa'immaqam*, and the southern by a Druze. In order to encourage a reconciliation between the two communities after the warfare of 1845, a council was established in each district with proportional representation for the major confessions. This was the first time that the principle of confessional power-sharing had been formally recognized in Lebanon, and it set a pattern for subsequent systems of government.

Following the Druze–Maronite war of 1860 (see below) and an intervention of French troops on the Christians' behalf, the governorates were combined and the autonomous Mutasarrifate (*mutasarrifiyya*) of Mount Lebanon was created in 1861. This was put under the governorship of a non-Lebanese, Ottoman Christian *mutasarrif*, supported by a council of four Maronites, three Druze, two Greek Orthodox, one Greek Catholic, one Sunni and one Shi'a. After the first world war, the French would combine Mount Lebanon with parts of the sanjaks (*sanajiq*) or districts of Beirut and Tripoli, and an area carved out from the vilayet (*wilaya*) or province of Damascus, to create *Grand Liban* within the borders that legally persist to this day.

Although the confessional conflicts of 1841 and 1845 involved Druze and Christian peasants and townspeople killing each other with a degree of enthusiasm, it seems that the origin of the disputes was largely an elite affair, at least as far as the Druze were concerned. Feudal lords, predominantly Druze, were intent on re-establishing control of their estates against the encroachments of an expanding middle class that had been encouraged first by Ibrahim Pasha and Bashir II, and then by Ottoman and British pressure on Bashir III. The intention of the pasha, emirs and Ottoman officials was not to champion the Christian cause, but that was how it appeared to the Druze lords. Owing to higher levels of education and greater contacts with French and other European traders, the Lebanese bourgeoisie was overwhelmingly Christian, and this contributed to a widespread feeling amongst the Druze that they were the victims of a Christian and particularly Maronite conspiracy against them.

All this was deeply humiliating for the Druze lords and their sense of personal honour. Their ancestors had encouraged Maronite peasants to migrate from the north to the Shouf in the seventeenth and eighteenth centuries in order to acquire a workforce for the expanding production of silk. As William Polk puts it, these peasants 'had come as serfs or artisans to practice those skills which Druze held to be degrading'. During the period of Egyptian rule many sharecropping peasant families acquired ownership of their land, and some became rich from the dramatic growth of the silk trade with Europe, to the extent that a few Maronites actually began to lend money to their former muqataajis. Thus, in one generation, some Druze lords found themselves in debt to some of their former 'serfs' (Polk 1963: 216 and 173–5).

The Christian artisans and merchants in the market towns of the Mountain came to see the Druze as vulgar and backward. Similar ideas also began to emerge amongst the Maronite peasantry, but these confessional prejudices were accompanied by the growth of something approaching a class opposition to the feudal domination of the Druze *and* the Maronite muqataajis. The politicization of this peasantry in the nineteenth century owed much to the activity of the Maronite church and its quarrel with the Maronite landlords.

Maronite monastic orders had become extremely effective economic organizations by the early nineteenth century. Through their collective labour the monks had transformed their monasteries and orders into wealthy corporate bodies. Farms had been acquired from gifts and in return for religious and secular services, such as schooling for example, for which the orders were often paid in land. Using modern techniques and diversifying into related activities like wine making and silk spinning, monasteries accumulated capital to the extent that they possibly owned almost a quarter of the Mountain by the middle of the century. Through example and instruction, monks and priests began to encourage peasants to cultivate cash crops using new methods, and one only needs to consider for a moment the religious and social role of the village priests to see how effective they might have been in transforming peasant perspectives. Many of them the sons of peasant families, they were closely in touch with their flock, hearing confession, baptizing babies, marrying couples, and burying the dead. They were well placed to provide the service of mediation, resolving family and village disputes, and many were literate and articulate champions of a peasant interest against the exactions of the landlords (Harik 1968: 111 ff; Khalaf 1987: 32–3).

As accumulators of land and capital, the monastic orders inevitably entered into competition with the muqataajis, and as 'fathers of the poor' many clerics came to resent a feudal system that prevented peasants from becoming accumulators themselves. As is well known, feudalism is a restraint on the development of capitalism. The personal tie between the peasant and the landlord prevents a free market in labour, and there is little to encourage an entrepreneurial peasant when the benefits of increased production are taken away in increased rental demands from his lord. Although some Lebanese sharecropping arrangements in the nineteenth century technically allowed the peasants to terminate their contracts with their landlords, usually they could only do so with the lord's permission or 'by actual physical flight' (Saba 1976: 6). And as the muqataajis and emirs became indebted to merchant capital and were subjected to higher tax demands from their Egyptian or Ottoman rulers, they imposed ever heavier burdens on the peasantry (Smilianskaya 1966).

Muqataajis borrowed money to invest in new techniques of production, but perhaps most of their borrowing was to finance their consumption of new imported commodities, to pay their armed retainers and to buy a continuing influence with the emir and imperial authorities. By the middle of the nineteenth century, a number of feudal families were heavily in debt to merchants and moneylenders who charged high rates of interest. Some were forced to sell parts of their estates to merchants or rich peasants, but many attempted to hold on to their land by increasing rents and other exactions. Some peasants were forced to work a greater number of days on their lord's home farm for no payment or share of the crop. Some women and girls, in addition to their agricultural and domestic tasks, were ordered to work as unpaid drudges in their lord's house. Muqataajis also demanded 'gifts' of farm produce and such items as sugar and coffee bought with hard-earned cash from the market. Increasingly larger shares of the peasant crop or its marketed value were taken by the lords, and some peasants who had managed to become secure tenants or buy their own land were forcibly reduced by their muqataajis to become sharecropping tenants-at-will (Saba 1976: 6–11).

Some impoverished peasants were forced to leave the land and seek a living in Beirut and other cities as beggars, day-workers on building sites, or as menials in the shops and homes of the merchant class. Many of those who remained on the land were bullied and harassed by the armed retainers of the lords. So great was the immiseration of the peasantry, one might expect rebellion to have been more widespread than it was. But the poorest, most dependent and oppressed rarely rebel. As we know from studies of the Russian and Chinese revolutions or of agrarian movements in India and elsewhere, it is the 'middle', more secure peasants, faced with a threat to their position, who take to arms; and even then they usually require an external leadership to help them (Alavi 1973; Wolf 1969).

Sections of the Maronite peasantry of Mount Lebanon fulfilled these conditions. Leadership was provided by the church, and at the start of the nineteenth century — prior to the subsequent immiseration — the rural economy was 'relatively prosperous and viable' (Khalaf 1987: 27). Land tenure was usually secure (Polk 1963: 75); the economy was self-sufficient in terms of food and handicrafts; the mountain climate was very conducive to the cultivation of mulberry trees, and the silkworms which fed on them provided the material for a village export industry that brought a degree of prosperity to all.

This rather fortunate state of affairs was perhaps first threatened by increased tax demands imposed on the emirate by the central authority. When Bashir II was forced by the Ottomans to send his collectors to the Maronite regions of the Matn and Kisrawan to raise more taxes in 1820, they were set upon by peasants whose subsequent uprising forced the emir into a temporary exile (from which he returned in 1821 to crush the rebels). While Kamal Salibi (1965: 25) sees this revolt as instigated by two cousins and rivals of Bashir who ruled in his stead while he was in exile, Samir Khalaf adds the Maronite clergy to the list. He points out that the rebellion did not extend to the Druze districts of the Shouf. In addition, a Maronite bishop, Yusuf Istfan (who apparently objected to Bashir's public denial of his Maronite faith), organized the peasants by writing a covenant of allegiance and encouraging them to select in each village a *wakil* (representative) to lead them (Khalaf 1987: 31–4). The wakils seem to have represented the first signs of a peasant leadership independent of the lords and their retainers. Such leaders were to emerge again in the peasant revolt of 1858–59, although by then they were more robust and violent in their style and intent.

In the four decades that followed 1820, the conditions of the Maronite peasantry deteriorated. When the peasants of the Kisrawan rebelled in 1858, their demands included: the abolition of forced labour, gifts and dues; reduced taxes and other levies; and the ending of the lords' rights to authorize marriages and impose the punishments of imprisonment and flogging. As in the previous uprisings of this turbulent century the revolt started with an essentially dynastic or elite dispute, but this time it did not end there. Despite a widespread popular involvement, the rebellion of 1840 had remained a war of the lords against Egyptian rule. Similarly, the uprising of 1820 could be seen in part as instigated by rivalries in the emir's family that had ended with the restored dominance of Bashir II. By contrast, the revolt in 1858–59 concluded with the expulsion of Maronite landlords. While some muqataajis, during 1857–58, were mobilizing their partisans against the recently appointed *qa'immaqam* of the northern governorate (a man they considered excessively corrupt and arrogant), the Maronite peasants of the Kisrawan seized the opportunity of political turmoil to mount a social revolution (Chevallier 1959; Porath 1966; Burke 1988; Choueiri 1988).

Their main target was the Maronite Khazin family whose members included the most powerful landlords of the district. A contemporary chronicler described them as follows:

They would say that the peasant and his possessions belonged to them, showing not the slightest regard for him. The most insignificant of the Khazins would insult the most reputable of the people, not to mention killing or imprisoning them and such like.

(Quoted in Salibi 1965: 84)

These, then, were repressive lords like the other warrior nobles we have come across before. Their honour was such that they had complete contempt for their peasants, imposing upon them arbitrary exactions and punishment according to their whim. Now, under the impulse of capitalism and modern ideas, they were to be swept away by those they despised. Unlike the peasants in *Fuenteovejuna* (see section 2 above), the rebels of the Kisrawan would not need to be pardoned by a higher authority. They represented a modern social current. The French consul in Beirut supported and encouraged them; the Ottoman authorities accorded them some 'moral backing' (Salibi 1965: 86); and later, in 1861, the Ottomans would announce the end of feudalism and enshrine the principle of equality before the law in the *Règlement Organique* (Organic Law) that constituted the new autonomous Mutasarrifate (governorate) of Lebanon.

Apart from the legitimation contained in such liberal principles as the 'rights of man', the rebels also had what for them, at that time, was probably a higher authority: that of the Maronite church. There can be no doubt that they were encouraged by their priests. Kamal Salibi (1965: 80) suggests that these were 'an ambitious clergy jealous of feudal power'. That might be true of some of the bishops who hankered after temporal as well as spiritual influence, or of the superiors of monastic orders who were rather like capitalist managers of agribusiness firms. But the church was more than a collection of jealous men. Some of the clerics also espoused the values of French liberal thought and capitalism: *liberté, égalité et fraternité* might have been a little too radical, but the right to 'life, liberty and property' was certainly the cause of many.

The notion of freedom held by the rebels, however, was conditioned by a culture of honour. The name used for a village organizer in 1858–59 was *shaykh shabab* (a sheikh or leader of young men). In 1820 it had been *wakil*, which simply meant something like an 'authorized representative'. A *shaykh shabab*, by contrast, was the name given to a village strong-arm leader whose local power was largely determined by his 'armed following of young men' (Salibi 1965: 210 n2). In other words he was a village 'qabaday', a man who claimed an honour similar if not equal to that of the lords. The overall leader of the peasant rebellion was a *shaykh shabab* from the village of Rayfoun, one Taniyus Shahin, described by Kamal Salibi (1965: 85–6) as 'a half literate farrier of forty-three who, according to some contemporaries, had little to recommend him other than his tall and muscular frame and his violent temper.' Worried spectators saw him as 'a ruffian of despicable character', but to the peasants he was their acknowledged leader, some addressing him as 'sheikh' (a title held by most of the landlords) and others as 'bey' (an Ottoman rank). As one chronicler wrote, 'In every village he entered, the people would prepare a grand reception for him amid joy and celebrations and continuous firing of rifles, as if it were the visit of a ruler to his subjects' (quoted in Salibi 1965: 85).

Led by Shahin, the Maronite peasants of the Kisrawan had bloodily expelled the landlords and their families by the spring of 1859. For a short time, it seemed as though the revolt might spread into the southern governorate where, after the wars of 1841 and 1845, a number of Druze lords had re-established their control of the peasantry. There were some 'stirrings' of discontent against them in a few Druze villages in the Shouf (Salibi 1965: 87), but the landlords were soon able to win the loyalty of their coreligionists, many of whom believed, with some justification, that the Maronites were more interested in usurping Druze lands than liberating the peasantry.

Both sides prepared themselves during the winter of 1859–60, and Taniyus Shahin boasted he could raise an army of some 50,000 men to defeat the Druze. Once the fighting started, however, Druze warriors inflicted a series of defeats on the numerically superior forces of their enemies. In May 1860 Christian civilians fled from their villages in the Matn and the Shouf, and many were killed on the way. A Druze custom or 'rule of war' imposed some restraint: only men and boys between the ages of seven and seventy could be killed (Alamuddin 1993: 102). But in the frenzy of massacre, some women and girls were slaughtered as well. Bodies were mutilated with the knives and machetes that had killed them, villages and towns were plundered, and homes destroyed and set on fire. As we have seen, some 11,000 Maronites and other Christians were killed in May and June, and around 4000 died from hunger, destitution and disease. Then, in July, after the end of the carnage in Lebanon, a Sunni mob attacked the Greek Catholic quarter of Damascus, apparently leaving the Greek Orthodox district 'virtually unscathed' and presumably wanting to punish the local Catholics whom they saw as in league with the Lebanese Maronites (Choueiri 1988: 73). In a single day perhaps as many as 5500 people were massacred, some women were raped and some of the younger ones were taken as concubines or forced into marriage (Salibi 1965: 107; Fawaz 1992: 73; Fawaz 1994: 89, 99 and 139).

When these events were recalled in the civil wars of the 1970s and 1980s, many Maronites and other Christians 'remembered' a primordial Muslim hostility to their community that went back through the Crusades to the early years of Islam in the seventh century. Muslims, on the other hand, tended to see the massacres of 1860 as the result of a French and British imperial rivalry in which the former had championed the Maronites and the latter the Druze. A more dispassionate view, however, would see confessionalism in the nineteenth century as partially a response to European ideas about nationalism and, more particularly, the result of the collapse of a feudal order. This is not a crude argument designed to blame everything on capitalism as some have blamed the manoeuvrings of wicked imperialists. It is simply the case that in the absence of a feudal order, the endogamous confessional community provided security and a sense of belonging to a group wider than the immediate family that was so often in economic competition with others.

I discuss the important kinship elements of 'blood and belonging' (Ignatieff 1993) in the next chapter. Here it is only necessary to reiterate some of the effects of capitalism in the nineteenth century to explain why people might have identified with their confession. As we have seen, the conditions of the peasantry deteriorated and some families were forced off the land. For the dispossessed peasantry and new middle classes, the perils of the market could bring reward to some but destitution to many others. Above all, both the gradual break up of feudal estates as a consequence of the lords' indebtedness, and the emergence of new centres of power and influence in Beirut and the market towns of the Mountain, led to an undermining of feudal hierarchy and order.

Previously, peasants had owed allegiance to their muqataajis. Most lords and their families lived in the villages they owned, and although they could be cruel and arbitrary they provided land and protection to their people. This order was based on a monopoly of economic and coercive resources, but it was buttressed by a hierarchy of honour that represented a consensual dependence of those who had less honour on those who had more. Although the Lebanese had always been conscious of their different religious identities, these were of little political importance in the villages where kinship loyalties to the extended family, and relations of dependence and adherence to the lord, determined most aspects of everyday life. The village represented a moral community in which religious attachment was largely irrelevant, and this seems to have been the case in mixed villages as much as in those where the inhabitants were all of the same faith.

Capitalism undermined this order and created an individualistic and competitive society. Among the Maronites, the church (itself a competitor in the market) provided a new sense of community and encouraged the development of a class consciousness within the peasantry. But this was an essentially confessional class identification. No serious attempt was made to establish links between Maronite and Druze peasants, and the extension of education served to create a sense of moral superiority among the Christians who had benefited from it. Speaking the languages of the foreign traders, some members of the educated elite became agents of European capital and were able to establish themselves as local merchants and moneylenders. Their poorer kinsfolk also came to see the advantages of the modern economy, and increasing numbers of peasants aspired to become owners of their land so they could invest in, and profit from, silk production and other forms of cash cropping. They became acquisitive, and it is scarcely surprising that having secured their own land by forcibly removing their landlords, some Maronite peasants of the Kisrawan should then consider the possibility of taking more land from the Druze muqataajis. After all, the lords had acquired their land through conquest or dynastic wars. Why should it be any different for Taniyus Shahin and the other leaders of the peasant uprising who had demonstrated their honour and were called 'sheikh' or 'bey' by their followers?

Meanwhile, comparatively untouched by the social changes occurring elsewhere on the Mountain, the Druze peasants had every reason to fear the Maronite army to the north. At best some Christians would replace the Druze landlords, and values of fealty ensured that the Druze peasants would fight for their own before submitting to another. At worst, the Maronites would simply settle the land and drive the existing occupants away. There was, after all, an historical precedent for this. When Maronites from the north had first migrated in large numbers to the Kisrawan region in the sixteenth century, the population was predominantly Shi'a. In the late seventeenth and eighteenth centuries, Khazin sheikhs bought land and villages from the Sunni overlords and Shi'a sheikhs of the Kisrawan, and they encouraged further migrations of Maronites from the north. Inevitably this led to conflict and eventually the Shi'a were evicted (Salibi 1988: 103–6). Sometimes this was achieved by the payment of compensation, but often enough by force and violence for 'memories' to be awakened in the nineteenth century. It was therefore not difficult for the Druze lords to protect their position by calling on their followers to fight. And of course, fight they did, with all the appalling consequences of 1860 and all the dark 'memories' that would be resurrected within a new generation of fighters a century later.

4. Honour and reproduction

The hierarchy of honour in feudal Mount Lebanon was similar to the one that we have seen persisting in twentieth-century Akkar (chapter 2, section 4). Status or prestige was largely determined by class and power, but was normatively (or 'morally') defined by genealogy. Druze and Maronite muqataajis could trace their descent back over many generations to the ancestors of their families, some as far as the sixteenth century or even earlier. In Akkar there were two ranks of honour: bey and agha. In feudal Mount Lebanon (which did not include Akkar) there were four. It seems there was no generally recognized status or term, comparable to agha, for armed retainers and bailiffs; but although all below the rank of sheikh were vulgar commoners (*'ammiyya*), some families or clans with a martial reputation could rise to become members of what William Polk (1963: 81) describes as the 'warrior class' that fought for the lords in factional wars. This 'class' was not, however, one of the noble ranks. It was the varying depths of the lords' lineages, and their closeness in marriage and other political alliances to the emir, that defined the four official ranks within the Lebanese aristocracy and nobility: *amir* (emir or prince), *muqaddam* (someone put before others), the 'great sheikhs' (*al-mashayikh al-kibar*) and ordinary sheikhs.

A crucial date in the history of these rankings was 1711, when Emir Haydar Shihab confirmed titles and grants of land for a number of families and bestowed new ones on others as a reward for their support in a decisive battle, at Ayn Dara, against a rival faction. This victory consolidated the Sunni Shihabi emirate and established a hierarchy that persisted into the nineteenth century. After the battle, one Druze family was raised from the rank of *muqaddam* to that of emir, to give a total of three princely families, one of them Sunni (the Shihabs who later converted to Maronite Christianity) and two Druze. One Druze family continued to hold the rank of *muqaddam*, and three Druze families were granted the title of sheikh to make a total of eight with the rank of 'great sheikh', five of them Druze and three Maronite. Below these great sheikhs were a number of lesser sheikhs, some of them effectively 'subletting' from larger tax farms (Salibi 1965: 8–10; Harik 1968; Khalaf 1987; Polk 1963).

In terms of prestige, the highest rank was the 'grand emir' (*al-amir al-kabir*) of Mount Lebanon and his family, the Shihabs. Second came the Druze Abillama (Abu'l-Lam') family who had been promoted from the rank of *muqaddam* in 1711 and with whom the Sunni Shihabs intermarried — a closeness that presumably explains why, after the Shihabs converted at the end of the eighteenth century, the Abillamas also adopted the Christian faith. Below them came the other princely family, the Druze Arslans, and the *muqaddam* family, the Druze Muzhirs. In terms of the extent of their feudal domains and military capacity, the Arslan and Muzhir families had less power than most of the sheikhs. Nevertheless, in terms of social honour their rank was higher. Among the great sheikhly families, although the fortunes of each one fluctuated over time, the wealthiest and most influential were the Druze Jumblats (whose descendant Kamal Jumblat would become the leader of the Lebanese National Movement in the 1970s).

All members of these families were able to use their title, even those with no land of their own, indicating that, as well as honour as domination or an enforced respect, there existed a sense of nobility that was a separate inherited quality similar to that which I define as the honour of nobility in modern Beirut (see chapter 2). As the nineteenth-century poet and chronicler Nasif al-Yaziji wrote about the honour (*karama*) of the muqataaji families, it did not 'vanish because of poverty' and was not 'upgraded because of wealth' (quoted in Harik 1968: 51).

Conscious of their inherited honour, the lords of Lebanon tended to marry within their status, the five Druze families of great sheikhs forming an almost entirely endogamous group; and they each held a meticulous record of their genealogy which showed their concern for past marriage alliances and the antiquity of their blood. Just as the European aristocracy and nobility constructed a sense of their superior qualities and their difference from other classes and statuses in terms of the 'symbolics of blood' (Foucault 1976: 197), so the emirs and muqataajis of Mount Lebanon legitimated their domination of the commoners in an ideology of honour and descent. Their history was one of factional feuds and wars in which their ancestors had been brave, quick-witted and ruthless. Heroic leaders of men in great battles, they had fought for the honour of their families and this established their right to rule. Their feudal fiefs had been granted to their families by the emirs, the fount of all honour to whom was owed tribute, both moral and material. And so long as they showed the emir the respect that was due to him and paid the taxes he requested, they were masters in their domains.

Although they were sometimes restrained by chivalric values, and by laws that limited their right to impose exactions and punishments, many lords continued to act in the arbitrary manner we saw (in section 3) in the case of the Khazins — one of the Maronite families of great sheikhs. Peasants and their household possessions were effectively the property of some of the muqataajis who could protect or abuse as they pleased. Protection of the villagers from external aggression was an important service, but abuse was a constant threat. There were commoners who could only marry with the consent of their lord, and a pretty girl might have to submit to a form of *droit du seigneur*. Similarly, although the law limited the lord's right of punishment to flogging and imprisonment, extrajudicial execution was not unknown. Property rights were also flouted, as when those peasants who had acquired ownership of their land were forcibly reduced to sharecropping or simply evicted. In the 1840s, for example, there were a number of bloody incidents when lords and their armed retainers tore up peasants' titles to land and threatened Ottoman officials conducting a cadastral survey (Saba 1976: 5–11). The latter would have legally determined ownership of land, and was abandoned in 1850 as a result of the muqataajis' harassment (Salibi 1965: 73).

As we have seen, honour as domination continued in some areas of Greater Lebanon into the second half of the twentieth century. Although the feudal system was formally abolished in 1861, and taxes were collected by state officials instead of tributary lords, landlordism continued. Even in the Kisrawan some of the Khazins who had survived the revolt of 1858–59 were able to return to their homes and reclaim their land (Burke 1988: 24; Choueiri 1988: 73; Salibi 1965: 112). Over time, more indebted landlords lost their estates to urban merchants and moneylenders, and more peasants were able to acquire ownership of their land, such that by the twentieth century much of Mount Lebanon was farmed by smallholding peasant proprietors and secure tenants (Warriner 1948: 84). But landed estates with sharecropping peasants persisted among the Sunnis of Akkar in the north, and the Shi'a in the Bekaa valley and southern Lebanon.

A further expansion of capitalist farming in the mid-twentieth century forced many peasants from the land, perhaps particularly during the reformist Shihabist period in the 1960s (see chapter 2, section 6, above). In that decade, state-sponsored extensions of electricity, piped water and roads, along with land reclamation, irrigation projects and an introduction of fruit trees and other new cash crops, were designed to help peasants in the underdeveloped regions of Lebanon. In practice, however, these reforms encouraged landlords to mechanize their estates and produce for the market directly, or to sell their land to merchants and financiers in the coastal cities (and regional centres such as Zahle) who were eager to profit from capitalist farming (Johnson 1986: 147–8). Sharecroppers had accounted for approximately 25 per cent of the active agrarian population in the 1950s, but by 1970 they represented only 5 per cent; and over 100,000 peasants had left the land during the 1960s (Nasr 1978: 6 and 10).

Rural–urban migrants brought the values of agrarian society with them when they moved to the city, and better roads and other communications presumably also served to encourage a mixing of urban and rural cultures. It is impossible to determine the extent to which a culture of domination was imported to the city. We have seen (in chapter 2, section 4) that the Sunni leader Sa'ib Salam believed the term za'im, with connotations of zulm (oppressive tyrannical rule), had been brought to Beirut during the 1920s or 1930s by Shi'a migrants from what he called a 'feudal' countryside. But elements of a similar political culture might always have existed in one form or another in the urban setting. Ira Lapidus's account (1967) of such Middle Eastern cities as Damascus and Cairo, for example, suggests that there were urban forms of arbitrary domination in the fifteenth and sixteenth centuries, and although gangs of zu'ar ('qabadays') had provided an avenue for common men to enhance their position vis-à-vis urban notables and imperial authorities, they were often allowed to prey on ordinary townspeople as a reward for support in elite factional conflicts.

What is clear, however, is that by the mid-nineteenth century new merchant leaders were emerging in Beirut and the other coastal cities of Tripoli and Sidon who, as a result of the *tanzimat* and other reforms, were able to participate in local councils for their city, sanjak (district) and vilayet (province) (Johnson 1986: 13–15 and 63–71). The development of mass democracy in the twentieth century led to some of these notables becoming powerful urban bosses or za'ims, but as we have seen (in chapter 2, sections 3 and 4) these leaders were necessarily far more responsive to the wishes of their followings than were the landlords to their peasants. Thus any rural influence on the political culture of the city was less one of *zulm* and probably more one of an 'egalitarian ethic' that had developed as the power of ascriptive or inherited honour on the Mountain had gradually been replaced by the more contingent and achieved notion of honour as something claimed and asserted by new leaders.

One of the first signs of this process of change in the countryside came in the mid-nineteenth century when Maronite peasants in the Kisrawan selected sheikhs of the *shabab* to lead them. The leaders of the uprising in 1858–59 were not mere representatives or 'wakils'. They were aggressive men of honour who controlled groups of armed followers. Some of these *shabab* and their leaders had acted as the retainers or bailiffs of the lords, and so they were not necessarily the self-abnegating peasant heroes of popular mythology. Rather, they were men who claimed the respect of others by being publicly jealous of their personal honour and ready to kill in defence of it. They mistrusted and were resentful of external authority, preferring to impose their own order through the private punishment of wrongs done to them, their family or their village. Ultimately they were competitive individualists, prepared to make alliances to achieve their ends, sometimes with their kin, sometimes their confession, but usually with their own self-interest paramount. Their sense of personal self-respect was such that they would rather die than risk the shame of ignoring an insult to their person or property, and their property included their women whose bodies and decorum enshrined the honour of their family.

As we shall see, a form of 'populist' honour already existed in those districts of the Mountain where the peasantry had not been fully subordinated to feudalism, and there can be little doubt that the peasants of the Kisrawan were influenced by this. But they were also reacting against the domination of their former lords. They were common men who in a sense adopted the honour code of the lords and made it their own. They laid claim to the title of sheikh, not in the sense of landlord but as a leader of lesser men — although an assertion of honour might also involve the acquisition of land. They became concerned about their genealogy, not in the sense of defining an ancient line of descent but as the controllers of their women and patrimony. And they formed marriage and other political alliances, not in the sense of establishing dynastic possession of large territories or domains but to consolidate a locally circumscribed leadership.

Similar forms of honour were found amongst the Druze as well as Maronites. Druze peasants might in a sense have remained subservient to their sheikhs in 1860, but they did not fight the Christians because they were forced to do so. First, in their treatment of Druze commoners, the lords of the Shouf region were almost certainly less repressive in the nineteenth century than the Maronite Khazins; and secondly, the Druze community was relatively small and had developed a fierce sense of communal solidarity. For some time, the Druze had been in a demographic, political and economic decline. As early as the mid-eighteenth century they were a minority even in their own districts of the Shouf, and factional rivalry between the Jumblat and Imad families was weakening the Druze sheikhs' hold on power in the emirate (Salibi 1965: 11). In the nineteenth century, some Druze lands were confiscated by Bashir II as he consolidated his rule and reduced his opponents; and as we have seen, the development of capitalism benefited the Maronites and other Christians disproportionately. Thus the Druze lords needed the willing support of their peasantry to defend what they had left, and this — coupled with a widespread sense of a minority united in adversity — seems to have contributed to more cordial relations between lord and vassal within their community.

But to understand Druze solidarity more fully it is important to consider the differences between forms of feudal organization on Mount Lebanon. Prior to the establishment of the feudal hierarchy, the mountains were largely controlled by 'tribal' authorities of dominant family or clan sheikhs who competed with each other for local influence and tribute, recruiting and protecting members of lower status families who were then identified with the leader's faction. As clients could change allegiance from a weak local patron to another stronger one, there were many opportunities for honourable men to lay claim to leadership positions by violently asserting themselves in feuding and other forms of local conflict. Only on Jabal Kisrawan (the Kisrawan mountain) was this factional system fully suppressed. In the eighteenth century the Maronite Khazins established themselves as feudal lords over a Maronite peasantry that had migrated from the north. As well as having the right to collect tribute from their tax farms, the Khazins also had legal ownership of most of the Kisrawan feudal district (*muqata'a*) that they had bought or confiscated from the previous Shi'a sheikhs and their Sunni overlords. On these lands their peasants were virtual serfs, with little or no honour or clan organization (Salibi 1988: 112–13).

By contrast, to the north of the Kisrawan on Jabal Lubnan (the Lebanese mountain proper) the Maronite peasants continued to owe their allegiance to a form of clan authority. When, for example, the Shihabi emir appointed the Dahir family as tax-farming muqataajis in the northern district of the Zawiya, the Maronites maintained allegiance to their 'tribal' sheikhs of whom the most powerful were those from the Karam clan of the village of Ehden. It seems that the Dahirs and other muqataajis were never able to suppress the local sheikhs and some, like the Karams, were officially incorporated into the feudal hier-archy (see section 5 below). A similar form of 'tribalism' existed south of the Kisrawan on Jabal ash-Shouf where, although Druze sheikhs had been made emirs and 'great sheikhs', close 'tribal allegiances' to the leading clans remained paramount (Salibi 1988: 112–13).

The 'tribal identification' of the Druze was related to a continuing factional conflict within their community. Initially they were divided into Qaysis and Yamanis (Yemenis), a division that was found in other Syrian communities and supposedly dated back to the tribal origins of the Arabs who had conquered the region in the seventh century. According to legend, the Qaysis were originally from northern Arabia, and the Yamanis from the south. The Yamani faction of the Druze was decisively defeated and its leaders killed at the battle of Ayn Dara in 1711 when the Qaysis rallied to the support of Emir Haydar Shihab. A new bifactional conflict then emerged among the Qaysis, this time between the Jumblatis and Yazbakis. The origins of the dispute are obscure (Polk 1963: 17–18), but the Yazbakis were initially led by the Imad family who were always weaker than their Jumblati rivals, and they allied with other Druze sheikhly families (the Talhuqs and the Abd al-Maliks) to form a balance of power, with a third faction headed by the Abu Nakad sheikhs remaining broadly neutral (Salibi 1965: 6–12; 1988: 111–12).

Later, in the twentieth century, the leadership of the Yazbaki faction had passed to the Arslan emirs (who still used their feudal title) and Emir Majid Arslan was a rival of Kamal Jumblat in the Lebanese parliament. As a clear demonstration of the continuing importance of the factional allegiances of families, a study conducted in 1980 identified all of the 333 family names in the Druze community and found that there was substantial agreement among the Druze as to which of the two factions each family belonged, only 16 families having apparently divided loyalties (Alamuddin and Starr 1980: 99 ff).

In the nineteenth century, this factional system and the requirement it imposed on muqataajis to earn the fighting support of their followers may have contributed to a greater security of tenure for the Druze peasantry of the Shouf region. William Polk's analysis of eighteenth and early nineteenth century documents held by some families in the mountain village of Ammatur (in the

Upper Shouf) suggests that many Druze and some Christians had legal owner-ship of their land or secure rights to it, and all peasants benefited from the rival lords' concern to keep the tax demands from the emir as low as possible (Polk 1963: chapters 4 and 5). In addition, the protection offered by the lords to their supporters enabled some Druze clans below the level of muqataaji — in what Polk (1963: 81) describes as the 'warrior class' — to acquire parcels of land and even whole villages that were farmed by Maronite peasants on a sharecropping basis. Thus commoner Druze clans tended to support one or other of the factional leaders from whom they received protection. And as Kamal Salibi (1988: 112) points out, only the Christian peasants of the Shouf saw the Druze sheikhs as their 'feudal overlords'.

A Druze chronicler wrote as follows, in the mid-nineteenth century, about the relations between Christians and Druze:

> Christians ... settled [in the Shouf] in the past century and they scattered in every village and hamlet in order to perform menial tasks and artisan's chores and to till the soil since the Druze do not themselves take to these matters, being raised above their performance not esteeming aught but the riding of horses and ... excelling in marksmanship and swordsman-ship and suchlike things of the habits of courage and chivalry, completely overlooking matters of learning.
>
> (Quoted in Polk 1963: 129–30)

This is a remarkable expression of a timocratic culture that can usefully be com-pared with Plato's account of Sparta, which I quote at the end of the second section of this chapter. Had it been written by a Maronite, we might consider it to be a prejudiced description — and it is presumably a somewhat exaggerated account of the Druze community as not all men would be adepts of the sword and horse. Nevertheless, such skills were traditional signs and markers for men of honour and were sometimes confined to distinct status groups in the Otto-man empire. Many members of the Turkish (or Turkified) nobility, for example, were descendants of officers in the cavalry, and the qualities of a chevalier were highly prized. Outside the sanctuaries of places like Mount Lebanon, and par-ticularly in the cities, Christians and Jews were at times not allowed to ride horses as one of the many signs of their inferior status.

What is particularly interesting about the description of Druze timocratic values is that it suggests Maronite commoners could not usually aspire to honour in the Shouf countryside to anything like the same degree as their Druze counterparts. Even if they were skilled artisans, they were assumed to be subor-dinate to Druze lords in a more fundamental sense than Druze peasants were.

And reading William Polk's account of the Egyptian period when the economic standing and social status of Maronites improved so considerably, one gets the impression that many Druze commoners felt humiliated by the humbling of their sheikhs and were spoiling for a fight to punish a community of former serfs who had forgotten the respect that was due not only to the lords but to all 'free' Druze (Polk 1963: 125–40).

This account of the nature of feudalism in the Shouf and Lubnan mountains indicates that forms of 'tribal' or factional honour which could be described as 'pre-feudal' might have persisted throughout the feudal period. But they were now structured by a hierarchy of prestige in which the honour of the sheikhs — even those who controlled relatively small areas of land — was clearly greater than that of the commoners and was usually supported and enforced by higher feudal authorities. Even in the northern districts such clan sheikhs as the Karams were eventually incorporated into the feudal system. In the nineteenth century this feudal hierarchy was challenged by capitalism and associated liberal and populist values, creating many more opportunities for common men to claim honour. And as we shall see in the next section of this chapter, a form of honour developed that was in some respects similar to that found in southern Italy where 'mafia honour' emerged in a competitive market economy.

The Lebanese mountain range was home to different sorts of societies in the latter decades of the nineteenth century, but all were increasingly penetrated by capitalism and, on the carefully constructed and tended terraces, the small farms were intensively cultivated by a market-oriented peasantry. In the north, on Jabal Lubnan, where the peasants had never completely submitted to a feudal overlord, clan loyalties to local leaders persisted alongside the development of smallholding agriculture, some of it on land held by peasant proprietors, some on rented property. On Jabal Kisrawan, despite the reassertion of Khazin rights to their estates, small-scale agriculture also developed after the abolition of feudal exactions and duties, as it did on Jabal ash-Shouf where some Maronite peasants returned with the growing security of the Mutasarrifate to work as free tenants or proprietors alongside the Druze peasantry. In all areas, there was agricultural growth and development, and the predominantly Christian market towns of Dayr al-Qamar in the centre of the Shouf, and Zahle on its eastern foothills, provided a sense of security for Christians in the countryside and contributed to agricultural improvement generally.

But the economy was highly competitive, and there was an undercurrent of violence, a familiarity with weapons and a willingness to use them. As a result of the recent wars against Egyptians and landlords, and between confessions, there was a martial culture in most communities, contributing to a self-image held by many Lebanese of a feuding mountain society in which men of honour fought for their family, clan and confession.

5. Mafia and feuding

In the previous chapter, I made a number of references to a Lebanese 'political mafia' of qabadays and za'ims operating in a modern urban context. Some historians have argued that a similar structure emerged in rural Mount Lebanon. In her article on the market towns of Zahle and Dayr al-Qamar in the mid-nineteenth century, Leila Fawaz refers to 'Zahle's *qabadayat* ... with their frontier mentality of self-reliance' and 'their vigilante style of law and order' (Fawaz 1988: 52; also see Fawaz 1994: 34 ff). These qabadays provided protection for the predominantly Greek Catholic population of Zahle, a relatively high proportion of which included peasants and 'semi-nomads' who had recently moved to the town for safety. Edmund Burke also refers to *qabadayat* in nineteenth-century Mount Lebanon, although he uses the word in the context of 'estate managers and their agents' who coerced and controlled the peasantry. Significantly, he sees the za'im–qabaday hierarchy as similar to the Sicilian mafia, whereby 'violent political middlemen' came to control the growing market in labour on behalf of 'urban absentee landlords and the state' (Burke 1988: 25).

The original Italian mafia developed in nineteenth-century Sicily when, after the abolition of feudalism in 1812, the *gabellotti* or bailiffs of the *latifondi* estates rented or forcibly acquired land from absentee landlords and then sublet to sharecroppers at extortionate rents. By establishing patron–client networks and manipulating the values of family honour, feuding and *omertà* (the code of silence), the *gabellotti* and their field guards (*campieri*) became *mafiosi*, offering votes to politicians, 'protection' and other services to clients, and gradually expanding, through theft and coercion, to gain leading positions in urban manufacturing and trade (Blok 1974; Schneider and Schneider 1976; Gambetta 1993).

It is possible that some lords' retainers acted in a similar way in modern Greater Lebanon, particularly on the landed estates of the Bekaa valley and in what Michael Gilsenan (1996: 79–84; and 1992) describes as the 'latifundia' of the coastal plain of Akkar that widens as it extends across the Syrian border. But despite Edmund Burke's assertions about za'ims and qabadays, there was nothing comparable to the Sicilian mafia in the *petit Liban* of the Mutasarrifate (which is Burke's geographical focus). The ecological and social conditions of the terraced and intensively farmed slopes of the Lebanese mountains were quite different from the Sicilian *latifondi*, large grain-producing estates with absentee landlords who rented or lost their land to *gabellotti* middlemen who, in turn, had a virtual monopoly of local power. Either the Lebanese landlords remained in their villages, or a complicated system of absentee landlordism, subletting and peasant proprietorship developed as feudal lords sold their land to urban merchants and rich peasants.

A number of developments helped Lebanese peasants accumulate land and expand their production by the use of seasonal and day labour. The official abolition of feudal dues and exactions led, in the 1860s and the decades that followed, to more lords selling land to their peasants, and to some peasants being free (or forced by necessity) to take employment as wage workers. The expanding market stimulated grain-growing on mountain terraces and increased acreages of mulberry and olive trees, tobacco and viniculture. Urban merchants often let out their land to rich peasants who employed wage labour and used other capitalist methods of production, and many of these 'yeomen farmers' expanded into processing industries producing silk, olive oil and wine (Saba 1976: 14–15).

This created a highly competitive economy quite unlike the Sicilian form of production determined by a monopoly control of land. If any comparison can be made, it should be with the Calabrian 'mafia' or 'ndrangheta that emerged on the plain of Gioia Tauro in southern Italy. There, in the late nineteenth and early twentieth centuries, peasants who either owned their land or had relatively secure tenancies produced, like their Lebanese equivalents, a variety of crops and agricultural products for the market such as olive oil and wine (and, in addition, citrus fruits). In this environment there were a number of commercial opportunities for entrepreneurial peasants, but fierce competition meant that while some became rich, others were ruined. It seems the 'ndrangheta emerged out of this competitive peasantry and was largely a response to the insecure economy of the Gioia Tauro.

In an article he wrote in 1979, Pino Arlacchi treated the Sicilian mafia and Calabrian 'ndrangheta as identical or at least similar phenomena. But a close reading of his later study of Calabrian agriculture and society (Arlacchi 1983) reveals crucial differences between the two forms of mafia. While it might be true to say that the 'most important Sicilian and Calabrian mafiosi of this century have all come from the lowest strata of society' (Arlacchi 1979: 58), the origins of the two mafias are different, the one based among the already privileged and powerful *gabellotti* middlemen and the other amongst the peasantry of the Gioia Tauro. It is only in respect to the Calabrian 'ndrangheta that it truly makes sense to say 'men of honour are not born, but self-made, on the basis of a free competition for honour that is open to everyone' (Arlacchi 1979: 54). Such men imposed a violent order on a competitive market, an order that was all the more effective because it encapsulated the economy they sought to control:

The 'functional necessity' of mafioso power and behaviour lies in the fact that it is simultaneously able to satisfy the need for organization and the need for mobility [in the society of Gioia Tauro]; that it is able to promote cohesion without denying the play of competitive forces.

(Arlacchi 1979: 57; cf Arlacchi 1983: 116)

Like the Beiruti qabadays, the Calabrian *'ndrangheta* intervened in a competitive economy in which individual social mobility could lead to either increasing wealth or extreme poverty. And although they provided a degree of organization, the mafiosi embodied many of the attributes of the society and economy in which they operated, combining aggressive competition with a concern for co-operation, rapid social mobility with a search for order.

This is the key comparison between mafia and the rural concept of individual honour in Mount Lebanon. There does not seem to be much evidence of any extensively organized mafia in rural Lebanon, but the honour systems in Calabria and Mount Lebanon did perform similar functions. The Calabrian *uomini d'onore* might have made more explicit use of the concept in a more organized fashion, but the sheikhs of the *shabab* were 'men of honour' too. These Lebanese strong-arm men did not take over marketing and agribusiness to the same extent as the *'ndrangheta*, but they did provide a local leadership and a degree of order based on the respect they earned through a violent defence and assertion of personal honour.

Particularly significant in the Calabrian and Lebanese cases is the way honour was associated with what might be called an 'egalitarian ethic' as compared with the ethic of domination imposed by the *gabellotti* middlemen on the Sicilian *latifondi* estates. Often, the only realistic avenue for peasants who aspired to a sense of honour in Sicily was to take to the mountains and become bandits. The power and domination of the mafiosi was such that the Sicilian sharecropping peasantry was as dependent and subordinate as it had been under the feudal lords. In Calabria, however, the existence of a free peasantry conditioned a different style of honour in the *'ndrangheta*. Members of this mainland mafia operated in an 'egalitarian' environment in which most men could enter and compete in the rural economy and potentially all could claim honour in the sense of respect. By behaving in an aggressively honourable fashion, by exercising 'courage, cunning, ferocity and the use of force and fraud' (Arlacchi 1983: 111), a man could earn the respect of his peers and acquire power, land and agribusiness. Nevertheless, the egalitarian ethic required the mafiosi to appear to be common men, even to the extent that their acquisition of wealth and power became something of a social 'embarrassment' to them, 'difficult either to protect or to justify' (Arlacchi 1979: 59).

Perhaps one should talk of an egalitarian 'myth', because of course there was great inequality in Calabria and Mount Lebanon. But the word 'ethic' is more useful as it describes a moral code that claims men are equal even when they are not. Probably in all agrarian societies peasants have some notion of 'rights' or, more precisely, of what James Scott (1976) calls a 'moral economy': a 'right to subsistence' and an ethical sense of an upper limit to the exactions that can be made upon them — by landlords, tax collectors and merchants — before they rebel or become bandits. We have seen something like this in the case of the Spanish peasants in *Fuenteovejuna* when they killed their cruelly oppressive lord (section 2 above), and clearly the Maronite peasants of the Kisrawan had a sense of a moral economy when they rebelled in 1858. However, perhaps particularly in societies where peasants own their land or hold relatively secure tenures, the idea of a moral economy and a 'subsistence ethic' (Scott 1976: 2–7) can be enhanced by a more strongly expressed notion of equality amongst the peasantry.

George Foster (1965), working in a modern Mexican context, called this the 'image' or idea of 'limited good'. Two key material goods are often limited in peasant societies: land and water. If one peasant acquires more land it is at the expense of another. This might not be the case where there is plentiful land for renting or where the land frontier has not been reached, but in many peasant societies, and certainly in most parts of the Mediterranean basin, there is a shortage of cultivable land. The same is true for the water necessary for irrigation. In Foster's Mexican village of Tzintzuntzan this seemed to determine a peasant ideology that all goods were limited, that one peasant's wealth was another's poverty, and the only legitimate way to become rich was through chance or fate — for example by discovering buried treasure or winning the national lottery.

So important was the ethic (or pretence) of equality in Tzintzuntzan that if, for example, a family of peasants were complimented on the fine quality of their crop, they would immediately go to great lengths to explain why it was no better than anyone else's. The whole of life was a 'zero-sum game'. Even good looks were limited, and telling a mother her baby was beautiful could imply the child's beauty had been stolen from another. In Lebanon, it is wise to invoke the name of God when looking at a child or complimenting someone on his or her good fortune, in order to ward off the 'evil eye'. But the idea of limited good does not extend as far as it appeared to go in Foster's Mexican case. Saying *b'ism allah*, 'in the name of God,' or *mabruk*, 'you are blessed' (by God), is designed to ward off the misfortune that attends hubris, not to cover up a theft. In many other respects, however, peasants on Mount Lebanon in the modern period did exhibit a notion of limited good, especially with regard to land and water.

In that part of his study of 'feuding societies' which deals with peasant forms of production in the Mediterranean region, Jacob Black-Michaud argues that shortages of land, water and other material resources, and the lack of opportunities for accumulation, tend to limit social differentiation and the development of a power structure based on monopoly ownership or control of economic resources. This 'total scarcity' gives rise to an 'egalitarian ethos' (or ethic) 'which reflects on the moral plane the material and institutional poverty of such societies' (Black-Michaud 1975: 121–2). But whereas George Foster concluded that peasants would prefer not to tolerate any stratification — including that of power — because this might result in the dominant gaining a larger share of the limited good, Black-Michaud argues that leaders do emerge in peasant societies and they achieve that rank by asserting their honour (for his critique of Foster, see Black-Michaud 1975: 174–5).

It is not altogether clear why peasants should treat honour differently from such other limited goods as land or water. It is obviously in short supply, otherwise everyone could lay claim to it. Nevertheless, Black-Michaud concludes that honour is a socially necessary and sanctioned 'affirmation of aptitude for leadership'. And because leaders gain privileged access to resources, honour is also 'a licit means of achieving an "illegal" material end'. The assertion of honour as a 'pretext' for a conflict over material ends enables that conflict to be prosecuted beyond the point where collective sanctions, based on an 'egalitarian ethos', would normally be invoked. At the same time, the rules and structure of feuding provide a mechanism for 'ensuring the non-proliferation of such conflicts throughout the social structure' (Black-Michaud 1975: 194).

Like Pino Arlacchi, Black-Michaud offers a functionalist explanation for honour. Unlike Arlacchi, however, he does not consider either the historical background to the emergence of a specific form of honour or its wider socio-economic context. For him virtually all societies that experience 'total scarcity' are prone to feuding, a controlled form of conflict that enables a necessary and functional differentiation of status and power, which in turn provides leadership and order. The nature of ecological poverty is different in nomadic pastoral societies, but here too Black-Michaud explains feuding and honour in terms of 'total scarcity' (a concept he always encloses in quotation marks). Whereas in peasant societies shortages of land and water can be ameliorated by a reduction in population, in herding societies, he argues, the size of the population does not affect levels of consumption and wealth. There is no absolute shortage of pasture and water in the pastoralist economy, and nomads migrate over varied ecological areas to avoid drought and overgrazed terrain. The scarcity, suggests Black-Michaud, is one of animals, and this is a result of the fixed ratio between the size of population and size of herd. Whatever the size of the human population, the conditions of pastoralism are such that there is always a shortage of food. An expanded population leads to an expanded herd, but the latter is never big enough to feed everyone adequately (Black-Michaud 1975: 162–8).

Black-Michaud's argument about the 'total scarcity' of pastoral society is expressed very tentatively, and he seems to be unsure of his ground. As such a society does not exist in Lebanon (except possibly for a few shepherds in the mountains and the Bekaa) we need not detain ourselves on this topic, although we should note that an ecological or other functionalist account of nomadic feuding is probably the only viable form of explanation for a phenomenon that has existed in some desert societies, apparently unchanged, for centuries.

The real problem with Black-Michaud's reluctance to consider his subject historically comes in his discussion of sedentary societies. For example, at various points in his book he refers to feuding in Merovingian France, and there are at least four references to Saint Gregory of Tours (538–94), the historian and contemporary chronicler of the kingdom of the Franks (Black-Michaud 1975: 14–15, 33, 51 and 149). How Gregory's accounts of noble feuds relate to the central argument about 'total scarcity' is never explained, and one wonders why Black-Michaud does not consider the difference between the honour and feuding behaviour of the warrior nobility, which is Gregory's subject (Gregory of Tours 1927; Wallace-Hadrill 1959), and the honour of peasant societies that is his own.

Large sections of his book deal with nineteenth and early twentieth-century accounts of feuding in Albania, and this is to be expected given that the Albanian mountains are home to perhaps the exemplar of a 'feuding society'. But it is frustrating that Black-Michaud provides no history of this society. It may well be the case that there have always been feuds among Albanian peasants and shepherds, but he has occasional references to 'princes' of the mountains (Black-Michaud 1975: 14 and 96 for example) and to hereditary *bajraktars* or 'tribal' leaders (Black-Michaud 1975: 157–8), and it is clear that a hierarchy of honour did exist. Unfortunately, we are not told how a system of something like 'feudal' domination might have been affected by the growth of a market economy, nor how socioeconomic change influenced the manipulation of honour and the conduct of feud.

It should not surprise us that a social anthropologist working within a structural-functional framework of analysis should be oblivious to history and the wider socioeconomic and political environments of the societies he studies. There have been many anthropologists — such as Talal Asad (1972; 1973; 1975) for example — who have criticized this sort of approach, and so here is another topic we can pass over fairly swiftly. But despite the methodological and analytical problems in Black-Michaud's work, his argument, taken together with Pino Arlacchi's, does provide some insights into the way honour seems to have become associated with an egalitarian ethic in nineteenth-century Lebanon.

Although precise historical evidence is rather scanty, it does appear to be the case that, under the impact of a capitalist market, honour became something that was no longer largely confined to the Lebanese nobility but could be claimed by any common man willing to assert himself through violence and thus make himself respected. Prior to the nineteenth century, there were undoubtedly men of honour in Lebanon who were not born to that status, perhaps particularly on Jabal Lubnan where clan forms of authority resisted feudal domination. But it is unlikely that many peasants, without a recognized genealogy and subject to the arbitrary power or *zulm* of their lords, could assert honour and be widely respected. There were possibilities for a peasant to demonstrate a violent prowess and come to the attention of a lord who might then make him an armed retainer or bailiff, but such opportunities were limited and associated with a hierarchical order, not an egalitarian ethic.

Ideas about equality and freedom were disseminated through Catholic mission schools in the nineteenth century, and these found a fertile soil in the changing socioeconomy of the Lebanese Mountain. Peasants began to assert themselves against their rulers and, significantly, to compete amongst themselves. As a result, feuding became something associated less with aristocratic rivalries and more with competition in the market. Arlacchi (1979: 62–3) argues that the 'very ancient "right of feud" ... re-emerges within any traditional society when it is penetrated by the market'; and although more research is needed into the history of Lebanese (and Calabrian) feuding, it is likely that this form of conflict became more widespread among peasants in a competitive socioeconomic environment.

The ecological conditions on Mount Lebanon were similar to those in other parts of the Mediterranean basin, such as Albania, discussed by Black-Michaud. It is also the case that the mountain communities of Maronites and Druze developed strong egalitarian ideologies that persisted into the twentieth century. For example, I once saw the Maronite warlord Bashir Gemayel in a television interview asserting, 'We Lebanese are all middle class, with a small house or apartment and a modest car.' For him the poor were either a fiction invented by Palestinians and communists or they were foreigners (Palestinians and others) who did not belong in Lebanon anyway.

To demonstrate that such an ideology existed, however, is not the same as saying that it bore any resemblance to how society was actually structured. One cannot assume, therefore, that honour created leaders in modern Lebanon in quite the way it might have done in Albania. With the development of a market economy there were many opportunities for accumulation, and the strongest leaders were usually those who already had access to their own or other people's wealth. First there were the former muqataajis. Although their feudal rights and status had been abolished, many kept their land and a number were appointed to the government of the Mutasarrifate. During the governorship of the first *mutasarrif*, Dawud Pasha (1861–68), 16 emirs or sheikhs were incorporated in leading administrative positions (Salibi 1965: 111–12), and subsequent governors employed the same strategy to prevent the old elite's alienation from a modern system and to maintain political stability in those areas where the lords continued to dominate their communities. Second, a new category of leaders emerged in the civil service of the Mutasarrifate, recruited from educated families that had acquired a degree of status as advisers or secretaries to the feudal aristocracy, as priests of the church, as minor feudal sheikhs or other landowners, or as merchants and other types of businessmen.

The Maronite Khouri family from the Shouf, for example, claimed ancestors who had been bishops and minor sheikhs. Bishara al-Khouri became a judge and his son, Khalil, a leading civil servant in the Mutasarrifate with the Ottoman title of bey. Khalil Bey's son — also named Bishara — was a lawyer and civil servant under the French Mandate who married the sister of Michel Chiha, a rich and successful Roman Catholic banker in Beirut. This marriage helped to cement the younger Bishara al-Khouri's links with leading members of the commercial-financial elite that were of immense importance to the patronage network he established after he became the first president of independent Lebanon in 1943 (Johnson 1986: 120–2). Also from the Shouf, the latter's successor, President Camille Chamoun (1952–58), was a lawyer and diplomat whose father had been a high-ranking official in the finance department of the Mutasarrifate. The already high status of this branch of the Chamoun family had been demonstrated in 1930 when Camille married Zelfa Thabit, the beautiful daughter of a notable merchant family (Goria 1985: 20 and 36–7; Harris 1997: 111–12).

The Gemayels were another powerful Maronite family. Although they rose to political prominence slightly later than the Khouris and Chamouns, they had a lineage that could be traced to the sixteenth century when they had established themselves in Bikfaya in the Matn region of the Mountain. There they acquired land and were awarded the title of sheikh by Emir Bashir II. They were never 'great sheikhs', however, and during the Mutasarrifate some of them became merchants. Others entered the professions. Sheikh Amin Gemayel was a medical doctor with business interests in Egypt where he and his immediate family spent time in exile from Turkish rule during the first world war (Harris 1997: 113–14; Goria 1985: 46). His son Pierre became a pharmacist in Beirut, founded the Phalanges party in 1936, and was first elected to parliament in 1960 after championing the Christian cause in the 1958 civil war. Later, Sheikh Pierre's son Bashir became commander of the Phalangist militia and, after forcibly uniting most of the Maronite militias into the Lebanese Forces, he was the most powerful leader of Christian Lebanon by the end of the 1970s. In 1982 he was elected by the parliament to become president of Lebanon, but was assassinated before he could take office. His place was taken by his brother Amin, a lawyer, who served as president from 1982 to 1990 (see chapter 2, sections 3 and 7, above).

As members of the professional and commercial-financial bourgeoisies, the Khouris, Chamouns and Gemayels could not be said to have established themselves as za'im families simply through an assertion of honour. Although, like other members of the post-independence political elite, Camille Chamoun and Pierre Gemayel became associated with a forceful style of leadership and recruited sheikhs of the *shabab* or qabadays to assist them, their rise to power had more to do with their educational, professional and commercial backgrounds. This was the typical route for the new Maronite leaders, and slightly below them in the status hierarchy a number of other Christian families benefited from Ottoman patronage during the Mutasarrifate (1861–1915) and French favours under the Mandate (1920–43).

The one place where new Maronite za'ims might have established themselves through feuding and aggression was the mountainous district of Zgharta in northern Lebanon, an area where feudal domination had never been fully established. As we have seen (in chapter 2, section 3), the Frangieh political dynasty could be said to have started when a member of the family was appointed a district administrator during the Mutasarrifate. His son, Kabalam (or Qadib) Frangieh, became a relatively successful merchant and served as the member of parliament for Zgharta from 1922 until he died in 1932 (Goria 1985: 123). In the elections of 1929 he was involved in a violent contest with a candidate supported by the French mandatory authorities and, in a gun battle near Tripoli, a group of Frangieh partisans killed 19 Senegalese soldiers who were members of the French security forces (Harris 1997: 112). Presumably the authorities did not consider Kabalam Frangieh to have been responsible, or they were forced to accept the situation, because he was re-elected and took his seat in the parliamentary assembly. After Kabalam's death, his eldest son Hamid inherited the political leadership of the family and served as member of parliament from 1932 until October 1957 when he was crippled by a cerebral haemorrhage. Hamid's brother and 'campaign manager' Suleiman then took over as leader of the family and eventually became president of Lebanon in 1970 (serving in that office until 1976).

Hamid Frangieh had had a distinguished career as a government minister, and at the time of his stroke was a leading contender for the Lebanese presidency. By contrast, Suleiman was little more than a strong-arm enforcer, dismissively described by one member of the political elite as *shaykh qabadayat*, a leader of qabadays or a gang boss (Goria 1985: 148 n46). He seems to have been of relatively modest means in 1957, working as a ship chandler and wool merchant (Randal 1990: 125; Goria 1985: 123), and was something of an embarrassment to his illustrious brother. According to the journalist Jonathan Randal (1990: 125), Suleiman affected a 'mafioso style. ... In keeping with [Zgharta] custom, he saw to it that a gunslinger ostentatiously shot dead a Tripoli Moslem every month or so to remind the potentially forgetful who was running the show.'

Four months before Hamid's stroke in 1957, Suleiman Frangieh had been involved in a shoot-out with a rival political clan, the Douaihis, in the village church of Mizyara. At the time, President Chamoun was encouraging Father Semaan Douaihi's political ambitions in an attempt to weaken the Frangiehs who opposed the president's plan to renew his term of office. This Maronite cleric was later to become known among the war correspondents in Beirut as 'the pistol-packing priest' (Glass 1990: 296), and Randal (1990: 125) describes his 'pleasure-loving' nature as 'not immune to the charms of money or female company'. His political challenge to the Frangiehs in the 1950s added to the already tense relations between the two clans that had apparently developed around a dispute about water rights on their farms. Accounts of the battle in the church vary, as do the estimates of the number of dead. Some say 23, others 25, people lost their lives, including women and children. Most of the dead were Douaihis, but a number of Frangiehs and members of other families were also killed. Representatives of Zgharta's four leading Maronite clans (Frangieh, Douaihi, Karam, and Moawad) were in the church for a requiem mass for the brother of a Maronite bishop. One family that was then allied with the Frangiehs was the Moawad clan. Here is how one of them, many years later, described the carnage to the journalist Charles Glass:

> Bishop Abed was saying Mass. Outside the church, there was a quarrel that led to the shooting. Those inside heard it, so they started firing. The place where [Suleiman] Frangieh was standing was surrounded by his men. He was standing with his back to a column that protected him. When the shooting started, that column was nearly destroyed. ... Some of both families went into the confessionals and shot from there. ... Some priests were killed. Many of the Douaihy family were killed.
>
> (Glass 1990: 300–1)

Suleiman Frangieh was forced to flee from the Lebanese authorities to Syria, but a year and a half later he was pardoned and returned a hero to Zgharta. By the time he became president of Lebanon in 1970, the feud had been contained for some time and Father Semaan Douaihi was his political ally. But hostilities between the two families had started again by the late 1980s and a new round of killings was witnessed by Charles Glass (1990: 287–325) when he visited Zgharta in 1987.

The leading clans of the district tended to live in the village of Zgharta which had become a small town with some 50,000 inhabitants by the 1980s (Glass 1990: 289). Some of the clans had originally come from such villages as Ehden high up in the mountains, but during the twentieth century they had moved to the district town in the foothills. There they established themselves in different quarters. Lesser families tended to be allied with one leading clan or another and often lived as neighbours to the leaders who protected them. Some of the Zalloua family, for example, were clients of the Karams and lived in the Karam quarter. It would be wrong to assume that all Zallouas supported all Karams, or that all Karams protected all Zallouas. But the various factions in Zgharta were clearly interpreted by local people as political units based on family traditions of loyalty to za'ims and other leaders who belonged to notable clans. When feuding erupted, people would return to their quarter for protection and some of the men would go to the clan chief's house for orders. In times of peace as well as war, men would visit their za'im to pay their respects, plot against enemies, ask for favours and while away time, drinking coffee and discussing politics and business. Samir Khalaf described as follows the 'open house' held in the 1970s by President Suleiman Frangieh in his summer residence in the village of Ehden:

> All protocol is lifted and any person, regardless of station or background, can seek [Frangieh's] audience without previous appointment. He personally enquires about each of his visitors' relatives, recalling nostalgic-ally past moments they might have shared together, listens to their grievances and promises prompt attention. Much like the fief holder of old, presiding over the private concerns of his estate, he is more the affable, benign and personable 'Bey' displaying genuine empathy and compassion in the lives of his subjects than a President carrying on with the affairs of state.
>
> (Khalaf 1977: 186–7)

This is of course an idealized account of Suleiman Frangieh's style of leadership, and certainly of the 'benign' and caring 'fief holder of old'. It is unlikely that a serf of the Khazin sheikhs would have received such solicitous care and attention if he had gone knocking at the door of his lord. At another extreme, Bashir Gemayel claimed that clients would kiss Frangieh's hand and bring him 'tribute' in the form of baskets of farm produce to obtain their za'im's favour, and even that Suleiman and his son Tony would sometimes demand a *droit du seigneur* with a client's fiancée before they gave their blessing to a proposed marriage (Goria 1985: 148–9 n47). Gemayel wanted to justify his war against the 'feudal' Frangiehs that had culminated in the 'Ehden massacre' of 1978 (see below, and chapter 2, section 3), so we should not attach too much significance to his more obscene claim. It would not be at all surprising, however, that peasants brought gifts of produce, or that they would kiss their za'im's hand; and clearly there was a social hierarchy at work in the Frangiehs' 'open house', just as there was in Kamal Jumblat's palace in the Shouf village of Mukhtara, or Sa'ib Salam's mansion in Beirut. But one is reminded more of a fictional mafia don than a cruel and rapacious landlord.

We are at the Long Island wedding of Don Vito Corleone's daughter, and guests are coming to pay their respects to their godfather (Puzo 1970: 11–40). The strong-arm Luca Brasi has said he hopes the first grandchild will be a boy and kisses his Don's hand. The audience in a Beirut cinema murmurs its approval. I am there with them, in 1972, watching *The Godfather* for the first time. This is their political system on the screen. There are one or two cheers when Don Corleone tells the pathetic undertaker, Amerigo Bonasera, that he should have asked for help earlier: 'If you had come to me for justice those scum who ruined your daughter would be weeping bitter tears this day.' There is applause when Bonasera bows before the Don and is told, 'You shall have your justice. Some day, and that day may never come, I will call upon you to do me a service in return.' Later, there is a huge roar of admiration when Don Corleone says of someone he will soon coerce rather nastily, 'He's a businessman. I'll make him an offer he can't refuse.'

In 1973, during a crisis in the government when President Suleiman Frangieh was having difficulty in forming a new cabinet, there was a cartoon in one of the Lebanese newspapers in which all the leading za'ims were showing Marlon Brando as Don Corleone to the prime ministerial chair. The cartoonist reflected a widespread perception that the Frangieh regime was a mafia. A few years later the civil war had created conditions even more conducive to such activity in the Zgharta region where the Frangiehs ran much of the war economy

By 1978 the Phalangist militia, under the leadership of Bashir Gemayel, was attempting to move in on protection rackets controlled by the Frangiehs in the cement and construction businesses of the industrialized region around the coastal town of Chekka, south of Tripoli (Hanf 1993: 235 ff). The Marada militia (*liwa al-marada*), led by Suleiman Frangieh's son Tony, was dynamiting or otherwise coercing banks, petrol stations and shops that refused to blacklist Phalangist customers. Many militiamen on both sides had been killed in outbreaks of fighting. In 1978 the local Phalangist leader in Zgharta was assassinated and the priests of the town refused to give him a church burial, allegedly at the instigation of the Marada. Bashir Gemayel then ordered Samir Geagea, a medical student at the American University hospital in Beirut, to take a group of Phalangist fighters to 'arrest' the killers. During the assault on Ehden, Tony Frangieh, his wife, their three-year-old daughter, the maid, the chauffeur, and at least 20 others were slaughtered. It was inevitable that Suleiman Frangieh should declare a vendetta against the Gemayels, and against Samir Geagea and his family who came from another northern Maronite stronghold, the village of Becharré, Zgharta town's traditional rival (Randal 1990: 118–22; Glass 1990: 312; and see chapter 2, section 3, above).

Their feuding relations and forceful assertion of their personal and family honour undoubtedly enhanced the local reputation of the Zgharta clans, and the Frangiehs, Douaihis and Moawads all, at one time or another, had family representatives in the Lebanese parliament. But they were not mere commoners when they were first recruited into the institutions of the Mutasarrifate. Some of them had land, others had entered the church, and others had established themselves in trade. The Douaihis, for example, could claim an illustrious ancestor who had lived in the seventeenth century. A graduate of the Maronite College in Rome, the historian Istifan Douaihi became patriarch (supreme bishop) of his church in 1668 and held that office until he died in 1704. He was fluent in Latin as well as Arabic and Syriac, and using a variety of sources wrote a number of works, perhaps the most important being a history of his own church and community (Hourani 1967: 57–8).

Other families had risen to prominence later, and by the nineteenth century the Karams were the most powerful Maronite clan in the district. The landlord and 'tribal' sheikh Yusuf Bey Karam was appointed *qa'immaqam* of the northern governorate after the 1860 confessional war and he restored order in the Kisrawan, enabling some of the Khazin landlords to return, and buying the acquiescence of the peasant leader Taniyus Shahin by making him a local district commissioner. Karam had ambitions to become the governor of an enlarged and united Lebanese province. When it became clear that his dream would not be realized, and the Mutasarrifate was established in 1861 under the governorship of a non-Lebanese, Ottoman Christian, he led a rebellion against a regime that seemed to be incorporating Druze leaders who had been involved in the recent massacres of Christians. He was eventually defeated and sent into exile in 1867, dying near Naples in 1889. His body was then taken home to

Ehden and kept in a glass coffin in the church of Saint George, outside which stood a statue of the local hero mounted on a horse as a general of cavalry (Salibi 1965: 112–13; Glass 1990: 319).

Aware of their ancestry, the leading clans of Zgharta tended to have some sense of genealogy. This was not necessarily a precisely written record of descent, but there was certainly a widely held belief that they were descended from the Crusaders, the French or other distinctive ancestors. Suleiman Frangieh thought that the Douaihis were the earliest family to settle in the area; then in the seventeenth century first the Karams and later the Frangiehs and Moawads became established. The Douaihis claimed that their ancestors came from the town of Douai in northern France. As for the Frangiehs, Suleiman referred to a 'story' or 'legend' that a brother of a Maronite bishop went to France during the reign of Louis XIV (1638–1715) and married a French woman. When he died, his widow brought up their children in Zgharta where she was called *al-ifranjiyya*, the 'Frankish woman' (Glass 1990: 323–4; Randal 1990: 36).

This detour into the clan politics of Zgharta has demonstrated that although their status was enhanced during the Mutasarrifate and French Mandate periods, the leading families of the district were already established in feudal Lebanon. The Frangiehs certainly overtook a clan like the Karams and, in part, they held on to their power through aggressive feuding. They were not, however, mere commoners when Suleiman Frangieh's grandfather was appointed as a district administrator during the Mutasarrifate. Despite some differences as compared with the new leaders in other parts of Mount Lebanon, leadership in Zgharta was similar in this respect: honour and feuding in an individualistic and stratified society might have contributed to the creation and maintenance of a post-feudal leadership, but they did not create za'ims from amongst the peasantry. Nevertheless, at the lower levels of society, the honour of the qabaday did provide a mechanism for peasants and other commoners to carve out for themselves a niche in the rural economy, and from there sometimes to develop into relatively wealthy farmers or businessmen and, at the village level, into relatively powerful local leaders. It was a violent culture where men were expected to behave with honour; and in spite of the clear stratification of leadership, the popular (or 'populist') culture was informed by an egalitarian ethic or myth.

As one man from Zgharta said in 1987 of the Maronite men of the Mountain and their aggressive egalitarianism:

Relations are based on violence. The mountains are rocky. The people are rocky. ... Look at the violence in the faces. They are not like the faces on the seashore. ... The people of the coast are fat. ... Here the people are thin and tough. They are suspicious. ... You can meet people in these mountains who have never been as far as Beirut. You can meet people who know Fifth Avenue in Manhattan. They are all the same, fighters, warriors. They came from the Turkish mountains in the eighth century, fleeing religious persecution. They were not farmers. They were mercenaries. They took part in all wars. Everyone in Zgharta and Becharré carries a gun.

(Glass 1990: 311)

Or as a Druze historian wrote about his people in the early 1990s:

One of the most deeply rooted aspects of Druze traditional behaviour is their extreme sensitivity and their dauntlessness in the exaction of revenge. Blood feuds are a stern reality. The duty of the avenger of blood is a sacred obligation. ... [F]or a majority of [Druze] the failure to honour it brings shame not only on the individual concerned but also on his whole family.

(Alamuddin 1993: 70)

Only in a place like Akkar was such honour largely confined to an ascribed 'caste' or kinship group of aghas (see chapter 2, section 4, above). Elsewhere in the countryside, qabadays and similar sorts of middle-level leaders tended to come from a broader social base. Also, at the head of the new hierarchy of power, za'ims had to be increasingly responsive to their electorates, producing what Albert Hourani (1976) called a 'populist' style of leadership out of a tradition started by people like Taniyus Shahin who led the peasants of the Kisrawan, and Yusuf Bey Karam who not only led a revolt against the Mutasarrifate in his own interest but also, at least in popular imagination, fought for 'the forlorn hope of the Maronites' against a political arrangement in which Druze killers were pardoned and incorporated. The Phalangists, wrote Hourani (1976: 37), were in some sense 'the heirs of this tradition'.

Perhaps paradoxically, given his record, the clearest exponent of an egalitarian ethic among the Maronite leaders in the civil wars of the 1970s and 1980s was Bashir Gemayel, the commander of the Phalangist forces, who claimed that all true Lebanese were 'middle class' (see above). Despite his ruthlessness and cruelty, he seems genuinely to have believed that he was fighting a war against 'feudalism' or what some Lebanese called 'political feudalism' (*al-iqta' as-siyasi*), the style of leadership exercised by the za'ims.

And among the Druze, Kamal Jumblat represented similar values, even though his position as za'im had been inherited from his feudal ancestors. He too claimed he wanted to reform Lebanon and reduce the power of the traditional za'ims. At the core of what he described as his 'socialist' beliefs was a populist small-property ethic, as evidenced in the political testament he completed just before he was assassinated in 1977:

> I myself have distributed 100 hectares to my tenants at Sibline, by the sea, and it was a source of real joy both for them and me. Big estates are unnatural, they distort the meaning of ownership: everybody likes to own something, it acts as an extension of people's senses, their hands, their bodies, their personalities. ... A sense of responsibility and a love of freedom go hand in hand with possession of land.
>
> (Joumblatt 1982: 33)

Kamal Jumblat and Bashir Gemayel were sworn enemies and the warlords of their respective communities. As such, they inevitably represented the values they claimed to despise. But their sense of honour was very different from that of the feudal lords of precapitalist Mount Lebanon. In a sense they were political schizophrenics, unable to distinguish the reality of a competitive and violent society from the idealized view they had of it and of their own role within it. They demanded something approaching submission from their followers, and yet they probably felt genuine affection for them. They did not despise them because they lacked a pedigree of noble blood. They believed that through the ownership of small-scale property their people were members of an egalitarian society in which all could respect each other. It was Kamal Jumblat who dictated the following, originally in French to the journalist Philippe Lapousterle, but it could just as well have been said by Bashir Gemayel in the colloquial Arabic he preferred to the language of the Lebanese elite: 'I am content to live as an honest man amongst the common folk. Mean with oneself, generous to others; a neighbour in need is as a brother, and stands as a symbol for God Himself' (Joumblatt 1982: 32).

6. Honour and confession

Whether the ideology of 'egalitarian honour' developed first in Mount Lebanon and was then introduced into the city by rural migrants is probably impossible to judge accurately. Some urban mythology, as related to me by my neighbours in Beirut, certainly saw the feud as an import from the countryside; and the historical account of Lebanese feuding given by Massoud Younes (1999: 139–99) situates its modern form in a transitional 'society between two orders', with an origin in a precapitalist agrarian society. Similarly, the Lebanese historian Kamal Salibi (1988: 163) sees the 'heritage of bitter mountain feuds' as one negative contribution that Mount Lebanon made to the political life of *Grand Liban*, and he compares this to 'the urbane and liberal Levantine tradition' of Beirut that had merged with the older heritage and 'succeeded, now and then, in rounding off its harsher edges.' Other myths, however, had it that the countryside was composed of village 'moral communities' and it was the city that created violence and anomie. As we shall see in the next chapter (section 4) this was a view at least partially articulated by Kamal Jumblat. In reality, however, there was so much interaction between the Mountain and the city in the nineteenth and twentieth centuries that it is likely both influenced the other.

And in terms of myths about the countryside, it is important to emphasize, as Pino Arlacchi (1979: 63) does in relation to Calabria, that although the 'precapitalist' values of community or *gemeinschaft* were exalted in twentieth-century Lebanon, they were actually applied selectively and instrumentally — certainly in the city, but also in the countryside. Obligations to kin and neighbours were whittled down in the political machine to become obligations to selected patrons, clients and allies; and honour, which could be construed as a value that should morally promote community, was used by the qabadays to prosecute an individualistic and violent competition for material ends.

Such competition and conflict became particularly pronounced in Muslim Beirut in the late 1970s after the military defeat of the National Movement by the Syrian 'peace-keeping' forces in 1976. Because there was no organized and powerful body that could impose a political order comparable to that estab-lished by the Phalangists in Christian East Beirut, rival gangs fought for control of their streets and quarters in the western half of the city. Although purporting to promote an ideology of Nasserism, socialism, or Islamicism, such militias — some of them funded from abroad by countries like Libya or Syria — were often little more than groups of racketeers who would extort money from the hapless local inhabitants in return for their 'protection'. In other words, the 'qabadays' were now preying on insiders rather than people outside the moral community of the neighbourhood. They were also, like their prewar predecessors, involved in smuggling, prostitution and black-marketeering; and competition over these lucrative operations gave rise to murderous blood feuds. By a complex process of fission and fusion, the various groups fought each other and then united to fight a common foe. Pro-Iraqi groups would unite to fight pro-Syrians or pro-Iranians; Shi'a would fight Sunnis; and all would unite together to fight Maronites or Israelis — although in 1982 there were even battles between rival militias over who would have the honour of defending which street from the advancing Israeli army (Johnson 1986: 196–8).

The conflicts between Muslim militias in Beirut were soon replicated by fighting between the Maronites: first, as we have seen (in chapter 2, section 3, and chapter 3, section 5), between Phalangists and the Frangieh militia; and later, in 1980, between Phalangists and the Tigers (*an-numur*) militia led by Dany Chamoun, the son of Camille, the former president of Lebanon. Later still, the various conflicts in Lebanon, both inter- and intra-confessional, became so byzantine that no useful purpose can be served by discussing them here.

What we can say by way of summary is that an honour code, originally associated with feudal domination, was reproduced in a competitive and increasingly urbanized society in the nineteenth century. With the extension of liberal democracy in the twentieth century it was again reproduced as an aggressive but socially legitimate resource in the clientelist system, where it served the interests of political control and order (see chapter 2, section 6, above). Finally, with the collapse of state authority after 1975, yet another form of honour became a resource in a war economy and society where warlords and militiamen fought for control of their respective enclaves or cantons. In the various wars that continued in one form or another until 1990, the emphasis soon shifted from *defending and enhancing personal honour* in relatively limited conflict to *imposing a collective shame on one's enemies* in massacres and annihilation.

Although very different in many respects, this latter form of honour shared some of the characteristics of the earlier form of honour as social domination. Rather like the way feudal lords imposed shame on commoners who lacked noble descent, the militiamen in the civil wars directed an essentially arbitrary violence against a despised Other. Also, much of the fighting in the late 1970s and throughout the 1980s resembled dynastic wars between rival feudal families. In a sense, some militiamen were the modern equivalents of lords' retainers, fighting for the honour not so much of themselves as their leaders. Despite claims that they were a modern political party, the Phalangists could be said to have represented the interests of the Gemayel family. The Tigers fought for the Chamouns, the Marada for the Frangiehs, and the Druze militia of the Progressive Socialist Party for the Jumblats. All of these were za'im families, two with a feudal pedigree (the Gemayel and Jumblati sheikhs) and two (the Chamouns and Frangiehs) that rose to prominence during the Mutasarrifate at the end of the nineteenth century.

We should not make too much of this parallel. Among the Sunni and Shi'a Muslims many new leaders emerged during the civil war. One example was Ibrahim Qulaylat, the former qabaday who led the Sunni Murabitun militia in Beirut. Another was Nabih Berri, a lawyer and the son of wealthy Lebanese emigrants to Sierra Leone, who became the leader of the Shi'a Amal (*amal*: 'hope') militia in 1980 (taking over from Hussein Husseini, a member of parliament and the son of a za'im–landlord family from the Bekaa valley). Nevertheless, many warlords, whether they came from old or new families, imposed an extremely oppressive domination on the people they 'protected', and we will return to this aspect of the civil wars in the next chapter (section 5).

Here, as a conclusion to this chapter, we should consider the difficult problem of honour and confessional conflict. Some might argue that the confessional wars were so different from feuding that the notion of honour as a link between the two is misplaced. But the *style* of communal warfare clearly involved striking at the roots of the Other's honour and imposing shame by cutting away his manhood, raping his women, and defiling his religious icons and places of worship. And at the other extreme, in periods of military stalemate, rival militiamen would trade insults across the wasteland of the 'Green Line' in Beirut that were sometimes as witty and clever as the 'manly performance' of honourable men described by Michael Gilsenan (1989; and see chapter 2, section 7, above). Many of the Lebanese fighters had been friends with their enemies on the other side of the line, and many would become friends again once the war was over. In other words, confessional conflict could sometimes be seen as a 'performance', a male banter, a kind of teasing, as well as pillage and atrocity.

Somewhere between these two extremes is a notion of honour intimately bound up with kinship relations, where the honour of the immediate family is extended into the honour of the confession, not necessarily in a violent way but simply in the sense that one's own honour is a function of family in its widest sense. As we shall see in the next chapter (section 2), in a society where confessional communities are ideally endogamous and where the overwhelming majority of marriages do actually take place within the confessional group, ideas about family honour are inevitably extended to the confession. For some authors, this implies that we are looking at a segmentary lineage system rather like those discussed at the start of this chapter. Kamal Salibi, for example, suggests that the Lebanese are a predominantly 'tribal' society with a history of mountain feuding (Salibi 1988: 163) in which, for example, Maronite clans might feud with each other but would ultimately band together in opposition to Muslims who belonged to an entirely different 'tribe'. Salibi is relatively specific about this, arguing that in the nineteenth century the politics of Mount Lebanon 'remained essentially tribal ... and this mountain tribalism was underlined and reinforced, and indeed perpetuated by religious and sectarian differences which provided it with confessional labels and fighting banners' (Salibi 1988: 165). After the first world war, the French expansion of the old Mutasarrifate of Lebanon — to include Akkar, Jabal Amil, the Bekaa valley and the coastal cities — brought in what Salibi describes as 'more tribes brandishing confessional banners' and this gave rise to problems that he seems to see as leading eventually to civil war (Salibi 1988: 165–6).

There are two problems with this approach. First, as I reiterate below, it confuses limited feuding with unlimited confessional war. Second, the definition of 'tribalism' is not at all clear, and a rather loose use of the concept conflates such distinct forms of social and political organization as tribe, faction, and confession. Sometimes even nations in the Arab world are described as little more than tribes, as for example when a retired Egyptian diplomat told the journalist Charles Glass, 'Egypt is the only nation-state in the Middle East. The rest are tribes with flags' (Glass 1990: 3). *Tribes with Flags* is an evocative title for a book about a journey through the Levant in the late 1980s, but it is not a useful starting point for an analysis of modern politics in the region.

A commonsense definition of 'tribe' is that it is a pre-modern (and, indeed, pre-feudal) form of political organization found in societies with a weak (or, in some cases, non-existent) central authority or state. The tribe is usually associated with a particular geographic territory in which political order is structured around lineages or kinship relations. Although the kinship organization of tribes can take many different forms, two ideal types can be distinguished. First there are tribes composed of a group of people claiming a common descent; and second, there are those where a collection of different families combine together for mutual defence, usually under the leadership of a dominant clan.

In the first type, the genealogy might be traced from a male or female ancestor through the paternal or maternal line; marriages might be virilocal (where the wife moves to live with the husband's family) or uxorilocal (where the married couple live in the village or homestead of the wife); and preferred marriages might be cross-cousin, parallel-cousin or exogamous. The distinguishing feature, though, is the claim of common descent. The exemplar of this type in the Arab world is the beduin tribe defined by patrilineal descent, virilocal marriage and a normative preference for parallel-cousin unions in which men marry their father's brother's daughter. The units or 'segments' of the tribe (*qabila*) might be the sub-tribe (*'ashira*), clan (*hamula*), and extended family (*'a'ila*); and the normative rules (although not necessarily the actual practice) of feuding would require extended families in one clan to unite to fight another clan, and clans to unite to fight another tribe. This is the segmentary lineage model discussed in the first section of this chapter, an analytical construction developed by E. E. Evans-Pritchard and others, and subjected to a variety of criticisms by Emrys Peters (1967) and his successors (Abu-Lughod 1990).

An example of the second type of tribe is found amongst the cattle-herding Nuer of southern Sudan, whom Evans-Pritchard (1940; 1970) studied in the 1930s. Although this is not necessarily the most useful example for a discussion of Lebanon, it is probably the best known in the literature. According to Evans-Pritchard's account, each Nuer tribe was associated with a dominant lineage or 'clan' but was composed of different families that could change tribal allegiance simply by moving from one tribal area to another. A clan was a patrilineal kinship group, composed of people who could trace their descent from a common ancestor and between whom marriage was forbidden. Members of the same clan could belong to different tribes, which were territorial groups divided into primary, secondary and tertiary sections or 'segments'. The villages of each segment were geographically separated from those of neighbouring segments — for example by a river or a relatively wide unpopulated area. In the feud, vengeance was initially the responsibility of close agnatic kinsmen, but this often led to conflict between the geographical tribal segments to which the feuding groups belonged, tertiary sections combining to fight a rival secondary section, and secondary sections combining to fight another primary section.

Although the original Arab conquerors of Lebanon and Syria might have been organized in tribes and segments that claimed a common descent, it is likely that the indigenous inhabitants were not. And it seems that over the centuries all 'tribes' in the Lebanese mountains became more like the Nuer. There were, however, important differences. First, Lebanese clans were not necessarily exogamous and the Arab practice of parallel-cousin marriage became an ideal in a number of communities. Second, whereas dominant clans among the Nuer did not seem to perform much of a leadership function, in Lebanon they clearly did. Leaders of dominant Lebanese families offered protection to less honourable families in return for support, and by asserting honour the dominant acquired control over land and water. Third, although Lebanese 'tribes' were associated with particular geographic areas, it seems that prior to the feudal period most areas of the Mountain were contested by rival clans. Some dominant sheikhs and their families were then incorporated into the feudal system as muqataajis, and local monopolies of power emerged in the landlords' estates. In Jabal Lubnan where the emirs were unable to suppress contending clans and thus failed to impose a full feudal authority, local leadership was competitive and village life was controlled by rival factions. As we have seen (in section 5) such a factional system continued into the twentieth century in the district of Zgharta where at times there were perhaps as many as four factions, led by the Frangieh, Douaihi, Karam, and Moawad clans.

In discussing the forms of leadership in feudal and modern Lebanon it makes much more sense to use the word 'factionalism' in place of 'tribalism'. Using the latter suggests that the inhabitants of the Mountain in the nineteenth and twentieth centuries thought in terms of an ancient or primordial form of leadership derived from the early period of Arab colonization. At the very least it implies a segmentary lineage structure in which rival sets of whole families had tribal allegiances to each other that were then, in response to an external threat, fused by a sense of common kinship into a confessional community. In the next chapter (section 2) I argue that confessional identity can be seen as an 'analogy' or 'metaphor' for the family, but we should not assume from this that the confession is a mechanical construction of families organized into otherwise hostile tribes. Even amongst the Druze where allegedly there is widespread agreement as to the factional allegiance of 317 of the 333 Druze families (see section 4 above), it is not the case that *all* members of a particular family will necessarily adhere to the Jumblati or Yazbaki 'tribe' to which the majority of family members feel they owe some sort of allegiance. The very fact that most accounts refer to two Druze 'factions' is an indication that political allegiance is not entirely determined by kinship loyalties.

Clan loyalty in modern Lebanon was an ideology and, although it seemed to be more pronounced in a community like the Druze, it should not be seen as a definitive guide to factional allegiance. This is illustrated by my own account of the 'politics of families' in the Sunni Muslim quarters of Beirut in the early 1970s (Johnson 1986: 53 ff and 90 ff). Although people told me that the Itani extended family or clan were traditionally supporters of the Salam family, a significant number of Itanis supported their kinsman Muhammad Zakariya Itani when he ran against the za'im Sa'ib Salam in the 1972 elections; and although the Fakhuri family had a long tradition of being opposed to and even direct political rivals of the Salams, I knew Fakhuris who were overtly and enthusiastically loyal to Sa'ib Salam. Factional ties in Lebanon might have been influenced by an ideology of family allegiances, but support for a particular za'im was also a function of complicated patronage networks of economic, social and political ties that often cut across kinship groups.

Stressing a supposed tribal origin for the Lebanese, and then assuming a continuity throughout the feudal and modern periods, gives the impression that they are a primitive people with primordial loyalties untouched by centuries of feudal domination and by the changes brought about by capitalism and modernization. Kamal Salibi wields the concept of tribalism as a rhetorical device to explain modern factional and confessional loyalties. If he uses 'tribe' as a metaphor, I have no real quarrel with him. But the problem is that his account gives the impression that feuds between kinship groups, feuds between political factions, and wars between confessional communities are not merely metaphorically 'tribal', but literally the same phenomenon.

It is certainly the case that there were a number of feuds in modern Lebanon with a confessional origin; and before discussing unlimited communal war, it is worthwhile to consider what might be called 'limited confessional feuds'. We have seen (in section 5 above) that Jonathan Randal (1990: 125) refers to the Frangiehs periodically killing a Muslim from Tripoli in the 1950s. Whether Suleiman Frangieh was responsible for this, and whether it happened as regularly as Randal implies, is a matter of myth. But there was a tradition of feuding between Maronite Zgharta and the predominantly Sunni city of Tripoli, and this inevitably took on confessional overtones. Similarly there was a tradition of honour killings among the qabadays of Beirut, and again this could involve Muslim–Christian rivalries as we have seen (in chapter 2, section 5) in the case of the two young heroes who shot each other dead in a nightclub in 1973.

During the late Ottoman period, in the decades either side of the turn of the century, there seems to have been a spate of sectarian killings in Beirut, and sometimes the tit-for-tat killings were so regular that people would stay at home if it was a night for one of their community to be knifed or shot (Fawaz 1983: 113–16; Johnson 1986: 18–22). The historian Leila Fawaz (1983: 114) explains this exchange of violence in terms of poor policing by the Ottoman authorities, Muslim resentment at a growing Christian mercantile wealth, and a certain aggressiveness on the part of Christian migrants from the Mountain who 'came devoid of the urban instinct for coexistence and compromise'. To slovenly policing we might add the lack of efficient arbitrating structures. In 1903, feuding between Greek Orthodox quarrymen and Sunni Muslim port workers degenerated into serious fighting. Merchant notables from both communities attempted to mediate, but their ability to arbitrate or impose a settlement was limited and it might be argued that the bloodshed only stopped when two American warships approached Beirut (Johnson 1986: 19). It was not until the latter years of the French Mandate that the za'ims' clientelist system of political control made mediation and arbitration more effective.

In independent Lebanon, feuding between Muslims and Christians could usually be contained by the za'ims relatively easily. Even after the start of the civil war in 1975 it was possible for Prime Minister Rashid Karami (the za'im of Tripoli) and President Suleiman Frangieh (the za'im of Zgharta) to agree on a deployment of the Lebanese army in September 1975 to separate Sunni and Maronite fighters in the Tripoli region. The protagonists were engaged in an essentially local war after Zgharta gunmen had kidnapped and murdered 12 Muslim passengers on a bus travelling from Tripoli to Beirut (Johnson 1986: 173). The fact that the Zgharta Maronites had killed a dozen Muslims indicated that things were getting out of hand, but the killings could still be classified as part of a feud: the Maronite gunmen were making an essentially limited statement about their honour, and were not envisaging an ethnic cleansing of Tripoli.

The situation was very different in Beirut where the Phalangists and their allies would embark, in January 1976, on the wholesale massacre of the Muslim population of the Karantina, a slum settlement on Maronite church land. Hundreds of men and some women were killed, bodies were piled in the streets, and at least one terrified victim shot his daughters rather than see them raped. After the slaughter and the expulsion of the Palestinians and Lebanese Muslims, the buildings and shacks of the quarter were bulldozed to create a level empty space (Johnson 1986: 191).

To imply that confessional massacre is an extension of a 'tribal' feud is to confuse a limited and proportional exchange of killing with disproportionate slaughter. Of course it is the case that the stress on damage-limitation in the feud (see chapter 2, section 7) is at least partly a function of a complicated balance of power that often does not exist in confessional warfare; and were it not for this balance of feuding groups, one lineage might seek to exterminate another. The requirements of social life and a 'social economy' mean that massacres of whole families or lineages in a feud cannot be tolerated, and equal access to knives and guns ensures that the balance between feuding 'segments' is maintained. One could argue that, given the opportunity, a lineage group with superior weaponry or numbers would massacre all their rivals if they had the opportunity. But this does not seem to happen, unless the opposing group is of a completely separate lineage or, in the Lebanese case, a completely separate confessional group. Even then, special circumstances are required to stimulate a confessional war. In the Shouf, for example, Druze and Christians were neighbours in a number of places until the war of 1860, and these mixed villages were re-established during the Mutasarrifate and the two communities lived and worked together again until the next Shouf war in 1983 (chapter 2, section 7). Apart from those wars, if there were incidents of violence between Druze and Christians they took the form of limited feuding, not confessional war.

Perhaps I am somewhat unfair to Kamal Salibi, but his argument about 'tribalism', and the implicit assumption that confessionalism is an extension of tribal feuding, does come perilously close to saying that confessional conflict is a 'given' of Lebanese history, a primordial view similar to that described by Clifford Geertz (1963) and discussed in the first chapter of this book (sections 5 and 6). My argument is quite different, as will become clearer in the next chapter. Confessionalism in Lebanon is a *modern* phenomenon, not an ancient one. It emerged in the nineteenth century under the impulse of capitalism, and it was reproduced after a century of relative harmony under the impulse of urbanization. If 'tribal' values played any part in the wars of the 1970s and 1980s, then like honour they were reproduced in a particular context in a different form from the contexts that might have existed earlier. Kinship loyalties were an essential ingredient of modern confessionalism; but it seems to me that before focusing on the wider 'tribal' unit, it is far more important to consider the nature of the *nuclear* family that developed within the new context of urbanization. As will be explained in the next chapter, it is the sexually repressive 'neopatriarchal family' in the city that turns honour into something far more nasty and unpleasant than the honour of a 'feuding society'.

4

Patriarchy and Surveillance

Patriarchal cultures of honour and shame certainly seem to have influenced —
albeit in different ways — both feuding and confessionalism in Lebanon. It is
difficult, however, to understand how a feuding system of contained and limited
violence could give way to the extremes of massacre and ethnic cleansing in
confessional war. An obvious point is that in the heat of battle men become
brutalized and commit acts of which they are later ashamed. But that provides
only a small part of the answer. This chapter seeks to provide a fuller explanation of confessional conflict in the 1970s and 1980s by investigating cultural
and social changes brought about by urbanization and other aspects of modernization.

In particular we need to consider the fact that a pronounced sense of
personal honour as 'respect' (see chapter 2, sections 1, 2 and 5) is primarily a
characteristic of young men, and it is this age group that provided the bulk of
militiamen and confessional fighters. These adolescents were the product of a
'neopatriarchal' and *modern* family that I discuss in this chapter. To prepare the
ground for an analysis of 'sexually repressive' families and their patriarchs'
attempts to control women and young men, it is helpful to look at comparative
material (drawn from Africa and the Indian subcontinent) on the relationship
between family structures and 'ethnicity', an umbrella term that includes African
'tribalism' and Indian 'communalism' as well as Lebanese confessionalism. This
subject matter is introduced in the second section of this chapter and stresses
the effects of urbanization as a key factor of modernity that stimulates ethnic
identity and conflict. Urbanization represents a threat to the extended family

and to patriarchy. As an analogy of the family, the ethnic group provides a sense of security and clearly defined roles for urban patriarchs, 'their' women and their adolescent sons.

In section 3 I look at some psychoanalytic explanations of communal violence, before considering a *sociology* of ethnic and confessional conflict in section 4. Although psychoanalytic accounts provide useful metaphors and analogies that help us understand the emotional passions involved in ethnic warfare, they do not give explanations that can be easily verified. Hence my emphasis on such sociological factors as urbanization, family structure and patriarchy. Although it is informed by some psychological insights, this sociology is hopefully much less speculative than a purely psychoanalytic approach.

A central concern in my sociology of ethnicity is the distinction between 'liberal' and 'romantic' nationalism. We have seen in the previous chapter (section 3) that nationalism was not a major determinant of confessional consciousness in the nineteenth century. A hundred years later it was, and the shift from liberal to romantic forms of this ideology would have profound consequences for the trajectory of confessional identity and conflict. In contrast to its liberal predecessor, romantic nationalism is authoritarian and exclusive, involving a submission to strict patriarchal leadership and an aggressive response to a feared Other who is excluded from the nation. Such an ideology appeals particularly to those people who are the 'casualties' of modernity, providing scapegoats who can be blamed for the insecurities and apparent anomie of urban life, and strong leaders who provide support and encouragement for threatened patriarchs in authoritarian families. Men fight for the ethnic cause, and women are highly valued as mothers of the nation and its martyrs. As the distinction between liberal, or 'civic', and romantic, or 'ethnic', nationalism informs many of the arguments in this chapter, I start in section 1 with an historical account of these ideologies in modern Europe and Lebanon.

The ideas of nationalism were important elements of the modernization process in Lebanon. Another development that formed part of the same process was the growth of 'surveillance', or the development of a system of 'micro-powers' in civil society that could possibly transcend confessional allegiance. While modernity provided the socioeconomic conditions for confessional conflict, it also generated social forms of 'self-surveillance' that promoted a nationalist 'counter-structure' competing with the values of narrow ethnic or confessional identity. This is discussed in section 5 as a prelude to a consideration in chapter 5 of the prospects for a secular political system in postwar Lebanon.

1. Arab and Lebanese nationalism

Most students of nationalism agree that their subject is a modern phenomenon (Anderson 1983; Gellner 1983; Hobsbawm 1990). There is certainly copious evidence to suggest that in Europe it was somehow associated with the economic and social changes ushered in by the industrial revolution in the eighteenth century, and few would disagree with the proposition that the French political revolution of 1789 marked a major turning point in its history. The subjects of Louis XVI became *citizens* of the republic, and the Declaration of the Rights of Man and the Citizen stated that 'sovereignty resides in the nation'. As we have seen (in chapter 3, section 3), these were revolutionary ideas and a challenge to monarchy everywhere, but perhaps the greatest threat was to the Habsburg emperor, the Russian tsar and Ottoman sultan, who all ruled multiethnic empires. The Greeks were the first to rebel successfully, and they won their independence from the Ottomans in 1830, the year Belgium broke away from the Kingdom of the Netherlands.

Throughout the nineteenth century new nations were created. The united kingdom of Italy was officially proclaimed in 1861. The Austro–Prussian (1866) and Franco–Prussian (1870–71) wars resulted in a united Germany, and the Russo–Turkish war ended with the Congress of Berlin recognizing the independence of Romania, Serbia and Montenegro in 1878. Despite an initial failure in 1876 when Ottoman troops had put down a rebellion with great savagery, the Bulgarians won full independence in 1908. In the same year, the Ottomans forfeited Bosnia and Herzegovina to the Austro–Hungarian (formerly Habsburg) empire and they were to lose virtually all their remaining territory in Europe when Macedonia was divided between Greece and Serbia after the Balkan wars of 1912–13. A few years later, it seemed that liberal nationalism was victorious in Europe with the dismemberment of the Ottoman and Austro–Hungarian empires after the first world war. Turkey's imperial status was permanently ended with the loss of its Arab provinces to Britain and France; and Austria and Hungary were divided and the new state of Czechoslovakia formed on their northern borders. In the Balkans the political union of the southern Slavs, or Yugoslavia, was created with the attachment of the formerly Austro–Hungarian territories of Slovenia, Croatia and Bosnia–Herzegovina to Serbia and Montenegro.

There are important differences in the historical detail or peculiarities of particular nationalist revolts and movements. Theda Skocpol's account (1979) of the French revolution, for example, suggests that the political crisis of the late 1780s owed more to aristocratic objections to the monarch's new tax demands than to any demands of a new bourgeois class. But as a broad generalization we can say that the leaders of nationalist movements and their most enthusiastic supporters were usually drawn from the middle classes: professionals such as lawyers and teachers, and the emerging bourgeoisie of merchants, artisans and industrial entrepreneurs.

Hence their preoccupation with liberal values. For them, political freedom meant free markets, free economic association, and an assertion of their individual rights to enter and participate in an expanding industrial economy. In many respects, nationalism was the ideology of national bourgeoisies, and it was not long before Marxists were explaining European wars between nations — not necessarily always accurately but at least with a degree of plausibility — in terms of competition between national capitalisms. But nationalism was, of course, attractive to other classes too. In the countryside, peasants were eager to benefit from the market economy and their opposition to tax collectors, land-lords and money-lenders often took a nationalist form. Their success in the national economy was, however, uneven. Some of them would become capitalist farmers, but many left the land and migrated to the cities — either attracted by the prospect of increased wealth or forced by debt, loss of land and a consequent rural impoverishment. Although some entrepreneurs won significant benefits during the industrial revolution, there were many more people who were losers. Among the recently urbanized populations and parts of the peasantry, a form of nationalism developed that expressed their grievances and was essentially romantic and reactionary rather than liberal and progressive.

The divorce between liberalism and reactionary nationalism in Europe occurred most dramatically during the interwar years in the twentieth century. An intense form of romantic nationalism developed in the 1920s and 1930s, and with it came a marked change of emphasis from individual to collective rights, coupled with a shift from inclusive to *exclusive* forms of nationalism. Part of the problem was that in eastern Europe and the Balkans there were significant ethnic divisions within the 'nation': Poland, Czechoslovakia and Yugoslavia being prominent examples. Conflicts between Poles and Germans, and Serbs and Croats, were to have bloody consequences during the second world war, but what is more significant is a widespread tendency in parts of Europe to define the nation in opposition to a 'demonized' Other that was technically or legally part of the nation. The Others who became the scapegoats of exclusive ultra-nationalism could be socialists, the establishment, intellectuals, immigrants or gypsies. Often they were Jews.

One needs to be careful in the use of the word 'romantic' to describe this form of nationalism. This is not the romanticism that first developed as an intellectual movement at the end of the eighteenth century. However contradictory it may have been, early European romanticism was usually characterized by individualism and a youthful rebellion against social convention and political tyranny. The English poet, Lord Byron, for example, sailed to Greece with arms and funds to support the war of independence. We are concerned with what might be described as the more unwholesome aspects of romanticism: passion and impulse instead of the rationality of the Enlightenment, cruelty and sub-mission rather than liberalism, and a romantic nostalgia for an ordered past instead of a sense of optimism about modern society. In other words, this is the romanticism that persisted into the latter half of the nineteenth century, per-haps particularly in Germany where it found expression, for example, in the philosophy of Friedrich Nietzsche (1844–1900).

Nietzsche's writings about the *Übermensch* (superman) and the 'will to power' were easily distorted to support notions of an Aryan master race; and given his commanding influence over the European mind at the turn of the century, and the publication of his work in cheap editions in Germany and Austria, we can be confident that many proto-fascists were inspired by a selec-tive reading of such works as *Also Sprach Zarathustra* (Thus Spoke Zarathustra). Of particular importance for our later discussion were his often vitriolic equations of women and weakness with liberalism, and of men and power with true freedom. Male pride, and fantasies of honour and glory, strength and severity, discipline and revenge, could easily be stimulated in the mind of an unsophisticated reader as he turned the pages of a Nietzschean text. And the German philosopher's excoriation of modernity appealed directly to the fascist's nostalgia for a pre-modern order. Although he might not have read him very closely, we know, for example, that Adolf Hitler counted Nietzsche as one of his intellectual influences (Brinton 1965: 200 ff; Cruise O'Brien 1988: 57–9).

Ultra-nationalism lay at the heart of Hitler's appeal. By annexing Austria and Czechoslovakia in 1938 and invading Poland in the following year, he avenged the humiliation imposed on Germany in the Versailles peace settlement of 1919. The German nation was reunited and the Third Reich established, tracing its origins back through the 'Second Reich' of Bismarck to the 'First', which was the Holy Roman Empire, and beyond that to the ancient Nordic and Teutonic legends. But the nostalgia of fascism and Nazism was more than a search for a glorious past. It also represented a romanticization of pre-industrial society. In practice, of course, fascism was thoroughly modernist — in Germany horrifi-cally so with the industrialization of genocide. But an important part of its popular appeal was a notion of healthy, happy, and self-sufficient rural com-munities, contrasted with the moral decadence of the urban centres. In *Mein Kampf*, Hitler (1939: 127–8) developed this theme, arguing that the German nation should be constructed on the foundation of a 'healthy peasant class'.

Romantic nationalism had clear ideas about the respective roles of women and men. Women were confined to the hearth and home where they served their menfolk and produced the nation's children. Men provided for their families and went to war on behalf of the nation. Women were housewives and nursemaids, men protectors and warriors. True men valued power and honour, were guided by impulse, and aspired to action and brave deeds. They were not so much irrational as anti-rational, rationalists being the hated intellectuals in the Enlightenment tradition who had done so much to undermine traditional values and who, in the Nazi romantic imagination, were either themselves Jewish or the champions of Jews. Jews became the repositories of everything that was bad or evil about modern society. They were the financiers and capitalists who exploited the people. They were socialists and communists who misled the working class. Morally degenerate, they had introduced corruption and ugliness into the national culture. They represented the threat of miscegenation poised to dilute a pure Aryan stock. They were the ultimate Other, frightful demons and thoroughly wicked, who were responsible for all the suffering brought about by capitalism and urbanization.

A similar transformation of ideas about nationalism occurred in Lebanon and the Middle East, although the romantic variant developed much later than in Europe. Even after democratic regimes were replaced in the mid-twentieth century by military dictatorships in Syria, Egypt and Iraq, Arab nationalism in those countries remained broadly secular and inclusive, and all who spoke Arabic, Christians as well as Muslims, were members of the nation. The status of Arab Jews, however, had become increasingly problematic with the development of Zionism in the late nineteenth and early twentieth centuries, particularly after the 'Balfour Declaration'. In November 1917 the British foreign secretary, Arthur Balfour, wrote to Lord Rothschild promising his government's support for a Jewish 'national home' in Palestine. This provocation to their nationalist sensitivities did not immediately create serious tensions between Arabs and a separate category of Jews, and Emir Faisal — one of the leaders of the Arab revolt against the Ottomans during the first world war — even signed an agreement of co-operation with the Zionist spokesman, Chaim Weizmann, in January 1919 (Laqueur and Rubin 1984: 17–20). But the events of the British Mandate period in Palestine and the creation of Israel in 1948 inevitably generated considerable hostility toward Jews throughout the Arab world. This was the first fissure in the Arab nation, although it was not until the Lebanese civil wars, the Iranian revolution of 1979, and the Iran–Iraq war in the 1980s, that the romantic nationalisms of the different Christian and Muslim communities were more fully developed.

During the nineteenth century, liberal Arab nationalism was initially expressed in an appreciation of literature and culture, and for some time was more concerned with achieving a greater autonomy for the Arab provinces within the Ottoman empire than with any serious ideas about independence. In 1847 two scholars of Arabic — Nasif al-Yaziji, a poet and former secretary of Emir Bashir II, and Butrus al-Bustani, compiler of an Arabic dictionary and a multi-volume encyclopaedia — helped to establish and administer a Society of Arts and Sciences in Beirut. This was associated with the American Presbyterian mission, and in 1850 the Catholic Jesuits created the rival Oriental Society. The membership of both organizations was apparently entirely Christian, but in 1857 another cultural group, the Syrian Scientific Society (*al-jam'iyya al-'ilmiyya as-suriyya*), brought together intellectuals from all the major sects. Its executive committee included the Druze emir, Muhammad Arslan, along with Husayn Bayhum, who was a member of the most prominent Sunni merchant family in Beirut, and a number of Christians including one of Bustani's sons (Antonius 1938: 51–3).

Of this early generation, Butrus al-Bustani was perhaps the most influential in laying the foundations of liberal Arab nationalism. He was educated at the Maronite seminary of Ayn Waraqa, where his teachers nominated him for a scholarship to the Maronite College in Rome. Instead, he went to Beirut in 1840 and became involved with the Presbyterian missionaries, helping them to translate the Bible into Arabic and teaching in their schools. He converted from the Maronite faith and became a Protestant, indicating his unease with the increasingly exclusive stance adopted by the Lebanese church. In his writings he took an ecumenical approach to all religions, and in his weekly journal, *Nafir Suriyya* (Clarion of Syria) published during the confessional crisis of 1860, he appealed to his fellow Christians to love their enemies, abjure vengeance and seek to create a national community united by a common culture and language.

Bustani's motto for a later political and literary review was 'love of country is an article of faith' (*hubb al-watan min al-iman*), a saying attributed to the Prophet Muhammad and popular among the 'Young Ottomans', the Turkish groups of liberal constitutionalists formed in Istanbul and Paris. In common with the latter, Bustani was loyal to the empire but wanted to reform it, and as an Arab he argued for a greater cultural autonomy for his Syrian *watan* (homeland). He addressed his appeals to his 'fellow countrymen' (*abna al-watan*) and, as Albert Hourani points out, he was 'perhaps the first writer to talk with pride of his "Arab blood"' (Hourani 1967: 101 and 99–102; see also Antonius 1938: 47–51; Tibi 1997: 102–4).

It is significant that Bustani should have propagated his ideas through the medium of the periodical press. As Benedict Anderson (1983) puts it, the nation is an 'imagined political community'. It is quite different from the pre-modern community of the village where all villagers know each other and interact on a face-to-face basis. The nation is so large that it is only in the imagination that people can relate to their compatriots. They cannot possibly all know each other, 'yet in the minds of each lives the image of their communion' (Anderson 1983: 15). Such an imagination was first stimulated and communicated to others by the printed word in the form of books and particularly mass-produced newspapers as a result of a technological revolution that Anderson describes as 'print-capitalism' (Anderson 1983: 37 ff and esp. 41–9). This began very early in Europe, which perhaps explains why nationalism first developed there and in the European colonies in northern America. But in Lebanon, Syria and Egypt, it was not until the 1860s that a widespread notion of nationalism was possible. In that decade, there was a dramatic increase in the number of Arabic printing presses, and for the next thirty years these were mostly owned by Lebanese Christians in Beirut, Cairo and Istanbul. Thus as Albert Hourani puts it, despite periods of censorship in the late nineteenth century 'a whole generation' of literate Arabs was exposed to 'the ideas of the new writers and thinkers of Lebanon' (Hourani 1967: 97 and 245 ff).

Hourani discusses a number of these writers and their newspapers and journals, and we need not consider them here; but there can be no doubt that the early Arab nationalists were usually Christian. As coreligionists of the Ottomans, most Sunni Muslims felt a stronger personal affinity to the empire. Christians, however, were second-class subjects and the more politically minded amongst them were faced with a choice between creating a small and marginal Christian nation in a homeland like Lebanon or appealing to a wider community of Arabs. Many of them chose the latter. As Egypt was a separate cultural entity with a distinct history, the focus for Arab nationalism in Beirut, Damascus and Lebanon was Syria, an area that for some included what would become the British mandated territories of Palestine and Iraq. Initially, however, the imagined community was largely confined to those who spoke Arabic in the Ottoman provinces of Beirut, Damascus and Lebanon.

In 1875 a small group of young Christian graduates of the Syrian Protestant College (later the American University of Beirut) formed a clandestine nationalist society in Beirut with close links to the recently formed Masonic lodge in the city. The group soon expanded to include Muslims, and by 1880 they and their associates were by night pasting proclamations on walls in Beirut, Tripoli, Sidon and Damascus, calling for the independence of Syria in union with Lebanon. Some of these handwritten notices included quotations from a poem written by Ibrahim al-Yaziji, the son of Nasif, that he had first recited at a secret meeting of the Syrian Scientific Society some 12 years earlier. This poem, which had been circulated and popularized by word of mouth, inveighed against the evils of confessional conflict and the Ottoman regime that had failed to prevent it. In emotive and rousing language, it spoke of a glorious Arab past and literature and called on Syrians to unite against Turkish tyranny (Antonius 1938: 54–5 and 79–89).

Owing to Ottoman repression, the Beirut nationalist society eventually broke up and some of its members went into exile in places like Paris and British Egypt. But in 1908 there was renewed optimism when, following their successful military revolt in Istanbul, the Young Turks' Committee of Union and Progress (CUP) forced the sultan to abolish censorship and implement a liberal constitution. It soon became clear, however, that the CUP was intent on a 'Turkification' policy to centralize the empire and bring the various ethnic and confessional communities more closely under the control of Istanbul. In response, Arab nationalists were forced back into clandestine politics, and a number of secret societies were formed. The *Qahtaniyya* (named after a legendary Arab 'ancestor') was founded by Arab army officers in 1909, and *al-'Ahd* (the Covenant) — almost entirely composed of army officers, most of them Iraqi — was formed in 1914. The most important civilian group was the Fatat or Young Arab Society (*jam'iyyat al-'arabiyya al-fatat*) founded in Paris in 1911 by a group of Muslim Arabs who were studying there. Two years later, while still not revealing their true identity, they organized an open Arab congress in Paris. This was attended by 24 delegates, almost equally divided between Muslims and Christians, some from Cairo and Baghdad, but mainly from Syria and Lebanon (Antonius 1938: 110–21; Tibi 1997: 106 ff).

The delegation from Beirut to the Paris congress was chosen by the committee of the city's Reform Society (*jam'iyyat bayrut al-islahiyya*) that had been elected in January 1913 by a meeting of local notables. The Beirut Reform Committee was composed of 13 Muslims, 12 Christians and one Jew, and included representatives of the leading merchant families of the city and vilayet (or province) of Beirut. These were moderate men, most of whom wanted to remain part of the empire, but they stood for a political autonomy for the Arab provinces and particularly for a greater local control over the economy. They were part of a more or less informal network of 'decentralizers' formed by the Ottoman Party of Administrative Decentralization (*hizb al-lamarkaziyya al-idariyya al-'uthmani*) which had been founded in Cairo in 1912 and had branches in most towns in Syria. The reforms agreed by the Beirut committee included calls for Arabic to be recognized as an official language and for government powers to be devolved. And significantly, given the mercantile interests of the committee, article 4 of its programme asked for the elected council of the vilayet to be given the right to issue licences to establish Ottoman limited companies instead of this being a prerogative of Istanbul (Hourani 1967: 282 ff; Johnson 1986: 16–18 and 64).

Although the CUP negotiated with the Arab congress and promised reforms, these did not materialize. Thus, when the Ottoman empire entered the first world war in alliance with Germany, many Arab nationalists looked to Britain and France for help in their liberation. Jemal Pasha, the Ottoman governor of Damascus, imposed military rule on Lebanon and Syria, and crushed the local nationalist movement by arresting, torturing and killing the activists whose names appeared in French consular papers. A Maronite priest from Lebanon was publicly hanged in Damascus in March 1915, and ten Muslims and one Christian were similarly executed in Beirut's main square in August 1915. In 1916 a Christian was executed in Beirut in April and 21 others were hanged in May, 7 in Damascus and 14 in Beirut. In this last batch of public executions, 17 of the victims were Muslim and 4 Christian. Faisal, the Arab emir from the Hejaz region of Arabia, had arrived in Damascus in January 1916, ostensibly at the head of an advance-guard of troops to support the Turkish war effort. He pleaded in vain with Jemal Pasha for the lives of the condemned, and on hearing of the executions he urged his father, the sharif of Mecca, to bring forward the start of a planned Arab revolt (Antonius 1938: 185–90).

Sharif Hussein (Husayn) of Mecca had been appointed guardian of the holy places of Islam by the CUP in 1908 after 15 years of enforced exile in Istanbul. He belonged to a Sunni lineage that traced its descent from the Prophet's family and many of his ancestors had held the title of 'grand sharif'. As the effective ruler of the Hejaz region of Arabia, he was well placed to lead a rebellion of the desert tribes against the Ottomans. After his lengthy correspondence between July 1915 and January 1916 with Sir Henry McMahon, the British high commissioner of Egypt, it was agreed that the 'Sharifian' Arabs under Hussein's leadership would give their armed support to the war against Germany and its Turkish ally. In return, the Arabs would be rewarded with an area of independence including most of what is now Syria, Jordan and Iraq, and the whole of the Arabian peninsular, with the exception of Aden, a British colony governed from Bombay in India. The other exceptions are disputed. The sharif accepted some British treaty obligations in Arabia, and a temporary British occupation of Iraq, but otherwise the major exclusion from the Arab constitutional monarchy was a region designated as lying to the west of the province of Damascus. This clearly included the Mutasarrifate of Lebanon but not, argue Arab nationalists to this day, the region that would become the British mandated territory of Palestine (Antonius 1938: esp. 164–83).

At the same time that McMahon was making unclear promises to Hussein, diplomats and other officials in Britain, France and Russia were agreeing to divide the region between Britain and France. The two leading negotiators were Sir Mark Sykes, secretary to the British cabinet, and F. Georges Picot, the French consul-general in prewar Beirut. The precise details of what came to be known as the Sykes–Picot agreement (finalized in May 1916) were overtaken by events, including the Russian revolution in 1917, but it formed the basis of the division of the region into mandated territories by the League of Nations. France would be granted the mandates for Lebanon and Syria, and Britain for Palestine, Transjordan, and Iraq.

In the autumn of 1918, with Damascus in the hands of British and Sharifian troops and Beirut about to fall to the allies, the Ottoman vali (*wali*) or governor of Beirut handed over the government of the city to the mayor, Omar ad-Da'uq, who formed a council of four other Sunnis and three Christians. They declared Beirut for Sharif Hussein, but with the arrival of British troops this government was disbanded and the city placed under military rule. Two years later, in August 1920, the new state of *Grand Liban* was established under the French Mandate, combining Mount Lebanon with parts of the Ottoman districts of Beirut and Tripoli, along with an area — which included the fertile Bekaa valley — carved out from the former province of Damascus. In the meantime, Emir Faisal had been crowned king of Syria by a congress of Sharifian notables in March 1920, but at the end of July French troops had occupied Damascus and Faisal had been forced to leave, eventually taking up the throne offered him by the British in Iraq (Johnson 1986: 22–3).

The imposition of French rule was intolerable for the Sunni communities in Syria and Lebanon. Only the Maronites and Greek Catholics were 'unhesitatingly for France' (Longrigg 1958: 91). Other Lebanese Christians were worried that they would lose ground in government to the Maronites whom the French were likely to favour. Emotionally, the Sunnis and many Orthodox Christians in Greater Lebanon felt part of Syria, and those merchant leaders who traded with Damascus and other Syrian cities were concerned that the new international border would undermine their businesses. In fact the latter fear was misplaced as Syria and Lebanon were treated as a customs union, but it took time for the Muslim merchants to realize that they might be better off within a Lebanese nation state. Most Sunnis boycotted the first Lebanese general election in 1922; and although they participated subsequently, parliamentary democracy was used as an expression of protest rather than a means to government. Periodically there were strikes and demonstrations against the Mandate, and in November 1936 the ratification of a Franco–Lebanese treaty, which prepared the way for independence within the disputed boundaries, stimulated violent confessional riots in Beirut (Johnson 1986: 23–5).

By the 1930s, however, a number of Muslim leaders had participated in government, and members of the Sunni bourgeoisie were beginning to feel that a reunification with Syria might lead to their political and economic subordination to Damascus. As for the Christian merchants, many of them had trading relations with the Arab world and they could see the folly of remaining dependent on France, divorced from other western as well as Arab markets. What was needed was a political formula that could re-integrate the confessionally divided bourgeoisie and create the conditions for self-rule. Among the Muslims it was a younger generation of notables who first began to speak of co-operation with Christians in a Lebanese context. In July 1936, for example, Salah Bayhum wrote a letter to a French-language newspaper, *L'Orient*, calling for an initial but credible accord for 'an effective union of all communities, necessary for the security of our national existence'. Soon he was joined by others; and eventually Riyad as-Sulh, a man recognized as the nationalist leader of the Lebanese Sunnis, was persuaded to settle for Lebanese independence rather than wait for a united Syria. From the late 1930s onwards, political integration developed until it found expression in the National Pact (*al-mithaq al-watani*) of 1943, the year of Lebanon's independence (Johnson 1986: 25–6).

The pact or covenant was an unwritten 'gentlemen's agreement' between Riyad as-Sulh and Bishara al-Khouri, respectively the first prime minister and president of independent Lebanon. Under the agreement, Maronite Christians accepted Lebanon as an independent and sovereign state within the Arab world and gave up their earlier preference for French protection, while Muslims accepted Greater Lebanon and abandoned their demand for a union with Syria. Both parties to the covenant also acknowledged Lebanon's links with Europe. As Riyad as-Sulh said in parliament, 'Lebanon is a nation with an Arab face, that accepts what is good and useful in western civilization.' Under the terms of such a vaguely defined pact, the Christian and Muslim bourgeoisies could agree that while their economic links with Europe and the West were essential, their moderate Arabism would also ensure they maintained their market in Syria and extended their access to the other Arab markets beyond (Johnson 1986: 26).

The central idea of the National Pact, at least as far as the Sunni Muslim elite was concerned, was that Lebanon was a multiconfessional nation that formed a separate part of a wider Arab entity (Hourani 1976: 39). This conception was a direct descendant of the liberal ideas of the nation contained in the writings of Butrus al-Bustani in the nineteenth century and the programme of the Beirut Reform Committee of 1913. Such 'nationalists' had then been essentially decentralizers, wanting not full independence but greater economic and political autonomy within the Ottoman empire for each *separate* Arab province within which Muslims, Christians and Jews would be equal citizens and where government would defend the freedom of the individual.

It was a peculiarly local and 'mercantile' conception of nationality, perhaps particularly in Beirut where most of the merchants of the Reform Committee made it quite clear that they did not support the aims of the secret societies that were working for independence from the Ottomans. They were even prepared to collaborate with the imperial authorities, as for example when a consortium of leading Beiruti and Lebanese families accepted a state land concession around Lake Hula in northern Palestine in 1914 (Johnson 1986: 64–5). And the fact that only two members of the Reform Committee (one a Christian and the other a Sunni) were executed by Jemal Pasha during the first world war demonstrates that most of the committee members were able to convince the Turkish regime of their loyalty to the empire (Johnson 1986: 17–18). This tradition of a moderate Arab nationalism, coupled with a willingness to compromise with the government of the day, continued during the French Mandate. While such nationalists as Salim Salam (see chapter 2, section 3) and Riyad as-Sulh spent time in exile, other Sunni Sharifians like Omar ad-Da'uq (the former mayor) stayed in Beirut, participated in the legislative assembly, and mediated between their followers and the French authorities (Johnson 1986: 65–6). Once it became apparent that a separate Lebanese entity, independent of Damascus, would be in the interests of the mercantile and financial elite in Beirut, it was not difficult for former Sharifians to become Lebanists.

Until then *Libanisme* was an identity largely confined to Maronites and other Catholics. It had a long history. The seventeenth-century Maronite patriarch, Istifan Douaihi (see chapter 3, section 5), had identified what he thought was a Byzantine origin for his community. He claimed the Maronites were originally descended from Mardaites, tribes from Anatolia (Turkey) established by the Byzantine authorities in the mountains between Antioch (Antakya) and Alexandretta (Iskenderun) in north-western Syria (now in Turkey). The Mardaites had been settled there in the seventh century by the eastern Christian empire as a bulwark against the Arab Umayyad caliphate based in Damascus, and for a number of years the warlike tribesmen were effective fighters against Arab forces in Syria. In 685, however, a treaty was made between the Byzantines and Umayyads, and the Mardaites were dispersed back to Anatolia. Douaihi mistakenly thought some of them went south to Mount Lebanon where their descendants established the Maronite community (Salibi 1988: 81–5). Thus a myth of origin developed that the Maronites were descended from frontier fighters against Islam, a claim reflected, for example, in the name of the Frangieh militia in the 1970s and 1980s: *liwa al-marada* or the 'Mardaite Brigade'.

After Douaihi, a number of other clerics and historians were to claim an ethnic identity distinct from the Muslim Arabs and the 'heretical' Christian sects. But it was not until the nineteenth century that the Catholic community was seen as intimately rooted in the homeland of Mount Lebanon. As Albert Hourani points out, this was scarcely surprising as it was only in the eighteenth century that the northern Maronite districts were incorporated into the Druze emirate, and only in the latter part of that century that the Shihabi emirs adopted the Maronite faith 'and so provided a focus for Christian loyalty' (Hourani 1976: 36).

It was Bishop Niqula Murad, while on a mission to Paris in the 1840s to gain French assistance against the Ottomans, who first wrote of a *nation Maronite* with an historic claim to the geographical and political entity of the emirate. Murad also claimed a martial Mardaite origin for the Maronites and was scathing in his description of the backward and lazy Druze. He saw them as fit for nothing better than working the soil as peasants, thus neatly turning the stereotype of Druze lords and Maronite 'serfs' on its head (Harik 1968: 139–43). Similar ideas were expressed by Yusuf Karam (see chapter 3, section 5, above) who in the 1860s led a revolt against the multiconfessional Mutasarrifate. The Maronites, he wrote, were 'the sons of one homeland' with 'one nationality' (quoted in Harik 1968: 151).

By contrast, a contemporary of Murad and Karam, the Maronite historian Tannus ash-Shidyaq, adopted a 'pluralist' approach, recognizing that the homeland of the emirate was ruled by an alliance of Maronite, Druze and Sunni families. But he too sought a non-Arab origin for the Lebanese, restating the old myth of a Maronite descent from the Mardaites, and being perhaps the first to trace the history of the Lebanese from the pre-Greek civilization of the Phoenicians (Harik 1968: 145–7). 'Phoenicianism' was to become a recurring theme in Lebanese nationalist discourse, taking its most developed form in the work of the Maronite poet, Charles Corm, published during the French Mandate period. Preferring to express himself in French rather than Arabic, he claimed the Lebanese were directly descended from the Phoenicians and were therefore part of a classical Mediterranean culture, a nation with its own '*formes ataviques de la sensibilité nationale*' (quoted in Hourani 1967: 320). Despite the use of modern languages and the adoption of European ways, Corm wrote, the 'atavistic forms' of an ancient culture continued to inform the 'national sensibility' of the Lebanese, a people who at their heart were also the sons of the church and living in 'the only Christian country in Asia' (Hourani 1976: 39).

The fanciful claims of Phoenicianism were toned down in the more sophisticated notion of 'Mediterraneanism' found in the writings of the person who, as secretary of the committee that drafted the Lebanese constitution in 1925–26, might be said to be the creator of the confessional political system in Greater Lebanon. Michel Chiha, the Roman Catholic banker and journalist, whose sister married Bishara al-Khouri, became a leading member of the post-independence elite. A liberal nationalist, he celebrated the different cultural influences in Lebanon and recognized the need for a pluralist system, although his ultimate aim was to see the creation of a truly secular state. He saw the confessional system of representation as something that would remain, in the words of the constitution, only 'on a transitional basis' (*à titre transitoire*). The various communities needed to grow to trust each other, and the tensions between Arab and European cultures resolved. This could be done if it were recognized that the purely Arab Middle East belonged to the Indian Ocean, whereas Lebanon properly belonged to the Near East lands of the Mediterranean from Greece to north Africa. The Lebanese occupied a special cultural space between the desert and Europe around an 'elect sea' (*mer élue*), the cradle of civilization where the Christian and Muslim peoples of its shores felt or would find a sense of blood relationship (*un air de parenté*) (Hourani 1976: 38; 1967: 321; Yamak 1966: 51–2).

Michel Chiha defined Lebanon in essentially secular terms and was careful to include more Muslim Arab than Christian European countries in his definition of the Near East. But although he provided an inclusive formula acceptable to most Muslims, it was inevitably something that would be more enthusiastically supported by francophile Maronites than Arab nationalist Sunnis. Similarly, the Sunni elite's limited Arabism was more acceptable to Muslims than to Christians who tended to look west to Europe rather than east to Damascus and Baghdad. So while Bishara al-Khouri and his brother-in-law could use Mediterraneanism as a counter to the extreme francophilia of a Maronite leader like Emile Eddé — the president of Lebanon between 1936 and 1941, and a man much more fluent in French than Arabic — they could not necessarily win the hearts and minds of the Sunni community. And while Riyad as-Sulh and other moderate Sunni leaders could stress their loyalty to the 'merchant republic', the Maronite Lebanists remained worried about a Muslim cultural and emotional attachment to the Arab world — which in the case of some Sunni merchants, for example, involved marriages with leading families in places like Damascus and Jerusalem. Most Maronites and Sunnis could agree on the necessity of a liberal democratic polity that would recognize the rights of individuals and include all confessions, and many people benefited from the liberal economy that developed after independence. But asserting liberal values did not fully overcome the differing emotional perceptions that the two communities had of the Lebanese nation and its place in the wider world.

The National Pact came under severe strain in the 1950s when, first, President Camille Chamoun refused to break off diplomatic relations with Britain and France after their invasion of Egypt in 1956, and second, when it appeared that the Sunni 'street' in Beirut, Tripoli and Sidon felt more loyalty to President Jamal Abdul Nasser of Egypt than Chamoun. Then, although the civil war of 1958 was largely a factional conflict between za'ims, the confessional killings demonstrated a continuing attachment to communal values (see chapter 2, section 3). As in 1943, the members of the consociational elite effected a compromise in 1958, agreeing on a Shihabist solution to confessional tensions and the unequal distribution of resources (chapter 2, section 6). But this created new problems when the diversion of development funds to the peripheries of Lebanon led to a growth of capitalist farming that forced sharecroppers off the land and into the suburbs of Beirut (chapter 3, section 4). There was growing dissatisfaction among the predominantly Shi'a Muslim immigrants to the city and, because they were now divorced from the za'ims and clientelist structures of their villages, many were recruited by radical parties backed by the Palestinian commandos. Some members of the Sunni middle class and sub-proletariat were similarly attracted to the cause of the Palestinians, and a number of these joined Nasserist groups that expressed their economic and political grievances. In response, the Maronites began to fear the 'state within a state' that the Palestinians had created and which appeared to be undermining the Muslims' loyalty to the National Pact (chapter 2, section 6).

Prior to the civil war, the increasingly violent conflicts of the early 1970s were closely associated with a series of strikes and demonstrations by factory workers, bakers, bank employees, teachers and students in Beirut, by share-croppers and workers in the tobacco industry in southern Lebanon, and by fishermen in Sidon (Johnson 1986: 164–77). With rising inflation and unem-ployment, a secular non-confessional trade union movement grew in strength. But the 'popular classes' among the Muslims tended to blame a system dominated by Christians; and while a few Maronites — particularly some students and intellectuals — joined the leftist National Movement, far greater numbers were drawn to their communal organizations. Such Maronites feared the loss of the privileges of patronage that stemmed both from Maronite control of the presidency and other high offices of state (such as the heads of the army and intelligence apparatus) and from a Christian dominance of large parts of the commercial and financial sectors of the economy.

It was a concern about the activities of the Palestinian commando groups that led to the Phalangists' break from the Shihabist coalition in parliament and their co-operation in the 1968 election with the other Maronite parties: Camille Chamoun's Liberal Nationalists (*hizb al-wataniyyin al-ahrar*) and Raymond Eddé's National Bloc (*al-kutla al-wataniyya*). Chamoun and Eddé had long resented the Phalanges party's support for the Shihabists. Camille Chamoun was thoroughly opposed to the latter because they were mostly made up of his former enemies in 1958, and he saw Phalangist support of them as a betrayal. Raymond Eddé (the son of Emile) had fallen out with the Phalanges party when his brother Pierre, the Maronite member of parliament for Beirut, was defeated by the Phalangist leader, Pierre Gemayel, in the 1960 elections after a campaign marked by strong-arm and intimidatory tactics tacitly supported by the security forces. And both Camille Chamoun and Raymond Eddé opposed what they saw as the authoritarian militarism of Shihabism, one example being their own defeats in the elections of 1964 — apparently as a result of interference by the *Deuxième Bureau* (army intelligence). The reconciliation between Pierre Gemayel and Chamoun and Eddé, and their tripartite alliance (supported by the Maronite patriarch who in 1958 had backed the predominantly Muslim rebels against President Chamoun), reunited the Maronite community, and the alliance was overwhelmingly successful in the 1968 parliamentary elections. Most importantly these developments returned the Phalanges party to its communal roots, and it soon overtook Chamoun's Liberal Nationalists who during the Shihabist era had more fully represented the Lebanese 'Christian ethos' (Salibi 1976: 4).

Pierre Gemayel had founded the paramilitary Phalanges party after attending the Berlin Olympic games in the summer of 1936. As a 22-year-old athlete representing the Lebanese soccer federation, he had been impressed by the Nazi links between physical fitness, discipline, order and nationalism. In 1968 he would write of his experiences in the German capital: 'I was struck with admiration. We orientals are, by nature, an unruly and individualistic people. In Germany I witnessed the perfect conduct of a whole, unified nation' (quoted in Entelis 1974: 46). On his way home, Gemayel visited Czechoslovakia were he was similarly taken by what he saw of the Sokol movement, whose name means 'falcon' with implications of bravery and heroism, and which had been founded in the nineteenth century to promote sports, youth education and national consciousness. Why, he asked himself, were the qualities of 'youth, zeal, strength' and nationalism 'so effectively mobilized in the West and not so in Lebanon?' (quoted in Entelis 1974: 46–7).

1936 was a year of strikes and demonstrations against the French Mandate in Beirut and Tripoli, culminating in confessional rioting after the adoption by the Lebanese parliament of the Franco–Lebanese treaty in November. A few days after these clashes, Pierre Gemayel and his young associates (including Charles Helou, the future president of Lebanon) announced the formation of the Lebanese Kata'ib (*al-kata'ib al-lubnaniyya*), usually known by its French translation, *Phalanges Libanaises*, using a name derived from the Spanish, fascist, Falange (phalanx) party. Also from Spain — this time from the royalist Carlist movement that supported the Falange in the 1936–39 Spanish civil war — came the Lebanese Phalangist motto, 'God, fatherland and family' (*allah, al-watan, al-'a'ila*). Both the Carlists and the Falange represented a Catholic romantic nationalism that accorded with Gemayel's own outlook as expressed in his party's national charter: 'the belief in God and family are the basic foundations of the Lebanese nation' (quoted in Entelis 1974: 69; also see Goria 1985: 45–6 and 55 n80).

John Entelis, an historian of the Lebanese Phalanges, argues that the 1930s 'can be described as the era of "shirts" in the Arab world' (Entelis 1974: 44) when a number of parties adopted the uniforms and militia structures of European fascist parties. In Cairo, the members of the nationalist Young Egypt (*misr al-fatat*) strutted and paraded in green shirts, while their rivals in the Wafd (*wafd*: 'delegation') youth movement did the same in blue. Similar organizations in Syria favoured grey and white shirts, in Iraq khaki, and in Lebanon tan. All of these groups had no real knowledge of the complexities of fascist or Nazi ideology; what motivated them was a strong sense of nationalism and a determination to adopt disciplined methods to recruit young men to the cause. Usually they acted like glorified boy scouts, but they were also paramilitary and they engaged in demonstrations against French or British imperial authority and in violent battles with their rivals, often using sticks and staves and occasionally knives or guns. They developed at a time of world recession and mounting opposition to colonial rule, and when Germany was challenging the power of Britain and France (Vatikiotis 1978: 27). Many of their members, like Pierre Gemayel, admired the order and strength of a people who had been humiliated by the treaty of Versailles in 1919 but had by discipline and effort restored their national honour.

One influence on nationalists in the Middle East was that of India, where the Congress movement's mass civil disobedience campaigns against British rule were having some success in the 1930s. It is possible that some of the 'shirts' in the Arab world knew about the militant Hindu-nationalist movement, the National Volunteer Organization or RSS (*rashtriya swayamsevak sangh*) which, in contrast to the liberal and inclusive nationalism of the Congress, advanced the romantic view that India was Hindu, and Muslims either did not belong there or should accept a subordinate status. Founded in 1925, the RSS was perhaps the first group in the colonized world to adopt the militia as a principle of organization, and its members wore a uniform of black caps, khaki shorts, and this time white shirts (Graham 1990: 16). However, although the RSS clearly espoused an exclusive form of nationalism, most paramilitary groups in the Middle East did not. Despite authoritarian tendencies, these militia parties usually conceived the particular nation that they 'imagined' — Lebanese, Syrian, Egyptian or Arab — to be open to all who lived within the boundaries of the homeland. Only the British and French should be excluded.

The most prominent exception was the Syrian Nationalist Party (*al-hizb as-suri al-qawmi*), whose leader seems to have adopted the title *az-za'im* as a translation of *der Führer*. Founded in 1932 by Antun Saadeh, a Greek Orthodox Lebanese who taught German at the American University of Beirut, the party was also known as the *Parti Populaire Syrien* (PPS) after a French official had mistranslated its name. Later it added the word *ijtima'i* to give a full title of the Syrian Social Nationalist Party (SSNP). Saadeh, the party's 'leader for life', was an admirer of Adolph Hitler and influenced by Nazi and fascist ideology. This went beyond adopting a reversed swastika as the party's symbol and singing the party's anthem to the tune of *Deutschland über Alles*, and included developing a cult of the leader, advocating totalitarian government, and glorifying an ancient pre-Christian past and the organic whole of the Syrian *Volk* or nation. Saadeh had a corporate view of the state, read fascist texts, and was allegedly in close touch with Italian fascists and the Nazis during the second world war.

He also shared with Nazism a racial prejudice against the Jews, not simply as a result of their association with the Zionist project in Palestine, but because they had 'alien and exclusive racial loyalties' that could not be assimilated into the Syrian nation (quoted in Suleiman 1967: 105). The SSNP claimed that the party brought all Syrians together in a secular movement. Its conception of the nation resolved the conflict between Maronite particularism and Muslim Arabism by determining a 'Canaanite' origin long before the Phoenicians, let alone the Christians and Arabs. Also its geographical definition of the homeland included the island of Cyprus and therefore Greek and Turkish speakers as well as Arabs. But despite this inclusivity, Lebanese and Syrian Jews were denied membership of the party, however anti-Zionist they might be (Suleiman 1967: 91–119; Yamak 1966; Johnson 1986: 168 and 187 n23).

In 1949 Antun Saadeh was executed by firing squad after an attempted rebellion against the Lebanese government; but his party continued after him, supporting President Camille Chamoun during the 1958 civil war and mounting an unsuccessful army *coup d'état* against President Fu'ad Shihab in 1961. Its leaders were imprisoned until the late 1960s, when the party split into factions, the dominant group allegedly moving to the left prior to its support of the National Movement in the civil wars of the 1970s.

The SSNP was unusual in its espousal of racist doctrines, and although the Phalangists were to develop an exclusive idea of nationalism in the 1970s they cannot properly be described as fascist. For many years they had a liberal conception of the state, were firmly committed to the democratic process, and declared that Lebanese Sunnis, Shi'a, Druze and Jews were full members of the nation. Nor was the Phalanges party a francophile group. It was actively involved in the independence movement, was suppressed by the French mandatory authorities on a number of occasions and, in the period leading up to the formal transfer of power in 1943, Pierre Gemayel and some 25 other Phalangists were briefly imprisoned along with President Bishara al-Khouri and his cabinet (Entelis 1974: 52–9).

The party's idea of Lebanon was heavily influenced by the Phoenicianism of Charles Corm and the Mediterraneanism of Michel Chiha, and it took pride in what it saw as the distinctive contribution of the Lebanese to European civilization. As Gemayel wrote in 1958:

> Even while they were only Phoenicians, the Lebanese already showed their sense of the universe, their attachment to liberal traditions, and a generosity of spirit and heart so great that it enabled them to love and understand even the most distant peoples. It is thus that they have contributed to the blossoming of Mediterranean civilization in the domain of art, science, religion, and material progress. Western humanism ... owes to them its first foundations.
>
> (Quoted in Entelis 1974: 77)

However, the Phalangists were emotionally the champions of Christian and particularly Maronite Lebanon. After President Fu'ad Shihab took office in September 1958, a new government was announced under the premiership of Rashid Karami, the Sunni insurrectionist leader of Tripoli. Pierre Gemayel condemned what he saw as a government dominated by those Arab nationalists who had rebelled against President Camille Chamoun; and after the kidnap and murder of one of their journalists, the Phalangist militias launched what came to be known as the 'counter-revolution'. A confessional war ensued between the quarters of East and West Beirut, and after fierce fighting and many deaths it finally ended when Gemayel was brought into Karami's new government of 'national unity'.

Clearly the Phalangists were vehemently opposed to Arab nationalism and to any suggestion that Lebanon might be drawn closer into the Nasserist bloc in the region. Nevertheless, many of them were enthusiastic supporters of President Shihab's reformism. In the words of Antoine Najm, perhaps the party's most influential philosopher or 'ideologue', the Phalangists rejected 'dogmatism' and adopted a more 'liberal' approach after their incorporation into the Shihabist regime. 'Whereas in the past,' he said, 'many of the party's beliefs were inimical to non-Maronites,' it became 'much more willing to accept different ideas' (Entelis 1974: 70–1). While still supporting a free and liberal economy, it helped to draft the social security law in 1963 and gave strong support to Shihab's 'green plan' to develop small-scale agriculture in the underdeveloped and predominantly Muslim regions of the countryside. In addition, it proposed a wide range of other reforms designed to promote 'social justice', including universal (and free) primary and secondary education, a national health insurance programme, low-cost housing projects, a degree of state control over banking, and a labour law guaranteeing free collective bargaining (Entelis 1974: 187–9). As early as 1952, the party had described itself as *hizb dimuqrati ijtima'i* (a social democratic party); in the 1960s it began to adopt policies that reflected its earlier claim.

It seems there were at least two factions within the party: one Maronite nationalist and the other social democratic. For some time the latter group was dominant, and the main aim of Phalangist nationalism was to modernize the Lebanese polity and, through the extension of state education and welfare, bind the Muslim communities into a genuinely inclusive Lebanese nation. The rise of the Palestinian resistance movement, however, led to a strengthening of the faction that saw Lebanon as a specifically Christian country. The Palestine Liberation Organization had been formed in 1964, and some commandos had started military training in the hills above Beirut. Initially the PLO was kept under the strict and at times brutal surveillance of the *Deuxième Bureau* (Sayigh 1994: 68–89); but in the aftermath of the devastating Arab defeat by Israel in the 'six day war' of 1967, the various Palestinian factions became far more militant. Yasser Arafat, the founder of the previously clandestine Fatah (*fath*: 'conquest') organization, became leader of the PLO, and commando raids into Israel from southern Lebanon increased in frequency.

In retaliation, Israel shelled and bombed Palestinian bases and Lebanese villages. Even Beirut was not immune from reprisals. In December 1968, after members of the radical PFLP (Popular Front for the Liberation of Palestine) had attacked an El Al airliner on the runway of Athens airport, killing one of the passengers, Israeli troops mounted a helicopter raid on Beirut's international airport. In a short and spectacular operation they destroyed 13 Lebanese airliners. The shareholders of Middle East Airlines (MEA) and other members of the Lebanese commercial and financial elite, Muslim as well as Christian, were thus forced to face the fact that tolerance of the 'armed Palestinian presence' could involve significant financial losses.

Under the informal rules of the 'consociational system' (see chapter 2, section 3), it was up to the Sunni za'ims to curb their followers' enthusiasm for a Palestinian cause that threatened commercial interests. But as a result of heavy-handed state action, this became more difficult. In April 1969 a demonstration in Beirut supporting the PLO resulted in 20 people being killed, and many wounded, when security forces opened fire on the crowd. This provoked a governmental crisis that forced the resignation of the prime minister, Rashid Karami. For some months there was fierce fighting between the Lebanese army and Palestinian commandos over control of the latter's supply routes from Syria to southern Lebanon, and during that time no Sunni leader was prepared to take the office of premier, fearing the loss of support from an increasingly pro-Palestinian Muslim community. President Charles Helou was eventually forced to compromise and, under the terms of the 'Cairo agreement' of November 1969, Palestinians were given the right to police their own camps and districts, thus releasing them from the control of the *Deuxième Bureau* (Khalidi 1979: 40–1, 163–4 and 185–7; Salibi 1976: 26–43; Sayigh 1994: 87–8).

These events, and especially the Cairo agreement, made the Phalangists determined to defend 'their' state by acting as its 'surrogate' (Stoakes 1975). A series of armed clashes between the party's militia and Palestinian fighters in the early 1970s led inexorably to civil war, and when Lebanese Muslims rallied to the defence of their 'brother Arabs' they became defined as the enemy too. When I lived in Beirut at that time, I was told by some middle-class Maronites that the way to deal with the Palestinians was to kill them all — something I took to be a joking hyperbole designed to shock me, but clearly a more fundamental desire than I realized. As for the Muslims, they were the trash swept up from the street, dirty people, either stupid and indolent or excitable and violent. The best thing to do with the Koran was to tie it to a rock and hurl it into the sea. Such prejudices were reflected in a more sophisticated way by the vice-president of the Phalanges party in an interview with John Entelis in 1969:

> [W]hile Christianity in the twentieth century is more spiritual than it was in the middle ages, Islam is today only in the fourteenth century although Lebanese Muslims, less fanatic than their coreligionists in other parts of the Arab world because of their contacts with Christians, are today in the eighteenth century, this in spite of their twentieth century appearances.
>
> (Entelis 1974: 81)

We have come a long way from the liberal nationalism of the nineteenth century, when even after the massacres of 1860 Butrus al-Bustani could call on his fellow Christians to love their enemies. With a sense of despair we read of another member of the Bustani family, this one called Fu'ad, a romantic nationalist who in the 1970s was a director of the Lebanese Front that provided political leadership to the Maronite forces in the civil war. An historian and former president of the Lebanese University in Beirut, he wrote that the attempt to create a *Grand Liban* had been a dreadful mistake. If even his holiness the pope called for a Christian–Muslim dialogue in Lebanon, Fu'ad al-Bustani wanted no part of it. He hoped for a final reckoning when the Christians of the Arab world would flee Muslim oppression and come to the sanctuary of

Lebanon. There they would swell the ranks of the Christian militias and make it possible to expel all Muslims from the Lebanese homeland (Helmick 1988: 312). All Muslims. And how, we might ask, would this ethnic cleansing be achieved? By an orderly evacuation? Or by genocide?

There were willing hands to perform the task. In 1976 an elderly Christian woman decided she wanted to leave the predominantly Maronite quarter of the Ashrafiyya in East Beirut. She was sickened by her neighbours. She had looked down from her window one day and seen a jeep dragging two bloodied bodies behind it: Achilles and his chariot. It stopped in the street and the driver and his accomplices began to dance round the corpses. Then they took out their knives and cut off the ears of their victims. A small crowd had gathered and the ears were passed around. People were smeared with blood and an excitement gripped them. 'It's Palestinian flesh,' they cried. 'It's Palestinian flesh!' (Tabbara 1979: 101).

2. Ethnicity and kinship

Ethnicity and such associated communal identities as confessionalism are, like nationalism, intimately connected with modernization. Of particular concern to us is the change that occurs in kinship structures with a shift from extended to nuclear families. Modernity undermines the extended family and threatens patriarchy, and a number of writers have seen an important relationship between this process and the development of extreme forms of ethnic identification (Brown 1994: 19; Eriksen 1993: 108). Associated with this, the key modernizing developments seem to be rural–urban migration and urbanization. Although many anthropologists and other social scientists writing in this field do not make the links between urbanization, the weakening of the extended family and the rise of ethnic identification fully explicit in their analyses, their ethnographies demonstrate that some form of relationship exists between these different aspects of modernization.

One of the earliest bodies of literature on urbanization and ethnicity was the set of studies conducted in the 1950s in the Copperbelt of Northern Rhodesia (Zambia) by such social anthropologists as J. Clyde Mitchell (1956) and A. L. Epstein (1958). Contrary to the received and conventional wisdom that 'tribalism' would decrease with the development of a modern economy, the Copperbelt studies showed that migrant workers from a countryside where social relations had little to do with ethnicity became far more conscious of their tribal identity in the new mining towns. Cut off from their families who often remained in the villages, many lived in all-male hostels. They faced difficulties, for example, in finding housing for their families and in adjusting to the disciplines of wage labour, and it seems that many of them dealt with the alienation of urban life by forming social relationships in venues like clubs and beer-halls with members of their ethnic group or tribe.

More recently, some of the papers in a collection on ethnic or communal conflict in the Indian subcontinent (Das 1992) illustrate a similar phenomenon. Dipesh Chakrabarty's account of communal riots in Bengal during the 1890s argues that Calcutta had been relatively free from such disturbances during the nineteenth century, but the arrival of Muslim migrants seeking work in the jute, paper and cotton mills led to violent conflicts with Hindus over the issue of 'cow sacrifice' in Muslim festivals. Although Chakrabarty does not go into detail about the breakdown of family structures, he does make the point that, 'In a life characterized by the preponderance of men, unstable marriages, [and] precarious living conditions, ... socialization usually took place along communal lines' (Chakrabarty 1992: 162–3). Similar points are made in the same volume by Akmal Hussain (1992) and Farida Shaheed (1992) in their studies of the 1986 violence in Karachi between Pathans, who had recently come to the city to work in the transport and trucking sector, and members of the local Muhajir community who had migrated to the city during the partition of India in 1947.

Specifying the origins of political violence in the city is a difficult task, and students of urbanization have adopted markedly different positions in relation to the subject. Some early accounts, influenced by the 'Chicago school' of urban studies, mistakenly argued that rural–urban migration would lead not simply to the undermining of the extended family but also, *inevitably*, to psychic disorder, social anomie and political unrest in the city (Cornelius 1969; Denoeux 1993: 15). Later, the work of sociologists like Wayne Cornelius (1974; 1975), who investigated the squatter settlements around Mexico City, showed how migrants in fact tended to be politically conservative and economically adaptive, devoting their time to finding work and accommodation, and then to improving their socioeconomic status. Based largely on the experience of Latin American cities, a new conventional wisdom emerged in the literature during the 1970s and 1980s. This emphasized the way political mobilization among the urban poor worked with, not against, the grain of established systems (Bienen 1984; Nelson 1979; 1987). Popular leaders of family, ethnic and patron–client networks were seen as conservative bulwarks against radical politics, and skilled negotiators for housing, jobs and other services. Then in the early 1990s, in a book on 'urban unrest' in Egypt, Iran and Lebanon, Guilain Denoeux (1993) took issue with this approach and demonstrated that under certain conditions 'informal networks' in the city could become 'destabilizing forces' and lead to radical opposition movements (militant Islam in Egypt), revolutionary politics (Iran) or ethnic conflict (Lebanon).

One key determinant of moderate politics among the urban poor seems to have been a sensitive and adaptable provision of patronage either by the state itself or by informal networks that the state assisted. Wayne Cornelius (1975; 1977), for example, made this quite clear in his work on Mexico City. In the 1970s, the governing Institutionalized Revolutionary Party (PRI) facilitated sophisticated patronage networks that helped migrants gain secure rights to their squatter settlements, and to water and electricity supplies. Leaders of the settlements were then co-opted as brokers by the PRI, and made responsible for the control of their followers and for the delivery of votes during elections. A similar clientelist system worked surprisingly well for the indigenous population in Beirut (see chapter 2, esp. section 6). It was not, however, adaptive or sensitive to the needs of migrants who found themselves excluded from the city's established patron–client networks. This was largely a result of an oddity in the Lebanese electoral law — presumably designed to strengthen conservative rural leadership — that people should vote not in the constituency where they lived, but where they had been born (Denoeux 1993: 115–16). With limited supplies of patronage, urban za'ims would not help those who could not vote for them (Johnson 1986: 94) and, as we shall see, many Maronite and Shi'a migrants responded to their exclusion by seeking patronage and other help from radical, sectarian, confessional organizations.

Communal violence is not confined to the city, and we have seen in the previous chapter how in Lebanon modern confessional warfare was first manifested in a rural setting. But it is significant that in India, for example, the increase in communal conflict (first between Hindus and Muslims and later between Hindus and Sikhs), which started in the late 1960s and became a relatively serious problem in the 1980s, occurred mainly in urban centres and only later (in the 1980s) spread to rural areas (Chhachhi 1991: 150–1). Having said that, however, it is also important to recognize that urban communal conflict in India was not confined to recent migrants from the countryside. Many Hindu–Muslim riots in the 1970s and 1980s seem to have been the result of Muslim entrepreneurs from established urban families moving into areas of economic activity that threatened similarly established Hindu businesses (Chhachhi 1991: 151). Nevertheless, in seeking an explanation for what appears to be a predominantly urban phenomenon, it is instructive to take note of the consequences of rural–urban migration.

To summarize an argument that is developed below, the move to the city tends to break the link between men and their rural extended families, and the ethnic group can provide a 'substitute family' that helps recent migrants make the transition to urban life, not just in the material provision of housing, jobs and other patronage services, but also in the moral promotion of emotional security. When families are re-established in the city, they tend to take a nuclear or only partially extended form. The patriarchal head of the urban family then finds himself in a difficult and emotionally uncertain role, responsible as the family's provider and protector of its public image. He has to operate in a competitive economic environment, and he fears the consequences of failing to provide a sufficient income to support his wife and children. He also fears that his family might become morally corrupted by the city and he imposes a strict repression on his wife and children to control their sexuality and general behaviour. This repression is in some respects similar to that which existed in the rural extended family, but in the city there are more opportunities for filial and marital rebellion and the responsibility for patriarchal control falls more heavily on the shoulders of the paterfamilias instead of being shared among the elders of the clan. This, then, is a new form of patriarchy, related to that which Hisham Sharabi (1988) calls 'neopatriarchy' (see section 5 below). I argue that ethnic or romantic nationalism helps resolve the contradictions within the 'sexually repressive family' by defining roles: first, for patriarchs who control the family as the ethnic leader dominates the 'nation'; second, for women who are elevated as 'mothers of the nation'; and third, for young men who become fighters for the nation's honour.

A very clear example of the link between urbanization, family crisis and ethnicity is found in modern Lebanon. Maronites first migrated to Beirut in large numbers during the late nineteenth century, and by the time of independence many were fully integrated in the social and political life of the city, living in such quarters as al-Ashrafiyya in East Beirut. In the 1950s, however, more Maronites came from Mount Lebanon and began to settle in the suburbs, creating a new area of settlement at Ayn ar-Rummaneh in orange groves to the south-east of the city (Salibi 1976: 9). Land shortage on the intensively farmed Mountain, and expanding opportunities in Beirut's trading and banking sectors, led to the growth of the Christian community in the city and its suburbs. But while these new migrants usually found work and housing, many felt excluded from the established patronage networks in East Beirut and were attracted to a Phalanges party that represented a predominantly lower-middle-class and Maronite interest. Significantly, this party also laid great emphasis on linking familial, nationalist and confessional values as expressed, for example, in its motto: 'God, fatherland and family'.

As one of the Phalanges party's theorists, Jamil Jabr al-Ashqar, wrote in 1949, the spirituality that stems from a belief in God 'raises society above itself' and 'constrains lust, and fosters a moralistic sense' that is an essential 'pillar' of the nation. The family is the 'cornerstone of all social action', promoting 'reverence, love and devotion' and providing the basic unit or building-block of the nation (Entelis 1974: 69–70). The necessity to contain lust is of immense significance to an argument about the patriarchal and sexually repressive family that I develop later. Here, however, we should note that in the 1950s many members of the Phalanges party had a familial and confessional conception of the nation. Although Phalangist ideologues often avoided specific references to Christianity, it is most likely that when a party whose membership was overwhelmingly Catholic referred to God it was the Christian deity that appeared in the members' imagination.

After the 1950s, the next wave of immigration to Beirut was predominantly Shi'a Muslim. During the 1960s over 100,000 people were forced to leave agriculture (Nasr 1978: 10) and most of them settled in the suburbs of Beirut. This was initially a result of landlords in the Shi'a periphery of Lebanon mechanizing their estates and expelling their sharecroppers, although the increasing frequency of Israeli reprisal raids against Palestinian bases in the south added to the exodus. More Shi'a moved to Beirut in the 1970s. A majority came from southern Lebanon, from where between 1960 and 1975 something like 60 per cent of the population had migrated. Migrants from the south and the Bekaa valley swelled the Shi'a community of the *hizam al-bu'us* or 'belt of misery' around the city to an estimated 315,000 in 1975, approximately a third of the total population of Greater Beirut (Nasr 1985: 11; Sayigh 1994: 164). Forced to settle in slums and shantytowns where they faced unemployment and great poverty, some Shi'a migrants were recruited into leftist movements, while a few — especially those who lived in Palestinian 'camps' or districts — joined one or other faction of the PLO. Most, however, were not so actively political, and amongst them there developed a greater consciousness of themselves as part of a somewhat amorphous mass of Shi'a, uprooted from their homes and adjusting to the difficulties of urban life.

In the suburbs of Beirut, Shi'a from southern Lebanon met their coreligionists from the Bekaa, and for perhaps the first time both groups began to 'imagine' themselves as part of the same community. This new identity was encouraged by some members of a Shi'a intelligentsia who had benefited from the expansion of state education during the Shihabist regimes of the 1960s. Such people as lower-level civil servants and teachers in government schools provided a new intellectual leadership that had been lacking in pre-Shihabist agrarian society where the provision of educational opportunity had been severely limited.

At first many of these educated Shi'a were attracted to socialist or communist parties, and the emerging communal consciousness was largely confined to a popular and growing interest in religious ritual. The annual festival of Ashura, for example, became increasingly central to a Shi'a urban identity. Ashura takes its name from the tenth day of the Muslim month of Muharram. On that day in

680 AD Husayn, the son of Ali and grandson of the Prophet Muhammad, was defeated and killed at Karbala in Iraq. The Sunni Caliph Yazid's forces also slaughtered the small band of soldiers who accompanied Husayn and captured their women and children. This ended the claims of the *shi'a* (party or faction) of Ali to the caliphate, and the martyrdom of Husayn and the dispersion of his followers can be said to have marked the beginning of a separate Shi'a sect within Islam. Shi'a remember this catastrophic event by processions of sorrow held during the first days of Muharram during which men and boys beat and cut themselves with chains and knives, culminating on the tenth day in performances of a passion play enacting the events of Karbala.

The developing importance of this festival is indicated in the words of a Lebanese Shi'a divine and former judge (*qadi*) in the shari'a religious court in Beirut. Interviewed by Fuad Khuri in 1982, he talked about how Ashura came to promote Shi'a consciousness not only in Beirut but, later, in the countryside too:

> It is Ashura that makes up the Shi'a identity. ... Great is the secret of Ashura: it keeps us going. ... Early in my career, as *qadi*, I used to address the brethren ... during the last three days of Ashura. Today, I spend more than four months working on Ashura commemorations; it is a continuous job for me. I go to Najaf [a Shi'a centre in Iraq] and sometimes to Iran to recruit speakers, approach the rich to subsidize local commemorations, and encourage Shi'a villages and towns to organize for Ashura rituals.
>
> (Khuri 1990: 187)

Ashura is a commemoration of martyrdom (*istishhad*), a central concept in the Shi'a religion. In Arabic the word for martyr (*shahid*) also means 'one who bears witness', and as it developed in Beirut during the 1960s and 1970s Ashura became a ritual of rebellion and renewal. Rather than simply mourning the deaths of Husayn and his companions, it also celebrated their lives and held them up as an example to the deprived and excluded Shi'a people in the suburbs of the city. In the countryside Ashura had originally been celebrated in a rather modest way; and the passion play was more a village festival than an assertion of Shi'a identity, to the extent that Christian villagers would sometimes take minor roles in it. In the city such 'ecumenicism' was rare. The processions, plays and speeches were a form of confessional mobilization, and although Christians might have been invited to join the audience, they were there as guests not participants (Khuri 1990: 45).

The leader of this popular Shi'a mobilization was the head of the religious hierarchy, the Imam Musa as-Sadr. In March 1974 he organized a mass rally outside the town of Baalbeck in the Bekaa valley. Close to 100,000 Shi'a from all parts of Lebanon attended, many of them carrying Kalashnikov automatic rifles, and some of them rocket launchers. In a speech punctuated by a militant and jubilant firing of guns into the air, the Imam told the crowd that 'arms are an ornament of men' (Salibi 1976: 78), and he called on his followers to rise up against the tyranny that oppressed them even if it meant paying with their blood as martyrs to the cause. Later Musa as-Sadr's Movement of the Deprived (*harakat al-mahrumin*) formed its own militia called Amal (from the Battalions of the Lebanese Resistance, or *afwaj al-muqawama al-lubnaniyya* which gives the acronym *amal* or 'hope').

The imam's use of martial rhetoric was apparently designed to promote a sense of communal pride and honour, not to incite an actual rebellion, for he was in fact someone who wanted to negotiate rather than force better conditions for his community. No doubt he intended negotiating from a position of armed strength, but he remained broadly neutral during the early rounds of the civil war and tried to contain the conflict. This might explain why he disappeared while on a visit to Libya. In August 1978 he and an aide had gone there for discussions with Colonel Mu'ammar Qadhafi. Although the Libyan authorities claimed the two men had left on a flight to Rome, they never arrived. The implication was that either the Libyan leader or some of his lieutenants had wanted to eliminate an influential man who was urging restraint in Lebanon. Whatever the truth of the matter, the 'vanished' or 'hidden' imam (see chapter 2, section 7) became a powerful Shi'a symbol, and Amal became a key player in the late 1970s and throughout the 1980s, often fighting pro-Libyan Sunnis whom they blamed for their leader's 'martyrdom' (Ajami 1986; Norton 1987).

In his studies of Maronite and Shi'a migrants in Beirut, Fuad Khuri (1972; 1975) shows how confessional identity was of little or no significance in the village. Family and clan allegiance was much more central in rural social networks, patronage-distribution and politics. It was only when the rural extended family was undermined by migration to the more individualistic society of the city that confessionalism and recruitment to communal parties developed to a significant extent. The Phalanges and Amal did recruit in the countryside, especially as the civil wars progressed; but they were initially urban movements and appealed mainly to relatively recent migrants to Beirut who found it difficult to find patrons to assist them. Registered to vote in their natal villages, migrants were not able to get help from the established za'ims of the city who reserved their patronage for their electors. So in one sense, migrants were attracted to communal parties because these organizations were prepared to offer assistance in finding jobs, housing and education.

Tewfik Khalaf (1976: 45) explained in the mid-1970s how 'the Phalange party has played a great role in establishing patronage relations and offering services ... on a supra-family, supra-zaim, supra-regional basis, in other words, on a true communal basis, thus increasing tremendously the cohesion of the community'. He then went on to compare this with the Communist Party's recruitment of Shi'a in the early 1970s, which was largely based on an ideological appeal directed against the Lebanese system. This, Khalaf argued, had a 'revolutionary and de-structuring effect' that he saw as a politically pro-gressive and secularizing development. But this was precisely why the left failed to keep Shi'a support beyond the mid-1970s. It was all very well adopting a moral stance over social inequality and exploitation; but without the means to earn a living and provide for one's family, the certainties and comforts of a socialist ideology were luxuries that few Shi'a could afford for a sustained period of time. Amal, on the other hand, had access to money donated by the Shi'a *émigrés* business communities in West Africa and Latin America, and perhaps more significantly by returned emigrants who felt themselves excluded from the Lebanese establishment. Bringing these disaffected *nouveaux riches* together with Shi'a intellectuals who provided an ideology and programme, and with young unemployed men who became the foot soldiers of the militia, Amal eventually became an effective communal organization like the Phalanges, using its funds to provide patronage to the poor in the slums of Beirut (Johnson 1986: 171–2).

What made the Phalanges and Amal so successful, however, was their ability to appeal to people's values as well as their material needs. Their programmes of romantic ethnic nationalism filled the moral vacuum created by the break from the ordered world of rural extended-kinship structures and, as we shall see, they also helped to resolve what were difficult tensions within the urban nuclear family.

The widespread adoption of ethnic identities as a partial substitute for kinship organization contributes to David Brown's discussion of ethnicity as an 'analogy' of the family (Brown 1994: xviii and 17–19) and Thomas Eriksen's of nationalism as 'metaphoric kinship' (Eriksen 1993: 107–8). What these and other authors are getting at is not just the way romantic nationalists talk about homelands as 'motherlands' or leaders as 'fathers' but the way they often identify their ethnic community as ascriptive and bound together by common descent. Such communal groups as Hindus and Muslims in India, or Maronites and Shi'a in Lebanon, are not absolutely endogamous but they are so as an ideal.

In Lebanon, marriages between Maronite and Greek Catholics, for example, are acceptable, between Maronites and Orthodox Christians less so, and between Maronites and Muslims virtually anathema. In 1970 only 10 per cent of Christian marriages involved a union between different Christian communities, and marriages between Christians and Muslims were 'statistically insignificant' (Hanf 1993: 81). In the mid-1980s the figures were similar. In a study of 1224 new-born children conducted at Beirut's American University hospital in 1984–85, 89 per cent of the babies had parents of the same sect (Maronite, Sunni, and so on), 9 per cent had parents from different sects but the same overall confession (Christian or Muslim), and only 2 per cent had one parent who was Christian and one Muslim (Khlat 1989: 44). On the rare occasions when Christian–Muslim marriages occurred outside the small liberal elite, the offending couple were often ostracized by their respective communities and there were some cases of young women being killed by their male relatives to prevent such an abhorrent union.

In many different parts of the world, the romantic ethnic community is 'imagined' and interpreted as a replication and, in some sense, an actual extension of the family via such other communities as clan, caste, tribe and, very significantly, sect or confession. Even where other aspects of the ethnic group such as language or a distinctive national history are perhaps more significant, religious confession is often important as well. Thus Sinhala and Tamils in Sri Lanka are differentiated by their respective allegiances to Buddhism and Hinduism as well as language, Greeks and Turks in Cyprus by Christianity and Islam, and Arabs and Israelis by Islam and Judaism. Insofar as these confessions are endogamous communities, then family relations can easily be imagined as extending into the religiously defined ethnic group. Also, the colonial or imperial experience of these groups often established the principle that personal or family law governing marriage, divorce and inheritance should be based on religious precepts. The British codified Hindu, Muslim and Buddhist personal law in India, and the Ottomans left such matters to the separate legal systems of the Muslim qadis, or religious judges, and the courts of the various Christian and Jewish millets (from the Arabic *milla*, 'community'; see chapter 1, section 1).

Such systems of religious law have usually survived in one form or another to the present day. The influence of secular ideas has meant that some aspects of personal status have been reformed. In the Middle East and Indian subcontinent, for example, laws limiting polygyny and the Muslim husband's right to immediate divorce by repudiation (*talaq*) were introduced in many countries during the 1950s and 1960s (Coulson and Hinchcliffe 1978). Nevertheless, laws governing key aspects of family life remain largely religious and help to reinforce the already powerful links between the confessional ethnic community and the kinship groups of which it is imaginatively composed.

As Erich Fromm (1955: 43–5) pointed out in relation to romantic forms of nationalism in Europe, ethnic identities are formed by people linked together by 'ties of blood that give man a sense of rootedness and belonging'; they respond to 'a deep craving ... to fight against being torn away from nature, from mother, blood and soil'. Fromm argued that the nationalism of Nazi Germany and other extreme forms of ethnic identification were a neurotic condition induced by the helplessness and despair that people suffered in modern society. Precapitalist agrarian society had provided a sense of community, order and security, while the freedom of the individual under capitalism was often a frighteningly lonely experience. In an attempt to rediscover community and order, people were attracted to a form of social identity that closely resembled the only model they had of full security: 'the tie of the child to the mother' (Fromm 1955: 43). Although organizations like the church could perform this function, it was often the nation that best provided an object of love and devotion to which the individual could submit and conform.

In a well-known passage, Fromm summarized his argument:

Man — freed from traditional bonds of the medieval community, afraid of the new freedom which transformed him into an isolated atom — escaped into a new idolatry of blood and soil, of which nationalism and racism are the two most evident expressions. ... Those who are not 'familiar' by bonds of blood and soil (expressed by common language, customs, food, songs, etc.) are looked upon with suspicion, and paranoid delusions about them can spring up at the slightest provocation. This incestuous fixation not only poisons the relationship of the individual to the stranger, but to the members of his own clan and to himself. The person who has not freed himself from the ties to blood and soil is not yet fully born as a human being; his capacity for love and reason are crippled; he does not experience himself nor his fellow man in their — and his own — human reality. Nationalism is our form of incest, is our idolatry, is our insanity.

(Fromm 1955: 59–60)

The last sentence encapsulates Fromm's insistence that romantic nationalism is a neurosis, replicating in part an incestuous fixation on the nationalist's mother. The psychoanalytic element of the argument is asserted rather than fully demonstrated, but it is significant that the discourse of nationalism often refers to the nation or homeland as a mother, not only in European languages (as in 'motherland') but throughout the world. The Islamic 'nation' or community is called the *umma* in Arabic (and the United Nations *al-umam al-muttahida*), derived from the same root as *umm* or mother. India has often been referred to as 'Mother India' or the 'Mother Goddess' (Chhachhi 1989: 569) and its long-serving Prime Minister, Indira Gandhi, was called the 'Mother of the Nation'. After Mrs Gandhi was assassinated by two Sikh security guards in 1984, Hindus in Delhi inflicted a violent reprisal on the local Sikh community in which hundreds of people were hacked or burnt to death. As the Hindus went about their grisly business, some were heard to chant, '*khun ka badla khun: tumne hamari ma ku mara*', 'Blood in vengeance of blood: you killed our mother' (Srinivasan 1992: 314).

The neo-Marxist psychoanalyst, Wilhelm Reich, a contemporary and associate of Erich Fromm in 1930s Berlin, also saw a crucial relationship between nationalism and motherhood. In his account of Nazism he wrote: 'In their *subjective emotional core* the notions of *homeland and nation are notions of mother and family*. Among the middle classes the mother is the homeland of the child, just as the family is the "nation in miniature"' (Reich 1970: 57, emphases in the original). The link made here between mother and *homeland* (or in Fromm's terms, between blood and *soil*) is significant. Ethnic or romantic nationalisms are usually replete with myths of origin making exclusive claims to a particular territory that has historically been the home of the national family. Hindu romantic nationalists believe that India is their homeland not the Muslims', and many Maronites in Lebanon see the Mountain as peculiarly 'theirs'. In making these claims, individuals supplement their 'escape' into a submissive 'idolatry of blood' (Fromm 1955: 59) with the emotional and physical security of hearth and home. As we have seen, Erich Fromm considered such romantic nationalism to be an 'incestuous fixation'. If as he and others have suggested it is a neurotic response to modernization, then as David Brown (1994: 17) points out 'it is a particularly widespread neurosis'.

This discussion helps to explain the emotional appeals of romantic ethnicity over other ideologies, such as socialism for example. We might argue that the secular 'socialisms' of President Nasser in Egypt or of Prime Minister Nehru in India ultimately lost their appeal because they failed to deliver significant economic benefits to large sections of the population. But there is also the important point that, despite their appeals to brotherhood, socialists are often intolerant of kinship organization and interpret 'the family as an obstacle to class consciousness' (Joseph 1978: 29). Thus, although Lebanese communist and socialist parties had some success in recruiting disaffected Shi'a during the early 1970s, they were ultimately unable to maintain such support, not only because they did not have access to patronage but also as a result of their failure to respond to the emotional needs of their supporters.

Family values are so powerful that social and political threats to them often provoke a romantic reaction. Amrita Chhachhi (1989), in her article on religious 'fundamentalism' in south Asia, provides a convincing argument that

Hindu and Muslim revivalist movements in India and Pakistan during the 1980s represented a patriarchal reaction to the improved status of women that had been a consequence of their increased participation in the formal economy and politics. Similarly, the growing support for Amal in Lebanon can be seen, in part, as a romantic reaction by Shi'a men whose patriarchal role in the family was threatened by difficulties in finding employment and by the ideas of gender-equality propagated by socialist and communist parties.

In Lebanon, the sociopolitical subordination of women was most marked in the Shi'a 'fundamentalist' Hizballah (*hizb allah*: the Party of God). This militia had been founded with the encouragement of Iranian 'revolutionary guards' who were allowed by Syria to operate in Baalbeck and the Bekaa valley in the early 1980s. Financed by Iran, Hizballah provided extensive educational, health and welfare services in the regions under its control, and it competed with Amal for the support of the Shi'a in Beirut. It was heavily influenced by conservative Shi'a clerics and, although it later moderated its theocratic ideas, at the start it was committed to the establishment of an Islamic state in at least part of Lebanon. Perhaps inevitably, Hizballah's attitude to women involved notions of their subordinate status and the need for their seclusion, modest dress, and the covering of their hair with the *hijab* or headscarf.

Threats to patriarchy and to clearly defined male roles are associated with the rise of nationalism, not just in its romantic but also its early liberal form. At a time when the ideas of liberal nationalism were hegemonic or dominant in nineteenth-century Europe, particularly middle-class women were kept in their place by a whole battery of Michel Foucault's 'machineries' of sexuality (Foucault 1976: 159–60). Apart from obvious forms of economic and social control, these included the 'hystericization' of the female body whereby the woman's central being was seen as thoroughly imbued with a sexuality that had to be brought under the surveillance of doctors and psychoanalysts so she could adequately perform her reproductive function within the family. Men were the guardians of women's honour, stern husbands and fathers, and the family's providers. With mass unemployment, and the ignominy of Germany's defeat in the first world war, these male roles were so severely threatened that it is easy to understand why the emotional and romantic appeals of 'national socialism' or Nazism were widely embraced, by the working as well as middle classes, in preference to the modernist leftist alternative (Reich 1970).

Similarly in the contemporary world, those countries afflicted by ethnic nationalism all seem to share a sexual or gender repression. This extends from perhaps rather subtle forms of patriarchy in Northern Ireland and the former Yugoslavia to arranged marriages and the seclusion of women in the Middle East, and even to the revival in north-western India of the ideals of *sati* or widow burning. In most of these societies, there is a pronounced sense of male honour and women's shame where it is incumbent on the male to prevent his women descending into a shameless state of being. Certainly until recently, Lebanese 'honour crimes' involving a man killing his sister or daughter for sexual misconduct were often only punished by a token prison sentence of a few months, and equally lenient treatment of men who 'discipline' their women is found in many other Arab countries (Badawi 1994: 94–5; but see also Younes 1999: 204 ff, and esp. 228–33, which suggests that Lebanese sentencing policy for honour and blood-vengeance crimes differs from court to court, with much longer prison sentences given in Beirut as compared with rural areas).

There is an agreement in much of the literature that there exists in the Middle East a widespread belief in a potentially destructive female sexuality (Hibri 1982; Ghoussoub 1987; Accad 1991; Kandiyoti 1991). Hence the need for constant surveillance to enforce women's modesty. As in nineteenth-century Europe, women's bodies are seen as being saturated with sexuality. The threat is not just to the woman's proper reproductive role within the family but also — through her ability to seduce healthy and 'normal' men — to the very structure of society and political order. As Kanan Makiya puts it in his devastating study of 'cruelty and silence' in the Arab world, 'Women's bodies are deemed simultaneously the font from which all honor derives and a source of *fitna*, or public sedition. That is why Arab tradition feels so threatened by female independence' (Makiya 1993: 298). This is not confined to the Middle East, or to Islamic societies. Similar male attitudes toward women are found in places as different as the province of Rajasthan in India and South African townships.

Amrita Chhachhi (1989; 1991), for example, discusses the predominantly male reactions to a case of *sati* in Rajasthan, in 1987, when an 18-year-old, recently married, widow immolated herself or was burnt by her relatives on her husband's funeral pyre. This act was hailed by her local caste community as a noble expression of 'wifely devotion' and a symbol of the Rajput 'warrior ideals of valour and honour'. Many pilgrims came to pay homage at the site of the sacrifice, and the associated commercial activity took on the character of a 'fairground'. Outrage expressed by feminists, reformist Hindus and human rights groups was interpreted by many Rajputs as an affront to their community; the provincial government refused to prosecute; some local politicians arrived to express their solidarity; and a group of Rajputs established a movement to propagate the ideals of *sati*, a practice that had been illegal since 1829 but which was nevertheless seen as a crucial element of communal identity (Chhachhi 1991: 146).

Chhachhi argues that, when interpreted alongside other cases of patriarchal reaction in India (amongst Muslims and Sikhs as well as Hindus), the events in

Rajasthan could be seen as part of a wider 'preoccupation' with the role of 'single women' who were increasingly being seen as a 'potential threat' to 'public peace', particularly when they might lay claim to their family's property. As she points out, the most common explanations for widow burning refer to the need to control the sexuality of widows and to keep patrimony within the family. Similarly, recent demands by Sikhs for their own personal code of law in India centred around the desire to restrict daughters' rights to inheritance and to strengthen the custom of 'levirate' or the marriage of a widow to her husband's brother (Chhachhi 1991: 165).

Chhachhi's accounts emphasize the interrelationships between communal identification, the assertion of martial values, and the threats to patriarchy consequent upon a limited emancipation of women in economic and sociopolitical arenas. By contrast, Catherine Campbell's discussion (1992) of male violence towards women in the townships of Natal in South Africa starts with an account of what she calls a 'crisis in masculinity' among Zulu males that was not a result of women's success but male failure. Unemployment and poverty in the 1980s had led to fathers being looked down on by their wives and children because they could not provide for their families. Young men lacked role models, and their inability to earn enough money for *lobola* or bride price meant they often felt as humiliated and emasculated as their fathers. Many men were recent migrants from the countryside and were recruited by the communal Zulu movement, the Inkatha Freedom Party. Others joined the African National Congress (ANC), and the clashes between these rival parties were violent and bloody.

The fighting in Natal, which continued into the 1990s, cannot properly be described as ethnic conflict as it involved Zulus killing Zulus, but the repertoire of violence, involving mutilation, rape and pillage, and the exaltation of heroic and martial values, was remarkably similar to communal or ethnic conflict elsewhere in the world. Inkatha considered those Zulus who supported the ANC to be traitors to their Zulu nation and collaborators with an organization that was interpreted as a movement favouring and promoting the interests of Nelson Mandela's Xhosa 'tribe'. Thus Zulu members of the ANC became a hated and despised Other and were punished accordingly (Adam and Moodley 1997; 1993: 121 ff).

Political violence was a 'male preserve' in the Zulu townships, and women were described as 'ashamed' to kill (Campbell 1992: 624). But what is striking about Campbell's account is the level of violence that men directed against 'their own' women. Men regularly beat their wives, girlfriends and sisters in an attempt to control them and reassert a sense of masculinity. One young man said that he liked his woman to 'bow down under [his] power all the time', another that he wanted to see his girlfriend 'always at home, cleaning the house

[and] keeping herself clean and neat'. A young woman said that if her man came to visit and found her absent, he would give her a 'five-finger' in the face when he next saw her. And women generally accepted this treatment as normal. As one said, 'I know that husbands beat their wives, sleep out and refuse to give them grocery money. But my parents have advised me that a wife should be tolerant of her husband, and bear all these problems patiently' (Campbell 1992: 626–7).

This account of familial violence in South Africa suggests that the appeals of a metaphorical ethnic family — in this case the Zulu nation — might be very attractive and reassuring to threatened patriarchs in dysfunctional families. But not all urban families are as violent and repressive as they appear to be in the townships of Natal. In Beirut, for example, they seem in some respects to have been able to adapt to urban conditions relatively successfully and quickly.

The migration of the male worker to the city undermines the extended family, but once he is joined by his wife, children, and other relations, family networks are often re-established. The economic role of the extended kinship group might be attenuated and there is a greater emphasis on the nuclear unit, but in many urban societies the 'partially extended' family does develop as an economic unit whereby, for example, brothers and cousins might work together as labourers on a building site, or open a shop together, or enter the wholesale trading sector and establish a family business in import and export.

The family was certainly an important economic unit in urban Lebanon before the civil war (Farsoun 1970; Khalaf 1987: 146–60). Small manufactories and trading houses were largely family concerns. Even joint-stock companies were often little more than family firms. Indeed the corporation became a way of dealing with disputes over the inheritance of non-divisible property such as real estate and factories. With regard to employment, managers of large scale companies would often recruit their kin as employees, and shopkeepers would employ members of their family. Similarly, kin-based labour gangs were common in factories and on building sites, as were family credit networks in the commercial sector. As the Lebanese sociologist Samih Farsoun wrote in an article at the end of the 1960s, 'A basic value-belief that is still current in Lebanon is that of "amoral familism" [and] suspicion of the outsider and trust of the family in-group are strong social-cultural patterns' (Farsoun 1970: 265).

The step from such familism to confessionalism was a short one. Lebanese personal law was confessional law; education was provided by missionary and indigenous religious foundations; and medical and welfare services were distributed by confessional charities. Laws that governed marriage, divorce and inheritance, and structures that educated the family's children, and tended its sick and needy, were usually confessional. The religious sect socialized and cared for the Lebanese family, and the two structures were bound together by a claim of common descent. Looked at in this way, it might seem that confessionalism in Lebanon was constructed from a base of functioning 'partially extended' families.

It seems that Lebanese urban society was unusually adaptive in restoring family solidarity among migrant communities. An illustration of this was the way many kinship groups sharing the same surname established family associations. These were formal organizations, with constitutions and membership rules, that acted as welfare and benevolent societies. Although similar associations might be found elsewhere, the relatively high number legally registered with the government, and the sophisticated nature of their formal structure, probably make the Lebanese case unique. What is interesting here is the historical pattern of their development. Samir Khalaf's study of the governmental records of family associations formed since 1930 shows that Christian families were the first to establish associations, followed to a much lesser extent by Sunni families (belonging to established urban communities in Beirut, Tripoli and Sidon) and then much later, and in significant numbers, by Shi'a Muslims. This pattern corresponds to the different historical periods when Christians and Shi'a were affected by the disruptive effects of urbanization, many Christians migrating to the predominantly Sunni city of Beirut in the latter decades of the nineteenth century, and Shi'a arriving nearly a century later. Of 108 Shi'a associations formed between 1930 and 1969, 77 (71 per cent) were established in the 1960s. It was not until then that large numbers of Shi'a migrated to Beirut and it is therefore significant that most of their family associations were founded during that decade (Khalaf 1987: 161–84).

Family associations seem to have been one response by Lebanese migrants to the difficulties of urban life. In place of the extended family structures of the villages that were so central to patronage distribution and self-help, the Maronite and Shi'a immigrants to the city established formally constituted benevolent societies. Within these organizations, richer or more influential members of the family or 'clan' assisted those who were less fortunately placed by helping to find housing, employment and education, providing information, credit and charity, and facilitating introductions to other patrons.

These societies should, however, be seen as an attempt to recreate the benefits of extended families, not as evidence for the vitality or persistence of extended kinship structures. Such families were breaking down into urban nuclear units. They might have co-operated in a benevolent association or a family business, but their members were increasingly living, working and marrying separately. One indication of this process was the decline of consanguine marriages in Beirut, documented in a study conducted by Myriam Khlat (1989). In 1983–84 Khlat selected a sample in Beirut of 2700 marriages contracted from before 1940 down to 1983. 675 of these marriages, or 25 per cent of the total, were between blood relatives, of which somewhat over half (379) were between first cousins (matrilateral as well as patrilateral) and the rest between more distant consanguine relatives (Khlat 1989: 49). Of all the sample's marriages contracted before 1940, 37 per cent were between blood relatives. In subsequent time-periods the percentages fluctuated but there was an overall decline. Among those marriages contracted in the period 1955–59, the proportion of consanguine unions had dropped to 25 per cent, in 1970–74 to 20 per cent, and in 1980–83 to 18 per cent. The decline was much more marked among Christians than Muslims. Before 1940, 40 per cent of Muslim marriages and 26 per cent of Christian marriages were between blood relatives. In 1970–74, the Muslim percentage had dropped to 23 per cent, but it rose again in 1980–83 to 25 per cent. By contrast the Christian figure dropped to 13 per cent in 1970–74 and to zero in 1980–83 (Khlat 1989: 46).

It seems that the comparative persistence of consanguine marriage amongst Muslims was in large part due to a relatively stable proportion of that population choosing to marry a first cousin. 14 per cent of Khlat's total sample (including Christians) were in this category and the proportion remained relatively stable over time, with only a slight decline from the 1950s to the 1980s (Khlat 1989: 46–9). Assuming all first-cousin marriages were between Muslims (because such unions are legally incestuous for Catholic and Orthodox Christians), then a substantial proportion — 21 per cent — of the Muslim marriages in the sample were of this type. Within this first-cousin category, the specific form of patrilateral parallel-cousin marriage (between a man and his father's brother's daughter) was an even more stable institution, accounting for 8 per cent of the Muslim marriages contracted in the 1950s, and 9 per cent of those in 1980–83 (Khlat 1989: 50). Reflected in this substantial minority is a residual preference among Muslims for a man to marry his father's brother's daughter. Such a marriage helps to keep property within the patrilineal family of those who practise it, but it also has wider social functions, promoting patriarchal ideas about the importance of endogamy and about the threat to patriarchal authority that comes from outside the moral community of agnatic kin (see chapter 2, section 5).

Despite the persistence of a preference for first-cousin marriage among a minority of the population, the overall decline of consanguine unions indicated a threat not only to the patriarchal heads of extended families but also to the very principle of endogamy. In fact, the only unit in society that came close to a truly endogamous 'family' before and during the civil war was the confession. As we have seen, about 90 per cent of marriages took place within the sect (Maronite, Shi'a, and so on), and probably less than 10 per cent between members of different sects but the same Christian or Muslim religion (for example, between a Sunni and a Shi'a). Only a very small number of Christians married Muslims, and these unions were largely confined to the liberal (and wealthy) elite in Beirut. It is no surprise that the confession became the source of an emotional bonding that was less and less provided by the family.

The transition to city life is difficult and sometimes frightening, and there is incontrovertible evidence that, as well as making use of family associations and other kinship ties, many migrants in communally divided societies find a sense of security in wider networks established within their ethnic community. What is new in the city is not the reassertion of family ties and values, but ethnic identity. As J. Clyde Mitchell (1956) and A. L. Epstein (1958) demonstrated in relation to the Copperbelt in southern Africa, and as Fuad Khuri (1972; 1975) showed in the case of Beirut, ethnic identity was not an issue in the countryside. It was only when people migrated to the city that ethnicity became politicized. In the case of the Copperbelt in southern Africa, this ethnic identification did not lead to violence; but when other factors — such as wider political tensions or difficulties in finding work and adequate housing — are brought in to play then ethnic conflict can be a result.

The 'external' threat of the armed Palestinians was a crucial determinant of the Lebanese war in 1975, but it is significant that the core of the Phalangist militias that took them on had been recruited from the families of Maronites who had migrated to suburban Beirut in the 1950s (Cobban 1985: 117). Similarly, many of the fighters in the 'leftist' militias supporting the Palestinians were Shi'a immigrants. With the prominent exception of the small group or gang called the Knights of Ali (see chapter 1, section 4), they did not usually fight in the early stages of the war as Shi'a communalists, partly because the leadership of the Amal militia had taken the decision to remain neutral. But by the late 1970s Amal was a crucial player, and in the 1980s it and Hizballah fought fiercely for the Shi'a cause.

Despite the arrival of women and children and the gradual re-establishment of family life, ethnic or communal organization continues to be a feature of city politics. It seems that this is at least related to, if not determined by, continuing threats to patriarchal authority and family values. Urban families might adopt complex mechanisms to encourage kinship solidarity in nuclear and extended groups. Also, patriarchal authority might seem to be more pronounced in the city than in the countryside: the veiling and seclusion of women, for example, tend to be urban rather than rural phenomena (because they are impractical in the countryside where women work in the fields, and because they are a mark of higher status). But the increased surveillance of female and adolescent members of the family in the city occurs precisely because the urban environment is so threatening. When women shop in the bazaar or souk they might meet other men, and social surveillance is much less efficient in the anonymous city than in the close-knit village community. Similarly, although adolescent sons can, for example, be tied into the family's urban business, they might be seduced by offers of a higher salary from a competitor.

As Wilhelm Reich pointed out in relation to Germany in the 1920s and 1930s, the urban patriarchal family is continually undermined by the suppression that sustains it (Mitchell 1990: 178–9). Husbands fear that their necessary but intrusive surveillance of their wives will drive their women into the arms of another. Also, of course, patriarchs might be seduced by those women who adopt a freer lifestyle in the city, and that is dangerous too. Fathers seek to bring up submissive children but, at the same time, they create the conditions for their sexual and other forms of youthful rebellion. And the big bad city is full of temptation. A walk downtown could introduce adolescents to all manner of vices.

Despite the reassertion of the family as a form of social and economic organization in the city, ethnic nationalism remains as a possibly more effective response to a threatened sense of patriarchy. The imagined community of the 'nation' or ethnic group provides an authoritarian leadership model for patriarchs, a highly valued maternal role for the mothers of the nation, and — very significantly — a normatively sanctioned outlet for the frustrations and aggression of sexually repressed young men.

In virtually all cultures, including my own, male adolescent rebellion is associated with a notion of honour. As we have seen (in chapter 2, section 1) some social anthropologists have argued that Mediterranean societies are peculiarly prone to this. The vocabulary and discourses of honour in Spain, southern Italy, Greece, Lebanon and north Africa are or were very sophisticated and elaborate; and the honour code seems to have been more embedded in these cultures, affecting adult as well as adolescent behaviour. But similar attitudes and values are found elsewhere. In many different societies, young men identify an Other who wears different clothes, comes from a different territory, supports a different football team, or has a different pigment in his skin, whom they can demonize and sometimes beat to a pulp on a Saturday night.

Such aggressive values are also closely bound up with petty crime and urban racketeering, and it is significant that the front-line fighters in ethnic wars and conflict are often local hoods and gangsters. Many of the Pathan fighters in the 1986 communal conflict in Karachi were involved either in racketeering in the city's taxi service or in the heroin mafia (Shaheed 1992), and the warlords of Lebanon ran the hashish and heroin export trade, piracy, and various other rackets like protection, real-estate speculation and construction, and the manufacture and sale of fake pharmaceuticals (Johnson 1986: 200–3).

Ethnic conflict is very macho and is often associated with aggressively virile activities. The gangster's or bandit's involvement in it has a dual role. In one sense he plays out a youthful rebellion against the repressive family, and the young men in communal militias or gangs can 'legitimately' engage in criminal activity that would otherwise earn them the disapproval of their elders. In another sense, however, the leaders of ethnic gangs can perform the role of patriarchal godfathers to mafia-style networks that include large parts of the local communities that they protect from assault by the Other. Thus, as we have seen in the case of Lebanese za'ims and qabadays, ethnic gangsters can provide some sense of order in the disordered urban world of familial insecurity and ethnic conflict.

3. Ethnic violence and psychoanalysis

Gangsters and members of the ethnic mafia might be accustomed to violence and cruelty as a result of competition or warfare with rivals. Most people, how-ever, are not. We know, for example, that many of the 'official' rapists in Bosnia felt themselves forced by their superiors to perform on the bodies of women who had often been their neighbours and even friends (Gutman 1993: 68–73, for example). Or at least that was their plea in mitigation. Reading a book like Susan Brownmiller's on rape (1976) makes one wonder if this extreme form of violence against women is not an ordinary behaviour of 'ordinary Joes'. Once men get used to the idea, it is remarkable the enthusiasm they show for the task.

How can we account for the sheer nastiness of ethnic and communal fight-ing? Perhaps we can explain the repertoire of violence symbolically (see chapter 2, section 7): male bodies are castrated to cut away their manhood, and women are raped to dishonour the men who should have protected them. In this inter-pretation the emphasis is on the values of honour and shame, but other authors stress a different symbolism, such as Heribert Adam and Kogila Moodley who have written about political violence within the Zulu community in South Africa. They argue that the mutilation of bodies in communal conflict 'symbolically appropriates' to the killer such qualities from the enemy as 'potency or eyesight or brains' that are highly valued by the emasculated and 'powerless' men who indulge in the violence (Adam and Moodley 1997: 324). Although Adam and Moodley suggest that their explanation might be general-ized to include other conflicts — they mention Bosnia and Azerbaijan — their argument is presumably influenced by the practice of ritual murder in South Africa. Some *muti* (magic) medicine requires human body parts, and so-called '*muti* killings' are not altogether uncommon and seem to be performed in order to acquire fresh and often very young limbs and organs that can be used in rituals to appropriate strength or health, virility or intelligence, or material power and fortune.

Thus in different cultures, different symbolic explanations can be advanced for very similar practices of mutilation. Given that Zulus in South Africa have a martial code of honour and heroism that is similar to the codes found in some societies of the Mediterranean, Middle East and south Asia, and given that most if not all these societies exhibit some form of a crisis in masculinity, it might be argued that mutilation in Natal is more a symbolic reflection of honour and shame than it is of a desire to acquire life-enhancing qualities from a slain enemy. But in a culture in which many people believe in the efficacy of *muti*, a notion of appropriation is presumably imagined along with ideas about shaming and humiliation. As is so often the case in considering the gruesome content of ethnic conflict, we are left floundering around in a sea of speculation. And even if we accept that the notions of honour and shame provide a more convincing cultural explanation for rape and mutilation, are we any further forward? Can such an interpretation really explain what motivates people to do such dreadful things to their Other?

In fact we need not be confused by different cultural explanations for the nastiness of ethnic conflict. We should expect that in a culture where communal fighters believe in the power of *muti* medicine, they would attempt to *appropriate* qualities from those they mutilate, while in a culture of honour and shame they would seek to *destroy* those qualities in the Other. What is important is that the mutilations are so similar, not that the symbolic explanations are different. Different cultures often interpret the same or similar phenomena differently. What we need is an underlying explanation that can explain the same style of violence found in virtually all cultures afflicted by communal or ethnic warfare.

Social psychology teaches us that identification with an in-group in opposition to an out-group is a normal characteristic of human behaviour (Brown 1988). We see this at work in the experiments of Muzafer Sherif (1966) on boys' teams at summer camps, and for ourselves in friendship cliques and factions, in neighbourhoods and workplaces, as well as in formal political structures like parties and parliaments. Indeed, the work of Henri Tajfel (1981) and others demonstrates that people can form groups based on the most minimal differences, and the mere fact of being categorized in one 'minimal group' can generate discrimination against members of another. But although quite ingenious experiments can be designed to show how people form group loyalties very easily and then discriminate against others, this does not help us explain why some groups are so all-encompassing and emotionally coercive that they engage in the rape, torture and slaughter of their Other.

To understand the emotional affectivity of ethnicity, and the horrific consequences it often entails, it is possibly more helpful to turn to the psychoanalysts and their texts about the development of the ego. Competition between groups can be a 'healthy' process, but ethnic conflict involves hatred and, very importantly, *fear* of the Other. Extreme forms of fear are of course a normal characteristic of childhood, whether it be a fear of the dark, of goblins and ghouls, or of parental discipline. And childhood fear, and the effect that this might have on adult behaviour, is pre-eminently the subject matter of psychoanalytic accounts of ego-formation. Whether we accept Melanie Klein's thesis that the ego is a real but fragile identity or Jacques Lacan's view that it is essentially a linguistic fiction, there are perhaps some lessons to be learned from this literature.

Jacques Lacan (1949) argued that the first phase in the creation of the ego comes before the development of language and is the 'mirror stage' when the baby child receives an external sense of a unified self from his or her reflection. It is, however, a misrecognition, and the image of integrated wholeness does not correspond to the child's experience of its fragmented bodily drives and desires. Even before language and social interaction the ego has been set on a 'fictional direction', built as it is on an imaginary identification. And, when it develops, although the ego acts as a defence against fragmentation it is always threatened by disintegration and collapse. Building on Frantz Fanon's interpretation of these themes in *Black Skin, White Masks* (1986, first published in French in 1952) Stephen Frosh presents a Lacanian explanation of racism in which some casualties of modernity are seen to perceive in the actual image of the Other 'a container' for their 'internal otherness' (Frosh 1989: 241). Frosh identifies an important link between Lacan's ideas about the ego and what he, Frosh, calls 'the *modern* experience' of 'multiplicity, contradiction and fragmentation' (Frosh 1989: 232). Racists — or in our terms, ethnic nationalists — experience 'immense terror' when confronted with someone who is so different by virtue of colour, language or culture. They perceive an undermining threat to their 'precarious sense of ego-integrity' that is already fragile because of 'the fragmentation that is central to the experience of infancy and, indeed, to the experience of modernity itself.' Crucially, though, it is the '*visibility* of difference' that 'undermines the abstract sense of homogeneity which so shakily supports the ego' (Frosh 1989: 241).

Melanie Klein (1946) has a somewhat different emphasis. She suggested that first at the mother's breast which represents both a plentiful ideal and a persecutory denial, and later through experience of the external environment, the child learns to differentiate between good and bad, and later between right and wrong. The child divides his or her self into two parts, one that is judge and the other that is judged. The 'paranoid-schizoid' phase is when the ego adopts the defence mechanism of 'splitting' and, as a protection against pain and guilt, projects on to others the bad, unacceptable or destructive aspects of the self.

The important implication is that this process causes children to view some individuals, groups or communities as embodying *the worst aspects of their selves*. The schizoid phase normally ends by the time the child is six or seven years old. By then he or she begins to deal with the good and bad aspects of the self and the external world in a more 'rational' way. Nevertheless, individuals who feel threatened by their environment can always revert to the defence mechanism of splitting and project their frustration and anger on to a socially defined Other (Brown 1994: 9–10; Frosh 1987: 113–29; Kakar 1992: 137–8; Mitchell 1986; Wright 1992: 191).

In his Kleinian account of ethnic violence in India, Sudhir Kakar (1992) shows how in many cases of *bhuta* or spirit possession that he investigated, the evil spirit inhabiting a Hindu was identified as Muslim. One possessing a Brahmin priest, for example, insisted on eating meat. Another wanted to kill her mother-in-law. This served to recognize and bring out into the open the desires and aggression of the Hindu, while at the same time demonstrating to the self and others that these emotions 'belonged to the Muslim destroyer of taboos' (Kakar 1992: 136). Thus the Muslim spirit represented the diabolic in opposition to the values of the rectitudinous and 'perfect' Hindu community. We could say that Hindus possessed by Muslim spirits were in a sense attracted to the demonic Other who expressed their repressed emotions, but the *bhuta* was a demon precisely because it represented the malignant and 'disavowed aspects' of the self. All this suggests that: first, the encounter with the Other is often a terrifying experience; second, it can lead to a demonization of the Other; and third, this demonology might involve a projection of the wicked and destructive aspects of the self on to the Other.

Having discussed splitting and 'projective identification', Kakar moves on to consider 'another set of analytic concepts' related this time to revenge and what he calls 'narcissistic hurt and rage'. The latter are the strong emotions felt when a community that has a developed sense of group identity, self-love, and honour, suffers humiliation or 'narcissistic injury'. To illustrate this, Kakar refers to the shame imposed on Sikh separatist insurgents in June 1984 when the Indian army stormed the Golden Temple of Amritsar where they had taken refuge. During the action many Sikh militants were killed, including their leader Sant Jarnail Singh Bhindranwale, and considerable damage was done to the sacred Sikh shrine. Such injury and destruction represented a tremendous loss of self-esteem and induced a compelling need for revenge to undo and heal the emotional hurt (Kakar 1992: 139–42). The extent of the affront to male honour was vividly encapsulated in the taunt of Sikh women to their menfolk after the army's action. 'Where is the starch in your moustache now?' they asked (Kakar 1992: 140), incidentally reminding us of the importance of this facial adornment for honourable men in many societies in the Mediterranean region as well as India, and of course making a deeply shaming allusion to the emasculation of their men.

Sudhir Kakar's discussion is an interesting interpretation of the emotional *need* for revenge, but he tends to treat narcissistic rage separately from his analysis of splitting and does not take the opportunity to develop the relationship between them. He seems to see the projection of 'disavowed aspects' of the self on to the Other as a characteristic of dominant groups, like upper-caste Hindus, and narcissistic hurt as an emotion felt by people who consider themselves exploited, subordinated or dishonoured. At first sight, his argument is compelling. One reading of the civil war in Lebanon might accord with his interpretation. There is certainly a tendency in much of the literature to blame the Maronite militias for introducing massacre as a strategy or tactic of war during 1975–76, and to exonerate Muslim and Palestinian atrocities as 'understandable' acts of revenge. One could therefore argue that the politically dominant Maronites demonized and sought to eliminate a subordinate Other, who then responded with narcissistic rage.

However, this would be an oversimplification. First, although the numbers killed were relatively few, one of the earliest atrocities in the war was the murder and mutilation of Christian civilians by a Shi'a Muslim gang (the Knights of Ali) in the Bashoura district of Beirut in May 1975 (see chapter 1, section 4). Thus it is not necessarily the case that the militias of a dominant community like the Maronites are the first to indulge in massacre or mutilation. Second, within the 'collective memory' of the Maronites was the narcissistic injury of the appalling massacres of thousands of their ancestors by the Druze and other Muslims in 1860 (chapter 3, section 3). Virtually all dominant ethnic groups have memories of past hurts and injuries inflicted on them and their honour by the Other, and it is difficult to separate motives of revenge from demonology.

Also, subordinate groups in Lebanon demonized their Other in much the same way as the dominant did. In the early 1980s, Samir Khalaf — influenced by the approach of the Group for the Advancement of Psychiatry (1978) — wrote of the 'demoralization of public life' in Lebanon:

> [T]he various warring factions ... engage in mutual debasement. Their media have developed elaborate and effective strategies for such mutual devaluation. Each group depicts the 'other' as the repository of all evil, wicked, and demonic attributes. ... All the unacknowledged and undesirable attributes of one's group are seen to reside in the 'other'. By evoking such imagery, the 'other' is transformed into a public menace, a threat to

security and national sovereignty. In this context, aggression against the 'other' assumes a purgative value. It becomes an act of liberation, the only way to preserve or restore national integrity and dignity.

(Khalaf 1987: 246–7)

Khalaf's account refers to all the major militias, not just those of the Maronite community; and Melanie Klein would have seen splitting and the projection on to others of the destructive aspects of the self as a universal defence mechanism, not merely a response by a threatened but otherwise dominant group. Sudhir Kakar's argument is useful for distinguishing different aspects of ethnic hostility, but surely revenge against the Other for a narcissistic hurt or injury can become entangled with a revenge against the self as well.

If it is the case that ethnic violence is a form of narcissistic revenge on the self as much as the Other, then this helps us understand the sheer nastiness and sadism involved in ethnic conflicts. The superego can be an exceptionally unkind and unforgiving judge. The individual knows, either consciously or subconsciously, that he or she has forbidden sexual and other desires and hatreds, has weaknesses such as fear and cowardice, and is possibly beyond redemption. The ego deserves heavy and uncompromising punishment for this shame, and it is necessary to wipe the slate clean. Hence the aggression directed against the Other who represents the vile and the weak aspects of the self; hence also the aim of annihilating all physical traces of the wicked self personified in the Other.

However we interpret the psychoanalytic origins of ethnic hostility, what is clear is that the Other is immensely frightening. This sense of fear, on its own, might provide an explanation for the general nastiness that accompanies ethnic violence. Specifically, it can resolve the differences between the symbolic explanations offered in different cultures for the mutilation of bodies. In Lebanon (and in places like Bosnia) the cutting away of ears or fingers, the gouging out of eyes, the castration of male bodies, and the removal of women's breasts — and their foetuses if they are pregnant — can all be seen as an imposition of shame on the Other. In South Africa the same or similar mutilations might be interpreted, as we have seen, as an attempt by the killers to appropriate from the Other such valued qualities as 'potency or eyesight or brains' (Adam and Moodley 1997: 324). The culturally specific explanations are different, but the underlying cause can be seen as the same. In both cultures, it is a fear of the Other that is being addressed, whether it be a fear of the Other's superior powers, the Other's evil intent, or the Other's encapsulation of disavowed aspects of the self. Imposing shame and appropriating qualities both serve to eliminate fear, and to enhance the sense of dominance of the killers who have a complete and unhindered power to demean the Other's honour or incorporate the Other's strengths.

A psychoanalytical approach to the study of ethnic conflict is suggestive. The problem is that this is often all it is. As Donald Horowitz (1985: 183–4) has pointed out, the 'individualist bias' of psychoanalysis makes it difficult to use its theories to explain the *social* phenomenon of ethnic conflict. Horowitz does not go into detail about this point, but we need only think for a moment about the focus of the psychoanalytic method to understand what he means. After months of therapy, an analyst might be able to uncover the childhood trauma of an individual patient that led the neurotic adult to kill and maim members of a different ethnic community. But how can such analysis reveal the way an ethnic *group* becomes 'neurotic'? Horowitz does admit that an analytic approach like that of Vamik Volkan might have something interesting to say about ethnic warfare. In his study of the Greek–Turkish conflict in Cyprus, Volkan (1979: 53–73) argued that the dynamics of the Cypriot extended family promoted the reaction of anxiety and the ego-defence mechanism of projection on to the Other. Commenting on this, Horowitz (1985: 184) recognizes there are important connections between ethnicity and kinship, and he agrees we cannot 'write childhood experience out of ethnic conflict altogether.' Nevertheless, he concludes, 'so strong are the structural similarities among culturally disparate groups like the Assamese, the Hausa, the Sinhalese, the Lulua, and the Malays that a focus on culturally conditioned processes like childhood development makes no sense for understanding ethnic conflict' (Horowitz 1985: 184).

Insofar as Volkan ties his explanation of conflict to the particular dynamics of a particular type of extended family found in Cyprus, then clearly his analysis cannot explain the same kind of conflict in Assam, Nigeria or Sri Lanka where different family and childhood development structures prevail. Thus Horowitz is right to insist on a sociological approach that seeks to identify the 'structural similarities' that determine ethnic identity and warfare. I think he is wrong, however, to dismiss the influence of childhood experience in the family to quite the extent that he does. I do not pretend to be an expert on all the ethnic communities that he considers, but I would expect that those which are engaged in conflict share some significant characteristics that have a lot to do with social, economic or political threats to established kinship structures and patriarchal domination. We shall return to this point in subsequent sections of this chapter. Here we should simply note that, despite the manifest differences between particular forms of kinship organization, it is likely that children brought up by authoritarian and threatened fathers are likely to share some latent psychological problems.

A more fundamental criticism of a psychoanalytic approach is that many of its propositions are simply not verifiable. In relation to ethnic warfare, how can we evaluate the different theories of regression to the insecurities and terrors of Lacan's 'mirror stage', Klein's 'splitting' or, if we want to return to the foundational source, Sigmund Freud's 'anal' and 'Oedipal' phases of development? The first problem is the lack of sufficient case material on the family histories of participants in ethnic conflicts. But the overriding difficulty is in formulating falsifiable (and therefore testable) hypotheses. It might be possible to identify and to some extent measure, as Sudhir Kakar has done in relation to spirit possession among Hindus, a process that seems to conform to Klein's theory of splitting. But how can we identify the extent or even the existence of the regression? Other psychoanalysts would situate the Hindus' demonization of Muslims in different theoretical contexts, perhaps all of them plausible but none of them properly verifiable in a way that would help us assess their comparative worth as explanations.

After reading various psychoanalytic accounts, it seems to me that the projection of disavowed aspects of the self contributes more to ethnic prejudice and hostility than such other ego-defence mechanisms as repression, denial and reaction-formation. Lacanian theory, as used by Stephen Frosh (1989), might explain ethnic prejudice in terms of the formation of the reactions of anxiety and fear (and particularly the latter) in response to a perception of the Other's difference. But while fear of difference is an important factor it does not, in my view, adequately explain the ferocity of ethnic conflict, nor can it explain fierce fighting between groups that are in many respects similar. Hindus and Muslims in India, Serbs and Muslims in Bosnia, and Christians and Muslims in Lebanon respectively share a number of cultural attributes, and in the townships of Natal in South Africa Zulus actually killed and mutilated each other. Kleinian theory seems a more useful avenue of psychoanalytic enquiry because of its stress on the projection on to the Other of the wicked and feared aspects of the self. But this is an intuitive judgement, not something that can easily be subjected to the requirements of scientific proof. We seem, therefore, to be left with suggestive insights, such as those in Kakar's account, or discussions at the level of what amounts to psychoanalytic analogy, metaphor or even 'mythology' (Coetzee 1991: 20) rather than explanation.

Some authors, particularly in the 'postmodern academy', have found psychoanalytic metaphors useful in discussing the complex affectivity of ethnicity, an identity that is so pervasive in so many societies and yet so puzzling and at times seemingly unintelligible. One interesting account of Arab–Israeli (and South African) identities, for example, that brings together Freudian theory, literary criticism, political analysis, and to some extent the author's own problems of identity, is Jacqueline Rose's discussion of 'states' and 'fantasy', concepts she deploys in place of 'culture' and 'identity' (Rose 1996: 14). It is certainly useful to question the analytic categories that have previously informed the study of ethnic identity; and as Saul Dubow (1994: 355–6) points out at the start of his essay on the emergence of the academic and political concept of 'ethnicity' in South Africa, postmodern theory does at least alert us to the importance of recognizing the 'ambiguous, contingent, and multiple nature of human identity'.

Nevertheless, I must confess to a continuing attachment to a form of 'logical positivism', which in effect places me in a modernist tradition dating back to the writings of philosophers like Auguste Comte or John Stuart Mill at the beginning of the nineteenth century or David Hume in the eighteenth. I accept that notions of societal rationality and historical progress need to be treated with some scepticism when we look at ethnic conflict. But in the end, I want to understand my subject in some rational sense, as indeed does Dubow who, after acknowledging the contribution of postmodernism, then proceeds to present us with a logical and carefully reasoned intellectual and political history. Too often the contributions of postmodern 'scholarship' are as unfathomable as their subjects of study. Even a psychologist like Stephen Frosh, who considers Jacques Lacan worthy of effort and careful study, makes despairing references to his 'dense prose', his posturing performance as a 'master of manipulation and paradox' and the nagging thought at the back of the mind that actually Lacan's works are 'devoid of meaningful content' (Frosh 1994: 70 and 67).

By contrast, two studies that make use of psychoanalytic theory and are entirely comprehensible are those of Wilhelm Reich (1970) on the 'mass psychology' of Nazism, which was originally published in German in the early 1930s, and A. L. Epstein (1978) who revisited some of his Copperbelt material (see section 2 above) and compared this with other accounts of ethnicity and identity in Melanesia and the United States. Apart from their clarity, what makes these works useful is their attempt to develop a *sociology* of ethnicity that draws on — but does not privilege — psychoanalysis in an attempt to understand 'the powerful emotional charge that appears to surround or to underlie so much of ethnic behaviour' (Epstein 1978: xi). Influenced by Erik Erikson (1963; 1968) who invariably situated his analyses of individual identity in a sociological context, Epstein (1978: xiii) argues that 'Ethnic identity, no more than ego-identity, is neither given nor innate; the way in which it is generated is always a psychosocial process.'

In other words, although early childhood experience and the nature and structure of the family are crucial determinants of identity, psychic development takes place within a social context. In the Copperbelt, ethnic identity was 'a response to the circumstances of urban life' (Epstein 1978: 10). And in Nazi

Germany, according to Reich (1970: 44 ff), fascism appealed to the 'honour' of the lower middle class or petty bourgeoisie, a class determined not simply by its sexually repressive 'family situation' but also by its 'position in the capitalist production process'. As Juliet Mitchell (1990) and many others have pointed out, there are serious flaws in Reich's analysis, but his emphasis on the social reproduction of authoritarian and repressive families has influenced my own approach to the subject of ethnicity, as has Epstein's discussion of urbanization.

What distinguishes the work of Reich and Epstein from that of many psychoanalytic theorists is that most of their hypotheses are falsifiable and therefore testable. In the next two sections of this chapter, I develop my own sociology of ethnicity or ethnic nationalism which, while informed by theories that deal with emotional affectivity, is nevertheless grounded in situational, structural or socioeconomic data that are accessible, and in theories that can be tested against the available evidence.

4. Ethnic conflict and sociology

I start my account of a sociology of ethnicity by considering the two types of nationalism discussed in the first section of this chapter. I shall argue that the rise of romantic nationalism and confessional conflict in Lebanon can, in a sense, be seen as a consequence of the failure of a liberal nationalism propagated by leaders of the independence movement. In particular, Lebanon's liberal regime presided over an uneven socioeconomic development that favoured the Christian communities as compared with the Shi'a Muslims. Confessional consciousness was thus reproduced among Muslims, who wanted to redress economic and social imbalances, and among Christians — especially Maronites — who were determined to maintain the status quo. The uneven development of capitalism can therefore explain the reproduction of confessional identity in the twentieth century. It does not, however, provide an adequate explanation for the outbreak of civil war, which had more to do with the militarization of politics by the Palestinian militias and their Maronite opponents. Nor can it explain the course of the wars in the 1970s and 1980s that were much more 'intra-class' conflicts than a struggle between 'poor Muslims' and 'rich Christians'. Towards the end of this section of the chapter, I develop the latter point by returning to a discussion of the way romantic or ethnic nationalism provided emotional support and security for those whose patriarchal family structures were threatened by urbanization. These people were the middle-class, proletarian and sub-proletarian casualties of modernization in *both* the Muslim and Christian communities. For them, romantic nationalism had great appeal as an ideology that could explain their failures, identify an Other to blame, and provide a sense of 'psychosocial' integration.

Perhaps the most significant difference between my two 'ideal types' of nationalism is that its romantic form is *exclusive*, while the other is liberal and *inclusive*. Although not exactly equivalent, ethnic nationalism, communalism and confessionalism are more akin to the romantic nationalism of German Nazism, and should be distinguished from a liberal tradition that can be traced, for example, to the French revolution and its slogans about freedom, equality and citizenship. According to the inclusive values of liberal nationalism — or what Anthony Smith (1991: 9–11) calls the 'civic' concept of the nation — all citizens who *choose* to recognize the state's authority are full members of the national community, regardless of their colour, ethnicity or creed. The nation is composed of equal citizens united by consent under a rule of law. Although all nations in practice impose immigration controls, the emphasis on choice is important. Romantic or ethnic nationalism does not allow for it: one is *born* an Aryan, a Christian or a Muslim, and one cannot escape from the obligations which that birth imposes. The romantic national community is thus defined less by law and contract, and more by a notion of common descent. The emphasis is on the collective rights of the organic community instead of the individual rights of citizens, and consequently romantic nationalism is associated with authoritarian as opposed to liberal-democratic forms of rule.

The extent of romantic nationalism's exclusivity is most clearly shown in its attempts to deny citizenship, or full citizenship, to groups that liberal nationalism recognizes as members of the nation. Thus Hindu nationalists in India and their Maronite equivalents in Lebanon tend to exclude Muslims from their respective nations. At the very least, they see Muslims as second-class citizens who should submit to the political and cultural dominance of the 'true' Indians or Lebanese. At worst they seek to 'cleanse' the nation by massacre and annihilation. Systematic ethnic cleansing took the extreme form of genocide in the Armenian provinces of the Ottoman empire, when the Turks attempted to extinguish the Armenians during the first world war, and in Nazi Germany and eastern Europe during the 1930s and 1940s. Also, degrees of genocide occurred, certainly in Rwanda, and to a lesser extent in Bosnia and Kosovo, in the 1990s. But similar attitudes to the Other are found in all communal or ethnic wars, and we have seen how they manifested themselves in Lebanon.

It might be assumed that exclusive nationalism in Lebanon was largely confined to those Maronites who defined their nation as a distinct Christian entity, descended from Phoenician or European ancestors, and quite separate from the foreign Arab nation that included the Palestinians and Lebanese Muslims. But a form of exclusivity also motivated the Druze when they fought to defend their 'homeland' and massacred Maronites in the Shouf war of 1983 (see chapter 2, section 7). Similarly, Shi'a militiamen adopted an exclusive stance when they turned against their former Palestinian allies and started the 'war of the camps' in 1985. In the mid-1970s some factions in the Palestine Liberation Organization had worked closely with popular Shi'a leaders, and Fatah had provided military training for the Amal militia. Over the years, however, the PLO came to act like an army of occupation in southern Lebanon, showing scant regard for the local Shi'a inhabitants who bore the brunt of Israeli reprisal raids. When, a few years after the Israeli invasion of 1982, Palestinian fighters began to infiltrate back into Beirut, Amal decided to keep them out; and the fighting in the southern suburbs of the city between 1985 and the end of 1987 was in many respects as brutal and nasty as the Maronite–Palestinian wars of the 1970s (Sayigh 1994: 187 ff).

Exclusivity took different forms in Lebanon. Palestinians were excluded from the Lebanese nation because they were legally non-citizens. Maronite romantic nationalism considered those Muslims who supported the PLO to be traitors, and this served to confirm their status as suspect, if not second-class, members of the Lebanese nation. Ultimately it served to justify their absolute exclusion in massacres. Muslim romantic nationalists, on the other hand, saw Maronites as traitors to the Arab cause, and this heightened the conception held by many that Christians were excluded from the wider Arab nation. Conceptually, the Jews had been excluded as a result of Zionism, and now the civil war in Lebanon excluded the Christians. When tensions between the radical Shi'a government in Iran and the predominantly Sunni regime in Iraq led to the Iran–Iraq war of 1980–88, Shi'a were excluded too. Thus, despite its liberal origins, Arab nationalism effectively became for some an exclusively Sunni phenomenon. And as it did so, it became increasingly irrelevant as a political force in Lebanon.

Violent manifestations of these exclusions were fought in Lebanon. Israelis fought Palestinians, eventually expelling most of the PLO fighters from Lebanon in 1982. Christians fought Muslims in various conflicts throughout the 1970s and 1980s. Shi'a fought Sunnis, taking over the Sunni quarters of western Beirut in 1984 and finally defeating the Murabitun militia in 1985. And then the Shi'a Amal militia fought the Druze for control of different parts of West Beirut. As the protagonists carved out their confessional enclaves in Lebanon, creating a patchwork of 'homelands', rival militias of the *same* confession fought each other for ultimate control of their respective territories. Maronite Phalangists fought Maronite supporters of the Frangieh family in the 1970s, and the Shi'a Amal fought the Iranian-backed Hizballah in the 1980s. Exclusions within exclusions occurred as each faction fought for the soul of its 'nation' and the right to lead it — much like the Zulus of Inkatha and the ANC fought in South Africa during the 1980s and 1990s (see sections 2 and 3 above).

Ethnic exclusivity and its facility for defining a demonized Other is one indication of the emotional content of romantic nationalism. Another is its sense of nostalgia. Both liberal and romantic nationalisms look back to a glorious past, but whereas the liberal form constructs historical myths to situate the nation on a forward path of development and progress, the values of its romantic cousin include the idea that the past is something worth returning to. There is a nostalgia for the rural idyll, a pre-modern society of ordered village communities. It is important to recognize that in its practice romantic nationalism is usually modernist: European fascism and Nazism particularly so. Nevertheless, a key theme in romantic discourse, and a central part of its emotional appeal, is an exaltation of rural values.

This rural nostalgia is expressed in different ways. In *Mein Kampf*, Adolf Hitler claimed to abhor industrialization and urban life, seeing the peasantry as the bedrock of the national community (Hitler 1939: 127–8) and the conquest of the Ukraine as an opportunity to build a society of German peasant colonizers (Carey 1992: 206–7). Hindu nationalism interprets Muslims as being associated with urban corruption, and claims that the heart of the Indian nation beats in the Hindu villages. And Maronites in Beirut often made a romantic distinction between the city and the Mountain (Hourani 1976), and saw themselves as the sons of Mount Lebanon, the personification of the rugged individualism of their peasant forefathers, as compared with the effete Orthodox Christians and slovenly Muslims who were the sons of the city.

Again, the Maronite community seems to be more closely attuned to this aspect of romanticism than other Lebanese confessions. Sunni Muslims and Greek Orthodox Christians, who mainly belonged to long-established urban communities, did not usually look back to a rural idyll. Nor, presumably, did those Shi'a whose memory of rural life was of domination by despotic landlords. But there was some sentimental feeling for the countryside among the dispossessed Shi'a peasantry forced to live in the slums of the city. This was encouraged by their Palestinian neighbours who had a memory — real for some, and imagined by their children and grandchildren — of the hills and villages of their homeland. As some of the Shi'a had moved to Beirut to escape Israeli reprisal raids, they could empathize with those who had fled from Palestine in 1948, and both communities had an idealized notion of what rural life could have been like if circumstances had been different.

The Druze za'im and warlord, Kamal Jumblat, also incorporated a rural nostalgia in his supposedly socialist interpretation of the proper direction for Lebanese nationalism (Joumblatt 1982: 43–4). He starts by telling us:

Lebanon is ... a country characterized by the widest possible cultural diversity, and it would be immensely rich if it came to recognize itself as such. ... The Lebanese formula could have been ideal, if only people had been content with this symbiosis of heart and spirit within a united and traditionally humane nation, this variety within a unity which went beyond multiplicity.

Alas, he continues, the Lebanese became gripped by the 'ideal' of 'modernity' and lost sight of their rural past of tolerance and cultural interaction: 'Many of our problems stem from a misinterpretation of Rousseau's egalitarianism, from a frantic individualism which cuts people off from their cultural or religious roots in the province or the village.' Then, in a manner typical of romantic discourse, Jumblat wheels in an authoritarian and charismatic leader to drive home the argument:

> General de Gaulle also wished for a return to regionalism, to save what could still be saved of [French] provincial or village entities. He knew what to keep from the old days. The village, where everything is on a human scale, contributes a specific ethnic entity. Can a State which lacks such specifications be truly viable in human terms? Can one live in it honestly? Does it allow one to breathe?
>
> (Joumblatt 1982: 43–4)

The lack of a cultural sense of rural nostalgia among the urban communities of the Sunnis and Greek Orthodox is, I think, significant. In each of the cities of Beirut, Tripoli and Sidon there were Sunni militias, but they tended to be relatively small and subject to factional rivalry. No dominant group emerged in the Sunni community of Lebanon that could rival, on its own, the Maronite Phalanges, the Shi'a Amal or the Druze PSP (Progressive Socialist Party). No Sunni organization captured the community's imagination in the way that the major parties of the Maronites, Shi'a and Druze did for their peoples. Similarly, although some Greek Orthodox had a traditional allegiance to the Syrian Social Nationalist Party (which had been founded by a member of their confession), its militia was not a specifically Greek Orthodox organization and was, anyway, a relatively minor player in the civil wars. It seems that the established urban communities of Lebanon were less prone to romantic nationalism and more opposed to the militias that claimed to represent them. They were perhaps more urbane, tolerant and liberal, more aloof from the conflict than those that had a recent or continuing connection with a rural life threatened by capitalism, urbanization and modernity.

More important than nostalgic ideas about the nation's agrarian past, however, are romantic nationalism's exaggerated myths of origin that date back many centuries to a golden age when the nation was born. By contrast, liberal nationalism — especially in the twentieth century — tends to look back to a more recent past to identify the 'collective memories' of the nation's culture. French nationalism, for example, draws heavily on the events and ideas of the revolution at the end of the eighteenth century, and British nationalism is (or was until recently) based on memories of the empire in the nineteenth century and ideas about an island race that stood alone against fascism in 1940.

This oversimplifies French and British nationalisms, but the point still holds that romantic nationalism tends to look back further into history than the liberal form, Spanish Falangism to the Catholic monarchy in the fifteenth century, Italian fascism to the Roman empire, and Nazism to Nordic and Teutonic legends. Arab (and predominantly Sunni Muslim) ethnic nationalists draw inspiration from the Umayyad empire in the seventh and eighth centuries, and their Shiʻa equivalents from their ancestors' resistance to it. Similarly, Maronites 'remember' their quarrel with the Byzantine empire in the seventh century (over the 'monothelete' doctrine), and their later alliance with the Catholic Crusaders and their union with Rome in the twelfth.

Whether it is documented in historical texts, as it is for the Roman, Umayyad and Indian Mogul empires, or recounted in such legends as the Hindu *Mahabharata* and *Ramayana* or the German epic poem, the *Nibelungenlied*, the myth of the golden age represents an exaltation of male martial values. The myths of origin tell stories of emotion, passion and impulse, and they glorify heroism, violence and cruelty. The army of the Umayyad Caliph Yazid, for example, showed no mercy to Husayn ibn Ali and his Shiʻa companions at Karbala in 680: the men were massacred and the women enslaved (see section 2 above). And in 1985, Ibrahim Qulaylat, the leader of the Sunni Murabitun militia in Beirut, issued threats against his Shiʻa enemies in the name of that same caliph (chapter 2, section 7). Similarly, Maronites in the 1970s and 1980s were inspired by their supposed origins as fierce and uncompromising Mardaites, front-line fighters against Islam in the seventh century; and the Frangieh militia in north Lebanon called itself the 'Mardaite Brigade' (see the first section of this chapter).

Such myths, and their re-interpretation in a modern context, stimulated the romantic imagination of fighters and their supporters, providing models of heroic and honourable men whose passion for their cause involved a severe and merciless contempt for their enemies. Romantic histories gave a sense of self and purpose to those who felt threatened by the stresses of modernity. They held up an image of hard and powerful men as an example to those whose everyday life made them feel weak and emasculated. Above all, they created a sense of a noble community, with a glorious past, that bound its individualistic and competitive members into an integrated whole under a ruthless leadership.

So great is the glorification of violent passions in romantic myths that, at their most extreme, they promote the values of martyrdom and a virtual 'cult' of death. The latter was expressed in the bizarre Spanish Falangist slogan, *Arriba la Muerte!* ('Up with Death'), and took its perhaps most extreme form in the Japanese admiration for the *bushido* code of the samurai knights that led to the kamikaze suicide pilots in the second world war. Such values were particularly pronounced in Lebanon among some members of the Shi'a community whose religion was, as we have seen (in section 2), to a large extent centred on the martyrdom of its founders. After Ali, the Prophet Muhammad's cousin and son-in-law, had been assassinated in 661, his son Hasan claimed the caliphate but was forced to withdraw by the Umayyads. Shi'a believe he was then killed by the latter in *circa* 669, as his brother Husayn would be in 680. These founding fathers are venerated as martyrs (*shuhada*), and martyrdom is highly valued in the Shi'a religion. In the 1980s, Shi'a militias — and particularly the 'fundamentalist' Hizballah — marshalled these values in the cause of war. All over the town of Baalbeck, where Hizballah had its headquarters, there were placards and slogans describing the fighters as 'lovers of martyrdom' and urging the Shi'a to seek 'salvation' by dying for their community (Fisk 1990: 468).

In 1983, Shi'a *shuhada* committed suicide when they drove lorries laden with explosives, first in April into the United States' embassy in Beirut, killing 63 people, 17 of them Americans, and then in October into two bases of the multinational peace-keeping force in Lebanon, slaughtering 241 US marines and 58 French soldiers (Fisk 1990: 479–80 and 511–20). In November another suicide truck-bombing killed 29 Israelis and 32 Lebanese at the Israeli army headquarters in Tyre in southern Lebanon (Johnson 1986: 208). These Shi'a martyrdoms later encouraged those Sunni militants in the Occupied Territories who had joined the relatively new Palestinian movement, Hamas (*hamas*: 'enthusiasm', 'zeal', an acronym for the Arabic for Islamic Resistance Movement). Uncharacteristically in terms of their religion's attitude to suicide, Hamas bombers from the Gaza strip and West Bank entered Israel in the 1990s, prepared to die in their struggle to liberate the homeland of Palestine.

The 'cult' of death associated with Shi'a suicide bombers included the belief that the martyrs would go straight to paradise. Mothers could feel joy that their sons had entered heaven, and funerals were sometimes more like marriage or birth ceremonies than expressions of grief. Similarly romantic attitudes to 'noble death' were apparent in other confessions. Although they did not embrace suicide bombing as a tactic of war, their martyrs were highly valued. Photographs of dead heroes were pasted on walls; and some of the more famous among them were virtually canonized, as we have seen in the case of Bashir Gemayel (chapter 2, section 7).

Values of emotion, violence and heroism, partly derived from historical myths of origin, are thus incorporated in modern or 'postmodern' ethnic nationalisms where they are expressed in an extremely submissive love of the nation, an enthusiasm for romantic, charismatic and often cruel leaders, and even a willingness to face certain death in an attempt to rid the homeland of a hated and demonized Other. In summary, we can say: first, that romantic or ethnic nationalism is much more exclusive and therefore more authoritarian than its liberal cousin, which is inclusive and democratic; and second, that the former is more nostalgic than the forward-looking latter. Liberal nationalism embraces Enlightenment values of progress and modernization, while romantic nationalism reacts against them and idealizes a pre-modern past that is usually defined in terms of a rural idyll and, invariably, in heroic myths about a glorious age.

At this stage an attentive reader might ask how such romantic values relate to a sociology of ethnic conflict. Tracing the origins of ethnic violence to a mythological history seems suspiciously like Clifford Geertz's description of primordialism (1963) discussed in the first chapter of this book (sections 5 and 6). Presumably Geertz would have seen romantic notions of an idealized past as a reflection of primordial loyalties and emotions, 'congruities of blood, speech, custom and so on' that are the 'assumed "givens" of social existence' with 'an ineffable, and at times overpowering, coerciveness in and of themselves' (Geertz 1963: 109).

But, however far back ethnic nationalists define their history, we should not fall into the primordial trap and assume their emotional exclusiveness has existed since the beginning of society. Theories about primordialism *reflect* rather than analyse the romanticism of those who stress the values of blood and soil. In a sociological as opposed to romantic sense, modern ethnic nationalisms have relatively recent origins. In the 'colonial world', we can see some signs of them in the nineteenth century when the effects of capitalism and modernization first began to transform agrarian societies in a general and widespread way. This transformation gave rise to varying degrees of ethnic conflict between Greeks and Turks in the Greek provinces of the Ottoman empire, Hindus and Muslims in British India, and Muslims and Christians in the Middle East. In the twentieth century, however, they were reproduced as reactions to a more developed modernity. In a sense, they were also reactions to what might be described as the 'failure' of liberal nationalism.

Once ethnic conflict had emerged or re-emerged in the nineteenth century, collective memories and exaggerated myths of origin began to be remembered, imagined or created. Nevertheless, despite romantic reactions to the rise of capitalism, and despite the use made of ethnic identity to provide a sense of community in an increasingly individualistic society, many members of the professional and commercial classes in the British, French and Ottoman empires absorbed the values of the European Enlightenment and adopted *liberal* forms of nationalism. These emphasized freedom from the imperial oppressor, and equality and citizenship thereafter, and such values characterized most independence movements. Although democratic government gave way to authoritarianism and dictatorship in many countries, independent regimes usually continued to subscribe to a secular and inclusive form of nationalism and were not seriously threatened by ethnic challengers until the 1970s and 1980s.

Many ethnic conflicts in the latter part of the twentieth century can be seen as a consequence of secular nationalism's failure to impose an ideological hegemony, which in part was a result of its proponents' failure to deliver a reasonably egalitarian distribution of economic 'goods' and other benefits. In response, disadvantaged groups demanded fairer shares, and advantaged communities sought to protect or extend their privileges. Despite varying local factors, it seems that ethnic identity has been closely related to uneven economic development.

The growth of capitalism is an unequal process, and in multiethnic societies what would elsewhere manifest itself as class (and regional) inequality often appears to be a difference between ethnic communities. In relation to Lebanon, this point is made particularly forcefully in an article written by Samih Farsoun who traces the history of what he calls 'sect-classes' from the Ottoman millet system (see chapter 1, section 1, above), through the 'uneven Western economic penetration' of feudal Mount Lebanon in the nineteenth century, to the 'more thorough' and 'more severely uneven' capitalist expansion after the second world war (Farsoun 1988: 125).

As we have seen in the previous chapter, the growth of mercantile capitalism in Mount Lebanon during the nineteenth century favoured the Maronites who benefited from the silk trade. In Beirut too, the mercantile bourgeoisie was predominantly Christian. Sharing the religion of the Europeans, better educated in mission schools, and therefore linguistically and culturally more able to form relationships with foreign merchants, Christians established themselves in the import and export sectors of the economy. In 1827, for example, the French consulate in Beirut reported that of 34 local and foreign firms trading with Europe, 15 were owned by local Christians and only six by Muslims (Issawi 1966: 71). In the late 1840s, of 29 local firms trading with England, only three were Muslim and the rest Christian (Fawaz 1983: 97). Christian merchants were predominantly Greek Orthodox and non-Maronite Catholic, but

Maronites were to benefit later from the favouritism of the French mandatory authorities.

In the first half of the twentieth century, Christians possibly enhanced their relative dominance of the economy. In a sample of 207 leading Lebanese businessmen in the early 1960s, only one sixth were Muslim, outnumbered by Christians in ratios of 10:2 in industry, 11:2 in banking and 16:2 in services (Sayigh 1962: 69–71). At that time, although the other urban classes were not so obviously dominated by one confession or another, the petty bourgeoisie or middle class was predominantly Christian, and the working class and sub-proletariat predominantly Muslim.

Using data from a variety of sources, Samih Farsoun (1988: 121 ff) shows how his 'sect-classes' were manifested by a number of indicators. To summarize his argument, he quotes Joseph Chamie (1980) who had conducted a quantitative survey in 1971:

> With whatever reasonable criterion one wishes to employ — such as education, occupation, female labor participation, income, movie attendance, membership in associations — the socioeconomic differentials which emerge between the religious groups are unmistakably clear: non-Catholic Christians and Catholics at the top, Druze around the middle, Sunnis near the bottom, and Shi'a at the very bottom.
>
> (Chamie 1980: 181)

This stratification of the various confessions helps explain both the reproduction of confessional consciousness in modern Lebanon and the eventual demise of the liberal nationalist ideals contained in the National Pact of 1943 (see the first section of this chapter). In the years leading up to the civil war, the za'im-leadership of the Muslims — particularly among the Shi'a — lost control of impoverished and increasingly resentful followings. By contrast, in the more homogenous Maronite community, leaders and followers developed a common purpose to defend their privileges from radical assault. 'It is no wonder,' concludes Farsoun (1988: 125), 'that the politically mobilized groups were eager for the civil conflict which broke out so dramatically and explosively in 1975.'

Although Farsoun is careful to avoid a simplistic reduction of his sect-classes to 'poor Muslims' and 'rich Christians', his analysis requires careful treatment. We have seen (in chapter 2, section 6) how Theodor Hanf argues that by the 1970s 'social and economic disparities' had 'narrowed enormously' in Lebanon, particularly since the Shihabist reforms of the 1960s. In a detailed discussion of a number of studies, Hanf (1993: 95–105) shows how the standard of living among Muslims had increased during that decade. One survey used a 'quality of life' index composed of indices for levels of 'hygiene, economic and technical standards, housing, schooling and cultural and social status'. This study revealed increases in the index between 1960 and 1970 of 36 per cent in the Bekaa (with a large community of Shi'a in the north) and 44 per cent in southern Lebanon (where the Shi'a formed the majority of the population), as compared with only 16 per cent in the central region. Another source showed that 53 per cent of university students in 1972–73 were Muslim — largely as a result of the expansion of the Lebanese University. And contrary to the notion of an almost entirely Muslim working class, a study of industrial workers in the eastern suburbs of Beirut demonstrated that, in 1974, as many as 45 per cent of them were Christian, mainly Maronites and Armenians. Hanf concludes that although Christians were still better represented in the upper and middle classes and Muslims in the sub-proletariat, the social stratifications of the two groups were 'similar' and confessional inequality appeared to be 'within bounds' (Hanf 1993: 105).

While this work raises important questions about Farsoun's analysis, we should also interrogate Hanf's data. First, there are problems in his discussion of the comparative increases of the 'quality of life' index between 1960 and 1970. Although an increase of 44 per cent in southern Lebanon 'which is 70 per cent Muslim', compared with only 16 per cent in the central region, suggests a 'narrowing of earlier disparities' (Hanf 1993: 101–2), another interpretation is immediately apparent when we remember that between 1960 and 1975 around 60 per cent of the population had migrated from the south (see section 2, and chapter 3, section 4, above). Sharecropping peasants were forced from the land by their landlords as agricultural estates were mechanized, and they faced many difficulties in finding work in the 'belt of misery' around Beirut. Farsoun cites an unpublished paper written by Salim Nasr to argue that, by 1975, as much as 65 per cent of the rural population of southern Lebanon, and 50 per cent of that of the Bekaa, 'had been driven out of their homes and off the land' (Nasr, quoted in Farsoun 1988: 124). Clearly, we can at least partly explain the higher increases in the 'quality of life' index in the south and the Bekaa in terms of a removal of the poor peasantry, and the lower increase in the central region by an expansion of the sub-proletariat in the suburbs of Beirut.

Second, the high percentage of Muslim university students in 1972–73 might not be all that significant if most of them were studying at the Lebanese University while Christian students tended to graduate from the elite, private universities of Saint Joseph (French-language) and the AUB (the English-language American University of Beirut). And third, it is not very surprising to find that in the predominantly Christian suburbs of eastern Beirut, populated by relatively recent migrants to the city, 45 per cent of the industrial workforce was

Christian. Also, as Hanf himself points out, within the 55 per cent figure for Muslims was an over-representation of lower-skilled workers, as compared with the more highly skilled Christian workforce. In fact, a reading of Hanf's sources shows that 76 per cent of Muslims and only 46 per cent of Christians were in the lower-skilled category, while only 12 per cent of Muslims, as compared with 21 per cent of Christians, were higher-skilled (Dubar and Nasr 1976: 90; Nasr and Nasr 1976).

Owing to the lack of any detailed census information on class and confession in Lebanon, it is impossible to provide a definitive account of the relationship between the two variables. The data Hanf uses are based on the quantitative class structure for the confessionally undifferentiated population of Lebanon that Claude Dubar and Salim Nasr (1976: 113) derived from a 1970 sample survey conducted by the ministry of planning (Government of Lebanon 1972). That in itself involves some difficulties as, in my opinion, the government survey did not make sufficiently clear distinctions between and within categories of employers, employees and self-employed. Hanf then applies other statistics from various sources to provide estimates for the class structures of the Muslim and Christian communities (reproduced in a simplified form in the first of the two tables below).

One problem with the way Hanf calculates his percentages is an implicit assumption that the relative sizes of the Muslim and Christian proletariats in the whole of Lebanon can be derived directly from statistics for industrial establishments in the eastern suburbs of Beirut. Nevertheless, the attempts made by Dubar and Nasr, and then by Hanf, to give estimates for the percentage size of social classes in Lebanon are probably no more inaccurate than my own indications (largely derived from the same 1970 survey) for the class structure of Beirut (Johnson 1986: 34).

I think Dubar and Nasr — and therefore Hanf — underestimate the size of the sub-proletariat and overestimate that of the proletariat, but this is more a matter of how those classes are defined than a result of different interpretations of the figures. Dubar and Nasr include all permanent and day-workers in 'nonfarm' employment as part of the proletariat (see notes in the table below), but I would only include workers in industrial employment. Thus my sub-proletariat is larger than theirs and comprises the unemployed and all those workers who have a 'clientelist relationship with their employer or with a supplier of essential resources'. For me, the sub-proletariat includes 'petty criminals, porters, pedlars, pimps and prostitutes', 'body guards and security guards', such homeworkers as tailors or seamstresses in a 'putting-out' system, and 'workers in very small workshops' (Johnson 1986: 36–9).

The major problem with Hanf's data, however, is that he gives an undifferentiated figure for the Muslim community, thus including Druze, who according to Joseph Chamie's study (1980) have a social stratification similar to

Percentage sizes of classes in Lebanon, 1970:
Theodor Hanf's data

Class	Christian %	Muslim %	Total population %
Bourgeoisie	4	2	3
Petty bourgeoisie	67	56	61
Proletariat	21	23	22
Sub-proletariat	8	19	14
	100	100	100

Source: Hanf 1993: 106, derived from Dubar and Nasr 1976 and other sources.
Notes: Bourgeoisie: heads of large commercial, financial and industrial companies. Petty bourgeoisie: small property holders (including independent farmers), the self-employed, and salaried staff (including top-level managers). Proletariat: full-time and day workers in non-farm employment. Sub-proletariat: farm workers, tenant farmers, temporary workers in the service sector, and the unemployed.

Percentage sizes of occupational groups in Lebanon, 1971:
Joseph Chamie's data

'Class'	Non-Cath. Christian %	Catholic %	Druze %	Sunni %	Shi'a %	Total popn%
Upper	27	23	23	20	15	22
Middle	50	53	53	48	41	49
Lower	17	18	21	26	39	24
Other	6	6	3	6	5	5
	100	100	100	100	100	100

Source: Chamie 1980: 182.
Notes: Upper 'class' (or occupational group): business and managerial, and professional and technical categories. Middle class: clerical, army, police, and craft. Lower class: labour and pedlars.

the Christians, along with Shi'a who have a markedly different one. Chamie's figures (given, in a simplified form, in the second of the tables) are organized differently from Hanf's, but the two sets of results can be usefully compared.

While the social stratification of the Druze in 1971 was remarkably similar to that of the Christians (and the Sunnis were not dramatically different), the Shi'a were under-represented in the 'upper' and 'middle' occupational groups and considerably over-represented in the 'lower' category. This helps to explain why, in the 1970s, many Shi'a sub-proletarians, workers, peasants, salaried staff, and students joined leftist parties like the Lebanese Communist Party (CPL), the Communist Action Organization (CAO) and the Arab Ba'th (*ba'th*: 'renaissance') Socialist Party. Some of the Shi'a intelligentsia held leading positions in these parties. For example, Husayn Mroueh and Hasan Hamdan were leaders of the CPL, and Muhsin Ibrahim led the CAO. This might have encouraged members of the Shi'a 'popular classes' to join the radical and secular militias, but it is clear that such people were also motivated by a sense of their socioeconomic deprivation (Sayigh 1994: 165).

Some further support for Farsoun's idea of 'sect-classes' can be found in the way Shi'a eventually deserted socialist parties and supported the confessional Amal militia. As we have seen (in section 2), Amal represented an extremely effective coalition of different Shi'a classes. Its mass following was recruited from an impoverished peasantry and sub-proletariat, while its organizational and political leadership came from an intelligentsia that had benefited from an expansion in educational opportunities. The lower levels of state employment in local government, the army and schools had been populated by Shi'a; and the schoolteachers, especially, had politicized their community. The other class drawn into this coalition was an *émigrée* bourgeoisie. From the time of the French Mandate, increasing numbers of Shi'a had gone to West Africa and Latin America to establish themselves in commerce. Having made their fortune, some returned home and attempted to enter the ranks of the Lebanese elite. But this was largely composed of Christians and Sunni Muslims, many of whom looked down on the *nouveaux riches* and appeared to be excluding Shi'a from positions of commercial and political influence. In reaction, members of this disaffected bourgeoisie found a common cause with their confessional community and contributed funds to Amal (Johnson 1986: 171–2).

Amal might be construed as a 'sect-class' organization, but as it included members of the bourgeoisie as well as sub-proletarians we cannot use Samih Farsoun's analysis to support an argument that the war was one between 'poor Muslims' and 'rich Christians'. This is the point that Theodor Hanf (1993: 97) is anxious to make. It is a misreading of the evidence, he argues, to see the conflicts between confessions as simply the manifestations of 'class struggles'.

As a response to relatively high rates of inflation and unemployment, leftist parties and trade unions organized a series of strikes and demonstrations in the early 1970s (Johnson 1986: 164 ff). Factory workers, firefighters, bank employees, teachers and students in Beirut, and sharecroppers and workers in the tobacco industry in southern Lebanon, were all involved in a struggle for better conditions and wages. And Hanf (1993: 109–10) is right to point out that the students', teachers' and workers' unions attracted the support of people from all confessions. It is true that more Muslims than Christians were involved in these secular struggles, and many Maronites became worried by the growing links between the left and the Palestinians. But although there were some violent incidents, the strikes and demonstrations were not usually confessional. In addition, they were relatively easily contained by the Lebanese police and security forces (see chapter 2, section 6). Also, concessions were made by employers and the state: working conditions were improved and the legal minimum wage was raised. As Hanf (1993: 110) says, 'there was little to distinguish these forms of conflict from those in homogeneous societies in times of economic crisis.'

Nevertheless, as Hanf himself recognizes, the poverty and politicization of the Shi'a community formed part of the explanation for the outbreak of civil war in Lebanon. And we should bear in mind, too, the way the labour movement became associated with the Palestinian cause and its mainly Muslim supporters. Many of those who demonstrated against higher prices and unemployment also joined demonstrations in support of the Palestine Liberation Organization. Then in February 1975, just two months before the start of the civil war, clashes between the army and Lebanese and Palestinian demonstrators in Sidon resulted in at least three deaths. One of those who died was Maarouf Saad, a popular Sunni leader and former member of parliament. When he was buried, his Lebanese body was wrapped in a Palestinian flag.

The PLO was not directly involved in the Sidon protests, which were directed against a mechanized fishing company (named 'Protein') that threatened the interests of local fishermen. But some Palestinians worked in the informal fishing industry alongside Lebanese Sunnis, some had married into local families, and many participated in the demonstrations. The honouring of Maarouf Saad's body was just one indication of the close links between the two communities. Significantly, the fishing dispute soon became confessionalized, first because the Protein company was headed by Camille Chamoun, the former president of Lebanon and leader of the Maronite Liberal National Party (PNL), and second because the Lebanese army was used to put down the popular movement in Sidon. A one-day strike was called in Beirut to protest against the killing of demonstrators, and there were Muslim calls for the resignation of the Maronite commander-in-chief of the armed forces, his replacement with a multi-confessional command council, and a general redistribution of power away from the Maronites. Such demands were passionately resisted by the PNL and Phalanges, and they organized counter-demonstrations in support of the army (Johnson 1986: 176–8).

But even if it can be shown, as Farsoun and others have tried to do, that class differences played a large part in the early rounds of the conflict, they cannot on their own be used to explain how a class struggle over socioeconomic conditions became a war. Had it not been for the militarization of Lebanese politics, the trade union movement could have been contained by police action and negotiation. The heavily armed PLO fighters' use of Lebanon as a base from which to attack Israel, and their unwillingness to compromise with the Lebanese authorities, were one set of factors. A second was the response of such Maronite parties as the Phalanges and PNL. Frustrated and angered by the Lebanese state's weakness, Maronite za'ims expanded their militias to fight the Palestinians, acquiring arms from the international market and obtaining some military training from the Jordanian security services (only later forming close links with Israel). Thirdly, the PLO armed and trained leftist and Muslim militias so they could fight as its allies. And finally, most Arab regimes entered the conflict and funded their various proxies. Because King Hussein's army had expelled the PLO fighters from Jordan in 1970–71, and his prime minister, Wasfi Tal, had been assassinated in November 1971 as an act of revenge, relations between Hussein's government and the Palestinians were very strained. Thus the Jordanians gave some help to the Maronites. Otherwise, the Arab regimes funded and gave military assistance to the Palestinian and Lebanese Muslim factions, Saudi Arabia helping Fatah and conservative Sunni za'ims, and Libya and Iraq backing the radical and leftist groups.

External patrons might be said to have militarized a Lebanese class struggle, but class factors cannot then explain the way the civil wars developed. They cannot, for example, explain why the relatively privileged Druze fought Maronites in the Shouf war of 1983 (see chapter 2, section 7), or why impoverished Shi'a fought equally impoverished Palestinians in the 'war of the camps' between 1985 and 1987. Nor can a class or 'sect-class' analysis adequately explain the *emotional* content of the massacres and mutilations that accompanied the warfare. Farsoun's account is persuasive insofar as it shows how confessional identities were reproduced during the modern period, but we need to look elsewhere for an explanation of how confessional identity gave rise to confessional violence.

It is not always the case that one community is predominantly 'upper' and another 'lower' class in ethnic disputes; and even where there is some overlap between class and ethnicity as there was in Lebanon, explaining a consequent conflict in such terms as 'poor Muslims' fighting 'rich Christians' is an over-simplification. The ethnic or confessional fighters in the Lebanese wars were largely recruited from the poor and lower-middle-class members of the Muslim *and* Christian communities. Some Muslims might have been motivated by a sense of 'relative deprivation' (Runciman 1966; Gurr 1970), and some Christians by a fear of losing relative privilege, but the fighting is much better interpreted as an 'intra-class' than an inter-class conflict.

It seems that intra-class competition expressed in ethnic terms is initially most pronounced within the 'state salariat' where members of different communities compete for government jobs, using ethnic patronage connections to assist their advancement, and normative values about a fair 'ethnic balance' to justify claims for a greater representation in the ranks of the bureaucracy. This does not necessarily lead to violence; but in interpreting the competition in ethnic terms, the salariat and those who aspire to that class provide articulate communal spokesmen who contribute to a growing polarization between communities.

Salaried employees of the British (along with members of the liberal professions) formed, for example, the rival leaderships of the inclusive Indian National Congress and exclusive Muslim League that respectively took power in 1947 after the partition of the Indian empire into India and Pakistan. Those members, or potential members, of the salariat who did not find adequate employment, or felt that their socioeconomic advancement was blocked by the new governing elites, soon used the discourse of ethnicity to explain their apparent disadvantage. At first this had little to do with confessional communalism, but different linguistic and regional interests defined themselves in opposition to the Hindi-speaking elite of northern India (Brass 1994: 157 ff), while the salariat in the East Bengal and Sindh provinces of Pakistan began to see themselves as Bengalis or Sindhis who were excluded from a fair share of state jobs by the dominant Punjabi elite (Alavi 1991).

Similarly, in the 1950s, members of the Muslim (mainly Sunni) salariat in Beirut objected to the dominance of the Lebanese state bureaucracy by Christians, and some of them joined such secular parties as the Arab Ba'th Socialists and Arab Nationalist Movement (*harakat al-qawmiyyin al-'arab*) in order to articulate their grievances. Others, however, adopted a confessional stance, and their best-known statement was the 1953 manifesto (translated into English as *Moslem Lebanon Today*) signed by representatives of a large number of educational, philanthropic, and religious, Muslim societies. The pamphlet complained that the 'fascist' Phalanges and other Maronites were in league with Zionism, the Christians' disloyalty to Arabism went back as far as the Crusades, and Lebanon was a Maronite-dominated state imposed by the French on a majority who favoured a united Arab Syria. These were familiar grievances, but in a significant section of the document the particular resentments of the salariat were more clearly expressed. The authors claimed that the Lebanese presidential secretariat was entirely Christian, and among the directors of civil service departments Christians outnumbered Muslims in a ratio of 7:3. The government, they argued, was not prepared to rectify this situation by improving the standard of Muslim education. On the contrary, 'foreign Christian missionary schools, colleges and universities' were given state encouragement and subsidies, while Muslim educational establishments were neglected (*Moslem Lebanon Today* 1953; Johnson 1986: 127–30; Gordon 1980: 162–3).

After independence, liberal nationalists in the Middle East, Indian sub-continent and elsewhere had attempted to modernize and develop their economies. But ultimately they failed to satisfy all the aspirations and demands of the followers and supporters of the independence movement. Very significantly, those members of the salariat who felt excluded became increasingly oppositional. Although they were not necessarily at the forefront of ethnic violence, they often played a leading role in promoting ethnic identity by claiming that 'so-called' liberal and inclusive nationalism actually favoured one or more ethnic groups at the expense of others.

Where liberal nationalism was relatively sophisticated and written down in political programmes, as it was in the case of the Indian National Congress, exclusive ethnic nationalism could be resisted for some time after independence. Despite the appalling communal massacres that had accompanied the 1947 partition of British India (leaving at least half a million dead), Prime Minister Jawaharlal Nehru and other Congress leaders were adamant that India was a secular state and Muslims were full members of the nation. It was not until the late 1960s that Hindu–Muslim conflict began again to increase in intensity, and not until the 1980s that it became a serious political problem (Banerjee 1992; Brass 1994: 228–47). In Lebanon, however, where inclusive nationalism derived its legitimacy mainly from an unwritten 'gentlemen's agreement' — the National Pact of 1943 — then threats from exclusive forms of Arab and Lebanese nationalism appeared after only a decade of independence, articulated respectively by Muslim members of the intelligentsia and salariat who wanted a greater share of resources and by Maronites eager to defend their privileges.

There was no doubt that Muslims were under-represented at all levels of the Lebanese state bureaucracy in the 1950s. But the concerns of the Sunni salariat were assuaged to a considerable extent by reforms instituted by President Fu'ad Shihab after the short civil war of 1958. These were designed to promote

Muslim–Christian parity in the civil service, and involved quotas and positive discrimination for Muslims. Because the Sunni and Druze communities had a higher standard of education, they benefited from the quota system far more than the Shi'a; and as more members of the latter community graduated from the new state schools — also established by Shihabist reformism to promote confessional equality — so some of them articulated a resentment about their under-representation in government employment. By the early 1970s the civil service was considerably over-staffed, and high-school and university graduates were competing more than ever for scarce positions. This created divisions in a student protest movement which, influenced by *les événements* of 1968 in Paris and elsewhere, had originally been broadly secular. Some students remained committed to leftist parties, but others lined up with their confessional organizations to press, for example, for the abolition of Muslim quotas, or for a census which would demonstrate that a larger share of state employment should go to Muslims in general and the Shi'a in particular (Grassmuck and Salibi 1964; Crow 1966; Salem 1973; Hanf 1993: 95–6).

As well as being articulate advocates of the values of ethnic nationalism, the salariat and other members of the middle classes are also central to an understanding of the relationship between ethnicity and kinship (see section 2). The break-up of the rural extended family clearly represents a threat to patriarchy, and rural–urban migration puts tremendous stress on men in all social classes who might then turn to their ethnic organizations for emotional and material help. However, for civil servants and teachers, and petty merchants and shop-keepers, the contradictions of the sexually repressive family are perhaps more significant than they are for other classes, especially because they are intimately related to notions of petty-bourgeois propriety and status.

Threatened by inflation and the prospect of economic crisis, and troubled by a perceived lack of fair opportunity in salaried employment, or by the competition of business rivals, the middle-class patriarch finds emotional security and demonstrates his social status in the proper behaviour of his family. If his wife and children bring him shame, then his life and precarious sense of well-being can fall apart. He faces potential chaos, and his fear of competitors outside the family can be projected on to a fear of betrayal within. It is this 'paranoia' that drives him to impose ever greater surveillance on the members of his family, but in so doing he creates the conditions for their rebellion and thus the need for more control in a miserable cycle of repression and despair. But what choice does he have? In the village, women and adolescents conform because inquisitive eyes are watching and loquacious tongues gossiping. In the anonymous city, the subordinates to patriarchal power might get away with any manner of social transgression if they were not constantly watched and controlled.

As romantic ethnicity appeals much more than liberal nationalism to family values, and manipulates with greater resonance such concepts as 'motherland' and 'father of the nation' (see section 2), it is warmly embraced by the patriarchal casualties of modernization. These include members of the working class and sub-proletariat as well as the salariat. The latter play a large part in teaching ethnicity to the poor, but soon some of the poor start to learn for themselves.

Romantic nationalism's stress on discipline and authoritarianism, and on strong and often despotic leadership, parallels the patriarch's role in his family. The notion that the only proper role for women is to be the mothers of the nation and its martyrs accords with his own desperate desire to keep his wife and daughters under control. The emphasis on submission to the ethnic group and its leadership provides him with an emotional and welcome relief from his awesome responsibilities as the family's leader and provider. And the demonization of the Other both feeds and explains his paranoia. It is possible that this demonology provides an opportunity for the patriarch to project, as the psycho-analysts would say, his weaknesses, fears, wicked and unclean thoughts — all the despised aspects of the self — on to the Other (see section 3). What is certain is that this Other can be blamed for the difficulties of urban life: a Muslim in Lebanon could blame the Christians for their dominance of an unfair economy and political system; a Christian could blame Muslims for their alliances with foreign Palestinians and 'international communism' that had given rise to disorder and chaos.

Romantic nationalism also provides help to women and adolescents. As we have seen, wives and mothers are highly valued. Although there is something approaching misogyny in romantic discourse, it is probably more a gynophobia, a fear rather than hatred of women; and although romanticism appeals to men's fears, it also reassures them and women that motherhood is a wonderful and noble aspiration. Romantic glorification of the mother provides women with a purpose. Despite the anxiety induced by the preference for sons, this helps them accept the restrictions imposed upon them and welcome their role as the reproducers of the family and the ethnic group.

In some ways, the problems presented to young men in the sexually repressive family are more difficult than those faced by women. Adolescent males introject the paternal authority figure so that their superego tells them they should conform to the values of patriarchy. This presumably explains why they are so disciplinarian with 'their' women, policing the behaviour of their sisters and girlfriends with beatings and sometimes murder. But they are driven by youthful rebellion as well, and they resent the patriarchy to which they feel they should submit. In addition, urbanization and other aspects of modernity undermine their sense of a clearly defined role. They need to establish themselves in a career before they can marry. If there is no family business for them to join, they have to enter a highly competitive market as members of the merchant, salaried, working or sub-proletarian classes. They are therefore subject to many of the anxieties of their fathers which, especially if they are cast adrift without the emotional security of wife and children, are often experienced in a more immediate and frightening form. They are also closer to the traumas associated with childhood; and whether or not we assign them to an Oedipal or 'splitting' source (section 3), these are nonetheless real and difficult.

The party and militia organizations of ethnic nationalism help by providing an outlet for youthful male rebellion while, at the same time, they promote the links between God, fatherland and family. Young men are encouraged to see themselves as belonging to a community that replicates the family but relieves them of its contradictions. Whether they are bachelors on their own in the alien city or the sons of repressive urban fathers, ethnicity provides them with a strong sense of self and of their place within a wider society. They can submit to the authority of their ethnic organization and its leader, and because they are part of a higher cause this submission is so much easier than the one forced on them by the tyranny of their fathers. Indeed it can be embraced enthusiastically because now they are fighters with a purpose and will be successful only if they accept the discipline of the group.

Ethnic parties and militias give the alienated adolescent an identity, and provide him with a sense of power and control. Such feelings are then enhanced in fighting the Other — as can be illustrated by the testimonies of the fighters themselves (Malarkey 1988: 291 and 297; also see Baghdadi and de Freige 1979; Fernea 1985). One Maronite militiaman said, in 1979, 'I think I liquidated in one day all my problems of identity. At the very moment I got behind the barricade, I became perfectly integrated, totally together.' Another told how the fighting meant 'taking one's future into one's own hands and *forgetting family conventions*' (my emphasis). And in the same year, a Shi'a militiaman spoke of how he and his comrades fought against 'the feeling of being the castoffs of the Arabs. All that was swept away with the first cartridges I fired. In my mind it was surely against all this nauseating rottenness that runs through this town: this war purified the country.' The fighter integrated with his group faces enemies who are so alien and Other that their Lebanese identity can be denied. As a Christian militiaman claimed in 1984, 'We are not fighting other Lebanese. We are fighting the Palestinians, the Syrians, the Libyans and all the stupid fanatics of the Third World. We're going to kill them all.'

As we have seen, a psychoanalytic approach suggests that such a demonized foe can provide a repository for the disavowed aspects of the self. For young men these might be sexual desire and promiscuity, jealousy of siblings and peers, and anger and hatred that would otherwise be directed against the father's repression or the mother's inability to provide constant and unconditional love. Certainly, the discourse and actions of ethnic conflict are replete with sexual imagery, fantasy and aggression, and these are associated with an idealization of the mother and all the pure women of one's own community as compared with the whores of the Other. In 1975 Lina Mikdadi Tabbara heard an exchange on the short-wave radio between a Palestinian and a Phalangist:

> They flew at each other immediately and, using the crudest language, accused their respective mothers of a whole range of sins and of all possible and imaginable vices. After fifteen minutes had elapsed the Palestinian seemed to be gaining. His adversary let him go on without answering. The Palestinian kept it up until he was finally nonplussed by the Phalangist's silence.
> 'You have nothing to say to all that, you son of a whore?'
> 'I'm much too busy with your sister' [came the sinister reply].
>
> (Tabbara 1979: 42)

A short step from this verbal shaming is the utter humiliation of the Other's honour by raping and killing his women. Of course, some fighters in Lebanon felt ashamed after the event. Some resorted to alcohol or tranquillizers, to hashish or crack cocaine. Others experienced post-traumatic stress disorders, induced by the general horrors of war (Malarkey 1988: 298; Abdennur 1980). It is not the case that ethnic conflict provides a constant sense of well-being, and one fighter in 1979 (quoted in Malarkey 1988: 304 n14) talked about 'the impression of having gone too far. You know, like when you fire a rocket and you hear the cries of children afterward. At the end, I was completely out of touch with everything.' Another said, 'When I think about it, I see myself vomiting gobs. I felt this incomprehensible need to go confess myself afterwards. But I couldn't tell the priest anything, nothing.'

In the heat of battle, however, many fighters experienced elation and a sense of purpose and integration. The fighting was cathartic and everything permissible: raping girls, castrating men, killing children, and cutting open the wombs of pregnant women. As a Shi'a militiaman said in 1984, 'War is my only friend. It's like my wife, I love it. In peace I feel afraid' (quoted in Malarkey 1988: 291).

There is nothing in these statements to suggest a sense of class consciousness. Even the Shi'a who spoke of his community being composed of the 'castoffs of the Arabs' expressed a resentment not against a dominant Maronite 'sect-class', but against Palestinians and Lebanese Sunnis who could be seen as members of the same deprived class as the impoverished Shi'a in the suburbs of Beirut. This was very different from the early stages of the war when many fighters might have expressed themselves in terms of a rightist or leftist ideology.

Before the war, Pierre Gemayel made a number of pronouncements in which he distinguished 'honourable commando action' from the actions of those Palestinians in alliance with what he called the 'international left'; and it is significant that in the first month of fighting, in April 1975, his Phalangist fighters seemed to concentrate their actions against the militias of the socialist and radical factions of the PLO (Johnson 1986: 176). Similarly, the Sunni leader of the Murabitun, Ibrahim Qulaylat, used the discourse of his 'sect-class' when he issued a press statement in January 1976 complaining about the 'decayed institutions' that had 'made Lebanon a country of privileges for the Maronite community' (Johnson 1986: 185).

By the late 1970s, however, few people talked in terms of a political left and right in Lebanon. In 1978 and 1980, Maronite factions fought each other for control of their enclave; and in the mid-eighties, after some years of tension between them, Amal turned on its former allies, defeating the Murabitun and closing its offices in 1985, the same year that it first laid siege to the Palestinian quarter of Shatila and started the 'war of the camps'.

If the concept of social class has any relevance at all in this context, it serves to draw attention to the fact that the civil wars were *intra*-class conflicts. The patronage structures of romantic or ethnic nationalism appealed to the material needs of various social classes: the sub-proletariat and working class whose members competed for scarce jobs and welfare services; the small-property holders who competed with business rivals for markets and government licences; and the salaried staff who competed for promotion in the office hierarchy. Economic competition, *within* rather than between classes, lay at the root of confessional conflict in Lebanon. But the reason romantic nationalism was so effective in recruiting support was that it supplemented socioeconomic appeals with an emotional affectivity that reached right to the heart of the self.

5. Neopatriarchy and surveillance

Samih Farsoun's analysis of 'sect-classes' explains the way confessional identities were reproduced in modern Lebanon. His discussion of the nineteenth century is similar to my own (see chapter 3), and his account of uneven development in the twentieth century shows how the various confessions continued to be associated with different levels of economic and social development. There can be no doubt that many of the protagonists in the first year of the civil war (1975–76) saw themselves as fighting either to redress economic and political imbalances between 'sect-classes' or to defend existing privileges. It is not surprising, therefore, that Farsoun and others saw the fighters as being motivated by factors related to the class structure of Lebanon. But, as we have seen, such an interpretation does not explain the subsequent course of the war or the emotional content of the conflict.

In *Class and Client* (Johnson 1986) I also adopted a class analysis. But rather than emphasizing the role of 'sect-classes', I stressed the individualistic and competitive nature of Lebanese society that was a consequence of what I called 'competitive service capitalism' (see chapter 2, section 6, above). In such a society, I argued, confessionalism provided a sense of security in an insecure market. What I failed to provide, however, was any detail about social insecurity beyond saying that it was determined by intra-class competition for jobs and services. Nor did I specify precisely enough how the confession provided a sense of community. Hopefully, by focusing on urbanization and the threats to patriarchal honour, and by discussing the 'comforts' of romantic nationalism, I have provided a much fuller explanation.

It should be abundantly clear by now that the nature of the sexually repressive family is central to my sociology of ethnicity and confessional conflict. Some support for this argument is found in Hisham Sharabi's important and provocative account of 'neopatriarchy' in the Arab world (1988) which seeks to locate repressive family structures in their historical and socioeconomic context. Reference has been made in chapter 2 (section 6) to the concept of 'permanent transition' that Pino Arlacchi uses to describe a social formation not fully transformed by capitalism, and in which values of honour and patriarchy are intimately involved in social and political organization. Similar notions are found in Sharabi's study, but here the emphasis is much more on the *contradictions* of patriarchy as compared with Arlacchi's essentially functionalist account.

Sharabi (1988: 5) argues that 'dependent' economic development in the Arab world produced a 'distorted' and 'peripheral' capitalism. Although he does not go into details, he is referring here to the way that an early European domination of the world economy discouraged the growth of industry in such 'peripheries' as the Middle East, where economies tended to be structured around the production of raw materials (for export to Europe) and associated trading and service sectors. These economies were dependent in the sense that they were subject to European levels of demand and pricing structures, and relied on Europe for imported manufactured items.

The social formation of dependent capitalism, Sharabi argues, had an 'underdeveloped bourgeoisie and proletariat' — presumably a result of a weak industrial sector. As a consequence, society became culturally dominated by a 'hybrid social class' which he calls the 'neopatriarchal petty bourgeoisie' (Sharabi 1988: 6). In Syria, Egypt, and Iraq, members of this class took power through *coups d'état*; but 'lacking internal unity and coherence', the petty-bourgeois regimes were 'utterly incapable' of promoting a sustained capitalist development. Indeed, they further weakened a bourgeoisie already in a state of 'enfeeblement' as a result of 'dependency and imperialism'. The failure of these regimes led in the 1980s to the spread of oppositional movements of militant Islam among 'the underprivileged and increasingly alienated petty bourgeois-proletarian masses' (Sharabi 1988: 5–9).

This analysis works best for those Arab societies in which the neopatriarchal middle class could be said to have taken direct control of the state, but Sharabi does attempt to extend the argument to 'semi-tribal' authorities in Saudi Arabia and the Gulf, and to the unique case of Lebanon. In fact, he sees the main tenets of his theory as applicable to all those cultures and societies in the world where 'modernization occurred under dependent conditions', leading to 'distorted, inauthentic modernity' and to 'modern' or 'modernized' patriarchy (Sharabi 1988: 22).

For our purposes, Sharabi's discussion of the neopatriarchal family is the most useful part of his book. He starts by suggesting there is a relationship between different kinship structures and different forms of economic organization: between the tribe and pastoralism or nomadism, between the clan or extended family and peasant agriculture, and between the nuclear family and urban capitalism. The nuclear family is 'an outcome and a motivating force of economic transformation'; and through the modern educational system, children in western societies acquire skills that as adults they can market independently of their father's will. They are no longer dependent on him for land or employment as they would have been in a 'rural or precapitalist setting', and this economic independence provides 'the basis of the nuclear family's democracy, the condition for the overthrow of patriarchal tyranny' (Sharabi 1988: 31–2).

The implication of this argument is that the persistence, or reproduction, of patriarchy in the nuclear (or partially extended) family in modern Arab society is due to a lack of significant economic opportunity outside the kinship group. Sharabi (1988: 4) also suggests that dependent capitalism has prevented the emergence of a *gesellschaft* of interest groups or associational forms of organization that might take the place of a 'distorted' (or partially modernized) *gemeinschaft* of such communities as family, clan, confession and ethnic group.

Sharabi develops his argument by referring to the work of the Lebanese psychologist, Ali Zayour, who has provided an 'analysis of the patriarchal family in Arab society'. Zayour describes the dominating and punishing role of the father and considers the effects of this on the child:

The family is relentless in its repression. [The child] is brought up to become an obedient youth, subservient to those above him — his father, older brother, clan chief, president. ... The main concern is that the child be obedient, well-mannered, ignorant about sexual matters, 'better' than his fellows. ... By being compared to others to underscore his failure he is driven to view himself negatively and to lose self-esteem (to the extent of self-punishment at times).

(Zayour 1977: 34, quoted in translation in Sharabi 1988: 41)

The repressive family makes considerable use of shaming and punishment in the socialization of children, and the incapacitated adolescent grows up to be subservient and ambivalent to authority. Interacting with this 'psychic structure of the individual' is a societal culture that values religion and 'magic' more than science and rationality, a culture that provides comfort in its myths about legacy, glory and heroism (Zayour 1977: 34; Zayour 1982; Sharabi 1988: 42; Barakat 1990: 144). Zayour sees this state of affairs not as an essential part of what he calls the 'Arab self' or 'ego' (*adh-dhat al-'arabiyya*), but as a product of particular social and historical conditions. As Sharabi (1988: 41) puts it, relations within the family are predominantly those of 'domination' and 'dependency', 'which both reflect and are reflected in the structure of social relations'. This social structure is a result of changes brought about by the development of capitalism, not something determined by a primordial Arab or Muslim culture. If this is properly understood, says Sharabi, then it might be possible to confront and reform the social and political authoritarianism that seems so prevalent in Arab societies.

Other authors have identified an authoritarian culture in the Arab world, but too often their accounts have been based on 'Orientalist' sources that assume an essential national character, largely determined by a rigid and authoritarian Islam. A prominent example is Raphael Patai's study of the 'Arab mind' (1973). This draws on an Orientalist canon represented by students of Islam and the Arabic language (Gibb and Bowen 1950; 1957; von Grunebaum 1962; and possibly Geertz 1968), and by the more subtle approach of modernization theorists (Lerner 1958; Berger 1964). Since the late 1970s, Orientalism has been subject to considerable criticism (Said 1978; Rodinson 1974; Gilsenan 1982; Asad and Owen 1983; *Review of Middle East Studies* 1975, 1976 and 1978). And in the light of this relatively new scholarship, we need to approach any conception of the 'Arab self' with great caution.

Put simply, the 'radical' critique of Orientalism argues, with considerable justification, that European and north-American accounts of the Middle East tend to be ahistorical or historically selective, and prejudiced or eurocentric.

Thus Orientalists interpret 'Islamic society' as more or less homogeneous, static and stagnant. This perception then colours the Orientalist view of the Arabs: although given to periodic acts of irrational rebellion, they are normally conservative, passive and fatalistic; they lack entrepreneurial skills and accept the lot that Allah has given them; they are submissive in political as well as religious life, and accept a subordination to despotic leaders in a tradition that dates back to the Islamic empires, both Ottoman and Arab.

Clearly, Hisham Sharabi wants to disassociate himself from an Orientalist academy; and in a collection of essays that he edited in 1990, he and Halim Barakat provide persuasive critiques of Raphael Patai's work (Sharabi 1990: 6–8; Barakat 1990: 133–7). But this is a sensitive subject, and in his consideration of what might be called 'Orientalist psychology' Barakat takes issue with Ali Zayour as well as western writers, and even has implicit criticisms of Sharabi's account of neopatriarchy (Barakat 1990: 143 ff). In Barakat's extended study of these issues (1984) is a careful analysis of the values of different classes and societies in the contemporary Arab world (summarized in Barakat 1990). Beduin nomads value 'respect for parents and ancestors', blood, honour and vengeance, individualism, hospitality and protection, and a 'knightly code' of 'chivalry', manliness and dignity. Peasant values reflect their dependence on the land and seasons: 'fertility', 'hope' and 'patience'; 'motherhood', family co-operation and honour; and 'faith', 'sainthood' and endurance. Urban classes, on the other hand, value 'affluence' and 'worldly enjoyments', 'compromise', 'self-reliance and discipline', and 'contractual relations, official laws and texts' (Barakat 1990: 145–6).

Obviously, Barakat wants to emphasize positive values instead of the negative ones analysed by Sharabi and Zayour. His account of the urban middle classes is very different from Sharabi's. They are more likely than other classes, he argues, 'to value ambition, success, self-reliance, achievement, individuality, freedom, and cleverness. On the level of ideology, they are more likely to subscribe to liberal values and reform of the prevailing system' (Barakat 1990: 145). This is certainly true of some members of the intelligentsia and the liberal and technical professions: academics, lawyers and bankers, economists, engineers and other 'technocrats'. Such people formed, for example, the 'elite core' of the social base of Shihabist reformism in Lebanon during the 1960s (Johnson 1986: 140–5). These *tiknuqratiyyin* (see chapter 2, section 8, above) were the optimistic beneficiaries of modernity and they subscribed to a liberal and inclusive form of Lebanese nationalism that they hoped would gain hegemony over exclusive and particularistic forms of romantic nationalism. But Barakat fails to take adequate account of the petty-bourgeois or middle-class casualties of modernization. Pessimistic about the future, such people in Lebanon — along with members of the working class and sub-proletariat — turned to the values of patriarchy, family and confession.

Barakat's account of the different values that are associated with different Arab societies and classes is a useful counterweight to any notion of an all-inclusive 'Arab mind'. Also, his insistence that socialization occurs in society as well as within the family underlines the importance of a sociological approach. Child-rearing structures are socially and historically determined; they are not the result of a specifically 'Arab' family. But Barakat is reluctant to accept the evidence in the work of Ali Zayour and others that authoritarian family structures might be relatively prevalent.

In the early 1950s, E. Terry Prothro and Levon Melikian (1953) administered an 'F-scale' questionnaire to a group of undergraduates at the American University of Beirut (AUB). The first F-scale was designed in the United States by Theodor Adorno and his colleagues (1950) to identify people with 'fascist' and other authoritarian tendencies, who were then interviewed to determine the nature of their families. Adorno's study argued that authoritarian personalities were a product of repressive and disciplinarian parents who were exceptionally concerned to see that their children conformed to conservative values. In choosing to conduct an F-scale enquiry in Lebanon, Prothro and Melikian were working with a theory and methodology that would attract considerable criticism (Christie and Jahoda 1954). Nevertheless, if treated carefully their investigation does provide some evidence of authoritarian personalities among the students they interviewed.

There were 130 undergraduates in the sample, all of them Arab and a majority (77) Lebanese. Slightly over half were Christian, and one intention was to identify differences between them and Muslims. The results confirmed the prior assumption of the researchers that the culture of 'Greater Syria' was authoritarian owing to the nature of 'Syrian family life, where the father is the absolute head of the household, and both wife and children obey him' (Prothro and Melikian 1953: 355). The mean F-scale score of the AUB sample was 5.03, while that of a sample of students in Oklahoma was 4.10, and in California and Oregon 3.56. Muslims were somewhat more authoritarian than Christians; but as Halim Barakat points out in his critique of the study, there was a degree of inconsistency in the responses that perhaps invalidates the researchers' conclusions on this issue (Barakat 1990: 138).

Rather surprisingly, Barakat does not refer to more general criticisms of the methodology of authoritarian personality studies. Instead he points out that Prothro and Melikian did not test for such variables as social class, rural/urban origins or 'conditions prevailing at the time of conducting the research'. Also, he says, the questionnaire was 'culturally loaded' insofar as the version of the F-scale adopted by the researchers in Lebanon was designed for use in America. In fact the researchers recognized the latter problem, but they did not seem to think it invalidated their results (Prothro and Melikian 1953: 361). In their defence we might argue that, despite its faults and shortcomings, their study represents one of the few attempts to provide statistical data on a subject about which there has been a lot of ill-informed speculation. Their results indicate a degree of authoritarianism in the 1950s, and their assertions about the nature of repressive families are supported by the more recent research of Ali Zayour.

We do not need to demonstrate that such families were overwhelmingly pre-dominant in Lebanon during the 1970s and 1980s. We are, after all, mainly concerned with explaining the behaviour of those people who expressed mili-tantly communal values: 10 per cent of Theodor Hanf's sample of the adult population in the 1980s (see chapter 1, section 3, above), or perhaps 20 per cent of the population if we accept the figures given by Salim Nasr (1990; and see chapter 5, section 1, below). In other words, we do not need to argue that authoritarian personalities were exceptionally numerous, or were a product of a specifically Arab family structure, or of a 'Lebanese mind', still less of an 'Arab self'. But although we cannot give a precise statistical account of the relationship between patriarchal families, romantic values and ethnic conflict in Lebanon, the qualitative evidence provided in this chapter — drawn from such places as the Indian subcontinent and Africa as well as Lebanon — suggests that fighters in ethnic wars are often motivated by socioeconomic threats to the family and authoritarian patriarchy.

The issue is less one of whether there was a tendency to authoritarian per-sonalities in Lebanese society than of precisely where that authoritarianism was located and why it might have existed in the first place. It is here that Barakat's questions about social class, rural/urban background and socio-political conditions are so apposite. It is to be regretted that Prothro and Melikian presented their findings as a manifestation of a problem in an undif-ferentiated Libano–Syrian culture instead of looking more closely at variables that could indicate a structural and historical context. And it is equally regret-table that Ali Zayour seems to work with a notion of an undifferentiated 'Arab self'.

In answer to the question about the location of authoritarianism, Hisham Sharabi argues that neopatriarchy and the repressive family are predominantly urban petty-bourgeois characteristics, although he tends to elide the middle class with others when he talks of the 'petty bourgeois-proletarian masses' (Sharabi 1988: 9) — which if not an oxymoron comes very close to it. We need to specify these classes more carefully, but Sharabi's account is basically in accordance with my own, which interprets authoritarian romantic nationalism as being at least functionally associated with the petty-bourgeois, proletarian and sub-proletarian casualties of modernity.

When it comes to the origins of authoritarianism, however, Sharabi and I have somewhat different arguments, as will become clear in the rest of this chapter. He sees neopatriarchy as a consequence of dependent capitalism, by which he means that the lack of a fully developed economy — perhaps particularly the lack of significant industrialization — has resulted in a situation where precapitalist social relations have not been completely changed, but have been partially incorporated into a 'distorted' social formation. Precapitalist social relations (for example between landlord and peasant) and precapitalist political authority (such as leadership of the beduin tribe) were, he says, patriarchal; and although they are partly transformed by capitalism, they persist — or in my terms, they are reproduced — under the conditions of dependent capitalism as neopatriarchy. The problem with this argument is that it does not fully explain the complexities of different transitions to capitalism. Specifically, it does not identify precisely enough the political, social and psychological changes associated with *independent* capitalism that transformed European, north-American and other social formations into 'modern' societies as compared with what Sharabi describes as the 'inauthentic modernity' of the Arab world. If one fails to provide this level of detail then one cannot specify adequately the social and historical 'conditions' that he wants to confront and, if possible, change.

As a way into my own argument about patriarchy and different forms of modernity, it is worth considering an extremely illuminating part of Sharabi's account where he deals with patron–client relations or clientelism. Although he is presumably describing the way patronage works under authoritarian regimes, Sharabi's discussion fits very well with my own analysis of the way the Lebanese clientelist system meshed with such cultural values as honour and patriarchy (see chapter 2). More importantly for our immediate purposes, his insights into the nature of law, crime and punishment pave the way to a fuller discussion of modernity in Lebanon.

Sharabi sees the '*wasta* (mediation) mechanism' of clientelism as an analogy for the neopatriarchal family:

> *Wasta*, in the form developed within the family, not only socializes the individual into accepting the supremacy of established authority but also trains one in the ways of dealing with it. Through the intercession of the mother, the uncle, a respected figure close to the family, and so forth, the child discovers that despite one's impotence one can still operate in the existing system of power.
>
> (Sharabi 1988: 46)

In the wider political system, patrons intervene in the relationship between client and government department, employer, or court of law, and they influence outcomes to the benefit of the otherwise powerless 'supplicant' who is forced 'to beg at the doors of the powerful and wealthy'. If the client were to attempt a direct approach and plead his or her case according to universal principles of law, contract or civil rights, the desired service would almost certainly not be forthcoming. To achieve one's end, one has to submit to the authority of the patron. Rights are 'not inherently possessed but bestowed from above'. There is no 'social contract' and, like the adolescent in relation to the paterfamilias, the client is subject to the sometimes capricious whim of a powerful patron. 'The law,' argues Sharabi, 'serves not the society but the established sociopolitical order; *crime* is not distinguished from *sacrilege* or *rebellion*; and punishment is intended not to reform but to restore the sanctity of the law and to safeguard existing social relations' (Sharabi 1988: 47, emphases in the original).

Again we should note that Sharabi's comments on patronage and the law are probably confined to authoritarian regimes in the Arab world. But although pre-civil war Lebanon had a relatively independent and liberal legal system, it was still the case that za'ims and other powerful people interfered in it. As we have seen in chapter 2, za'ims would offer protection from the law to the qabadays and this 'service' could be used to impose a personalized political control at the expense of the rule of law. Often the regime itself would manipulate the legal process: during election campaigns, it was not uncommon for the government to order the arrest of those qabadays who worked for opposition za'ims, holding them in prison until after the election; and throughout the 1960s the *Deuxième Bureau* (military intelligence) gave protection to those qabadays who collaborated with the Shihabist regime, and harassed or imprisoned those who were associated with the parliamentary opposition (Johnson 1986: 141–2).

The corruption of public life was not confined to the qabadays and their relations with the political elite. Politicians used their positions to enrich themselves, taking bribes and obtaining government contracts to create business opportunities for themselves or their friends and relations. The already rudimentary planning laws and customs regulations were regularly flouted, and tax avoidance was widespread. A blind eye was often turned to honour crimes and to violence associated with political or economic rivalry. If you knew the right people you could usually, in one way or another, buy your way out of trouble. In effect people were punished if they had no protector, and living without protection could be construed as a statement of opposition to the political order.

It is in this sense that we can talk, as Sharabi does, of rights being 'bestowed from above', of criminal activity only being treated as crime if it was also in some sense a 'rebellion', and of punishment being something meted out more to restore the dominance of the establishment than to reform the criminal or to create an order based on universal principles.

With the collapse of established order in the Lebanese civil war, these characteristics became even more pronounced. Warlords and their militias held a power of life and death over the ordinary citizenry. Indeed, it is more accurate to describe Lebanese civilians during the wars of the 1970s and 1980s as subjects rather than citizens. They had no civil rights worth the name and were vulnerable more than ever to the whim of despotic leaders, who could now punish disloyalty by kidnap, torture and murder. The worst punishments were usually reserved for the enemy, but those who refused to pay protection money to the local militia, or failed to show sufficient loyalty and respect, were often subjected to arbitrary retribution.

One is reminded of Michel Foucault's study of surveillance and punishment (1975). Crime under the *ancien régime* in Europe attacked the monarch, as well as the immediate victim, because the law was an extension of the sovereign's will. Punishment was a spectacle that manifested the enormity of the crime in the body of the criminal as he or she died in public, often under torture. Modern punishment, by contrast, represented a shift from retribution to reform. The public display of spectacular punishment gave way to the spectacle or display of the trial and rule of law. The imposition of pain and destruction *on* the body was replaced by the surveillance and training *of* the body. Public execution and gross cruelty were abolished in favour of the essentially private punishment of a designated term of imprisonment designed to fit with the severity of the crime. Most crimes became a form of social deviance. They were no longer sacrilege or a rebellion against the sovereign. They were treated as legally graduated degrees of harm done to a society that had to be protected from assault, but which also needed to reform the criminal.

Drawing on insights from his earlier works on the history of medicine and psychiatry, Foucault developed his analysis of European surveillance. From around the start of the nineteenth century, society created 'carceral' or prison-like organizations such as hospitals, asylums, workhouses, factories, barracks and schools which, like the panoptican designed by Jeremy Bentham as a model prison, kept the patients, workers, soldiers, pupils and other inmates under the constant 'gaze' of social authority.

Thus in modern Europe, argues Foucault, it is not just the obviously repressive apparatuses of the state, such as the police and army, that maintain a stable social order, but also civil society itself through 'machineries' of institutional control, through calibrated discipline, self-discipline and timetabling, and through the fragmented, diffuse, but interconnected 'micro-powers' that permeate the carceral structures and their environments.

Foucault seems to trace the origins of this surveillance to the monastic system. Monks' cells in monasteries became the model for the divisions of schools into classes, armies into barracks, factories into the separate stages of production lines, and hospitals into specialized wards. Like the cellular structure of the prison, all these divisions and sub-divisions controlled the space in which people were subjected to discipline, and split them into manageable units. But carceral organization also served to combine people into a disciplined whole. Monks were not isolated individuals pursuing their own projects in their cells, but were part of a corporate monastery with clearly defined religious, social and economic goals. Similarly, the marauding soldiers of the past, who had sometimes looted and deserted at will, were confined to their various barracks and drilled into a disciplined fighting force. Under a strict hierarchy of command, platoons combined into companies, battalions and regiments, and the emphasis was no longer on individual strength, honour and heroism but rather on obeying orders and acting as part of an overall strategy of war.

The monastic timetable with set hours for prayer, work and private study was another influence on carceral organizations. The school day was divided into timed classes, each for specific subjects of learning, and like the monastic timetable punctuated by the ringing of bells. Factory workers were required to take their designated place on the production line at specified times — of necessity, we might add, as the line could not work properly if all the specialized tasks were not covered. The body was made to work like a machine or to be an extension of the machine with which it worked: the soldier an extension of the rifle, the textile worker of the loom. And to ensure that the body developed properly as an efficient machine, children in schools and soldiers in armies were subjected to 'exercise' in its widest sense, modelled on 'spiritual exercise' and designed to strengthen the body and discipline the mind:

> Exercises, not signs: time-tables, compulsory movements, regular activities, solitary meditation, work in common, silence, application, respect, good habits. ... [All these create] the obedient subject, the individual subjected to habits, rules, orders, an authority that is exercised continually around him and upon him, and which he must allow to function automatically in him.
>
> (Foucault 1975: 131–2; translation from Sheridan 1980: 148)

Discipline promoted self-discipline and both were the main elements of a power that was no longer absolute, overwhelming and concentrated, but temperate, measured and diffuse. This was not simply a power imposed from above, but something that was also generated within the individuals who together formed civil society. Foucault is quite clear that such power was not a negative repression. On the contrary, its extension throughout society was a positive development that produced active individuals and knowledge:

> We must cease once and for all to describe the effects of power in negative terms: it 'excludes', it 'represses', ... it 'conceals'. In fact power produces; it produces reality; it produces domains of objects and rituals of truth. The individual and the knowledge that may be gained of him belong to this production.
>
> (Foucault 1975: 196; translation from Sheridan 1980: 165)

This discussion of Foucault could possibly help us understand why societal order in Lebanon appeared so fragile as compared with the 'surveillance societies' that developed in nineteenth-century Europe and elsewhere. But we should proceed carefully and not immediately assume that Lebanon lacked European-style carceral institutions. It is argued below that, despite limitations, such structures were evolving in independent Lebanon. The problem is in deciding how far that evolution had gone and in assessing the effectiveness of surveillance in the institutions of civil society.

Drawing on the work of Talal Asad (1992) and Anthony Giddens (1985) as well as Foucault, John Gledhill (1994) suggests that while authoritarian regimes in postcolonial societies have at their disposal many of the attributes of a modern state — bureaucracies, armies, police forces and so on — they have not developed the subtle structures of administrative control associated with a 'penetration' and manipulation of society. They thus govern through 'weak' state structures and are forced to rely on 'physical coercion' and repression (Gledhill 1994: 17–21). In the context of the Middle East, we can see how this reliance on repression is either exercised overtly, as in the case of such police-states as Iraq or Syria, or through the more benign methods employed in the Lebanese clientelist system.

A problem with this sort of approach, however, is a tendency to over-emphasize the role of the state as the agent that creates (or fails to create) machineries of surveillance. Foucault, on the other hand, looks more closely at the workings of civil society. The problem emerges, for example, in the analysis of the modern nation state offered by Anthony Giddens (1985). Although in many respects he provides a much more persuasive account than Foucault's of the growth of surveillance societies in Europe, his emphasis is more on how the state and industrial capitalism created the structures of modern nation states than on what happened among those who 'imagined' the nation.

Giddens is certainly right to stress the role of capitalism, and particularly industrialization, in the development of surveillance. It makes much more sense to see the requirements of factory production for disciplined, organized and timekeeping workers as the motor of carceral structures than to interpret them as an off-shoot of monastic organization. And it is important to recognize the significance of state repression at the start of the process. Workhouses, and to a certain extent prisons, were established by the state to control the impoverished migrants from the countryside and forcibly expose them to the disciplines of wage-labour (Giddens 1985: 144–5 and 184–6).

However, although Giddens by no means posits a simple link between the requirements of industrial capital and the development of a surveillance state, his focus on the way the state and industrial forms of discipline penetrated society and established a pervasive administrative power perhaps needs to be supplemented by a closer analysis of relatively autonomous developments within civil society. This is necessary if we are to understand the development of *self*-discipline in modern society and move away from the idea — common enough elsewhere if not in the pages of Giddens — that order is invariably imposed from above. It is also important if we are to give a full explanation for the apparent lack of 'civil' surveillance in the Arab world.

At first sight, the reworking of Foucault by Giddens helps explain why industrialized societies have systems of surveillance and pre-industrial or developing societies do not. This in turn adds a meaningful content to Hisham Sharabi's bald assertion that neopatriarchy is a result of dependent capitalism. Clearly, the relative lack of industrial forms of organization in Lebanon and elsewhere in the Arab world has some bearing on the fact that neopatriarchal repression has not been superseded by societal surveillance. We could say, by way of illustration, that the lack of widespread industrialization helps to explain a corresponding deficiency, in some societies, of timekeeping, punctuality and associated forms of industrial discipline.

In a sense, industrialization must be the key because it is the only significant factor that is missing in Lebanon and the Arab world. Apart from large-scale factories and workhouses, most of the other carceral organizations are in place: schools, hospitals, barracks and prisons. We could add that Lebanon has monasteries as well.

All joking aside, we need to address a potential flaw in this argument. Yes, industrialization makes an important contribution to the development of 'modernity', universalism, carceral structures and surveillance. But is it not remarkable that even without industrialization, surveillance has not emerged in an Arab world where all the other carceral organizations are established? All the prisons, armies, bureaucracies, all the rote learning and discipline in schools, all the emphasis on physical exercise, all the repression within the family — all this and no surveillance?

It is only by appreciating Foucault's point about power developing *within* civil society that we can make sense of this. Social surveillance in Europe was perhaps less a result of the administrative penetration of society by the state than a consequence of actions taken by a large number of different people, either as individuals or in combination. It was not the state but entrepreneurs, inventors and engineers who developed the production line in factories. Doctors and nurses organized the hospital into wards. Generals and other officers turned the army into a disciplined fighting force. Teachers divided the school into classes. Humanitarians reformed the prison and systems of punishment. People in one carceral organization would learn from another and adopt its techniques, and I would concede that some of the lessons were probably learnt from monasteries.

This upsurge of intellectual and organizing activity was immensely exciting and empowering. Gradually the citizenry asserted their rights against the state. Property owners and tax-payers claimed the right of representation. Later, workers' friendly societies and trade unions also demanded political rights and the suffrage was extended. Very importantly, the courts asserted their authority against the executive and a rule of law was established. Some will argue that such structures as courts, schools and even hospitals are part of the state, but to go too far down that road makes the distinction between state and society meaningless. A much better way of looking at it is to say that the distinctive feature of modernization in Europe was not just that the state penetrated society, but that civil society also penetrated the state.

Partly under pressure, partly by default, and partly as a result of enlightened government, the state gradually left civil society to get on with it. Employers came to recognize trade unions and entered into negotiations that led to the improvement of workers' conditions; teachers abandoned rote learning and adopted more progressive methods of education; and the sexually repressive family was slowly transformed by a complicated set of circumstances that included the advice of child psychologists and feminist demands, as well as broad economic and social changes.

By contrast, in much of the colonized world civil society was virtually powerless vis-à-vis the state. The colonial state sometimes forcibly introduced the notion of private property and capitalist social relations. It imposed armies and martial law. It established bureaucracies to collect taxes, police to root out sedition, and courts to impose strict punishment on the recalcitrant. The judiciary was an arm of the executive, rarely a control on it. Similarly the schools were not designed to stimulate enquiring minds, but used learning by rote to produce collaborators and subalterns trained to obey orders. Schools, hospitals, agricultural co-operatives and institutions of local government were usually run like quasi-military structures as extensions of the state. Few of them were truly civil or civic. Part of their authoritarianism was derived from the models of institutions operating 'at home' in Europe. But because these colonial organizations were introduced or imposed from outside, there was little opportunity for innovation and reform from within.

Thus the carceral structures of colonialism failed to generate a power from below that could increase knowledge and activity. Instead, the requirements of political control and the racism of colonial officials reinforced or inculcated a culture of domination, dependency and submission. In some colonial possessions such as India, where a long and drawn out struggle for independence had wrung concessions from the imperial rulers, the organizations of civil society were able to make advances. But most societies in the Middle East had to wait for independence until this could happen to any meaningful extent, and then military intervention in politics soon established a neocolonial form of rule in which power was again imposed from above.

Lebanon was one prominent exception where power was decentralized. There were a number of reasons for this. First, the French administration in Lebanon did not have to impose capitalist social relations because in much of the society these were already in existence. As we have seen in chapter 3, feudalism was formally abolished in 1861. Peasants and farmers produced silk, grain and other cash crops, and there was a developed market in land. By the late nineteenth century, Beirut had become a relatively prosperous port and trading centre, and other market towns had been increasingly drawn into local, as well as long-distance, trading. Secondly, missionaries and indigenous philanthropists had set up schools and hospitals, so that some important carceral institutions were already well-established in civil society when the French arrived. Thirdly, the merchant elite and landlords had been used to exercising local power, and bargaining with each other, in the councils and assemblies of the Ottoman provinces, and many of them continued to do so in the democratic institutions of the Mandate. And finally, the mountainous terrain had been conducive to a long tradition of relative local autonomy from central authority that the French wisely worked with rather than markedly against.

One could argue that some of these conditions existed in other societies in the Middle East when Britain or France took direct control of Egypt in 1882, and Iraq, Transjordan, Palestine and Syria after the first world war. But in terms of the institutionalization of civil society, Lebanon was further advanced than elsewhere, and its political elite seemed more determined to build on this experience after independence. Free trade, finance and banking were encouraged, the state hardly intervened in the economy at all, and leading merchants and financiers, as well as landlords, were incorporated into the parliament and government (Johnson 1986: 119 ff). Lebanese democracy had its faults and the clientelist system did impose power from above, but the post-independence regimes were rarely oppressive. Za'ims and other influential people did interfere in the legal process, but the courts were hardly an extension of the executive as they were in most Middle Eastern states. There was a free press; and although a number of leftist parties were technically illegal until 1969, their newspapers and other publications were usually tolerated. Welfare services, hospitals, schools and universities were largely provided by private individuals, charities and foreign missions, and thus many carceral organizations remained almost entirely independent of administrative penetration by the state. Partly as a result of this, Lebanese civil society gradually created innovative medical and educational systems of an extremely high standard.

Of course, such services were not available to all, but neither were they in nineteenth-century Europe when surveillance societies first began to emerge. It is also the case that an active civil society in Lebanon could not, on its own, provide civic order, but again that was true for Europe as well. The self-discipline of modern European surveillance societies emerged from an evolving interaction and negotiation between the administrative power of the state and the diffuse micro-powers of civil society. And just as European states had to impose a degree of political control, by using police forces, prisons and the like, and then eventually contributed to an overall order by providing educational, medical and other welfare services, so too did the Lebanese state move in that direction in the 1960s. Shihabist reformism did this by strengthening the role of the repressive apparatuses of the liberal state (principally the *Deuxième Bureau*) and by extending public education and welfare to the poorer sections of society (see chapter 2, section 6).

What needs to be emphasized here, however, is that despite all the tensions and conflicts that had given rise to a civil war in 1958, Lebanese civil society had developed its own structures of surveillance. Moreover, given time, these could have generated the self-discipline and social order that Foucault saw as characteristics of modern Europe. Against the background of the disruption caused by the French Mandate, this was a remarkable achievement. The high point of eastern Arab unity in the second decade of the twentieth century, and the autonomous development of liberal nationalism and self-surveillance, had been indubitably undermined by the creation of *Grand Liban* in 1920. That Muslims and non-Catholic Christians could participate with Maronites in creating a liberal independent Lebanon a quarter of a century later was a great success for civil society (see the first section of this chapter).

In the latter part of the nineteenth century, liberal Islamic thinking had represented a development comparable to the Protestant reformation in

European Christianity (Hourani 1967; Ahmed 1960), and the Arab intellectual and nationalist 'awakening' (Antonius 1938; Salibi 1965: 120 ff) promised all sorts of possibilities for civil society despite the tension between Arabists and Lebanists. The separation of Lebanon from Syria after the first world war, however, created considerable hostility between Muslims and Maronites (and between Orthodox and Catholic Christians), not just at the 'popular' level of society but significantly within the elite as well. Nevertheless, the idea of a separate Lebanese nation — adumbrated earlier by a number of Maronites but given a more concrete and *inclusive* form by such people as Michel Chiha, the architect of the Lebanese constitution (see section 1) — eventually convinced the Muslim bourgeoisie that they would be better off in what amounted to the city-state of Beirut with all its potential as an entrepôt and financial centre.

Once the idea of the Lebanese project had been accepted by a majority in the economic elite, such politicians as Bishara al-Khouri and Riyad as-Sulh (respectively the first president and prime minister after independence) helped to build a liberal political system that drew upon the micro-power structures of the society. It might not have been ideal, but at least it reflected many of the realities of civil society and was not entirely imposed from above. And its reliance on kinship allegiance and patriarchal leadership was not necessarily a weakness. As we have seen, the creation of family associations mitigated some of the disruptive effects of urbanization (section 2), and the manipulation of family loyalty and honour played an important part in creating a relatively stable political order (chapter 2, section 6).

Indeed, the point needs to be made that patriarchy and the sexually repressive family are not simply the residues of traditional or pre-modern society, but are actually central features of modernization.

A stress on the values of patriarchy is certainly an important part of the appeal of romantic nationalism, but the sexually repressive family in Europe first developed during the early part of the nineteenth century when it was associated with modernization and the rise of *liberal* nationalism. Some, particularly Marxists, have seen this as connected to industrial capitalism and the need for a disciplined workforce. In his 'history of sexuality', however, Foucault (1976) makes the obvious point that if the functions of sexual repression were to provide such discipline, then the full weight of repression should have been applied to the working class. Surely it was essential to prevent the workers from dissipating their energies in the pursuit of pleasure and to confine their sexual activity as much as possible to their reproduction? In fact, the machinery of sexual repression was directed not at the proletariat, but at the women and children of the bourgeoisie. In the early nineteenth century, the upper-middle classes began to develop theories about their sexuality that were to lead to an obsessive concern with the control of women and children, with health and cleanliness, and eventually with eugenic notions of class and racial purity.

Middle-class women were 'invested by the machinery of sexuality', and theories developed about the 'idle', 'nervous' or 'hysterical' female. Similarly, great attention was paid by parents, teachers and doctors to the masturbating adolescent, 'wasting his future substance in secret pleasures':

> [T]his was not the child of the people, the future worker who had to be taught the disciplines of the body, but rather the schoolboy, the child surrounded by servants, tutors and governesses, who was in danger of compromising not so much his physical strength as his intellectual capacity, his moral duties and his obligation to preserve a healthy line of descent for his family and his social class.
>
> (Foucault 1976: 159–60; translation from Sheridan 1980: 190)

Machineries of sexuality were directed by the bourgeoisie against itself, as a way of defining a class identity and of demonstrating to itself and others its inherent superiority. Put simply, it represented a concern for a class-based and forward-looking genealogy. The old aristocracy — like the landlords of Lebanon — had worked with notions of blood and honour, the historical depth of their lineages, and the kinship alliances that had helped to preserve their absolute power. By contrast, the European bourgeoisie affirmed itself by a repressed sexuality, by the control of hysterical women and masturbating children, by a concern for pure and healthy descent, and by the promotion of honour, not as a manifestation of absolute domination, but as an expression of the intellectual and genetic hegemony of the new middle classes. Hence their almost neurotic concern for physical and mental health, their careful definition and classification of different diseases of the mind and body, and — in spite or perhaps because of the private hypocrisy of prostitution — their public preaching against the dangers of immorality and venereal disease.

Later, this form of surveillance was to lead to a science of eugenics and to notions of racial superiority. But we should not deduce from Foucault's account of the bourgeois family that the racist aspects of Nazism and other forms of romantic nationalism in Europe were merely an extension of the bourgeoisie's concern for a healthy genealogy. The latter represented an assertion of class superiority by those who had benefited from the modern economy. This did not mean that the dominant class sought to exclude others from the nation. On the contrary, liberal nationalism served the interests of the bourgeoisie by legitimating the social integration of different classes and ethnic groups into a linguistically and culturally standardized population, necessary for the efficient functioning of an industrialized national economy (Gellner 1983). Nazism, by contrast, was a corporatist ideology that sought to create an ethnically exclusive coalition based particularly on the petty-bourgeois and proletarian casualties of modernization. Part of fascism's success as a political movement was its appeal to a nostalgia for pre-modern values about blood and honour. And these were then combined with the values of the sexually repressive family that had, certainly by the early part of the twentieth century if not earlier, permeated the aspiring lower classes as well as the bourgeoisie.

In Foucault's account of this development, he writes of the re-emergence of pre-modern 'symbolics of blood' in the modern 'analytics of sexuality' (Foucault 1976: 197). The Third Reich made extremely effective use of imposed carceral institutions and 'disciplinary power' in maintaining its rule, preparing for war and implementing the holocaust. But this was intimately related to the private surveillance of Aryan women and the family by threatened patriarchs who were encouraged by fascist notions of eugenics, health, and 'the nation's blood and the triumph of the race' (Sheridan 1980: 193).

It seems that a substantial minority of the Lebanese, during the 1970s and 1980s, were attracted by 'symbolics of blood' that provided an emotional release from the 'analytics of sexuality'. It also seems that this had a lot to do with neopatriarchy, and it is significant that Hisham Sharabi starts the preface of his book with an account of two men of the 'wrong' confession who were shot dead at a roadblock, 'on their knees, crying and begging for mercy' (Sharabi 1988: vii). It would be oversimplistic, however, to assume that the patriarchal repressive family was necessarily a 'sickness' afflicting Lebanese society and politics in the way that Sharabi suggests it affected other Arab countries. It is also oversimplified to say that neopatriarchy in Lebanon was a result of 'distorted, dependent capitalism' (Sharabi 1988: 5). Patriarchal power and the repression of women, adolescents and children were no doubt extremely unpleasant for the recipients, but the evidence of nineteenth-century Europe shows they could be a 'normal' part of the modernization process.

The argument of Anthony Giddens leads us to conclude that neopatriarchy could have been eliminated had Lebanon industrialized, but a close reading of Foucault suggests that large parts of Lebanese society were nevertheless subject to the self-discipline and order of civil surveillance. Sharabi (1988: 61–83) is right to devote a whole chapter of his book to the 'colonial' or 'imperial' period for it was then, for most societies in the Middle East, that the conditions for an *imposed* form of surveillance and what might be called a 'pathological patriarchy' were created. In Lebanon, however, the historical experience of imperialism was different. Civil society was badly affected by the imposition of French rule and the separation of Greater Lebanon from Syria, but it had sufficient reserves of past experience — along with lessons learnt during the Mandate — to create a relatively self-disciplined, independent nation state in 1943.

Lebanese liberal nationalism was also able to hold its own against romantic challengers for much of the time until the 1970s. Sectarian identity was reproduced as a result of urbanization (see section 2 above) and the uneven development of the economy (section 4); and this reproduction of ethnicity was, of course, encouraged by the confessional systems of politics, education, welfare provision, and personal law. But special conditions brought about the triumph of romantic ethnic nationalisms and the collapse of liberalism. The civil wars were not inevitable, and they could have been avoided had it not been for external interference in Lebanese affairs. The problems and contradictions of neopatriarchy and the authoritarian family were real threats to the liberal project, but they might well have been no greater than similar threats in Europe during the nineteenth and early twentieth centuries.

6. Conclusion: external determinants of ethnic nationalism

It is worth repeating the points made towards the end of the last section. Patriarchy and the sexually repressive family are not merely the residues of a pre-modern society. They are better seen as phenomena that are reproduced in a new, modern, competitive and individualistic context. My treatment of Michel Foucault's account of surveillance suggests how, in Europe, they were gradually transformed as a result of the vitality and liberalism of civil society. But there were many setbacks in the forward march of liberalism, particularly in the 1920s, 1930s and 1940s. Extreme and intolerant forms of romanticism were especially attractive to those who were the casualties of modernization; and romantic nationalism conceptualized role models for patriarchs and their families, provided explanations for individual failures, and also identified demonized Others who could be blamed for the negative aspects of modernity.

Particular conditions bring about a combination of the modern 'analytics of sexuality' with pre-modern 'symbolics of blood' to create a widespread and aggressive form of exclusive nationalism. In Europe this had to do with the economic depression of the 1920s, the social and political grievances that it generated, and the cynical exploitation of emotions by determined leaders. In independent Lebanon, however, levels of inflation and unemployment were never anywhere near as high as they were in Germany after the first world war. Socioeconomic grievances, urbanization and threats to patriarchy contributed to the growth of romantic forms of identity, but it was largely external factors that undermined civil order to the extent of militarizing Lebanese politics, first in the late 1950s and then devastatingly so in the 1970s.

There is little doubt that the civil war of 1958 was in part due to the incompetence of President Camille Chamoun who made a series of foreign-policy blunders in relation to Egypt and rigged the 1957 elections to provide a parliamentary majority that would elect him for a second term of office (see chapter 2, section 3). It is also true that some Muslim classes — particularly the salariat — were motivated by a sense of relative deprivation. It is still the case, however, that the interference in Lebanese politics by President Jamal Abdul Nasser and the Egyptian intelligence service made a major contribution to the stimulation of Maronite fears about Muslim domination, and to the radicalization of Sunnis who perceived themselves to be deprived as compared with their Christian neighbours. This destabilization was further encouraged by the protagonists in the global cold war, who attempted to draw Lebanon into their respective spheres of influence. There was United States pressure on Lebanon to join the anti-Soviet Baghdad Pact, for example; and during the 1957 elections, the American CIA funded President Chamoun, while the Soviet Union advanced money to the opposition za'ims. Such activity by the Americans, Soviets and Egyptians, which included the provision of weapons to the opposing factions, increased tensions between Muslims and Christians, and contributed to a militarization of disputes that might otherwise have been settled by mediation (Qubain 1961; Copeland 1969).

As we have seen (in section 4), the confessional inequality of the 1950s had been at least partially rectified by the 1970s. Despite the increased militancy of workers' organizations, the pressures from society on the state could have been contained — by negotiation between the civil organizations of employers and workers, as well as police action — had it not been for another period of militarization in Lebanese politics. They might have over-reacted, but the increased intolerance of the Maronite parties is understandable when one considers the way Palestinian commandos acted like a 'state within a state', controlling strategic positions in and around Beirut, and — along with various Arab regimes — arming and training Muslim and leftist militias.

The civil warfare cooled after the Syrians invaded to prevent a victory by their former Palestinian and Lebanese-leftist clients. Worried about a radical pro-Palestinian government in Lebanon, which might provoke an Israeli invasion that would threaten Syrian security, President Hafiz al-Asad ordered his army to impose a settlement in the summer of 1976. The Syrians, however, were unwilling and unable to suppress the various militias, and the Israelis' encouragement of Maronite confessionalism and their invasion of 1982 stimulated many more conflicts. Israeli forces expelled the Palestinian fighters from Beirut and ensured the election of the Maronite warlord, Bashir Gemayel (see chapter 3, section 5), as president of Lebanon. After he was assassinated by an agent of Syria, the Phalangists blamed the Palestinians and took their revenge on the civilian inhabitants of Sabra and Shatila (chapter 1, section 4). Later, as Israeli troops withdrew from Lebanon, fighting broke out between the Syrian-backed Druze militia and the Israeli-supported Phalanges in the Shouf. Then, the military assistance given by the United States and its 'peace-keeping' forces to the Phalangist-dominated regime of President Amin Gemayel led to an intensification of the fighting. Encouraged and materially supported by the Soviet-armed Syrians, Druze fighters massacred Maronites, and the Shi'a Amal took over the Sunni quarters of West Beirut, conducting wars against the Murabitun militia and the Palestinians (see section 4 and chapter 2, section 7).

And so it went on. In 1988 Amin Gemayel's six-year presidential term ended, and the Lebanese parliament was unable to elect a successor. The Maronite commander-in-chief of what was left of the army, General Michel Aoun, claimed an executive position, but his predominantly Maronite enclave in East Beirut and part of Mount Lebanon was attacked by Syrian forces in 1989. In the same year, the parliament met in the secure environment of Ta'if in Saudi Arabia and negotiated a possible end to the civil war. But their chosen president, René Moawad, was assassinated soon after he took office, perhaps by agents of General Aoun or his Iraqi backers, but probably by Syrian interests that preferred to deal with a more compliant Maronite. Moawad was replaced by Elias Hrawi, and hesitant steps were taken to end the conflict. Then in 1990, at a time when even a faction of the Maronite Lebanese Forces (under the leadership of Samir Geagea: see chapter 3, section 5) was engaged in a bloody war to topple Aoun, the general fought on with Iraqi support. Finally, Iraq's invasion of Kuwait, and Syria's support of the USA and the allies in the Gulf war, led to a political situation in which the Americans, and indirectly Israel, could accept a final Syrian solution to the Lebanese wars. In October 1990, Michel Aoun's resistance was crushed by Syrian troops; and in the following year all the militias were disarmed, except for Hizballah that was allowed to fight on as a guerrilla force in the Israeli 'security zone' in southern Lebanon.

Although Syria eventually ended the war, it had, like Iraq, Libya, Israel, the US, and others, done much to prolong it at different times since 1975. It would be naive to think that the Lebanese fighters were innocents manipulated by outside forces. They were, of course, equally adept at manipulating their backers and were even capable of inflicting defeats on foreign forces in Lebanon. Also they were determined to continue the warfare, and they fought with enthusiasm for their respective 'homelands' and the honour of their communities. But they were a minority of the population. As we have seen in the first chapter (section 2), an overwhelming majority of Lebanese in the 1980s wanted a liberal-democratic end to the war, and an antiwar movement had developed in civil society. The militias became increasingly unpopular and, although they had responded to and emerged out of some of the contradictions within 'Lebanese modernity', they could not have fought for as long and as fiercely as they did without material and political support from outside.

This argument does not absolve the Lebanese militias of responsibility for the horrors of 'uncivil' fighting. Once the war had provoked the first confessional split in the Lebanese army in early 1976, there was no force strong enough to contain it. A war economy developed in which militia leaders could accumulate profits from the local arms trade, from such rackets as illegal construction and real-estate speculation, and from the export of the refined products of cannabis and the opium poppy — both grown in the Bekaa valley. Money was also raised by 'taxes' imposed on civilians and on goods passing through the various ports controlled by each of the major militias on the coast. As warlords became richer, they could buy arms on the international market and they became less dependent on external political support. It would have been difficult for the civilian anti-war movement to end the warfare entirely, and some foreign peace-keeping force was probably essential. The problem was that, until 1990, such potential peace-keepers as Syria, Israel, and the USA, all had rival agendas for Lebanon.

The real issue, however, is not why the war went on for so long, but how it started in the first place. Whatever sympathy we might have for the plight of the Palestinian refugees, it cannot be denied that their armed liberation movement — along with associated interferences by Arab and Israeli governments — contributed more than any other factor to the militarization of Lebanese politics. We should not idealize the prewar political system. The za'ims had, after all, co-operated with, and often encouraged, a violent culture of honour and feuding. But as we have seen in earlier chapters, the feud was a limited and mediated form of conflict. It was not conducted at a level of violence that threatened social order to anything like the destabilizing degree that confessional and ethnic warfare would achieve in the 1970s and 1980s. Also, Shihabist reformism in the 1960s had demonstrated that, at a time of relative regional stability, groups as different as Kamal Jumblat's Progressive Socialist Party, the Maronite Phalanges, and the technocrats and their professional organizations could co-operate with an astute president in an essentially liberal project to create a united Lebanese nation.

Perhaps it cannot be demonstrated categorically that the civil wars would not have happened without external interference. Nevertheless, the potential partnership between a liberal state and the surveillance structures of civil society was massively undermined by the violent activities of Palestinian commandos and a minority of the Lebanese people who received material aid and encouragement from their external sponsors.

5

Civil Society and Confessionalism in Postwar Lebanon

1. Liberal nationalism and patriarchal honour

Theodor Hanf's argument about Lebanese reactions to the civil war is encapsulated in the title of his book: *Coexistence in Wartime Lebanon: Decline of a State and Rise of a Nation* (1993). Despite the collapse of state authority, most civilians managed to co-operate during the years of fighting, and many developed a strong sense of Lebanese nationalism in reaction to the romantic ethnicities promoted by the militias. As we have seen in chapter 1 (section 2), 80 per cent of Hanf's sample of the adult population in 1987 supported a democratic resolution to the nation's problems, and by then such organizations as women's movements, trade unions and professional associations had become increasingly assertive in their opposition to the war.

Salim Nasr (1990), who assisted Hanf in conducting attitude surveys in the 1980s, was similarly optimistic about the future of civil society. He argued that at no time did the total number of fighters in all the Lebanese militias exceed 30,000, and during 15 years of war perhaps only 90,000 or 100,000 people (approximately 3 per cent of the total population) were ever members of a militia. He accepted that many others sympathized with the fighters, but concluded that less than 20 per cent of the population was part of a 'war society' in the sense of being actively involved in supporting one faction or another (Nasr 1990: 7).

The analyses offered by Hanf and Nasr demonstrate an important fact about the civil war: the vast majority of Lebanese played no active role in the fighting and wanted it to end in an intercommunal and democratic solution. This serves as a useful antidote to those accounts, such as my own, that concluded with pessimistic predictions about 'communal feeling and vengeance' making 'any truly Lebanese community an impossibility' (Johnson 1986: 226).

It should also caution us against generalizing too much about some of the literature discussed in this book in relation to the prewar society and culture of Lebanon. In her critique of anthropological accounts of male honour and violence in the Arab world, Lila Abu-Lughod (1990: 100–1) makes the telling point that 'the threat of violence may be less pronounced in the societies than in the relevant studies of them.' Such studies can be seen as part of an essentially masculine discourse written by European and north-American men who some-times seem to have a vicarious admiration for the violence they describe in their ethnographies. Certainly, we should not assume that because they were a part of Lebanese culture, the values of honour and feuding were necessarily endorsed by a majority of Lebanese people. Even where such norms appeared to be embedded in a local culture, men could find ways of avoiding their impli-cations, as Michael Gilsenan (1976) seems to suggest in his discussion of 'lying' and story-telling in the Akkar region of northern Lebanon. Abu-Lughod (1990: 101) argues that, by telling exaggerated tales, Akkari men were able to 'circum-vent in their social action the seemingly rigid rules of violence associated with a concern about honor.'

In a later article, Gilsenan describes the performance involved in recounting joking stories about the actions of honourable men:

> Much of the joking turns on fear ... represented grotesquely in panto-mime rolling of eyes, snivelling tones, shaking hands and the roars of the victim beneath the blows, which come complete with their own masterly sound effects. Virtuoso gestures mimic ... the ruin of the aesthetics of honour in often wonderfully contrived comedy. The nightmare of fear and the revealing of fear within the core of honour and respect becomes a performance generating explosive laughter and unrestrained amusement.
>
> (Gilsenan 1989: 207)

In other words, although the values of honour and heroism were often admired in Lebanon, they could also be mocked and derided. The 'individual' with his 'all-powerful will', who should have been the hero of the honour narrative, could be 'shown in comic realism as all too human' (Gilsenan 1989: 207). Nevertheless, the stories heard by Gilsenan dealt with a real 'nightmare of fear' and were, as he makes clear, a reflection of values that some men sought to emulate when they could (see chapter 2, section 4, above). Thus, although Abu-

Lughod's points might alert us to potential difficulties in the study of honour and shame, they cannot be used to deny entirely the cultural and social significance of such values.

Among those who normally eschewed the norms of honour in prewar Lebanon, their actual behaviour sometimes demonstrated they were influenced by an 'heroic culture'. Most of my neighbours in Sunni Muslim Beirut, for example, complained about the local qabadays and other aspects of the za'ims' clientelist structures of control, but it soon became apparent that many of them did support one or other of the local leaders. When challenged about their inconsistency, they would explain that their qabaday was different from the others, that he was honourable and 'helped the poor' (see chapter 2, section 5).

In the civil wars, the values of individual honour were reproduced as confessional pride and vengeance. Even secular and liberal people could feel the strong emotions of communal revenge at different stages of the fighting, as is illustrated by the quotation from Lina Mikdadi Tabbara's diary given in the first chapter of this book. She did not herself go out and slaughter Christians in revenge for the 'Black Saturday' massacres, and indeed she was eventually to work for reconciliation. But in the first months of the war, Tabbara felt 'the seeds of hatred and the desire for revenge taking root in [her] very depths':

> A call for sanity from Pierre Gemayel [the leader of the Phalanges] who, it is said, no longer believes in Christ because Christ was a Palestinian! I am thoroughly convinced of it now: all these regrets and fine speeches are nothing but lies. You do not listen to someone ... who has shed the blood of three hundred and sixty-five people to cleanse his honour. ... [N]o one in Lebanon can pretend any longer not to have taken sides. ... I am Lebanese, Moslem and Palestinian. ... I would like [the fighters of the Sunni Murabitun militia] to go into offices and kill the first seven hundred and thirty defenceless Christians they can lay their hands on. One shouldn't fall into the trap of blind sectarianism, but an end has got to be put to this cowardly indifference.
>
> (Tabbara 1979: 54)

We should be grateful to Tabbara for her honesty in telling us that she wanted to see twice as many Christians killed in revenge for the Muslims massacred by the Phalanges and other Maronite militias on the first Saturday of December 1975. We cannot begin to estimate what proportion of the Lebanese population experienced similar emotions. As we have seen in chapter 4 (section 3), psychoanalytic accounts suggest that fear and hatred of the Other, and feelings of narcissistic hurt and vengeance, are relatively common among those who become involved in ethnic conflict, either as protagonists or as the recipients or spectators of the violence. However, to recognize that many people can, like Tabbara, experience such emotions from time to time does not mean they will necessarily sustain their hatred and engage in the violence themselves. Clearly, there were far more victims than perpetrators in the Lebanese civil wars, and most people simply wanted the killing to end. They might have subscribed to patriarchal and kinship values that encouraged ethnic or confessional identity, but unless they were suddenly swept up in both emotion and circumstance they were unlikely to become directly involved in the fighting.

It is difficult to determine the number of people who were actually committed to communal warfare. There are all sorts of reasons for this, not the least of which is that some of those who said they wanted a democratic end to the conflict might well have been prepared under particular circumstances to engage in it. We do know that of Theodor Hanf's respondents in 1987 (79 per cent of whom were male) as many as 10 per cent were militant communalists, prepared to fight on and eliminate the Other from their territory (Hanf 1993: 533). Thus, despite the lessons that might have been learned from over a decade of warfare and the thorough 'demoralization of public life' (Khalaf 1987: 238 ff), a relatively large minority was still ready to prosecute the war to a 'final solution'. This group was smaller than the 20 per cent of the total population identified by Salim Nasr as belonging to what he called a 'war society', and included the most extreme supporters of the various political factions. But in addition to those who believed members of other communities should be massacred or expelled, there were others who felt Lebanon should be partitioned into confessional enclaves where minority confessions should accept the rule of the locally dominant community. Although the data presented by Hanf and Nasr are not directly comparable, it is clear that a substantial minority was committed to the values of romantic 'ethno-confessionalism'.

Hanf's evidence suggests that the militant group was 'economically frustrated' (Hanf 1993: 533). It included some high-school and university graduates, and some who were rich, but most confessional militants had lower levels of education and income. This accords with my argument that the adherents of ethnic or romantic nationalism were usually the casualties of modernization (see chapter 4). Forced migrants to the city, the unemployed, and those whose lower-middle-class livelihood was precarious, were all potentially prone to demonize their Other as they sought to resolve the perceived contradictions of modernity and the associated conflicts of the self.

In a society composed of different confessional groups, it seems almost inevitable that dissatisfaction about economic and social opportunities should be expressed in communal terms. When a society such as Lebanon's is structured around the principles of confessional representation in politics, confessional family law, and the confessional provision of educational, medical and welfare services, then the prospects for a national identification are reduced. It is not surprising, therefore, that disgruntled young men in Lebanon's civil wars should have identified their Other as a member of a different religion, particularly if they were encouraged to do so by their political leaders.

All societies develop methods for containing youthful rebellion, and in prewar Lebanon the za'ims might be said to have contributed to an overall order by incorporating the aggressiveness of youth into the clientelist structures of the state (see chapter 2, sections 5 and 6). We have seen (in chapter 3) that the values of honour and violent heroism had a long history, and when they were reproduced in modern society they were not merely there as a result of encouragement by leaders. Nevertheless, the manipulation by the za'ims of an heroic culture did serve to perpetuate communal pride and the desire for vengeance against those who threatened that pride. These emotions were then translated in a magnified form into the imposition of shame on the Other once the system of control broke down in the 1970s.

A much more effective method of controlling violence would have been to generate machineries of surveillance in civil society (see chapter 4, section 5). Here Lebanon had a degree of success with its schools, hospitals, army barracks and other 'carceral' organizations, including the sexually repressive family. But for surveillance to work effectively, it is essential that the carceral institutions mesh with each other to create a web of micro-powers that together provide an overall societal order in which the more repressive forms of surveillance (such as the patriarchal family) can be gradually transformed and liberalized. If the carceral structures are divided each from the other by confession, then interaction cannot take place very effectively. Thus, despite the developments within civil society outlined in chapter 4, surveillance in Lebanon never achieved the degree of sophistication it did in Europe.

We might argue that had it not been for external interference, the separation between Lebanese micro-powers could have been overcome, and it is certainly the case that the relative stability of civil society was seriously undermined by the intervention of Palestinian militias and Arab and Israeli intelligence agencies. But if we are interested in a stable future for Lebanon, it would be sensible to encourage the promotion of inclusive, as opposed to confessionally exclusive, carceral organizations.

It is therefore worrying that the new Lebanon has been constructed along the same confessional lines as the old. Under the terms of the 'Ta'if agreement' negotiated by the Lebanese parliament when it met in Saudi Arabia in October 1989, the political imbalance in favour of Christians has been changed. The powers of the Maronite president have been limited, the remits of the prime minister and the speaker of the parliamentary assembly have been extended, and the ratio of Christian to Muslim members of parliament has been changed from 6:5 to an equal representation of the two communities. But the presidency is still reserved for a Maronite Christian, the premiership for a Sunni Muslim, and the seats in parliament for the different sects according to their rough size in the population. There is an obvious injustice here in that the Shiʻa are now the largest sect; and according to the conventions of the original confessional compact, they ought to be given the presidency instead of the chair of the parliament. But the real problem is the continuance of the confessional principle in political representation.

Secular and multiconfessional women's organizations and trade unions were at the forefront of civil society's antiwar movement. Yet, as we shall see, they were virtually ignored in a *pax Syriana* that for most of the 1990s seemed intent upon incorporating into Lebanon's 'Second Republic' the sectarian confessional warlords who had done so much to destroy the country in the 1970s and 1980s. Perhaps the local power of the militia leaders made such an incorporation a pragmatic necessity, and we know from Hanf's study that there was popular support for confessional representation in the political system. But although 80 per cent of the 1987 sample favoured a democratic confessional solution, 71 per cent of respondents supported the creation of a secular party system and government by the majority party or coalition. If we differentiate these over-lapping groups, they break down into three as follows. A 'progressive' minority of 17 per cent (nearly 16 per cent of the total sample) was opposed to con-fessional representation and supported only simple majority rule. A 'conser-vative' group of 23 per cent explicitly rejected a secular democracy and insisted on power-sharing between the confessions. A 'liberal majority' of 60 per cent, however, would have been happy with either system (Hanf 1993: 523–34).

In the immediate aftermath of the civil wars, it might well have been sensible to opt for the more popular form of confessional representation, just as Michel Chiha and others had felt it was a temporary necessity in the 1920s to heal divi-sions and create the conditions for a truly liberal and inclusive nationalism (see chapter 4, section 1). But in the longer term it would surely be advisable to build on the relatively large majority of people who support the idea of a secular system.

Confessional representation inevitably favours strong communal leaders whose behaviour as militia warlords had encouraged the destructive values of neopatriarchy. As we have seen in chapter 4 (section 5) patriarchy and the sexually repressive family can be interpreted as 'normal' aspects of moderniz-ation. Also, confessional and other forms of ethnic identification are not uncommon responses to the disruptive effects of urbanization and the under-mining of the extended family (chapter 4, section 2). Neither patriarchy nor ethnicity need be dangerous. When, however, the 'symbolics of blood' enter the 'analytics of sexuality' (chapter 4, section 5) then a threatened patriarchy can contribute to a situation in which ethnic identification develops into fierce conflict.

Unfortunately, many of the prewar za'ims and virtually all the warlords encouraged the 'symbolics of blood'. Even those za'ims who had worked hard to contain communal conflict were in effect confessional leaders, and they had cer-tainly laid great emphasis on the values of patriarchal honour when it came to managing their clienteles. Because macho values of honour and violence were built into the clientelist structures of the prewar state, some young men had been encouraged by the political establishment to assert their masculinity in an heroic culture of pride and vengeance. This could be controlled in what I describe in chapter 2 (section 7) as the 'damage-limitation exercise' of the feud, a form of conflict that prescribed rules for mediation and restricted levels of violence. The conditions of warfare, however, unleashed all the powerful emotions of revenge and hatred against the Other.

It is oversimplified to see a direct link between political feuding and confessional war (see chapter 2, sections 7 and 8; and chapter 3, section 6). Nevertheless, the values of personal honour and vengeance, coupled with ideas about authoritarian and patriarchal leadership, are characteristics of romantic or ethnic nationalism which, when they are combined with notions of common ancestors and a shared blood, can encourage extreme forms of ethnic identity and hostility. The weaving together of romantic ideas about male honour and heroism with the sophisticated formulations of ethnic nationalists about pre-modern 'symbolics of blood' provides an emotional release from the modern family's 'analytics of sexuality'. The undermining of the extended family and the emergence of nuclear units, and the need to control patrimony and the sexuality of women and adolescent men, all create the contradictions of the sexually repressive family. In reaction, threatened patriarchs, frustrated young men and oppressed women seek solace in symbolic ideas about leadership and pro-tection, motherhood and the kinship of blood. As we have seen in chapter 4, whether it takes the form of Nazi anti-Semitism, Maronite particularism, Muslim Arabism, or Islamic militancy, romantic nationalism is an exclusive and nostalgic reaction against modernity, as compared with an inclusive, and forward-looking, liberal nationalism that embraces the modern with enthu-siasm.

An inclusive form of nationalism was central to the ideas of the National Pact, which paved the way to Lebanese independence in 1943. It was also a dominant ideology during the reformist regime of President Fu'ad Shihab (1958–64) and during at least the early part of Charles Helou's presidency (1964–70). Given that liberal nationalism was so influential in modern Lebanon and that, left alone by the men of violence, many Lebanese were entrepreneurial in their economic activity and 'modern' in their approach to such matters as the education of their children, it is perhaps surprising that neopatriarchy and romanticism seemed so prominent in the political culture. When I lived in Beirut in the early 1970s, I met many Shihabists and other reformists who wanted to replace the confessional and clientelist system with a modern liberal democracy. Some of them stood for election to parliament in 1972; but they did not win many votes and most electors supported the patriarchal za'ims and their allies (Johnson 1986: 162). Similarly, while some 'new' and secular leaders (including women) were elected to the Lebanese parliament in the postwar elections of 1992, 1996 and 2000 many of the most successful candidates were communal militants. Despite the growth of a sense of Lebanese nationalism in civil society in reaction to the confessional warlords and their violent depredations, there was still considerable electoral support for the former militias that had now become influential political parties in the Second Republic.

There is obviously a continuing tension in Lebanese civil society between the values of liberal and romantic nationalism. Hanf's sample survey of 1987 suggests that while a minority of the population was fully committed to political reform and a thorough secularization, a larger group gave support to patriarchal and confessional leaders. The majority, however, was prepared to accept some form of secular government so long as there were confessional safeguards. This solution was suggested by the 1989 Ta'if agreement that talked of the eventual establishment of a bicameral parliament, with a lower house elected on a secular basis, and a senate selected by confessional representation. The agreement stated that 'the abolition of confessionalism' was 'a vital national objective' and should be achieved 'in stages' (Hanf 1993: 585–8). But no timetable was set for a new political system; and although there was some popular support for the idea, there has been little sign of any governmental momentum towards it.

2. Reconstruction and economic growth

In many respects, the recovery of Lebanon after the war was impressive. A considerable amount of economic activity was generated by reconstruction. Electricity and water supplies were repaired and enhanced, telecommunications expanded, old hotels like the Phoenicia were renovated and new ones built, and the Beirut property company, Solidere, embarked on an ambitious programme to rebuild the city's central business district. Even banking made a modest recovery, for example through the issue of Eurobonds.

Initially, however, there were setbacks. As a result of continued fighting in the south between Shi'a Hizballah forces and Israel and its Lebanese proxy militia, there was a crisis of investor confidence in 1991 that led to a projected increase in government borrowing and yet another devaluation of the Lebanese currency in 1992. In May 1992, strikes and demonstrations stimulated by the currency crisis and inflation took on the character of a 'popular uprising' (Hanf 1993: 624). The prime minister's office, a hotel owned by the speaker of parliament, petrol stations owned by the president's son, and the finance minister's house were attacked and vandalized. The prime minister (Omar Karami, the brother of Rashid who had been assassinated in 1987) and his government resigned and a new cabinet (with Rashid as-Sulh as premier) was formed to supervise parliamentary elections — the first since 1972.

Four years later, in February 1996, the *Confédération Générale des Travailleurs Libanais* (CGTL) organised a general strike, demanding a 76 per cent increase in public-sector salaries and a 100 per cent increase in the minimum wage. This time, however, the protest was put down by the Lebanese army, and a curfew was imposed in the major towns and cities (Europa Publications 1998: 752). Repression became the standard response to groups within civil society that challenged the political order. As we shall see, the CGTL labour union confederation, and other opposition groups, protested in October and November 1996 against bans on public demonstrations and the closing down of a number of radio and television stations. And once again, troops were deployed on the streets of Beirut to prevent a general strike and demonstrations.

After the 1992 elections, a new cabinet was formed under an extra-parliamentary prime minister, Rafiq al-Hariri, a billionaire with Saudi as well as Lebanese citizenship and close ties to the governments of Saudi Arabia and the United States. His appointment stimulated confidence, particularly because he was prepared to invest much of his personal fortune in reconstruction. International and local confidence in him was demonstrated by an increase in the value of the Lebanese pound when he took office, and declines when he threatened to resign in December 1994 and May 1995. During Hariri's premiership, the currency stabilized, rates of inflation and unemployment fell, and impressive economic growth rates of Gross Domestic Product were achieved at 9 per cent in 1994 and 6.5 per cent in 1995 (Perthes 1997).

Nevertheless, the government relied on heavy borrowing requirements and in 1997 the budget deficit rose to 59 per cent of state expenditure (*MEED*, 19 June 1998). As a result, interest rates were high and this meant that lending to the private sector had been squeezed, delaying the start of revenue-earning projects and contributing to a lower rate of annual economic growth at 4 per cent in 1996 and 1997. Some argued that the government should raise taxes: income and corporation tax had been lowered to a flat rate of 10 per cent, and there was certainly a case for an increase. But for many, including the government, the answer lay in foreign aid, concessionary finance, and private investment. The problem was that these would not be as forthcoming as expected while the security situation in relation to Israel was so uncertain.

The refusal to raise taxes was seen as an example of the government's intention to favour the economic elite at the expense of the poor. It was estimated that more than 25 per cent of the population lived below the poverty line in 1996 (Perthes 1997), while those close to the regime made fabulous profits from an extraordinarily corrupt and 'politicized' economy. Stories of bribes and kickbacks were legion. It was estimated, for example, that the successful tender for the southern extension of the coastal motorway was overpriced by millions of dollars, and much was made of the fact that the firm that had won the contract was run by the wife of Nabih Berri, the leader of Amal and speaker of the parliament (Perthes 1997: 17).

In 1998, President Elias Hrawi's extended period of office came to an end, and Emile Lahoud, the commander of the Lebanese army, was elected in his place with a commitment to stamp out corruption and deal with the budget deficit. The new president worked closely with a technocratic government under the premiership of Salim al-Huss, and in April 1999 a reformist budget was presented to parliament. Although the deficit had decreased in Rafiq al-Hariri's last year of office to 43 per cent of government expenditure, it was still large, and the new finance minister, George Corm, announced his intention of reducing it much further — to approximately 6 per cent of Gross Domestic Product within three years — from its current level of 14 per cent of GDP. The budget raised income and corporation taxes to a rate of 15 per cent, and increased indirect taxes on a wide range of goods and services. Along with plans to privatize governmental holdings in utilities, these measures stimulated a degree of renewed confidence among foreign investors, and the growth rate of real GDP was predicted to rise in the new millennium (*MEED*, 11 December 1998 and 23 April 1999).

It was clear that the government needed to increase its revenue by raising taxes and dealing with tax evasion, and these were two aims associated with Corm's fiscal adjustment programme approved by parliament in June 1999. This five-year plan forecast a doubling of government gross revenues through increasing tax income, and a reduction of the budget deficit to less than 20 per cent of expenditure (*MEED*, 19 November 1999). A year later there was no improvement. Indeed, the situation was worse than ever. Total public debt was estimated as being as high as 130 per cent of GDP, the budget deficit had increased to nearly 52 per cent of government expenditure or about 15 per cent of GDP, and some economists claimed that GDP had actually fallen by around 1 per cent in the previous year (*MEED*, 16 June 2000; *MEIB*, 'Intelligence Briefs', 1 June 2000). The prospects for lifting the economy out of recession in 2000 were very limited so long as investors were discouraged by the lack of progress in a peace agreement between Israel and Syria. And as we shall see, the government's failure to deal with the economic crisis would shortly have severe electoral consequences.

3. Elections and confessionalism

Initial disillusionment with the new political order, and opposition to Syrian military occupation, were reflected in low turnout figures for the general election in 1992 (Bahout 1993; Hanf 1993: 625–34). It soon became apparent that the constituency boundaries had been drawn to favour those politicians, many of them former warlords and their lieutenants, who were close to the Syrians. According to the Ta'if proposals, Mount Lebanon, for example, should have been one constituency, but in the event was divided into six. This appeared to be a blatant act of gerrymandering to ensure the election in the Shouf constituency of the Druze warlord, Walid Jumblat, who would otherwise have had to win the support of the overwhelmingly Christian electorate in Mount Lebanon — an electorate with reason to hate him for the massacres that had occurred in the 1983 Druze–Maronite war (see chapter 2, section 7).

The subsequent Christian boycott of the elections meant that pro-Syrian placemen were elected to Maronite seats. Among these was Elie Hobeika, the former Phalangist, considered by many to have been the mastermind behind the 1982 massacres of Palestinians in Sabra and Shatila, who had switched his allegiance to Syria in 1985. He was elected in the Baabda constituency (where there was a 12 per cent turnout of the electorate) with about 3 per cent of the potential vote. Such Maronite leaders as General Michel Aoun (leader of the resistance to Syrian hegemony in 1989–90), Dory Chamoun (son of the former president, Camille Chamoun) and Amin Gemayel (president of Lebanon from 1982 to 1988) remained in exile, so that the popular Maronite parties constituted an extra-parliamentary opposition. The main exception to this was in the northern districts in and around Zgharta, where pro-Syrian Maronites were popular leaders and Tony Frangieh's son, Suleiman, and his allies were elected (Hanf 1993: 633–4).

In Beirut neither the former Sunni za'im, Sa'ib Salam, nor his son Tamam stood, presumably fearing Syrian sanctions, and this contributed to the alienation of some of the city's Sunni community. Coupled with the Maronite boycott, this resulted in a very low turnout in Beirut of 10 per cent, compared with

47 per cent in 1972. Overall, only 20 per cent of the Lebanese electorate voted in 1992 and, if we exclude the relatively high number of potential electors living abroad, this meant that less than a third of those able to vote did so, as compared with approximately 60 per cent in previous elections. (For the 1992 elections, see: Bahout 1993; and Hanf 1993: 625–34).

The highest voting rates occurred in the predominantly Shi'a constituencies in the northern Bekaa valley and southern Lebanon. Although it was about a third less than in 1972, a turnout of 40 per cent was at least relatively representative. Not surprisingly, the traditional za'im leadership in these regions was swept aside by candidates of the Amal and Hizballah parties, who along with the Syrian regime were the main beneficiaries of the elections (Hanf 1993: 631–3).

Between the general elections of 1992 and 1996, the economy improved and there was renewed optimism in civil society. Until his harsh treatment of civic opposition and the extensive corruption of his regime tarnished his image, Rafiq al-Hariri was a popular prime minister. His position was considerably strengthened by winning nearly 79,000 votes in the Beirut constituency in the 1996 elections, the largest number won by any candidate, and by the success of his electoral list that won 14 of the 19 seats in the city. Despite a low turnout of 30 per cent and allegations of vote-buying and corruption, this result in his first election established Hariri as the most powerful za'im in Beirut, eclipsing the traditional political elite. But opposition candidates were successful too. Salim al-Huss, a former prime minister who headed an opposition list, won with 64,000 votes, and Tamam Salam won as an independent. The leftist Greek Orthodox member of parliament, Najah Wakim, a vocal critic of Hariri, also won, but with a reduced share of the vote compared with his 1992 result (*MEED*, 13 September 1996).

The 1996 election was much more representative than the previous one. The most obvious case of gerrymandering was in Mount Lebanon, again to ensure the success of Walid Jumblat and his allies. Nevertheless, the calls for a Christian boycott from exiled Maronite leaders were largely ignored. Turnout in the Mount Lebanon constituencies averaged 45 per cent, one point higher than the national average; and after a copious distribution of state patronage and some electoral fraud, government ministers and their clients won 32 out of 35 seats, a colossal defeat for the exiles. Again, the highest turnouts were in the northern Bekaa (53 per cent) and southern Lebanon (48 per cent) where Amal and Hizballah won most of the seats. Overall, Hizballah lost some of the seats it had won in 1992, and this was interpreted as an indication of some tension with the Syrians, as well as closer relations between Hariri and the leader of Amal, Nabih Berri, who had been the parliamentary speaker since the election of 1992. In the

128-seat parliament in November 1996, Hariri's bloc of between 30 and 40 deputies and Berri's of 20 to 25 contributed to political stability. But the overwhelming majority of pro-Syrian members of parliament confirmed an external hegemony over Lebanon that was already apparent in the subordination to Damascus of the Lebanese army and of such leading politicians as President Hrawi, Prime Minister Hariri, Nabih Berri and Walid Jumblat. (For the 1996 elections, see: *MEED*, 6–27 September 1996; *Oxford Analytica Daily Brief*, 27 September 1996: 11–12; and Salem 1997).

In November 1996, Rafiq al-Hariri was forced to form a new cabinet that included some of his staunchest pro-Syrian critics. Two new ministers (who had served in earlier postwar cabinets) were Suleiman Tony Frangieh, the Maronite za'im from Zgharta and grandson of Suleiman, the former president of Lebanon, and Talal Arslan, a Druze emir and rival of Walid Jumblat. Both were very close to Damascus, and their return to government (Frangieh as minister of health, and Arslan as minister for emigrant affairs) was seen as a reminder to Hariri and the others as to who were the true masters in Lebanon (*Oxford Analytica Daily Brief*, 12 November 1996: 12–13).

The other noteworthy feature of this government was that former warlords who had ended the civil war in alliance with Syria continued to hold ministries. As well as Suleiman Tony Frangieh whose family had led the Marada fighters in northern Lebanon, three other members of Hariri's cabinet had been associated with militias. The Druze leader, Walid Jumblat, remained as minister for displaced persons; the former Phalangist, Elie Hobeika, retained his position as minister of electricity; and Asad Hardan of the Syrian Social Nationalist Party (SSNP) also continued as a minister, holding the labour portfolio.

This continuing incorporation of warlords — including Nabih Berri as parliamentary speaker — should be contrasted with the repression directed against ordinary Lebanese citizens. Soon after the new government had taken office in November 1996, the Lebanese army was deployed to prevent civil disobedience and a general strike by trade unionists. The latter were campaigning for an end to a 1993 ban on public demonstrations and for the rescinding of legislation that would restrict broadcasting to six television and 12 radio stations. There was no doubt that the civil war had contributed to a chaotic state of broadcasting, with many small stations representing narrow sectarian interests. But the government's intention to license only a limited number of companies was seen as an attempt to restrict freedom of expression in the political and financial interests of the regime. Of four private (as opposed to state-run) television networks granted licences under the new law, one belonged to Rafiq al-Hariri, one to Nabih Berri, and another to the brother of Michel al-Murr, the minister of the interior. Only 11 private radio stations from an estimated total of 150 had been granted licences; and of the three allowed to broadcast news, one was owned by Hariri and another by Berri. Then in late December 1996, after a mysterious machine-rifle attack on a bus carrying Syrian migrant workers, some fifty people were arrested, including a journalist for the prestigious daily newspaper *An-Nahar*. Concern was expressed that these arrests, along with restrictions on the media, represented an excessively heavy security-clampdown by the government and Syrian authorities (*MEED*, 11 October 1996 to 17 January 1997).

In addition to trade union opposition, there were signs of a Maronite disenchantment that might threaten the Second Republic. Many Christians had supported General Michel Aoun's failed attempt to unite the Lebanese against the Syrians in 1989–90 (see chapter 4, section 6). Shortly after the defeat of Aoun's forces in October 1990, one of his lieutenants, Dany Chamoun, the leader of the Liberal National Party's militia and son of the former president, Camille Chamoun, was assassinated along with his wife and two children in their home near the general's headquarters. Suspicion fell on another Maronite warlord, Samir Geagea, who had led his faction of the Lebanese Forces (LF) against Aoun in favour of an accommodation with the Syrian-sponsored Ta'if agreement. Geagea's apparent collaboration with Damascus meant he was unpopular in his community, but he soon demonstrated he was not prepared to accept a permanent Syrian rule. His relations with the postwar government deteriorated, and he began to articulate a Maronite opposition to the continued occupation of Lebanon by Syrian troops.

Then, in February 1994, when Geagea's LF was transforming itself into a political party, a bomb exploded in a Maronite church, killing ten people. The government immediately claimed 'Zionist agents' were responsible, but many Christians blamed the Syrians and Lebanon's security forces, arguing that it was an attempt to terrorize the Maronites and justify further repression. The LF was banned and, in April 1994, in what seemed a masterstroke by the regime, Samir Geagea was arrested and charged with organizing both the bombing and the murder of Dany Chamoun and his family. During a nine-month trial in which the judges appeared to be following Syria's bidding, the bombing charge came to lack credibility, but Geagea was found guilty of the Chamoun assassination and sentenced to life imprisonment (Harris 1997: 277, 290 and 300–1).

Many Maronites believed Geagea was singled out for a retribution that should have been directed at other warlords as well, and his continued incarceration became a growing source of resentment. In 1996 he was given 10 years imprisonment for maintaining the Lebanese Forces militia and trying to rearm it during the early part of 1994. Then, in the years that followed, further charges were brought against him and, at different trials, he was sentenced to life imprisonment for the attempted murder of Michel al-Murr in 1991, life for the assassination of the Lebanese prime minister, Rashid Karami, in 1987, and life again for the murder of an LF official in 1989. At his 1999 trial for the assassination of Rashid Karami, Geagea complained of 'selective justice'. He pointed out that, although it possessed intelligence about their identities, the Lebanese government had not charged those who had killed the Lebanese president René Moawad in November 1989, the Lebanese *mufti* (Sunni juriconsult and 'archbishop') Sheikh Hasan Khalid in May 1989, and the Druze leader Kamal Jumblat in 1977 (*MEIB*, July 1999). The implication was clear: the assassins had all been agents of Syria and were therefore immune. Car bombs had killed Moawad and Khalid because they had wanted to negotiate with Syria's enemy Michel Aoun, and Jumblat had been shot because he had opposed the first intervention in Lebanon of Syrian troops in 1976. Why were some warlords and other killers granted an amnesty and not the leader of the Lebanese Forces?

In spite of the participation of some major Maronite groups in the 1996 elections, the allegiance of the largest Christian confession to the post-Ta'if regime remained problematic. The Lebanese Forces produced a hagiography of Samir Geagea on their internet website (www.lebanese-forces.org) alongside a similar treatment of another victim of the Syrians, Bashir Gemayel (see chapter 2, section 7), the LF leader and Lebanese president-elect who had been murdered in 1982, and whose assassin had been freed from prison when the Syrian army took control of East Beirut in 1990. This and other websites talked of a plucky and tenacious Maronite resistance to Syrian hegemony, and provided details of political prisoners, torture and other abuses of human rights. Maronite rivals of the LF were also active. In Paris, for example, General Michel Aoun, Dory Chamoun (Dany's brother) and Amin Gemayel formed an alliance to press for Syrian withdrawal and the re-establishment of Lebanese sovereignty. Although this group and Geagea's LF were unable to exercise any significant influence over events in a Lebanon so much under the control of Damascus, they did represent a considerable degree of privately expressed hostility within the Maronite community.

In the summer of 1998 Lebanon went to the polls again, this time to elect district and municipal councils. For the first time in over three decades, voters were able to choose local councillors and there was a ready response to the opportunity. The elections were conducted in an atmosphere of considerable freedom, without any marked Syrian interference, and there was a very high rate of turnout — 70 per cent of registered electors in some districts (Europa Publications 1998: 754). Seats were not reserved for members of particular confessions, and thousands of people presented themselves as candidates. Secular representation at the local level of politics was a modest new departure, and the enthusiasm of the electorate demonstrated the vitality of civil society. Commenting on the large number of candidates, Paul Salem of the Lebanese Centre for Policy Studies said: 'It's very healthy to get these people involved in politics — the young, women, environmentalists, professionals. This will change the face of political elites' (*MEED*, 19 June 1998: 10).

Optimism was high within the Maronite community. Dory Chamoun returned from exile and won a seat in his family's home town of Dayr al-Qamar, and other candidates opposed to the government were either elected or came close to it in other parts of Mount Lebanon, including supporters of Samir Geagea. Nevertheless, the result in Tripoli, where only one Christian was elected to a council of 24, stimulated or confirmed fears that Christians were being excluded from political life. Clearly, confessional identities were still prominent as compared with any desire for a genuine secularization.

Notwithstanding Syria's low profile in the local elections, opposition persisted in all communities to the occupying power. Although there had been some Syrian troop withdrawals, the Syrian and Lebanese security services continued to maintain a police state. Throughout the 1990s, there was little action on the part of Lebanese governments to trace the whereabouts of Lebanese and Palestinians, Christians and Muslims, who had 'disappeared' and were thought to be imprisoned in Syria; and opponents of the regime were arbitrarily arrested, tortured and held incommunicado (Sherry 1997).

The annual reports of Amnesty International (1997–2000) suggest there was some improvement in the government's human rights record toward the end of the 1990s. For example, although each year dozens of people were arrested on political grounds, most were released without charge after a few hours or days. Some long-term prisoners were freed too. In March 1998, 121 political detainees were transferred from Syrian to Lebanese custody, and 103 were immediately released. And in June 1999, the Lebanese court of appeal released two people, Antoinette Chahin and Jihad Abi Ramia, after they had served five years of their life sentences imposed for the political murder of a monk who had supposedly betrayed the Lebanese Forces. The government also entered into a dialogue with Amnesty about the use of execution as a punishment for murder. Two people were executed in 1996, five in 1997, two (in public) in 1998, and none in 1999 — the latter coinciding with a statement by Prime Minister Salim al-Huss that he did not support capital punishment.

Despite some encouraging signs, however, there were still many abuses of human rights. The practice of the judicial process in political cases fell short of international fair-trial standards, and scores of political prisoners said they had been tortured. Even when there was independent evidence of torture, the authorities were not prepared or able to do anything about it. For example, a doctor who examined Antoinette Chahin in June 1994 found bruises and swellings on her body consistent with her claims that she had been beaten while suspended from the ceiling and that her feet had been scalded in hot water (Amnesty International 1997: 3). But despite her being declared innocent five years later, the court did not order any investigation into the conduct of her interrogation.

Students were arrested during demonstrations, political activists were tortured, and some simply 'disappeared', all with the aim of terrorizing the Lebanese into accepting the new order. Meanwhile, Syrians and Lebanese close to the corrupt regime enriched themselves, with apparently little regard for the rest of the population. Large numbers of people eked out a living below the poverty line, forced to compete with a massive influx of migrant workers from Syria who had flooded the labour market. Representing some of the poorest members of its community, Hizballah became increasingly oppositional, participating with the trade unions in anti-government protests, and winning widespread Shi'a support in the 1998 local elections in the poverty-stricken suburbs of Beirut (MEED, 19 June 1998). Also, resentment about the hundreds of thousands of migrant workers in Lebanon led to violence, and in 2000 there was a series of dynamite attacks against shantytowns and other districts housing Syrian workers (MEIB, April/May 2000).

Poverty probably contributed to confessional as well as Libano-Syrian tension. There were some violent incidents, for example, between supporters of Beiruti soccer clubs, with Sunnis championing the Ansar (Partisans) and Shi'a the Najma (Star) team (Harris 1997: 297). Perhaps we should not attach too much significance to football violence that is found in Europe as well as Lebanon, this case being comparable to conflicts between the respectively Catholic and Protestant supporters of the Celtic and Rangers clubs in Scotland. Nevertheless, communal rivalry between sports teams in Lebanon reflected underlying problems in a society in which confessional identity informed so much of everyday life, from family law to the provision of welfare and employment.

Confessionalism continued to pose threats to Lebanese unity, not just among those Maronites who were alienated from the postwar settlement. Another example was the resentment periodically expressed in all communities about Hizballah's guerrilla war against the Israeli forces and their client militia in southern Lebanon. A regional peace settlement would have ended the fighting, but Damascus was in no hurry to achieve this and the warfare was interpreted as a ploy by the Syrian president, Hafiz al-Asad, to strengthen his hand in any negotiation over the future status of the Golan Heights (Syrian territory occupied by Israel since 1967). Israeli reprisal raids undermined the prospects for foreign investment and job-creation in the Lebanese economy. Thus, although Hizballah was seen by some as part of the opposition movement in civil society, others saw it as a collaborator with an occupying power that was using the Lebanese people and their political integrity as pawns in a dispute with Israel.

The Lebanese government could not negotiate with Israel in its own right, which was yet another example of its subordination to Damascus. But while there was discontent with this state of affairs, there was also a sense of anger directed against Israel's occupation of southern Lebanon and the repressive rule of its proxy militia. The latter was the South Lebanese Army (SLA), composed mainly of local Maronites and other Christians who were seen as traitors to their nation. In July 1993, the Israeli army and airforce mounted 'Operation Account-ability' against Shi'a villages in southern Lebanon in retaliation for Hizballah's Katyusha rocket attacks against northern Israel. 128 Lebanese were killed and around 300,000 fled north. Worried that Israel might strike against Syria, President Asad ordered Hizballah to cease its cross-border attacks and confine its operations to the Israeli 'security zone' in Lebanese territory. While Hizballah agreed to this limitation, fighting in the occupied zone brought further Israeli reprisals. Over subsequent years, a number of SLA fighters and Israeli troops were killed, and Israel responded with aerial bombardments of Hizballah bases in the Bekaa as well as the south, and with a naval blockade of Tyre and Sidon in 1995 that disrupted local fishing for months (Harris 1997: 316–18).

When Hizballah resumed its Katyusha attacks, Israel launched a massive air and artillery reprisal in April 1996. 'Operation Grapes of Wrath' involved some 600 air raids against Hizballah and civilian targets in a little over a fortnight. Two power substations in Beirut were destroyed, in retaliation for a disruption of electricity caused by rockets launched against the Israeli town of Qiryat Shimona. 400,000 people were forcibly displaced — including most of the population of Tyre — from an area of southern Lebanon much larger than the security zone, and many were killed or maimed. In the most horrific incident of the operation, Israeli artillery fired on a United Nations observation post at Qana where a number of civilians had taken shelter. Over a hundred people were killed in the UN compound and a similar number wounded. Such carnage, accompanied by the influx of frightened and exhausted refugees into Beirut, prompted an upsurge of national feeling throughout Lebanon. Individuals and non-governmental organizations provided help to the homeless, there were demonstrations of solidarity with the south, and a national day of mourning was declared for the victims (Harris 1997: 319; Hollis and Shehadi 1996).

Once more, when faced with adversity, large sections of civil society revealed a significant sense of unity. This was short-lived, however, and as the election campaign got underway, in the late summer and autumn of 1996, tensions developed between Hizballah and the more mainstream parties and factions. People close to Prime Minister Hariri raised the slogan, 'What Hizballah won in the aggression, they must lose in the elections,' and Hariri complained of the militia's 'boastful behaviour and its logic of constantly defying the state' (*MEED*, 21 June 1996). Such attitudes reflected a wider Lebanese opposition to an Iranian-backed militia that threatened the stability of the Second Republic. Despite moderating its theocratic stance, Hizballah still represented militant Islamic values that were alien to Lebanese culture, and this was a matter of concern to Amal as well as Sunnis and Christians. Nabih Berri and the other urbane and liberal leaders of the moderate Shi'a party took exception to the way Iranian funding gave Hizballah patronage resources, which it could use to buy support and seduce people away from Amal's more secular approach.

Rafiq al-Hariri, of course, could not have voiced his criticisms of Hizballah without the backing of Damascus. President Asad had allowed the militia to keep its arms so that it could fight a restricted war against Israel and keep his enemy under pressure. What he could not tolerate was a situation that might provoke reprisals against Syria. He needed to rein in Hizballah, and so rival politicians felt able to criticize a party that had previously been favoured by the occupying power. Given the close control exercised by the Syrian and Lebanese security agencies over the political process, it is not surprising that Hizballah subsequently lost some seats in the 1996 parliamentary elections.

Overall, however, Hizballah was seen by many as a force committed to the restoration of Lebanese territory, a reputation that was considerably enhanced when, after more fighting in February 2000 between the militia and Israel, and more reprisal bombing raids against Lebanese power stations, Israel unilaterally withdrew from south Lebanon in May. As 1500 members of the SLA and their families fled to Israel, and their prisoners were freed from the notorious Khiam torture and detention centre, crowds gathered all over the country to celebrate a liberation brought about by the tenacity and bravery of the Hizballah fighters (*MEED*, 18 February 2000 and 2 June 2000). Hizballah's victory generated tensions with Amal as both groups competed for the leadership of the Shi'a community, and there were armed clashes between them in June and July after Amal had sought to claim some of the credit for the Israeli withdrawal (*MEIB*, 1 July 2000; *MEIB*, 'Intelligence Briefs', 5 August 2000). Hizballah, however, was clearly the moral victor, and — back in favour with Damascus — it was rewarded by the Syrian decision to give it equal representation with Amal on the 'official' lists in the 2000 parliamentary elections.

The Syrians were not prepared to allow in the general elections of August–September 2000 a repeat of the 1998 local elections. One story had it that the then prime minister, Rafiq al-Hariri, had persuaded Damascus to grant a degree of freedom in 1998 in order to boost Lebanon's 'democratic credentials' without giving any significant concessions to the opposition (Gambill 1999: 1). The fact that some 40 per cent of government candidates had been defeated angered Syrian officials, who were now determined to control closely the outcome of the parliamentary elections.

The new electoral law passed at the end of 1999 adjusted already gerry-mandered constituencies to help pro-government candidates. In north Lebanon, for example, electoral districts were combined to favour such Syrian allies as Suleiman Tony Frangieh and weaken Maronite candidates from areas sym-pathetic to Samir Geagea and the Lebanese Forces, while the constituency in Beirut was divided into three to weaken Rafiq al-Hariri in Beirut 1 and promote the prospects of the prime minister, Salim al-Huss in Beirut 3, and his tem-porary ally, Tamam Salam in Beirut 2. Perhaps more important, 'grand lists' in southern Lebanon and the Bekaa ensured the election of pro-Syrian candidates from such diverse parties — and unlikely allies — as Amal, Hizballah, the Syrian Social Nationalist Party and the Phalanges. By bringing political oppon-ents together in this way, Damascus was able to create coalition lists that would both command widespread popular support and lead to a balance of forces in parliament that could be manipulated and controlled. (For the 2000 elections, see: Gambill and Nassif 2000; *IDREL*; and *Daily Star*, August–September 2000).

Once again there was extensive electoral malpractice. Government vehicles were used to drive voters to the polls, security forces were present inside polling stations, and often it was impossible to vote secretly. Through a process of cen-sorship, vote-buying, and the intimidation of electors and candidates, the Syrians manipulated the elections to produce a parliament much like the one elected in 1996. Although some supporters of Samir Geagea and Michel Aoun refused to have anything to do with this travesty, Christian participation in 2000 probably remained the same or increased compared with the 1996 election; and it was noteworthy that the former president, Amin Gemayel, nego-tiated his return to Lebanon to support the successful election campaign of his son Pierre in the Matn region of Mount Lebanon. Amin's rehabilitation required a solemn undertaking not to criticize the Syrian presence, and left only Aoun as a significant Maronite leader in exile. Pierre Amin Gemayel's election perhaps demonstrated that Damascus did not entirely control the electoral process, as did the defeat of the pro-Syrian Maronite, Elie Hobeika, in Baabda. But the Gemayels were forced to accept Syrian hegemony; otherwise Pierre would not have been allowed to stand. Najah Wakim, the radical Greek Orthodox member of parliament in Beirut, stood down in 2000 rather than tolerate what he described as Syrian interference in the electoral process. Even if he had surrendered to intimidation by the security forces — and there was no evidence that he had — Wakim was still widely admired in Beirut. By comparison, Amin Gemayel's reputation was tarnished. Allowing him to return on such humiliating terms was really another victory for the occupiers.

Only in Beirut did the Syrians suffer what some saw as a significant setback when the opposition candidate, Rafiq al-Hariri, not only won but also surpassed his electoral success of 1996. However, as we shall see, even the defeat of the prime minister, Salim al-Huss, in his carefully gerrymandered constituency was not a disaster for Damascus, and a change of government was effected without any difficulty.

Rafiq al-Hariri had been a fierce critic of the Lebanese regime that had come to power after parliament had elected General Emile Lahoud as the new president of Lebanon. When he took over from President Elias Hrawi in November 1998, Lahoud had given a warmly received address to the parliament in which he pledged his 'intent and determination' to address issues of governmental corruption and what he called the 'sectarian' or confessional 'protection' of those who abused their offices:

> The people want an administration that will be strictly supervised, characterised by honesty and expertise, run by officials whose immunity is derived from their professional performance, not from political or sectarian protection. They want an administration from which they can obtain services by paying taxes, not by bribery as well as taxes.
>
> (*MEED*, 11 December 1998: 2)

This was a thinly veiled attack on Prime Minister Hariri and a regime of corrupt politicians, many of whom owed their position in government to connections with the confessional leaders of former militias. Hariri was soon replaced as premier by Salim al-Huss, a highly respected member of parliament for Beirut. A former banker, Huss was a technocrat in the Shihabist mould who had established his political reputation when he first served as premier (1976–80) during the regime of President Elias Sarkis, a man who had run Fu'ad Shihab's presidential office in the 1960s. It seemed appropriate that Huss should now be prime minister to a president who, like Shihab, had previously been commander-in-chief of the army. In place of Rafiq al-Hariri's 30-member cabinet, Huss formed a government of 15 ministers, none of whom had been a militia leader. Among the technocrats appointed to the cabinet were Nasser Saidi, a former vice-president of the Lebanese central bank (*Banque du Liban*), and George Corm, an economist who had long been opposed to Hariri's economic policies. As finance minister, Corm presented the reformist budget to parliament in April 1999 that increased income and corporation taxes (*MEED*, 18 December 1998 and 23 April 1999; and see section 2 above).

Many Lebanese had turned against the corrupt and repressive government of Rafiq al-Hariri, and so Emile Lahoud's regime, with its promises to root out corruption and deal with the budget deficit, was greeted with a renewed sense of public optimism. There was also considerable Christian support for a president who was seen as a much stronger Maronite leader than Elias Hrawi had ever been. But there was still a clear recognition that the government was ultimately subservient to Syria. Although Salim al-Huss had had difficult relations with Damascus in the past, he had served as prime minister (in 1976–80 and 1987–90) only with President Hafiz al-Asad's blessing. Similarly, Lahoud would not have been elected president if he had been in any way out of favour with the masters of his country. Indeed, he was apparently very close to Bashar al-Asad, the Syrian president's son who had been given charge of Lebanon as part of a process to prepare him for succeeding his father. While serving as commander of the Lebanese army Lahoud had, of course, co-operated in the suppression of opponents of the Syrian regime, but it seems he also shared with Bashar a determination to stamp out governmental corruption. In any case, Lahoud was quick to advertise his continuing loyalty from the start of his presidency. 'Our relationship with Syria is one of history, land and people,' he said in his speech to parliament in November 1998. 'It cannot be a wager or temporary adaptation, but a historic destiny, and a strategic option' (*MEED*, 11 December 1998: 3).

There were suggestions that Bashar al-Asad had wanted to remove Rafiq al-Hariri from the premiership in 1998 because he was closely associated with a Syrian 'old-guard' in Lebanon that might have posed a threat to Bashar's presidential ambitions (Gambill 2000: 2–3). In the event, the succession proceeded smoothly after Hafiz al-Asad died in June 2000. But although the two new presidents seemed so close, they were not able to prevent Hariri's comeback in the elections of 2000. The problem was the poor performance of the Lebanese government in managing the economy. President Emile Lahoud and Prime Minister Salim al-Huss had promised to end the corruption of Hariri's regime and promote economic recovery. Instead the public debt increased, the recession deepened, and in consequence people turned against a failed technocratic government. Despite the attempt to weaken him by dividing the large Beirut constituency into three, Hariri and his allies took all 19 seats in Beirut, defeating the lists of Salim al-Huss and Tamam Salam in their respective constituencies of Beirut 3 and 2.

There was never any doubt, however, about Hariri's willingness to co-operate with the Syrian regime. Although he was the 'opposition candidate', some of his electoral allies were business associates and friends of Bashar al-Asad (Gambill and Nassif 2000: 2), and it was soon confirmed Hariri was back in favour again. In October 2000 he became prime minister and formed a new government — mainly composed of his own, Emile Lahoud's and Nabih Berri's allies, but all of them manifestly close to Damascus. Hizballah pursued its quasi-neutral strategy and remained outside the government, while the major exclusion was a strong Maronite or any other voice critical of Syrian hegemony (*Daily Star*, 28 October and 8 November 2000).

4. Neopatriarchy and the future

The Syrian occupation has provided the sort of neopatriarchal order described by Hisham Sharabi (see chapter 4, section 5). Still influenced by democratic traditions, the Lebanese regime might not be as overtly repressive as the unfettered dictatorship in Syria, but it is obviously far more authoritarian than the prewar political system. Relatively powerful groups like Hizballah, Amal and the Druze Progressive Socialist Party, along with more informal clientelist structures led by a variety of Sunni and Christian politicians, might attempt to manipulate Damascus but all are subservient to its directives. The Syrian president is the ultimate patriarch, and Lebanese leaders are subordinate to his rule. The succession of Bashar al-Asad might eventually lead to some liberalization, but for the foreseeable future the different clientelist factions in Lebanon are firmly controlled by a Syrian patriarchy.

Sometimes two or more Lebanese factions form temporary alliances, but each has a different constituency that is primarily a confessional grouping still suspicious of the others. There is little consistent co-operation between them, and within the confessions there is considerable division between patriarchal leaders. Hizballah and Amal compete for Shi'a support and government patronage, as do the sub-factional leaders within them. Walid Jumblat's party competes with the Yazbaki Druze (see chapter 3, section 4) led by the Arslan emirs. In the Beiruti Sunni community, rival groups are led by Rafiq al-Hariri, Salim al-Huss and Tamam Salam, while in the different Maronite regions there are similar divisions like those, for example, between the Frangiehs and other leading clans in the northern district of Zgharta (see chapter 3, section 5).

The postwar za'ims play the clientelist game as individuals, competing for influence within the regime and for favours extended by Damascus. In the byzantine world of Lebanese politics, alliances can change from day to day as the notables jockey for power and influence. Salim al-Huss had won his parliamentary seat in 1996 at the head of an opposition list, but on his elevation to the premiership in 1998 he soon received overtures from former supporters of Rafiq al-Hariri, anxious to demonstrate their loyalty to the new government.

Similarly, supporters of Huss defected to Prime Minister Hariri in 2000. Few leaders have a political programme, and many seem to play the game for their own personal advantage and enrichment without any real sense of responsibility for the interests of their clients. Despite the reformist intentions of President Lahoud, the system is as corrupt as the one that existed before the civil wars, the significant difference being that now there are 'super-patrons' — members of the Syrian regime — controlling the state and imposing their will by the threat of political exclusion, imprisonment, torture and assassination.

Only a few Lebanese, because of their particular status, seem to be protected from Syrian punishment. The Maronite patriarch (or supreme bishop), Nasrallah Sfeir, is perhaps the most obvious example. He has long made clear his opposition to the Syrians. In November 2000 he once again called for their withdrawal, arguing for proper diplomatic relations between two sovereign governments instead of the 'current Syrian hegemony', and complaining of various abuses — including the case of the Syrian students who were able to register in the medical and engineering faculties of the Lebanese University without having to pass entrance examinations (*Daily Star*, 14 November 2000). Sfeir's statement came less than two months after he had chaired a Maronite bishops' council in September that had issued a document (translated in *MEIB*, 5 October 2000) condemning the corrupt parliamentary elections, the dire state of the economy and the coercive political system. This remarkably critical declaration by the bishops spoke of citizens who 'feign loyalty' to the government, but who in reality were 'full of resentment', and who if they protested openly would be 'tracked down' and imprisoned in Syria. After an astute reference to the recent Israeli withdrawal from south Lebanon, the document asked when, 'pursuant to the Ta'if Accord,' the Syrians might follow suit.

President Emile Lahoud immediately accused the bishops' council of 'encouraging sectarian bigotry', but the Lebanese and Syrian regimes felt unable to act any more severely against a body protected by the Catholic church and the Vatican. Instead, they encouraged Muslim spiritual leaders to condemn the council's declaration. The Sunni *mufti* and other leading Sunni, Shi'a and Druze sheikhs spoke of their 'astonishment' and reminded their people of the 'very big sacrifices' made by 'sisterly Syria' to preserve a united Lebanon (Gibreel and Gambill 2000: 2). In so doing, of course, they encouraged the confessional enmity that Lahoud had earlier condemned. Thus, even when dissent is allowed in Lebanon, it is manipulated in an attempt to sow division between the confessions and divide and weaken any wider opposition to the patriarchal regime.

As well as the limited immunity granted to the Maronite bishops, some powerful za'ims are also able to exercise a degree of independence. In 1999, for example, Walid Jumblat was seen as a sort of spokesperson for those politicians who had been marginalized after Emile Lahoud became president. At a time when power seemed to be slipping away from the former warlords to security and intelligence officers appointed by Lahoud, Jumblat even complained of a 'neo-military regime' (*MEIB*, August 1999). During the 2000 elections he wisely became reconciled with the government, but he was soon disaffected again when his parliamentary bloc was not given what he thought was an adequate representation in Prime Minister Hariri's new government (*Daily Star*, 28 October 2000). There was speculation that Jumblat wanted to build on the success of his bloc in the elections by improving his relations with the Maronite community; and in a carefully worded speech to parliament, he seemed to call for at least a partial Syrian withdrawal from Lebanon. During the ensuing parliamentary debate, a member of the Ba'th party threatened that 'enemy agents' like the Druze leader would not escape 'the rifles of the resistance'; and in Damascus it was announced that Jumblat and his parliamentary allies would henceforth be denied entry to Syria in any official capacity. This was for saying that he hoped the Syrians would 'reconsider' some of their military locations that were not related to 'strategic purposes' (*Daily Star*, 8 November 2000).

The rapid response from the Syrians and their Lebanese allies indicated again the limits of opposition. Jumblat's statement, however, was directed less at the Syrian occupiers than the population of the Shouf where the Druze leader wanted to win support from his Maronite neighbours. His implied criticism of the Syrians came at a time when Maronites were resentful that their interests were not properly represented in a regime angered by the bishops' September declaration. If Jumblat could win their support, he might be able to strengthen himself vis-à-vis his Druze rival, Talal Arslan. In this context, Jumblat's actions can be seen as part of the acceptable game of inter-factional rivalry, and the removal of his privileged status in Syria was merely a reminder to one of the players that he and the others could only operate within closely defined limits.

Tolerating and even encouraging factionalism within the confessions helped Syria's strategy of divide and rule. Sometimes such conflict was controlled as, for example, in the case of the Shi'a community in 2000. After members of Amal and Hizballah had fought and killed each other following the Israeli withdrawal in the summer, the two parties were not allowed to run against each other in the elections and were ordered to form joint lists, not just with each other but also with their former enemies in the Maronite community. In Mount Lebanon, by contrast, relatively fierce competition was allowed between Maronites and between Druze, as it was in Beirut between the followers of the Sunni za'ims, Rafiq al-Hariri and Salim al-Huss. So long as all or at least most of those who entered the elections were ultimately loyal to Syria, a little healthy conflict between them was beneficial, creating the illusion of a free election and dividing the Lebanese electorate along narrow, intra-confessional lines.

Just as the za'ims are subordinate to the Syrian 'super-patrons' led by President Bashar al-Asad, so are clients in turn subordinate to their za'ims. Well-connected individuals at the various levels of the clientelist hierarchy can obtain services from their patrons in return for electoral support in the often artificial conflict between factional leaders. The patronage might include such typical prewar services as jobs, education and welfare, but these are now supplemented by the patron's ability to intercede with the security forces and maybe help secure the release of political prisoners. This provides some assistance to people who feel disadvantaged; but once again, there are no universal rights but merely favours granted by the mighty. The systems of politics and law serve the Syrian and Lebanese establishments, not civil society. Occasionally crumbs are offered to that society, as for example when Damascus allowed relatively free elections to local councils in 1998. But it is significant that the institutions of local democracy have few powers and resources, and they are completely subordinate to regional governors appointed by the central government. By contrast, when trade unions and other independent civic organizations protest, they are deemed guilty of rebellion and suppressed.

As we have seen in chapter 4 (section 5), Hisham Sharabi provides a devastating critical review of neopatriarchal clientelism:

> Clearly, in the context of patronage based on impotence and submission, the concept of social contract is inconceivable. Society in actuality is only subject to the will of the rich and powerful. ... The law serves not the society but the established sociopolitical order; *crime* is not distinguished from *sacrilege* or *rebellion*; and punishment is intended not to reform but to restore the sanctity of the law and to safeguard existing social relations.
>
> (Sharabi 1988: 47, emphases in the original)

Sharabi sees these phenomena as replicating the structure of the patriarchal and sexually repressive family. The relationship between an authoritarian father and submissive women and adolescents provides a model for the roles of patron and clients. Thus the private and public spheres reinforce each other and contribute to a depressing environment of repression and fear in which creativity and knowledge are discouraged in favour of a mediocre uniformity of dull obedience.

Patriarchal families not only contribute to repressive forms of rule. They also inform ethnic identification. If we were to consider communal conflicts in the

Middle East, Europe, the Indian subcontinent and Africa in any detail, we would be able to point to a range of differences between them. What they share, however, is a sense of unity between kinship and ethnicity. As we have seen in the last chapter, romantic nationalism claims a common descent for members of the nation or ethnic group. Confessional groups in Lebanon and India are ideally endogamous, and there are strong pressures and sanctions against those who want to marry outside the moral community.

Threats to patriarchal domination in the family can lead to a romantic reaction. In the previous chapter, I stressed the disruptive effects of urbaniz-ation in the twentieth century. To these we might add any number of threats to an established order: the socioeconomic mobilization of women in India; the collapse of a feudal authority in nineteenth-century Lebanon; or the end of a communist order in Yugoslavia. What is common is not the different causes for an undermining of patriarchal authority, but something that underpins a particular form of patriarchy — the notion of a common blood and line of descent. It is this that defines the difference between the Other and the self. The logic of endogamy not only protects the patrimony of the family and promotes patriarchal control: it also reinforces communal divisions.

In chapter 4 (section 3) I have argued that Kleinian theory seems more useful than other psychoanalytic approaches to the study of ethnicity. In particular, I made the intuitive judgement that projection of disavowed aspects of the self on to the Other contributes more to ethnic conflict than the reaction-formation of anxiety and fear in response to a sense of the Other's difference. Christians and Muslims in Lebanon share a number of cultural attributes, and in South Africa Zulus killed and mutilated each other. So rather than a simple fear of the Other's difference, it is more likely that people fear the despised aspects of the self embodied in a similar Other. Cultural differences between, say, Lebanon and South Africa mean that ethnic nationalists in Beirut seek to destroy the Other's honour, while Zulus in the Natal townships kill to appropriate it. In both cases, however, the fighters seem to be motivated by a fear of their ene-mies' embodiment of such disavowed aspects of the self as sexual and other desires and hatreds.

This reference back to my discussion of psychoanalytic theory is not meant to reopen a consideration of the somewhat nebulous 'metaphors' discussed in chapter 4. My intention is merely to stress that fear of the Other's difference is not necessarily what motivates ethnic fighters. It might well be that the sense of fright stems more from a fear of the self. Nevertheless, having made this point, it is still important to recognize that in ethnic conflict the various groups of protagonists are usually defined in terms of descent from different ancestors or — in the case of the Zulus in South Africa and intra-communal fighters within the Maronite and Shi'a communities in Lebanon — in terms of their betrayal of the kinship group. A notion of common descent, of a shared blood, lies at the root of ethnic identity. One is born a Sunni or a Maronite and one has no choice in the matter. Even if a Muslim converts to Christianity, or a Christian to Islam, the convert can never be a 'proper' Christian or Muslim, and the natal confession can still claim the convert as its own. So difficult is the transition from one ethnic community to another, and so great is the taboo against it, that sometimes families will kill transgressors to eliminate the colossal assault on their honour.

Until endogamy is challenged, ethnic identities can always be reproduced in any socio-political conjuncture. It is thus a matter of concern that there continues to be a powerful resistance to civil marriage in Lebanon. It is not simply a problem of a strong norm of confessional endogamy in civil society. Even if two people from different confessions want to marry and would be allowed to do so by their families, they are unable to be legally married unless one converts to the other's faith. When, in March 1998, President Elias Hrawi proposed to his government that they draw up a civil marital code, he was opposed not only by virtually all the religious authorities in Lebanon but also by the prime minister, Rafiq al-Hariri, who said he was afraid of offending confessional values and interests (Europa Publications 1998: 754–5). Although some Lebanese saw President Hrawi's proposal as a welcome step in the direction of a secularization that might help to bridge sectarian divisions, there was no sense of any widespread disapproval when Prime Minister Hariri refused to submit legislation to parliament.

It is the failure of Arab politicians and intellectuals to confront this sort of issue that so concerns Hisham Sharabi. One reading of his analysis of neopatriarchal domination might give the impression that he is blaming imperialism and 'dependent' capitalism for the modern problems of the Middle East (see chapter 4, section 5). But in fact he provides a damning critique of contemporary Arab society and politics. His book concludes with an affirmation of the trends within civil societies that are moving toward the triumph of 'modernity, secular democracy, and libertarian socialism' over authoritarian regimes — and over the Islamic 'fundamentalist destroyers-redeemers' who are, of course, as patriarchal as the repressive systems they oppose (Sharabi 1988: 155). We need not be drawn into a discussion of Sharabi's moderate socialism. The precise form of government in a secular democracy is a matter to be decided by the electorate. What is important is his advocacy of a liberal system in place of patriarchal repression.

Sharabi's treatment of neopatriarchy is similar to the polemic written by Kanan Makiya (1993) against 'cruelty and silence' in the Arab world. This Iraqi opposition author provides us with an account of appalling cruelties, not simply of despotic rule in Iraq, Syria and Saudi Arabia, but also of a culture of honour and shame that involves the suppression of women. In Saddam Hussein's prisons, rape is a method of torture designed to shame the families of political dissidents precisely because the values of family honour are so widespread; and 'husbands are therefore — wittingly or not — as complicit as the Iraqi secret police in the victimization of the women of Iraq' (Makiya 1993: 291). After documenting 'honour crimes' in contemporary Palestine and other parts of the Arab Middle East, Makiya concludes:

> All over the Mashriq [the eastern Arab world] and around the Mediter-ranean (north and south) there are women ... who are beaten, brutalized, and not infrequently murdered in order to preserve the 'honor' of their families. So important is this honor that sometimes mothers and grandmothers become active participants; they egg on the menfolk to murder their own daughters.
>
> (Makiya 1993: 290)

At the end of his book, Makiya (1993: 312 ff) discusses the relative silence of those members of the Arab intelligentsia who have turned blind eyes to the faults of their societies. As he points out, so many intellectuals have sought to blame monsters of exploitation and ethnocentrism in Israel and the metro-politan centres of the western or northern worlds. Of course, some of the major problems of the Middle East are a legacy of the imperial designs of Britain, France, and later the USA and its Israeli client. Such malign influences helped to destroy the prospects for liberal nationalism after the first world war, and encouraged — either actively or through the indirect consequences of neo-imperialism — patriarchal forms of rule in the latter half of the century. But Kanan Makiya and Hisham Sharabi are concerned to question the easy response that all the faults of the Arab world stem from the intervention of external powers. Local intellectuals, they say, have a responsibility to confront the fail-ings of the societies and cultures in which they live.

We could argue that now is the time for the Lebanese intelligentsia, at any rate, to confront the patriarchal failings in civil society in preparation for a reform of the political system. This might be a naive conclusion, and we should not underestimate the problems faced by a society in which ethno-confessional warfare was ended by a neopatriarchal and repressive regime with its own agenda. But although the full potential of civil society will not be realized until Syria itself democratizes, it is the Lebanese who will have to find long-term solutions. They have demonstrated they have the potential to do so, despite the gloomy predictions of foreign observers such as myself; and if the efforts of those groups involved in the antiwar movement can be sustained, patriarchy and the related values of honour and shame could be transformed.

Significantly, women were at the forefront of the peace movement in the 1980s. In 1985 'Women Against War' — at considerable risk to themselves — marched on parliament, defying the militiamen who threatened to fire on them. Wives and mothers of hostages taken by the militias formed multiconfessional groups to press for the release of their men and to support each other in facing the horror of not knowing what fate had befallen their loved ones. These were brave people, whose efforts to restore decency to their lives, and to Lebanon as a whole, have received little academic attention compared with the cruel atrocities of the 'men of honour'. In their struggles against the war, such women literally shamed those fighters and their leaders who peddled hatred, selfishness and domination.

It was an often private struggle, dealing with grief and the pain of war, bringing up children and protecting them from the terrors of street fighting, fetching food and water, and tending the sick and wounded. Perhaps as a result of these essentially domestic rather than public experiences, a relatively large number of intellectual women expressed opposition to the war by writing personal diaries, poems and novels. The novelist Hanan al-Shaykh in *The Story of Zahra* (Shaykh 1986), for example, described the dismal and depressing reality obscured by the superficial excitement of violence. Such other writers as Ghada al-Samman, Andrée Chedid and Etel Adnan took a similar approach, confronting the cruelties of war and the cultural silence that surrounded them. Antiwar novels often reflected the private fears and hopes of their authors, but there can be little doubt that gradually these 'other voices' of the Lebanese wars (Cooke 1987) were heard by a larger audience.

In her discussion of this literature, Evelyne Accad (1990) makes an interesting comparison between the approaches of female and male authors. While both women and men who wrote novels about the Lebanese wars described the fighting and the often violent interactions between genders 'in the bleakest terms', women tried to search in their writing for non-violent alternatives and for different ways of managing their relations with men and families. Male novelists, on the other hand, tended to emphasize 'heroism, revenge, and violence as catharsis' (Accad 1990: 167). This might seem a rather harsh judgement, and at least one male writer, Halim Barakat, took great exception to Accad's interpretations of one of his novels (Accad 1990: 130–4). Whether Accad has merely read the values of the fighters into the novels of men, or has uncovered a specifically male discourse about war, is beyond the scope of this concluding chapter. What is clear, as Miriam Cooke (1987) argues in her book on the same subject, is that Lebanese women wrote novels not simply about men fighting a pointless war over their honour, and women suffering the consequences: they were pre-eminently concerned to confront the fragmenting patriarchal society in which they, as women, had been imprisoned. They advocated not only a 'collective responsibility' of women, but also a responsibility for themselves as individuals. To survive the war, women had to take 'responsibility for the self' (Cooke 1987: 12). They needed to confront the patriarchy of those closest to them in order to understand and change a society that, in its collapse, revealed its fundamental flaws.

As women became more vocal, men joined them. The multiconfessional trade union movement (the CGTL) organized large demonstrations against the war in the latter half of the 1980s, and professional organizations of doctors, lawyers and engineers excluded members of militia parties from their elected executive committees (Hanf 1993: 639–40). Women's groups, trade unions and professional associations continued to be active in civil society in the 1990s, in spite of their repression by the postwar regime. Many journalists, novelists, theatre groups and film-makers also contributed to a culture of secularism and modernity. Although they worked under very difficult conditions, such people were able to get their message across and provide encouragement to each other, creating a sense of national unity after the ruination of war.

Jean Chamoun, for example, is a Maronite from a notable family whose most illustrious members were the former president, Camille Chamoun, and his sons, Dany and Dory, who together had led the Liberal National Party and its Tigers militia. Yet Jean and his Palestinian wife, Mai Masri, have made films that expose the warlords, promote the Palestinian case, and demonstrate the potential for peace in Lebanon. In *War Generation: Beirut* (Chamoun and Masri 1988), militiamen are shown as rather pathetic people fighting for causes that have long gone sour and are ultimately of benefit only to their leaders who have made personal fortunes from the war economy. In *Suspended Dreams* (Chamoun and Masri 1992), two former enemies — one a Christian and the other a Muslim — are shown working together as painter-decorators, repairing the war-damaged home of a woman whose husband had been kidnapped some years before. The men joke about the way they had shelled and shot at each other across the 'Green Line' that used to divide Beirut. They have come to realize that, as business partners, they have far more in common than they ever had with their respective confessional warlords. While they fill in the pock marks on the walls of the apartment, their employer asks them whether it is easier to destroy or rebuild. One man laughs to hide his embarrassment, and he tells her that destruction was easy compared with the difficult but necessary tasks of reconciliation and reconstruction. Later the mother looks at a photograph album with her two young sons, fondly remembering a father who was taken from the street and disappeared without trace.

There is great sadness in this film, but no sense of a continuing despair. The mother attends meetings with other women whose men were captured during the war. Some wear the *hijab* headscarf, others western fashions, but all are united in support of each other, and together they lobby the government for information, insisting on their right to know the fate of the hostages and the whereabouts of the bodies of those who were killed. Women who have suffered enormous loss and emotional pain are shown taking control of their lives. They are angry about what has happened to them and their families, and about the fact that some of the kidnappers are members of the postwar government. But they do not speak of vengeance. They want to know about the fate of those who died in some squalid place that the militias called a homeland. Above all, they want to make a better future for their children.

It will not be easy to create a new Lebanon. It will eventually require a sensitive series of negotiations with Syria, and there might well be many setbacks. Economic problems and political repression have, for example, contributed to a huge increase in the number of people — many of them well-educated — emigrating from Lebanon. The *As-Safir* newspaper even reported (on 7 April 2000) that the number of emigrants in 1995–99 was the same as that for the entire civil war period of 1975–90 (*MEIB*, 'Intelligence Briefs', April/May 2000). Nevertheless, Lebanese emigrants maintain close ties with their country, and many return for regular visits. And among those who remain, the voices of opposition have not been silenced. In March 2000 the editor of *An-Nahar* wrote in his newspaper an 'open letter' to Bashar al-Asad, calling for Syria to withdraw. This was followed by similar editorials in other Lebanese newspapers and critical statements by community leaders, professional associations and human rights groups (Gambill 2000: 3; *MEIB*, April/May 2000 and June 2000).

In April 2000 student protests against the Syrian presence, although organized by Michel Aoun's rather small opposition group, drew in hundreds of students from many campuses in and outside Beirut. When the demonstrations were broken up with teargas and beatings, and a number of activists were arrested and imprisoned (for relatively short terms of between ten days and six months), there were protests from such groups as the Beirut Bar Association and the Lebanese Communist Party, as well as an expected condemnation from the Lebanese Forces and other groups on the Christian right (*MEIB*, April/May 2000). Also in April 2000, on the 25th anniversary of the start of the civil war, over a thousand demonstrators in Beirut demanded more resources be devoted to uncovering the fate of the 17,000 hostages and other people who had disappeared since 1975 (*MEIB*, April/May 2000). This was part of a campaign of demonstrations and vigils, mainly involving women who were seeking inform-ation about their lost husbands and sons. And the campaign was of considerable embarrassment to the Lebanese regime, not only because of the government's continuing collaboration with warlords in parliament, but also because some members of this movement claimed their missing relatives were being held incommunicado in Syrian jails.

There is a vibrant, multifaceted, and often optimistic, counter-cultural movement in Lebanese civil society. In a calm but persistent way, it informs private discourse and even some aspects of public life. Different ideas are repre-sented within it, and different strategies are offered. What is common is a belief in a united and free country in which inclusive liberal nationalism can finally overcome those exclusive ethnicities motivated by the romantic ideologies of blood and soil, honour and shame, patriarchy and vengeance.

I end with a concept I hoped I could avoid. 'Globalization' of economic and information systems makes authoritarian forms of rule increasingly anachro-nistic. Free markets and free information imply free individuals. Whatever the negative effects of the dependent capitalism to which Hisham Sharabi alludes — and there are many — one positive aspect of globalization is the hesitant shift to more democratic forms of government in the developing world. Neopatriarchal forms of rule in the Middle East will not last for ever. There will, of course, be a reactionary resistance from romantic nationalists and authoritarian patriarchs. That is to be expected, but no one need fear it will ultimately prevail. In 1789, the year of the French revolution, the German poet and novelist, Christoph Martin Wieland, noticed cartloads of pamphlets against the Enlightenment on sale at the Leipzig book fair. 'Birds of the night,' he wrote, 'cry loudest when the sun dazzles them.'

When the mother in *Suspended Dreams* talks with her sister about how her experiences have strengthened them both, she smiles with a degree of contentment. Tears are in the eyes of the viewer, who gazes in admiration as he listens to the voices of light.

References

Abdennur, Alexander (1980) 'Conflict Reactions among a Sample of Fighters in the Lebanese Civil War', *The Psychiatric Journal of the University of Ottawa*, 5:2

Abu-Lughod, Lila (1990) 'Anthropology's Orient: The Boundaries of Theory on the Arab World', in Hisham Sharabi (ed.) *Theory, Politics and the Arab World: Critical Responses*, New York and London: Routledge

Accad, Evelyne (1990) *Sexuality and War: Literary Masks of the Middle East*, New York: New York University Press

(1991) 'Sexuality and Sexual Politics: Conflicts and Contradictions for Contemporary Women in the Middle East', in Chandra Talpade Mohanty, Ann Russo and Lourdes Torres (eds) *Third World Women and the Politics of Feminism*, Bloomington and Indianapolis: Indiana University Press

Adam, Heribert and Kogila Moodley (1993) *The Negotiated Revolution: Society and Politics in Post-Apartheid South Africa*, Johannesburg: Jonathan Ball

(1997) '"Tribalism" and Political Violence in South Africa', in Josef Gugler (ed.) *Cities in the Developing World: Issues, Theory, and Policy*, New York and Oxford: Oxford University Press

Adorno, T. W. et al (1950) *The Authoritarian Personality*, New York: Harper & Row

Ahmed, J. M. (1960) *The Intellectual Origins of Egyptian Nationalism*, London: Oxford University Press

Ajami, Fouad (1986) *The Vanished Imam: Musa al Sadr and the Shia of Lebanon*, London: I.B.Tauris

Alamuddin, Najib (1993) *Turmoil: The Druzes, Lebanon and the Arab–Israeli Conflict*, London: Quartet Books

Alamuddin, Nura S. and Paul D. Starr (1980) *Crucial Bonds: Marriage Among the Druze*, Delmar, New York: Caravan Books

Alavi, Hamza (1973) 'Peasants and Revolution', in Kathleen Gough and Hari P. Sharma (eds) *Imperialism and Revolution in South Asia*, New York: Monthly Review Press

(1991) 'Nationhood and Communal Violence in Pakistan', *Journal of Contemporary Asia*, 21:2

Amnesty International (1997–2000) *Annual Reports: Lebanon*, published on the website www.amnesty.org

(1997) 'Antoinette Chahin: Torture and Unfair Trial', *Lebanon Documents*, published on the website www.amnesty.org

An-Nahar, Lebanese (Arabic language) newspaper, published in Beirut

Anderson, Benedict (1983) *Imagined Communities: Reflections on the Origins and Spread of Nationalism*, London: Verso

Antonius, George (1938) *The Arab Awakening: The Story of the Arab National Movement*, London: Hamish Hamilton

Arlacchi, Pino (1979) 'The Mafioso: From Man of Honour to Entrepreneur', *New Left Review*, 118

(1983) *Mafia, Peasants and Great Estates: Society in Traditional Calabria*, Cambridge: Cambridge University Press

As-Safir, Lebanese (Arabic language) newspaper, published in Beirut

Asad, Talal (1972) 'Market Model, Class Structure and Consent: A Reconsideration of Swat Political Organisation', *Man*, 7:1

(ed.) (1973) *Anthropology and the Colonial Encounter*, London: Ithaca Press

(1975) 'Anthropological Texts and Ideological Problems: An Analysis of Cohen on Arab Villages in Israel', *Review of Middle East Studies*, 1

(1992) 'Conscripts of Western Civilization', in Christine Ward Gailey (ed.) *Civilization in Crisis: Anthropological Perspectives* (vol. 1 of *Dialectical Anthropology: Essays in Honour of Stanley Diamond*), Gainsville: University of Florida Press

Asad, Talal and Roger Owen (eds) (1983) *The Sociology of 'Developing Societies': The Middle East*, London: Macmillan

Badawi, Leila (1994) 'Islam', in Jean Holm and John Bowker (eds) *Women in Religion*, London and New York: Pinter

Baghdadi, Maroun and Nayla de Freige (1979) 'La génération de kalachnikov', *L'Orient-Le Jour*, (Beirut newspaper), five-part series published in the spring

Bahout, Joseph (1993) 'Liban: Les élections législatives de l'été 1992', *Monde arabe: Maghreb-Machrek*, 139

Banerjee, Ashish (1992) '"Comparative Curfew": Changing Dimensions of Communal Politics in India', in Veena Das (ed.) *Mirrors of Violence: Communities, Riots and Survivors in South Asia*, Delhi: Oxford University Press

Barakat, Halim (1977) *Lebanon in Strife: Student Preludes to the Civil War*, Austin: University of Texas Press

(1984) *Al-mujtama' al-'arabi al-mu'asir* (Contemporary Arab Society), Beirut: Markaz Dirasat al-Wihda al-'Arabiyya

(ed.) (1988) *Toward a Viable Lebanon*, London and Sydney: Croom Helm

(1990) 'Beyond the Always and the Never: A Critique of Social Psychological Interpretations of Arab Society and Culture', in Hisham Sharabi (ed.) *Theory,*

Politics and the Arab World: Critical Responses, New York and London: Routledge

Beattie, John (1966) *Other Cultures: Aims, Methods and Achievements in Social Anthropology*, London: Routledge & Kegan Paul

Berger, Morroe (1964) *The Arab World Today*, New York: Doubleday

Bienen, Henry (1984) 'Urbanization and Third World Stability', *World Development*, 12 (July)

Binder, Leonard (ed.) (1966) *Politics in Lebanon*, New York: Wiley

Black-Michaud, Jacob (1975) *Feuding Societies*, Oxford: Blackwell

Blok, Anton (1974) *The Mafia of a Sicilian Village, 1860–1900: A Study of Violent Peasant Entrepreneurs*, Oxford: Blackwell

Brandes, Stanley (1987) 'Reflections on Honor and Shame in the Mediterranean', in David D. Gilmore (ed.) *Honor and Shame and the Unity of the Mediterranean*, Washington, DC: Special Publication of the American Anthropological Association, no. 22

Brass, Paul R. (1994) *The Politics of India Since Independence (The New Cambridge History of India IV:1)*, Cambridge: Cambridge University Press (2nd edn)

Brinton, Crane (1965) *Nietzsche*, New York: Harper & Row

Brown, David (1994) *The State and Ethnic Politics in Southeast Asia*, London and New York: Routledge

Brown, Rupert (1988) *Group Processes: Dynamics Within and Between Groups*, Oxford: Blackwell

Brownmiller, Susan (1976) *Against Our Will: Men, Women and Rape*, Harmondsworth: Penguin

Burke III, Edmund (1988) 'Rural Collective Action and the Emergence of Modern Lebanon: A Comparative Historical Perspective', in Nadim Shehadi and Dana Haffar Mills (eds) *Lebanon: A History of Conflict and Consensus*, London: I.B.Tauris

Calderón de la Barca, Pedro (1991) *Plays: One* (The Surgeon of Honour and others), translated and introduced by Gwynne Edwards, London: Methuen Drama

Campbell, Catherine (1992) 'Learning to Kill? Masculinity, the Family and Violence in Natal', *Journal of Southern African Studies*, 18:3

Campbell, J. K. (1964) *Honour, Family and Patronage: A Study of Institutions and Moral Values in a Greek Mountain Village*, Oxford: Clarendon Press

Carey, John (1992) *The Intellectuals and the Masses: Pride and Prejudice among the Literary Intelligentsia, 1880–1939*, London and Boston: Faber & Faber

Chakrabarty, Dipesh (1992) 'Communal Riots and Labour: Bengal's Jute Mill-hands in the 1890s', in Veena Das (ed.) *Mirrors of Violence: Communities, Riots and Survivors in South Asia*, Delhi: Oxford University Press

Chamie, Joseph (1980) 'Religious Groups in Lebanon: A Descriptive Investigation', *International Journal of Middle East Studies*, 11:2

Chamoun, Jean and Mai Masri (1988) *War Generation: Beirut*, film, International Broadcasting Trust production with MTC (Beirut) for BBC Television

(1992) *Suspended Dreams*, film, MTC (Beirut) production with Television Trust for the Environment and the One World Group of Broadcasters for BBC Television

Chevallier, Dominique (1959) 'Aux origines des troubles agraires libanais en 1858', *Annales*, 14

(1971) *La société du Mont Liban à l'époque de la révolution industrielle en Europe*, Paris: Libraire orientaliste, Paul Geuthner

Chhachhi, Amrita (1989) 'The State, Religious Fundamentalism and Women: Trends in South Asia', *Economic and Political Weekly*, 24 (18 March)

(1991) 'Forced Identities: The State, Communalism, Fundamentalism and Women in India', in Deniz Kandiyoti (ed.) *Women, Islam and the State*, London: Macmillan

Choueiri, Youssef M. (1988) 'Ottoman Reform and Lebanese Patriotism', in Nadim Shehadi and Dana Haffar Mills (eds) *Lebanon: A History of Conflict and Consensus*, London: I.B.Tauris

Christie, Richard and Marie Jahoda (eds) (1954) *Studies in the Scope and Method of the Authoritarian Personality*, New York: Free Press

Churchill, Colonel Charles Henry (1853) *Mount Lebanon: A Ten Years' Residence from 1842 to 1852* (3 vols), London: Saunders & Otley

Cobban, Helena (1985) *The Making of Modern Lebanon*, London: Hutchinson

Coetzee, J. M. (1991) 'The Mind of Apartheid: Geoffrey Cronjé', *Social Dynamics*, 17:1

Cooke, Miriam (1987) *War's Other Voices: Women Writers on the Lebanese Civil War*, Cambridge: Cambridge University Press

Cooley, John K. (1973) *Green March, Black September: The Story of the Palestinian Arabs*, London: Frank Cass

Copeland, Miles (1969) *The Game of Nations: The Amorality of Power Politics*, London: Weidenfeld & Nicolson

Cornelius, Wayne A. (1969) 'Urbanization as an Agent in Latin American Political Instability: The Case of Mexico', *American Political Science Review*, 63: 3

(1974) 'Urbanization and Political Demand Making: Political Participation among the Migrant Poor in Latin American Cities', *American Political Science Review*, 68: 3

(1975) *Politics and the Migrant Poor in Mexico City*, Stanford: Stanford University Press

(1977) 'Leaders, Followers, and Official Patrons in Urban Mexico', in Steffen Schmidt et al. (eds) *Friends, Followers, and Factions: A Reader in Political Clientelism*, Berkeley and Los Angeles: University of California Press

Coulson, Noel and Doreen Hinchcliffe (1978) 'Women and Law in Contemporary Islam', in Lois Beck and Nikki Keddie (eds) *Women in the Muslim World*, Cambridge, MA and London: Harvard University Press

Crow, Ralph E. (1966) 'Confessionalism, Public Administration, and Efficiency in Lebanon', in Leonard Binder (ed.) *Politics in Lebanon*, New York: Wiley

Cruise O'Brien, Conor (1988) *The Siege: The Saga of Israel and Zionism*, London: Paladin/Grafton Books

Daily Star (The) Lebanese (English language) newspaper, published in Beirut

Das, Veena (ed.) (1992) *Mirrors of Violence: Communities, Riots and Survivors in South Asia*, Delhi: Oxford University Press

Davis, John (1977) *People of the Mediterranean: An Essay in Comparative Social Anthropology*, London: Routledge & Kegan Paul

(1987) 'Family and State in the Mediterranean', in David D. Gilmore (ed.) *Honor and Shame and the Unity of the Mediterranean*, Washington, DC: Special Publication of the American Anthropological Association, no. 22

Daw, Butrus (1978) *Tarikh al-mawarina: al-wajh al-'askari al-maruni* (History of the Maronites: The Maronite Military Aspect), Junieh: Dar al-Bulisiyya

Dekmejian, Hrair Richard (1978) 'Consociational Democracy in Crisis: The Case of Lebanon', *Comparative Politics*, 10

Delaney, Carol (1987) 'Seeds of Honor, Fields of Shame', in David D. Gilmore (ed.) *Honor and Shame and the Unity of the Mediterranean*, Washington, DC: Special Publication of the American Anthropological Association, no. 22

Denoeux, Guilain (1993) *Urban Unrest in the Middle East: A Comparative Study of Informal Networks in Egypt, Iran, and Lebanon*. Albany: State University of New York Press

Dromgoole, Nicholas (1997) 'Introduction', in Lope de Vega, *Fuente Ovejuna and Lost in a Mirror: Two Plays*, adapted by Adrian Mitchell, London: Oberon Books/Absolute Classics

Dubar, Claude and Salim Nasr (1976) *Les classes sociales au Liban*, Paris: Fondation Nationale des Sciences Politiques

Dubow, Saul (1994) 'Ethnic Euphemisms and Racial Echoes', *Journal of Southern African Studies*, 20:3

Economist (The) British journal, published in London

Eickelman, Dale F. (1967) 'Musaylima: An Approach to the Social Anthropology of Seventh Century Arabia', *Journal of Economic and Social History of the Orient*, 10

El-Messiri, Sawsan (1977) 'The Changing Role of the *futuwwa* in the Social Structure of Cairo', in Ernest Gellner and John Waterbury (eds) *Patrons and Clients in Mediterranean Societies*, London: Duckworth

Entelis, John P. (1974) *Pluralism and Party Transformation in Lebanon: al-Kata'ib, 1936–1970*, Leiden: Brill

Epstein, A. L. (1958) *Politics in an Urban African Community*, Manchester: Manchester University Press

(1978) *Ethos and Identity: Three Studies in Ethnicity*, London: Tavistock

Eriksen, Thomas H. (1993) *Ethnicity and Nationalism: Anthropological Perspectives*, London and Boulder, CO: Pluto Press

Erikson, Erik H. (1963) *Childhood and Society*, New York: Norton

(1968) *Identity: Youth and Crisis*, New York: Norton

Europa Publications (1988) *The Middle East and North Africa 1999*, London: Europa Publications (45th edn)

Evans-Pritchard, E. E. (1940) *The Nuer*, Oxford: Clarendon Press

(1949) *The Sanusi of Cyrenaica*, Oxford: Clarendon Press

(1970) 'The Nuer of Southern Sudan', in M. Fortes and E. E. Evans-Pritchard (eds) *African Political Systems*, London and Oxford: Oxford University Press

Fanon, Frantz (1986) *Black Skin, White Masks*, London: Pluto Press

Farsoun, Samih K. (1970) 'Family Structure and Society in Modern Lebanon', in Louise E. Sweet (ed.) *Peoples and Cultures of the Middle East: An Anthropological Reader*, Volume II: *Life in Cities, Towns and Countryside*, Garden City, New York: Natural History Press

(1988) 'E Pluribus Plura or E Pluribus Unum? Cultural Pluralism and Social Class in Lebanon', in Halim Barakat (ed.) *Toward a Viable Lebanon*, London and Sydney: Croom Helm

Farsoun, Samih K. and Lisa Hajjar (1990) 'The Contemporary Sociology of the Middle East: An Assessment', in Hisham Sharabi (ed.) *Theory, Politics and the Arab World: Critical Responses*, New York and London: Routledge

Fawaz, Leila Tarazi (1983) *Merchants and Migrants in Nineteenth-Century Beirut*, Cambridge, MA: Harvard University Press

(1988) 'Zahle and Dayr al-Qamar: Two Market Towns of Mount Lebanon during the Civil War of 1860', in Nadim Shehadi and Dana Haffar Mills (eds) *Lebanon: A History of Conflict and Consensus*, London: I.B.Tauris

(1992) 'Women and Conflict in Lebanon', in John P. Spagnolo (ed.) *Problems of the Modern Middle East in Historical Perspective: Essays in Honour of Albert Hourani*, Reading: Ithaca Press

(1994) *An Occasion for War: Civil Conflict in Lebanon and Damascus in 1860*, London and New York: I.B.Tauris

Fernea, Elizabeth (1985) *Women and the Family in the Middle East: New Voices of Change*, Austin: University of Texas Press

Fisk, Robert (1990) *Pity the Nation: Lebanon at War*, London: André Deutsch

Foster, George M. (1965) 'Peasant Society and the Image of Limited Good', *American Anthropologist*, 67

Foucault, Michel (1975) *Surveiller et punir*, Paris: Gallimard. Translated by Alan Sheridan as *Discipline and Punish* (London: Allen Lane) 1977

(1976) *La volonté de savoir*, Paris: Gallimard. Translated by Robert Hurley as *The History of Sexuality: Vol. 1: An Introduction* (London: Allen Lane) 1979

Frank, André Gunder (1969) 'Sociology of Development and Underdevelopment of Sociology', in André Gunder Frank, *Latin America: Underdevelopment or Revolution*, New York: Monthly Review Press

Franklin, John Hope (1964) *The Militant South*, Boston: Beacon Press

Fromm, Erich (1955) *The Sane Society*, New York: Fawcett

Frosh, Stephen (1987) *The Politics of Psychoanalysis: An Introduction to Freudian and Post-Freudian Theory*, London: Macmillan

(1989) 'Psychoanalysis and Racism', in Barry Richards (ed.) *Crises of the Self: Further Essays on Psychoanalysis and Politics*, London: Free Association Books

(1994) *Sexual Difference: Masculinity and Psychoanalysis*, London and New York: Routledge

Gambetta, Diego (1993) *The Sicilian Mafia: The Business of Private Protection*, Cambridge, MA: Harvard University Press

Gambill, Gary C. (1999) 'Syria Restructures Lebanon's Electoral Law', *Middle East Intelligence Bulletin*, 1:12, published on the website www.meib.org

(2000) 'Lebanon after Assad', *Middle East Intelligence Bulletin*, 2:6, published on the website www.meib.org

Gambill, Gary C. and Daniel Nassif (2000) 'Lebanon's Parliamentary Elections: Manufacturing Dissent', *Middle East Intelligence Bulletin*, 2:8, published on the website www.meib.org

Geertz, Clifford (1963) 'The Integrative Revolution: Primordial Sentiments and Civil Politics in New States', in Clifford Geertz (ed.) *Old Societies and New States: The Quest for Modernity in Asia and Africa*, New York: Free Press

(1968) *Islam Observed: Religious Development in Morocco and Indonesia*, New Haven: Yale University Press

(1971) 'In Search of North Africa', *The New York Review of Books*, 22 April, XVI:7

Gellner, Ernest (1969) *Saints of the Atlas*, Chicago: University of Chicago Press
(1983) *Nations and Nationalism*, Oxford: Blackwell

Ghoussoub, Mai (1987) 'Feminism — or the Eternal Masculine — in the Arab World', *New Left Review*, 161

Gibb, H. A. R. and Harold Bowen (1950, 1957) *Islamic Society and the West: A Study of the Impact of Western Civilization on Moslem Culture in the Near East* (2 vols), London: Oxford University Press

Gibreel, G. and Gary C. Gambill (2000) 'A Return to Religious Extremism? Not Quite', *Middle East Intelligence Bulletin*, 2:9, published on the website www.meib.org

Giddens, Anthony (1985) *The Nation State and Violence: Volume Two of A Contemporary Critique of Historical Materialism*, Cambridge: Polity Press

Gilmore, David D. (1987) 'Introduction: The Shame of Dishonor', in David D. Gilmore (ed.) *Honor and Shame and the Unity of the Mediterranean*, Washington, DC: Special Publication of the American Anthropological Association, no. 22

Gilmour, David (1983) *Lebanon: The Fractured Country*, Oxford: Martin Robertson

Gilsenan, Michael (1976) 'Lying, Honor and Contradiction', in Bruce Kapferer (ed.) *Transaction and Meaning: Directions in the Anthropology of Exchange and Symbolic Behavior*, Philadelphia: Institute for the Study of Human Issues
(1977) 'Against Patron–client Relations', in Ernest Gellner and John Waterbury (eds) *Patrons and Clients in Mediterranean Societies*, London: Duckworth
(1982) *Recognizing Islam: An Anthropologist's Introduction*, London and Sydney: Croom Helm
(1989) 'Word of Honour', in Ralph Grillo (ed.) *Social Anthropology and the Politics of Language*, London and New York: Routledge
(1992) '*Nizam ma fi*: Discourses of Order, Disorder and History in a Lebanese Context', in John P. Spagnolo (ed.) *Problems of the Modern Middle East in Historical Perspective: Essays in Honour of Albert Hourani*, Reading: Ithaca Press
(1996) *Lords of the Lebanese Marches: Violence and Narrative in an Arab Society*, London: I.B.Tauris

Glass, Charles (1990) *Tribes with Flags: A Journey Curtailed*, London: Secker & Warburg

Gledhill, John (1994) *Power and its Disguises: Anthropological Perspectives on Politics*, London (and Boulder, CO): Pluto Press

Goodwin, Jan (1995) *Price of Honour: Muslim Women Lift the Veil of Silence on the Islamic World*, London: Warner Books

Gordon, David C. (1980) *Lebanon: The Fragmented Nation*, London: Croom Helm

Goria, Wade R. (1985) *Sovereignty and Leadership in Lebanon 1943–1976*, London: Ithaca Press

Government of Lebanon (1972) *L'enquête par sondage sur la population active au Liban: novembre 1970*, Beirut: Direction Centrale de la Statistique, Ministère du Plan

Graham, B. D. (1990) *Hindu Nationalism and Indian Politics: The Origins and Development of the Bharatiya Jana Sangh*, Cambridge: Cambridge University Press

Grassmuck, George and Kamal Salibi (1964) *Reformed Administration in Lebanon*, Beirut: Catholic Press

Greenberg, Kenneth S. (1996) *Honor and Slavery*, Princeton: Princeton University Press

Gregory of Tours (1927) *The History of the Franks* (2 vols), translated with an introduction by O. M. Dalton, Oxford: Clarendon Press

Group for the Advancement of Psychiatry (1978) *Self-Involvement in the Middle East*, New York: Group for the Advancement of Psychiatry

Gurr, Ted Robert (1970) *Why Men Rebel*, Princeton: Princeton University Press
(1993) *Minorities at Risk: A Global View of Ethnopolitical Conflicts*, Washington, DC: United States Institute of Peace

Gutman, Roy (1993) *A Witness to Genocide: The First Inside Account of the Horrors of 'Ethnic Cleansing' in Bosnia*, Shaftesbury, Dorset: Element Books

Hage, Ghassan (1989) *The Fetishism of Identity: Class, Politics, and Processes of Identification in Lebanon*, Ph.D. thesis, University of Macquarie, Australia

Haley, Edward P. and Lewis W. Snider (eds) (1979) *Lebanon in Crisis: Participants and Issues*, Syracuse: Syracuse University Press

Hanf, Theodor (1993) *Coexistence in Wartime Lebanon: Decline of a State and Rise of a Nation*, London: Centre for Lebanese Studies and I.B.Tauris

Harik, Ilya (1968) *Politics and Change in a Traditional Society: Lebanon, 1711–1845*, Princeton: Princeton University Press

Harris, William W. (1997) *Faces of Lebanon: Sects, Wars, and Global Extensions*, Princeton: Markus Weiner

Hechter, Michael (1975) *Internal Colonialism: The Celtic Fringe in British National Development, 1536–1966*, London: Routledge
(1986) 'Rational Choice Theory and the Study of Race and Ethnic Relations', in John Rex and David Mason (eds) *Theories of Race and Ethnic Relations*, Cambridge: Cambridge University Press

Helmick, Raymond G. (1988) 'Internal Lebanese Politics: The Lebanese Front and Forces', in Halim Barakat (ed.) *Toward a Viable Lebanon*, London and Sydney: Croom Helm

Herzfeld, Michael (1980) 'Honour and Shame: Problems in the Comparative Analysis of Moral Systems', *Man*, 15

(1984) 'The Horns of the Mediterraneanist Dilemma', *American Ethnologist*, 11

(1985) *The Poetics of Manhood: Contest and Identity in a Cretan Mountain Village*, Princeton: Princeton University Press

Hibri, Azizah al- (ed.) (1982) *Women and Islam*, Oxford: Pergamon Press

Hitler, Adolf (1939) *Mein Kampf*, translated with an introduction by James Murphy, London: Hurst & Blackett

Hitti, Philip K. (1957) *Lebanon in History: From Earliest Times to the Present*, London: Macmillan

Hobbes, Thomas (1909) *Leviathan* (1651), with an introduction by W. G. Pogson Smith, Oxford: Clarendon Press

Hobsbawm, Eric J. (1959) *Primitive Rebels: Studies in Archaic Forms of Social Movement in the 19th and 20th Centuries*, Manchester: Manchester University Press

(1990) *Nations and Nationalism since the 1780s: Programme, Myth, Reality*, Cambridge: Cambridge University Press

Hollis, Rosemary and Nadim Shehadi (eds) (1996) *Lebanon on Hold: Implications for Middle East Peace*, London: Royal Institute for International Affairs

Homer (1950) *The Iliad*, translated with an introduction by E. V. Rieu, Harmondsworth: Penguin

Horowitz, Donald L. (1985) *Ethnic Groups in Conflict*, Berkeley, Los Angeles and London: University of California Press

Hourani, Albert H. (1946) *Syria and Lebanon: A Political Essay*, London: Oxford University Press and Royal Institute of International Affairs

(1966) 'Lebanon: The Development of a Political Society', in Leonard Binder (ed.) *Politics in Lebanon*, New York: Wiley

(1967) *Arabic Thought in the Liberal Age, 1798–1939*, London: Oxford University Press and Royal Institute of International Affairs (revised edition, first published 1962)

(1976) 'Ideologies of the Mountain and City', in Roger Owen (ed.) *Essays on the Crisis in Lebanon*, London: Ithaca Press

(1981) *The Emergence of the Modern Middle East*, London: Macmillan

Hudson, Michael C. (1968) *The Precarious Republic: Political Modernization in Lebanon*, New York: Random House

(1976) 'The Lebanese Crisis: The Limits of Consociational Democracy', *Journal of Palestine Studies*, 19/20

Hussain, Akmal (1992) 'The Karachi Riots of December 1986: Crisis of State and Civil Society in Pakistan', in Veena Das (ed.) *Mirrors of Violence: Communities, Riots and Survivors in South Asia*, Delhi: Oxford University Press

IDREL: Lebanon's Memory, published on the website www.idrel.com.lb/elect2k

Ignatieff, Michael (1993) *Blood and Belonging: Journeys into the New Nationalism*, London: BBC Books/Chatto & Windus

Issawi, Charles (1966) 'Economic Development and Political Liberalism in Lebanon', in Leonard Binder (ed.) *Politics in Lebanon*, New York: Wiley

Johnson, Michael (1978) 'Factional Politics in Lebanon: The Case of the "Islamic Society of Benevolent Intentions" (Al-Maqasid) in Beirut', *Middle Eastern Studies*, 14:1

(1986) *Class and Client in Beirut: The Sunni Muslim Community and the Lebanese State, 1840–1985*, London and Atlantic Highlands: Ithaca Press

(1997) 'Political Bosses and Strong-Arm Retainers in the Sunni Muslim Quarters of Beirut, 1943–1992', in Josef Gugler (ed.) *Cities in the Developing World: Issues, Theory, and Policy*, New York and Oxford: Oxford University Press

Joseph, Suad (1978) 'Muslim–Christian Conflicts: A Theoretical Perspective', in Suad Joseph and Barbara L. K. Pillsbury (eds) *Muslim–Christian Conflicts: Economic, Political and Social Origins*, Boulder, CO: Westview Press

Joumblatt, Kamal (1982) *I Speak for Lebanon*, as recorded by Philippe Lapousterle, translated by Michael Pallis, London: Zed Press

Kakar, Sudhir (1992) 'Some Unconscious Aspects of Ethnic Violence in India', in Veena Das (ed.) *Mirrors of Violence: Communities, Riots and Survivors in South Asia*, Delhi: Oxford University Press

Kandiyoti, Deniz (ed.) (1991) *Women, Islam and the State*, London: Macmillan

Kedourie, Elie (1992) *Politics in the Middle East*, Oxford: Oxford University Press

Kerr, Malcolm H. (1960) 'The 1960 Lebanese Parliamentary Elections', *Middle Eastern Affairs*, 11:9

Khalaf, Samir (1977) 'Changing Forms of Political Patronage in Lebanon', in Ernest Gellner and John Waterbury (eds) *Patrons and Clients in Mediterranean Societies*, London: Duckworth

(1987) *Lebanon's Predicament*, New York: Columbia University Press

Khalaf, Tewfik (1976) 'The Phalange and the Maronite Community: From Lebanonism to Maronitism', in Roger Owen (ed.) *Essays on the Crisis in Lebanon*, London: Ithaca Press

Khalidi, Walid (1979) *Conflict and Violence in Lebanon: Confrontation in the Middle East*, Cambridge, MA: Harvard Center for International Affairs

Khayyat, Sana al- (1990) *Honour and Shame: Women in Modern Iraq*, London: Saqi Books

Khazen, Farid El (2000) *The Breakdown of the State in Lebanon, 1967–1976*, London and New York: I.B.Tauris

Khlat, Myriam (1989) *Les mariages consanguins à Beyrouth: traditions matrimoniales et santé publique*, Évry Cedex: INED/Presses Universitaires de France

Khuri, Fuad I. (1972) 'Sectarian Loyalty Among Rural Migrants in Two Lebanese Suburbs: A Stage Between Family and National Allegiance', in Richard Antoun and Ilya Harik (eds) *Rural Politics and Social Change in the Middle East*, Bloomington: Indiana University Press

   (1975) *From Village to Suburb: Order and Change in Greater Beirut*, Chicago and London: Chicago University Press

   (1990) *Imams and Emirs: State, Religion and Sects in Islam*, London: Saqi Books

Klein, Melanie (1946) 'Notes on Some Schizoid Mechanisms', reprinted in Juliet Mitchell (1986) *The Selected Melanie Klein*, Harmondsworth: Penguin

Kressel, Gideon M. (1988) 'More on Honour and Shame' (correspondence), *Man*, 23

   (1992) 'Shame and Gender', *Anthropological Quarterly*, 65:1

Lacan, Jacques (1949) 'The Mirror Stage as Formative of the Function of the I as Revealed in Psychoanalytic Experience', in Jacques Lacan (1977) *Écrits: A Selection*, translated by Alan Sheridan, London: Tavistock

Lamb, Franklin P. (1984) *Reason not the Need: Eyewitness Chronicles of Israel's War in Lebanon*, Nottingham: Nottingham Spokesman

Lapidus, Ira Marvin (1967) *Muslim Cities in the Later Middle Ages*, Cambridge, MA: Harvard University Press

Laqueur, Walter and Barry Rubin (eds) (1984) *The Israel–Arab Reader: A Documentary History of the Middle East Conflict* (revised and updated), New York and Harmondsworth: Penguin

Lerner, Daniel (1958) *The Passing of Traditional Society: Modernizing in the Middle East*, Glencoe, IL: Free Press

Lichtenstadter, Ilse (1974) *Introduction to Classical Arabic Literature*, New York: Schocken Books

Lijphart, Arend (1977) *Democracy in Plural Societies: A Comparative Exploration*, New Haven and London: Yale University Press

Lison-Tolosana, C. (1966) *Belmonte de los Cabelleros: A Sociological Study of a Spanish Town*, Oxford: Clarendon Press

Locke, John (1960) *Two Treatises of Government* (1690), with an introduction by Peter Laslett, Cambridge: Cambridge University Press

Longrigg, Stephen Hemsley (1958) *Syria and Lebanon under French Mandate*, London: Oxford University Press

Lope de Vega (1997) *Fuente Ovejuna and Lost in a Mirror: Two Plays*, adapted by Adrian Mitchell, London: Oberon Books/Absolute Classics

Machiavelli, Niccolò (1961) *The Prince*, translated with an introduction by George Bull, Harmondsworth: Penguin

McKay, James (1982) 'An Exploratory Synthesis of Primordial and Mobilizationist Approaches to Ethnic Phenomena', *Ethnic and Racial Studies*, 5:4

McKendrick, Melveena (1992) *Theatre in Spain: 1490–1700*, Cambridge: Cambridge University Press

Makiya, Kanan (1993) *Cruelty and Silence: War, Tyranny, Uprising, and the Arab World*, London: Jonathan Cape

Malarkey, James M. (1988) 'Notes on the Psychology of War in Lebanon', in Halim Barakat (ed.) *Toward a Viable Lebanon*, London and Sydney: Croom Helm

Mansfield, Peter (1985) *The Arabs*, Harmondsworth: Penguin

MEED Middle East Economic Digest, business weekly, published in London

MEIB Middle East Intelligence Bulletin, journal of the United States Committee for a Free Lebanon, published on the website www.meib.org

Meo, Leila M. T. (1965) *Lebanon: Improbable Nation: A Study in Political Development*, Bloomington: Indiana University Press

Middleton, John and David Tait (1958) 'Introduction', in John Middleton and David Tait (eds) *Tribes Without Rulers: Studies in African Segmentary Systems*, London: Routledge & Kegan Paul

Mitchell, J. Clyde (1956) *The Kalela Dance*, Manchester: Manchester University Press (Rhodes-Livingstone Papers, no. 27)

Mitchell, Juliet (ed.) (1986) *The Selected Melanie Klein*, Harmondsworth: Penguin

—— (1990) *Psychoanalysis and Feminism*, Harmondsworth: Penguin (first published in 1974 by Allen Lane)

Moslem Lebanon Today (1953) Beirut: n.p.

Nasr, Marlène and Salim Nasr (1976) 'Morphologie sociale de la banlieue-est de Beyrouth', *Maghreb-Machrek*, 73

Nasr, Salim (1978) 'The Crisis of Lebanese Capitalism', *MERIP Reports*, 73

—— (1985) 'Roots of the Shi'i Movement', *MERIP Reports*, 15:5

—— (1990) 'Lebanon's War: Is the End in Sight?' *Middle East Report*, 20:1

Nelson, Joan M. (1979) *Access to Power: Politics and the Urban Poor in Developing Nations*, Princeton: Princeton University Press

—— (1987) 'Political Participation', in Myron Weiner and Samuel P. Huntington (eds) *Understanding Political Development*, Boston: Little Brown

Nordlinger, Eric A. (1972) *Conflict Regulation in Divided Societies*, Cambridge, MA: Harvard University Center for International Affairs

Norton, Augustus Richard (1987) *Amal and the Shi'a: Struggle for the Soul of Lebanon*, Austin: University of Texas Press

Owen, Roger (ed.) (1976) *Essays on the Crisis in Lebanon*, London: Ithaca Press

Oxford Analytica Daily Brief, published in Oxford

Parsons, Talcott (1952) *The Social System*, London: Tavistock

Parsons, Talcott, and Edward A. Shils (1951) *Toward a General Theory of Action*, Cambridge, MA: Harvard University Press

Patai, Raphael (1973) *The Arab Mind*, New York: Scribner's

Patterson, Orlando (1982) *Slavery and Social Death: A Comparative Study*, Cambridge, MA: Harvard University Press

Peristiany, John G. (ed.) (1965) *Honour and Shame: The Values of Mediterranean Society*, London: Weidenfeld & Nicolson

Perthes, Volker (1997) 'Myths and Money: Four Years of Hariri and Lebanon's Preparation for a New Middle East', *Middle East Report*, 27:2

Peters, Emrys L. (1967) 'Some Structural Aspects of the Feud among the Camel-Herding Bedouin of Cyrenaica', *Africa*, 37

Pitt-Rivers, Julian (1961) *The People of the Sierra*, Chicago: Chicago University Press

   (1965) 'Honour and Social Status', in John G. Peristiany (ed.) *Honour and Shame: The Values of Mediterranean Society*, London: Weidenfeld & Nicolson

Plato (1955) *The Republic*, translated with an introduction by H. D. P. Lee, Harmondsworth: Penguin

Polk, William R. (1963) *The Opening of South Lebanon, 1788–1840: A Study of the Impact of the West on the Middle East*, Cambridge, MA: Harvard University Press

Porath, Yeheshua (1966) 'The Peasant Revolt of 1858–1861 in Kisrawan', *Asian and African Studies*, 2

Prothro, E. Terry and Levon Melikian (1953) 'The California Public Opinion Scale in an Authoritarian Culture', *Public Opinion Quarterly*, 17

Puzo, Mario (1970) *The Godfather*, London: Pan Books

Qubain, Fahim I. (1961) *Crisis in Lebanon*, Washington, DC: Middle East Institute

Rabinovich, Itamar (1984) *The War for Lebanon, 1970–1983*, Ithaca and London: Cornell University Press

Randal, Jonathan (1990) *The Tragedy of Lebanon: Christian Warlords, Israeli Adventurers and American Bunglers*, London: Hogarth Press

Reich, Wilhelm (1970) *The Mass Psychology of Fascism*, New York: Simon & Schuster

Review of Middle East Studies (1975, 1976 and 1978) London: Ithaca Press

Rodinson, Maxime (1974) *Islam and Capitalism*, London: Allen Lane

Rose, Jacqueline (1996) *States of Fantasy*, Oxford: Clarendon Press

Runciman, Steven (1978) *A History of the Crusades* (3 vols), Harmondsworth: Penguin

Runciman, W. G. (1966) *Relative Deprivation and Social Justice*, London: Routledge & Kegan Paul

Saba, Paul (1976) 'The Creation of the Lebanese Economy: Economic Growth in the Nineteenth and Twentieth Centuries', in Roger Owen (ed.) *Essays on the Crisis in Lebanon*, London: Ithaca Press

Said, Edward (1978) *Orientalism*, New York: Pantheon

Salem, Elie (1973) *Modernization without Revolution: Lebanon's Experience*, Bloomington: University of Indiana Press

Salem, Paul (1997) 'Skirting Democracy: Lebanon's 1996 Elections and Beyond', *Middle East Report*, 27:2

Salibi, Kamal S. (1965) *The Modern History of Lebanon*, London: Weidenfeld & Nicolson

  (1976) *Crossroads to Civil War: Lebanon, 1958–1976*, London: Ithaca Press

  (1988) *A House of Many Mansions: The History of Lebanon Reconsidered*, London: I.B.Tauris

Sayigh, Rosemary (1994) *Too Many Enemies: The Palestinian Experience in Lebanon*, London and New Jersey: Zed Books

Sayigh, Yusuf A. (1962) *Entrepreneurs of Lebanon: The Role of the Business Leader in a Developing Economy*, Cambridge, MA: Harvard University Press

Schiff, Ze'ev, and Ehud Ya'ari (1986) *Israel's Lebanon War*, London: Unwin

Schneider, Jane (1971) 'Of Vigilance and Virgins', *Ethnology*, 9

Schneider, Jane and Peter Schneider (1976) *Culture and Political Economy in Western Sicily*, New York: Academic Press

Scott, James C. (1976) *The Moral Economy of the Peasant: Rebellion and Subsistence in Southeast Asia*, New Haven and London: Yale University Press

Scott, George M. Jr (1990) 'A Resynthesis of the Primordial and Circumstantial Approaches to Ethnic Group Solidarity: Towards an Explanatory Model', *Ethnic and Racial Studies*, 13:2

Shaheed, Farida (1992) 'The Pathan–Muhajir Conflicts, 1985–86: A National Perspective', in Veena Das (ed.) *Mirrors of Violence: Communities, Riots and Survivors in South Asia*, Delhi: Oxford University Press

Sharabi, Hisham (1988) *Neopatriarchy: A Theory of Distorted Change in Arab Society*, New York and Oxford: Oxford University Press

(1990) 'The Scholarly Point of View: Politics, Perspective, Paradigm', in Hisham Sharabi (ed.) *Theory, Politics and the Arab World: Critical Responses*, New York and London: Routledge

Sharara, Yolla Polity (1978) 'Women and Politics in Lebanon', *Khamsin*, 6, London: Pluto Press

Shaykh, Hanan al- (1986) *The Story of Zahra*, London: Quartet Books

Sheridan, Alan (1980) *Michel Foucault: The Will to Truth*, London and New York: Tavistock

Sherif, Muzafer (1966) *Group Conflict and Cooperation: Their Social Psychology*, London: Routledge & Kegan Paul

Sherry, Virginia N. (1997) 'Disappearances: Syrian Impunity in Lebanon', *Middle East Report*, 27:2

Skocpol, Theda (1979) *The State and Social Revolutions: A Comparative Analysis of France, Russia and China*, Cambridge: Cambridge University Press

Smilianskaya, I. M. (1966) 'From Subsistence to Market Economy, 1850s', in Charles Issawi (ed.) *The Economic History of the Middle East, 1800–1914*, Chicago and London: The University of Chicago Press

Smith, Anthony D. (1991) *National Identity*, Harmondsworth: Penguin

Srinivasan, Amrit (1992) 'The Survivor in the Study of Violence', in Veena Das (ed.) *Mirrors of Violence: Communities, Riots and Survivors in South Asia*, Delhi: Oxford University Press

Stoakes, Frank (1975) 'The Supervigilantes: The Lebanese Kata'eb Party as a Builder, Surrogate and Defender of the State', *Middle Eastern Studies*, 11:3

Suleiman, Michael W. (1967) *Political Parties in Lebanon: The Challenge of a Fragmented Political Culture*, Ithaca: Cornell University Press

Tabbara, Lina Mikdadi (1979) *Survival in Beirut: A Diary of Civil War*, London: Onyx Press

Tajfel, Henri (1981) *Human Groups and Social Categories: Studies in Social Psychology*, Cambridge: Cambridge University Press

Tibi, Bassam (1997) *Arab Nationalism: Between Islam and the Nation-State*. Basingstoke and London: Macmillan (3rd edn)

Vatikiotis, P. J. (1978) *Nasser and his Generation*, London: Croom Helm

Volkan, Vamik D. (1979) *Cyprus — War and Adaptation: A Psychoanalytic History of Two Ethnic Groups in Conflict*, Charlottesville: University Press of Virginia

Volney, C. F (1959) *Voyage en Egypte et en Syrie*, Paris: Mouton (1st published 1787)

von Grunebaum, G. E. (1962) *Modern Islam: The Search for Cultural Identity*, Berkeley and Los Angeles: University of California Press

Wallace-Hadrill, J. M. (1959) 'The Bloodfeud of the Franks', *Bulletin of the John Rylands Library* (Manchester), 41:2

Warriner, Doreen (1948) *Land and Poverty in the Middle East*, London and New York: Royal Institute of International Affairs

Weber, Max (1948) 'Class, Status and Party', in H. H. Gerth and C. Wright Mills (eds) *From Max Weber: Essays in Sociology*, London and Boston: Routledge & Kegan Paul

(1966) *The Sociology of Religion*, London: Methuen

Wikan, Unni (1984) 'Shame and Honour: A Contestable Pair', *Man*, 19

Wolf, Eric R. (1969) *Peasant Wars of the Twentieth Century*, New York: Harper & Row

Wright, Elizabeth (1992) *Feminism and Psychoanalysis: A Critical Dictionary*, Oxford: Blackwell

Yamak, Labib Zuwiyya (1966) *The Syrian Social Nationalist Party: An Ideological Analysis*, Cambridge, MA: Harvard University Press

Younes, Massoud (1999) *Ces morts qui nous tuent: la vengeance du sang dans la société libanaise contemporaine*, Beyrouth: Editions Almassar

Zayour, Ali (1977) *Al-tahlil al-nafsi li al-dhat al-'arabiyya* (The Psychoanalysis of the Arab Self), Beirut: Dar al-Tali'a

(1982) *Qita' al-butula wa al-narjisiyya fi al-dhat al-'arabiyya* (Fragments of Heroism and Narcissism in the Arab Self), Beirut: Dar al-Tali'a

Index

neopatriarchy, 17, 19, 21, 47, 131,
132, 157, 205–13, 216, 222–3,
232, 234, 249–55, 259; *see also*
patriarchy
Netherlands, 134
New York, 6, 121
Nietzsche, Friedrich, 136
Nigeria, 179
Nizami, 79
nomads, *see* beduin and nomads
Nordic legends, 136, 187
Nordlinger, Eric A., 37
Northern Ireland, 165
Norton, Augustus Richard, 61, 66, 160
nostalgia, romantic, 136, 185–6, 189,
222, 233
notables, 25, 28, 30, 31, 33, 34–5, 40, 45,
57–8, 102, 114, 117, 129, 140, 142–3,
249, 257
Nuer, 29, 72, 126–7

Oedipal phase, 180, 202
omertà (code of silence), 107
Operation Accountability, 244
Operation Grapes of Wrath, 244
opium, 226
Oriental Society, 138
Orientalism, 61, 81, 207–8
Orthodox Christians, 2–4, 47, 91, 96, 129,
142, 150, 161, 170, 185–6, 190, 220,
238, 246; *see also* Armenians; Greek
Orthodox; Syrian Catholics and
Orthodox
Other, 7, 9, 13, 17, 20, 61–2, 68, 124–5,
133, 135, 137, 167, 172–80, 182–4,
189, 201–3, 223, 229–31, 233, 253; *see
also* demonization of the Other
Ottoman empire, 4, 15, 22, 34, 40, 42, 44,
47, 70, 74, 81, 85–96, 100, 105, 114–
15, 119, 129, 134, 137–45, 162, 183,
189, 190, 208, 218
Ottoman Party of Administrative
Decentralization, 140
Owen, Roger, 61, 207

Oxford Analytica Daily Brief, 239

Pakistan, 165, 198
Palestine, 22, 24, 137, 139, 141–2, 144,
150, 185, 188, 218, 255
Palestine Liberation Organization (PLO),
6, 22, 24, 55–6, 152, 158, 184, 196–7,
204
Palestinian Liberation Army, 22
Palestinians, 3–4, 6, 9–12, 16, 22, 35,
54–6, 60–3, 66, 113, 130, 147, 152–4,
158, 171, 177, 182–5, 188, 196–7,
201–4, 224–6, 229, 231, 237, 242, 257
Paris, 6, 138, 140, 145, 200, 241
parliament, Lebanese, 4, 7, 15, 25, 28,
34–5, 39, 45–6, 52–3, 60, 68, 71, 104,
115, 119, 124, 142–3, 144, 147–8, 196,
212, 218–19, 224–5, 231–2, 234, 235–9,
245–51, 254, 256, 259
Parsons, Talcott, 18
partition of India (1947), 155, 198–9
pashas (governors), 86–9, 91, 114, 141,
144
Patai, Raphael, 207–8
Pathans, 155
patriarchy, 1, 5, 16–21, 26, 28–9, 31–2,
47, 48, 57–8, 67–8, 132–3, 136–7,
148–9, 154, 156–8, 164–8, 170–3, 179,
182, 200–3, 205–12, 220–3, 227–34,
249–50, 252–7, 259; *see also*
neopatriarchy
patron-client relations, *see* clientelism and
patronage
Patterson, Orlando, 84
peasants, 2, 14–15, 19–20, 23–4, 25, 30–1,
34, 40–4, 46, 57, 67, 69, 70–2, 76–80,
83–4, 86–7, 89–98, 100–13, 118–21,
135–6, 145, 185, 192, 195, 206, 208,
211, 218; *see also* commoners; *fellahin*
Peristiany, John G., 26
personal and family law, 4, 162, 168, 223,
231, 243, 254
Perthes, Volker, 235–6
Peter, Saint, 1

timocracy, 70, 83–5, 105
Toledo, 76
torture, 61, 78, 80, 174, 213, 241–3, 245, 250, 255
transmigration of souls (reincarnation), 2, 64–5
tribalism and tribes, 16, 18, 23, 72–3, 80–1, 84, 87, 103–4, 106, 112, 119, 125–8, 130–2, 141, 144, 154–5, 162, 167, 206, 211; *see also* clans
Tripoli, 4, 42–4, 55, 85, 91, 102, 115–16, 118, 129, 139, 142, 146, 148, 151, 169, 186, 242
Trissino, Giangiorgio, 75
Troy, 76, 79
Turkey and Turks, 79, 88–9, 105, 114, 121, 134, 138, 140–1, 144, 150, 162, 179, 183, 189; *see also* Ottoman empire
Turkish language, 47–8, 86
Tuscany, 74
Tyre, 188, 244
Tzintzuntzan, 110

Ukraine, 185
Umayyads, 144, 187–8
unions, trade, 7, 21, 43, 147, 196–7, 217, 227, 232, 235, 239–40, 243, 252, 257
United Nations, 163, 244
United States of America, 33, 38–9, 83–4, 88, 129, 138, 181, 188, 209–10, 224–6, 228, 235, 255
Urban, Pope, 23
urbanization, 16–19, 20, 24, 47, 67–9, 72, 101, 124, 130–3, 135, 137, 154–8, 168–9, 171–3, 181–2, 185–6, 200–2, 205, 220, 223, 233, 253
Urdu, 79

valis (governors), 85–6, 90, 142
Vatican, 73–4, 250
Vatikiotis, P. J., 149
vendetta, 29, 35–7, 119; *see also* feuding

vengeance, 8–9, 11, 14, 26, 29, 32, 36, 43, 45–6, 49, 51, 60–1, 64–5, 77–80, 121, 127, 136, 138, 164, 166, 176–8, 197, 208, 225, 228–31, 233, 256, 258–9
Versailles treaty (1919), 136, 149
vilayets (Ottoman provinces), 91, 102, 140
Volkan, Vamik D., 179
Volney, Constantin François de, 86
von Grunebaum, G. E., 207

Wafd (Egyptian party), 149
wajih (notable), 31
wakil (representative), 94–5, 102
Wakim, Najah, 238, 246–7
Wallace-Hadrill, J. M., 112
war economy, 7, 118, 124, 172, 226, 257
war of the camps, 11, 184, 197, 204
warlords, 21, 34, 37, 113, 122, 124–5, 172, 185, 213, 224, 226, 232–4, 237, 239–41, 251, 257, 259
Warriner, Doreen, 101
wasta (intermediary), 51, 211–12
Weber, Max, 27, 30, 57, 82
Weizmann, Chiam, 137
widows, 120, 165–7
Wieland, Christoph Martin, 259
Wikan, Unni, 26
Wolf, Eric R., 93
women, 5, 7, 9–13, 19–20, 26–7, 31–3, 43–4, 47, 61–2, 65, 67–8, 73, 77–80, 81, 83–4, 93, 96, 102–3, 116, 120, 125, 130, 132–3, 136–7, 157, 159, 162–4, 165–8, 171–3, 176, 178, 187, 200–1, 203, 220–2, 227, 232–4, 242, 252–3, 255–9
Women Against War, 7, 256
women novelists, Lebanese, 256–7
Wood, Richard, 90–1
working class, 55, 137, 165, 191–2, 196, 201–2, 204, 209, 220; *see also* proletariat